MODERN PUBLIC FINANCE

MODERN PUBLIC FINANCE

EDITED BY

JOHN M. QUIGLEY

AND

EUGENE SMOLENSKY

HARVARD UNIVERSITY PRESS

Cambridge, Massachusetts, and London, England   1994

Library of Congress Cataloging-in-Publication Data

Modern public finance / edited by John M. Quigley and Eugene
Smolensky.
    p. cm.
  Includes bibliographical references and index.
  ISBN 0-674-58054-0 (alk. paper)
  1. Finance, Public. I. Quigley, John M. II. Smolensky, Eugene.
HJ141.M634 1994
336—dc20

93-23838
  CIP

This volume is dedicated to
George F. Break and Richard A. Musgrave
and to the memory of Joseph A. Pechman
by their many students, colleagues, and friends.

Contents

PART III. TAX POLICY

PART IV. OPTIMAL TAXATION AND EXTENSIONS

MODERN PUBLIC FINANCE

JOHN M. QUIGLEY AND
EUGENE SMOLENSKY

1

Introduction

How can collective action improve resource allocation and economic efficiency
and also alter the distribution of income in socially desired ways? This central
question—which challenges us to improve our understanding and execution of
government policy in pursuit of efficiency and equity objectives—has been
debated by public finance specialists from the beginning. Nevertheless, the state
of knowledge in the late 1950s constitutes a natural and important baseline from
which to examine important developments in modern public finance addressed
to such issues. We begin with the years in which Richard Musgrave's *Theory
of Public Finance* first appeared. Musgrave's *Theory* represented the zenith of
partial equilibrium analysis and introduced general equilibrium modeling of
taxation. It also demonstrated the first sustained effort to integrate the theory
of public goods with "standard" price theory.

Shortly afterward, partial equilibrium analysis of taxation and public expenditure was replaced for most purposes by a general equilibrium treatment—at
first the analysis of two sectors (for example, Harberger, 1962), and ultimately
the analysis of complex simultaneity (for example, Fullerton et al., 1980). More
generally, diagrammatic analyses of individual and market equilibria gave way
to the familiar constrained maximization paradigm now used to represent individual and collective choice.

This volume reviews the developments in public finance theory within these
new paradigms—selectively, to be sure—and bears witness to the advances
that have been made in the application of economic principles to important

1

problems in the positive economics of taxation and public expenditure. The chapters are not intended primarily as "review papers," nor are they intended to be comprehensive surveys of the field. Most of them do provide focused surveys of recent developments in the various subfields. But they also report new work that significantly advances our understanding; they illustrate the power of modern public finance and draw specific attention to fertile areas for future research. The chapters define the state of the art for specialists in other research fields and also suggest fruitful research topics for graduate students (as well as public finance specialists). A major objective of the book is to motivate research by advanced graduate students.

Although the topics covered here are diverse, they are unified in their methodological perspective. Each of the chapters considers the implications of public sector decisions from a general equilibrium perspective, where that perspective is derived from an explicit optimizing framework. In Chapter 2, Anthony Atkinson provides a general equilibrium analysis of tax incidence using the employer payroll tax as an example; he analyzes the ultimate burden of payroll taxation in a two-sector model which includes primary and secondary labor markets. The general framework for the model is an extension of the methodology developed in the now-famous Harberger model of corporate taxation. Yet the specific application developed by Atkinson is highly original and yields rich and novel insights. Moreover, the formulation of the model serves as a blueprint for the incorporation of modern notions of labor economics in public finance. Atkinson's model incorporates such non-neoclassical features as unemployment queues, efficiency wages, and the matching of vacancies with available workers. It vividly indicates how tax changes can qualitatively alter the equilibrium of an entire economy. It also recognizes the distinct possibility that taxes may lead to nonuniqueness in economic equilibria, and thus that tax policy may greatly alter the equilibrium of the economy.

Atkinson also contrasts modern equilibrium notions of tax incidence with previous analyses. He demonstrates that the incidence of taxation is properly *deduced* from the characterization of the market and from the behavior of economic actors; it is not *assumed* as a series of postulates—even postulates representing sophisticated exercises in economic accounting.

By incorporating modern notions of labor economics into the analysis of tax incidence, Atkinson implicitly raises a series of analogous applications of microeconomic theory to public finance—for example, the relationship between industrial organization and the burden of payroll or profits taxes or taxes on real property, or the relationship between the features of international competitiveness and tax incidence. It appears that we can better understand the economic effects of taxation if we embed recent developments in industrial organization or international economics within a general equilibrium model of tax incidence. More generally, tax incidence and distributional analyses can be enriched by the explicit incorporation of imperfections in markets—for products and capital, as well as for labor.

Atkinson also raises a more fundamental question about the meaning of incidence. Ultimately, the burden of taxation is borne by identifiable households or the individuals who constitute them. These individuals simultaneously supply labor, consume products, and receive nonlabor income. In a modern economy, the distinctions between laborers and capitalists as separate "classes" may be far less salient than distinctions among individuals on the basis of productivity, inherited advantage, or random experiences. Furthermore, the burden of taxation will vary according to the way these individuals are distributed across firms of differing sizes, industries, and competitive environments.

In Chapter 3, Alan Auerbach considers the dynamic and intertemporal implications of related issues. In particular, he reviews three aspects of dynamic tax incidence: the taxation of lifetime income as compared to annual income; the taxation of capital accumulation; and the long-run versus short-run view of tax incidence. In each case, dynamic considerations can lead to surprising implications for the burden of taxation.

The heart of Auerbach's contribution, however, is his synthesis of modern research on the nature of the public debt and the link between current and future fiscal choices. Auerbach reviews the profound implications of the Barro proposition of Ricardian equivalence: government debt is not perceived as net wealth by taxpayers because they recognize that the future taxes required to retire this debt represent a liability of equal magnitude. Auerbach also reviews the assumptions that generate Ricardian equivalence and the ambiguous empirical evidence about its validity.

If Ricardian equivalence holds, then the federal deficit cannot be a vehicle for allocating the burden of public expenditures across generations (and social insurance schemes that transfer resources to the elderly have no effect on aggregate saving). Auerbach shows that even under these conditions fiscal policy can still be used to improve welfare, by smoothing tax rates over time and thus reducing the deadweight loss from taxation.

Finally, Auerbach raises important and troubling issues in the measurement of public debt, especially when this is compared with the definition and measurement of debt for private corporations. The ambiguity in the definition of public debt, in turn, raises further questions about the nature of "tests" of the importance of Ricardian equivalence in the real world.

Auerbach's analysis pays particular attention to the transition from one tax regime to another and to the distinction between tax design and tax reform; government incentives for individual savings (such as individual retirement accounts) and for corporate investment (such as investment tax credits) are important examples. These issues will have even greater salience as nations in western Europe reform their tax systems to encourage fiscal harmonization and as nations in eastern Europe seek to design tax and expenditure policies to assist in the transition to market economies.

Suzanne Scotchmer takes seriously the possibility that the private profit motive can call forth the appropriate supply of public goods and thereby reduce the branches of Musgravian public finance from three to two (distribution and stabilization). She analyzes the potential role of the profit-maximizing "proprietor" of a community or club. Her points of departure are the classic informal models of Tiebout (1956) and Buchanan (1965).

Scotchmer distinguishes between local public goods and clubs. Local public goods are available in the same amount to all "members" of a community—members who may pay different prices. Clubs consist of "members" who may pay identical prices, but whose willingness to pay for the goods depends upon the number (and perhaps the identities) of others sharing in the consumption.

The distinction between clubs and local public goods reflects the role of space or location as a means of rationing entry. In the former, space is irrelevant and admission fees can be charged directly. In the latter, space is important because it provides the indirect mechanism for restricting entry.

Scotchmer shows that, for a reasonable set of assumptions, a competitive equilibrium in clubs with costless entry generates a fully efficient outcome. She argues, more strongly, that the theory of clubs can be defined as the theory underlying the efficient pricing of the externalities, which identify consumers in groups.

The efficiency of the club model helps explain the magnitude and sources of inefficiency in the local public goods economy. First, efficiency in the local public goods market is limited by the arbitrary and exogenous partitioning of space into communities. Second, to achieve economic efficiency the proprietor of the community must somehow forecast the land price capitalization of all possible tax and expenditure policies. The proprietor must somehow know the preferences of consumers for packages of goods which are not observed in the market. Third, the efficiency analysis depends upon circumstances in which all residents are landowners and all landowners are residents.

Evidently, efficiency in the provision of goods by the local public sector is far more problematic than efficiency in the provision of goods by exclusive clubs.

Wallace Oates gives more institutional relevance to the microeconomics of the local public sector. His discussion of the allocation of revenue-raising authority among different levels of government indicates how tax exporting can lead to inefficient levels of public spending by state and local governments. Oates finds that when additional and more realistic tax instruments are considered (in comparison to sparse models such as those relied on by Scotchmer), the potential for inefficiency in resource allocation in public goods provision is much larger. As emphasized originally by Break (1967), the distorting effects of fiscal competition among communities provides a justification for grants to local governments—a justification based on economic efficiency.

Oates reviews the general theory of grants-in-aid among governments and the recent literature on the "flypaper effect." This latter anomaly may suggest that local government officials are able to manipulate the citizenry to "overspend" the proceeds of grant money on public services. Indeed, this anomaly provides almost the only empirical evidence on the existence of the Leviathan government postulated by Brennan and Buchanan (1980). An alternative and more benign explanation, in terms of transactions costs, can also be held responsible (Quigley and Smolensky, 1993). In any case, Oates demonstrates that there is a real need to devise sharper empirical tests to distinguish among alternative explanations for the phenomenon. More generally, he concludes that careful analysis and reform of the grant system may yield large positive returns, in realizing allocative and distributional goals.

Oates also raises for the first time (at least to our knowledge) the potential importance of "regulatory federalism" in the analysis of public finance. He considers the example of varying regulations governing pollution across areas or regions of the country. This may be but one example of an increasingly important theoretical and empirical problem in intergovernmental fiscal relations—namely, the role of mandates and rules imposed by the federal government upon states and by state governments upon localities. Devising positive and normative models of the imposition of mandates (or the use of mandates as matching requirements) will not be an easy task. But increasingly, the actions of lower-level governments, and the fiscal choices available to them, are restricted by regulations imposed by higher levels of government. The notion of "price" must be expanded to accommodate this reality.

In chapter 6, Charles McLure and George Zodrow consider the way in which public finance theory, and the advances in that theory, have been translated into usable knowledge in the design and execution of tax policy. They consider specifically the interplay between economic analysis and the federal income tax policies actually undertaken in the United States during the past three decades.

McLure and Zodrow begin by characterizing the consensus on theoretical issues that prevailed in 1960, paying particular attention to the logic of those principles that underlay informed scholarly and professional opinion at that time. They discuss the definition of the tax base, the role of the Haig-Simons definition of income, and the implications of this definition for the treatment of inflation, investment, and the timing of taxation.

The authors provide powerful illustrations of the way in which advances in theory and new empirical evidence affected the economic consensus from 1960 to 1985. This analysis of the development of economic thinking during a quarter-century, though selective, is enormously instructive.

McLure and Zodrow indicate, for example, the operational importance of the controversial empirical findings that labor supply behavior is quite sensitive to taxation (Hausman, 1981b), that the amount of savings is affected by its after-tax return (Boskin, 1978a), and that the sensitivity of human capital investment decisions to taxation further increases the long-run labor supply and savings elasticities with respect to tax rates.

The authors also demonstrate the importance of modern computable general equilibrium models in analyzing plausible interactions among economic entities. They provide a careful and balanced review of recent work on the choice between consumption and income tax bases and the controversies over tax expenditures and tax shelters.

The heart of the McLure-Zodrow contribution, however, is the analysis of the interaction between these theoretical advances (and the controversial nature of many of them) and their actual implementation in the Tax Reform Act of 1986. The authors find a major paradox in the application of modern public finance theory. The complexity and subtlety of modern analysis make it ever more difficult to argue convincingly to those who make tax policy in the legislative process. But the difficulty goes deeper than explication, because the complexity of modern analysis also means that empirical results are more fragile and uncertainties are greater. Finally, the diffusion of highly competent public finance talent throughout the federal government—from the Treasury Department to the legislative staff—encourages the use of sophisticated economic analysis in an adversarial setting. Adding to the adversarial nature of public economics is the fact that strong analytical staffs are now working at the major consulting and accounting firms and are thus available to interest groups and private sector advocates.

This volume includes four chapters analyzing issues in optimal taxation and public finance. As suggested by McLure and Zodrow, a central finding of this new literature—that high or increasing marginal tax rates may not be appropriate, even if the social welfare function is strongly egalitarian—was an important consideration in legislating tax reform. The chapters by James Mirrlees and Peter Diamond provide elegant theoretical analyses extending the paradigm of optimal taxation. Mirrlees addresses the goods produced by tax revenues, while Diamond addresses optimal stabilization policy. The final two chapters, by Robert Haveman and Richard Arnott, provide an interpretation and assessment of the importance of the theory of optimal taxation.

James Mirrlees, the founder and original innovator of the optimal tax literature, analyzes the relationship between optimal taxation and the finance of public expenditures, thus formulating the first linkage between optimal tax (in the sense of tax rates applied to labor and commodities) and the "optimal" amount of revenue to be spent on public production. Mirrlees considers the circumstances under which this intricate problem has a well-defined solution. He also examines the relationship between this model and more conventional macroeconomic problems of adjustment and stabilization.

Mirrlees offers an extensive analysis of this challenging class of problems in his consideration of the optimal level of public expenditures in a second-best economy. Much of his work also requires an integrated analysis of the effects of public expenditures on tax revenues. Generalizing the optimal taxation paradigm to include the effects of government production on consumers is no easy task and is a fertile area for theoretical research. It appears that it may be possible to provide a stylized model of the "optimal government" using the techniques developed for the study of taxation.

Peter Diamond presents a complementary analysis of optimal stabilization policy, clearly illuminating the potential tradeoff between economic efficiency and stabilization objectives. His notion of stabilization encompasses situations in which demand is unstable or uncertain, as well as those in which there is some single large shock to the economy. He also discusses circumstances in which there is a prolonged period of low aggregate demand and idle resources.

In the latter case, Diamond sketches out a model that enables one to determine the number of additional public sector jobs required to stabilize the aggregate economy. In this model, public sector job creation depends upon the investment costs required to produce jobs and the substitutability of different kinds of jobs in stimulating aggregate employment and total output. The allocation and stabilization objectives are reconciled by considering explicitly the number of jobs and their division between the public and private sectors.

In his analysis of stabilization policy in response to shocks to the economy, Diamond builds on Musgravian analyses of built-in stabilizers. He asks whether a particular set of tax and transfer mechanisms—which, in effect, insures producers and workers against an exogenous shock in the economy—also provides appropriate incentives to job suppliers and to workers. In several stylized cases, he solves for the optimal stabilization policy and for its effects upon the otherwise optimal tax rate in the economy. He also extends these models informally to address price level changes in an inflationary environment.

Robert Haveman examines the policy lessons that can be learned from the optimal tax literature, considering both commodity and income taxation. He raises important questions about the relevance of this literature to public policy and to the debate about desirable tax reforms. He describes a dozen difficulties in getting unambiguous results from the theory that could be applied in practice. Havemen concludes that popular ''lessons'' from optimal tax models for tax policies are unwarranted and perhaps misleading. His analysis reinforces the caution expressed by McLure and Zodrow about the fragility of many policy conclusions.

In chapter 10, Richard Arnott addresses two technical issues that complement the analysis presented by Mirrlees. First, what is the relationship between the level of public goods production in the second-best circumstance and the level in the first-best circumstance? Second, how can Mirrlees' attempt to incorporate macroeconomics into optimal taxation be interpreted? Arnott complements Haveman's analysis by asking: How has the theory of optimal taxation contributed to public economics?

Arnott extends Mirrlees' comparison of first-best and second-best public goods provision and demonstrates an alternative and simpler way of approaching the problem. He continues by analyzing a series of models that bring stabilization objectives into the optimal tax framework. In extending and complementing the work of Diamond and Mirrlees, Arnott makes an important contribution to further research.

The third part of Chapter 10 offers a spirited defense of optimal tax theory and its contributions to public economics. The reader will judge the success of this effort. The argument should be compared not only with the chapters by Mirrlees and Haveman but also with the more general treatment by McLure and Zodrow.

The authors of this book furnish provocative analyses of the most salient issues in the public finance component of public economics, but they do not analyze specific public expenditures. It is not difficult to envision a separate volume, roughly the same size as this, which would be devoted entirely to modern public expenditure analysis—health care, social insurance, agriculture subsidy, the economics of defense spending, and so forth. Such a volume would have a different theoretical basis from the general equilibrium model emphasized here, but it would be a welcome companion to this book.

PART I

DISTRIBUTION, STABILIZATION, DYNAMICS

2

The Distribution of the Tax Burden

The distribution of the tax burden has been a subject of central concern in the public finance literature. In the United States, one thinks of the landmark study of the tax burden by Musgrave, written with Carroll, Cook, and Frane (1951). Musgrave returned to the subject in Musgrave, Case, and Leonard (1974). In the same year, Pechman and Okner published their celebrated book *Who Bears the Tax Burden?* Pechman wrote a sequel (1985) and gave calculations up to 1988 in his presidential address to the American Economic Association, which he was unable to deliver before he died (Pechman, 1990). This chapter focuses on the relation between theory and empirical evidence in understanding the distribution of the tax burden.

The findings of Musgrave et al. (1974) show that in the United States in 1968, on the basis of progressive assumptions about incidence, the tax burden as a percentage of total income increased from 20 percent for the lowest group (broadly, the bottom 20 percent of families) to between 26 and 30 percent for the rest of the population, rising above this only for the top 5 percent. With regressive assumptions about incidence, the tax burden starts at 32 percent, rises to around 35 percent in the middle, and falls below 30 percent for the top 5 percent. (The assumptions about incidence are described more fully below.) For 1980, Pechman, using similar but not identical methods, found that "under the most progressive assumptions effective tax rates in 1980 ran from about 20 percent at the lowest end of the income scale to 27 percent at the top. Under the least progressive assumptions effective tax rates declined from over 30 percent at the lowest end of the distribution to about 25 percent in the second decile and remained at that level until they declined to 22 percent in the top percentile'' (Pechman, 1985, p. 4). His estimates for 1988 (Pechman, 1990, Table 3) show, on the most progressive assumptions, that the changes in the United States since 1980, of which the most important was the Tax Reform Act of 1986, have reduced the tax burden for the bottom three deciles, increased the burden for the next six deciles, and reduced it for the top 10 percent (the overall burden being little changed).

The reasons for making these calculations, and the reasons for investigating them more fully, are well explained by the president of the Brookings Institution in his foreword to Pechman's 1985 book: ''The distribution of tax burdens by income class is of major concern to the general public, political leaders, and social scientists, yet the information regarding this distribution is scanty. The lack of information is attributable to the difficulty of making such estimates and to the conceptual problems of deciding who actually pays the various taxes'' (MacLaury, in Pechman, 1985, p. viii).

The question of tax burdens is of considerable interest to the policy debate—yet at the same time there are major issues to be examined. In this chapter, I review some of the key developments in our understanding of the distribution of the tax burden, and identify topics for future research. I have chosen to concentrate on two aspects. The first is the problem of incidence, which is mentioned in the quotation above and which is one of the central issues of tax analysis. The second is the relationship between factor incomes, in terms of which incidence is typically discussed, and the incomes received by individual taxpayers, which are the concern of the empirical studies.

Part I is about incidence. From Musgrave's *Theory of Public Finance* (1959a, Part III), through Arnold Harberger's general equilibrium analysis of corporate taxation (1962), to computable general equilibrium models, we have seen a growth in understanding of the economics of tax incidence. The Harberger model in particular has proved its value in modern public finance, showing the general equilibrium impact of taxation on factor prices and product prices, and it is with this that I begin. In order to illustrate the analysis, I take a particular example—the incidence of the employer payroll tax—because it is both an important tax and one where the issue of incidence is vexed. At the same time, from this and other applications, it is evident that there are major limitations to the simple two-sector model, and that we need to leave the world of a frictionless, static Walrasian economy. The implications for tax incidence of such departures form the subject of the second section of Part I.

Part II of this chapter takes up the relation between the functional distribution of income (factor prices)—the primary focus of the Harberger model—and the personal distribution. The general equilibrium analysis can be informative in answering the question "Who bears the tax burden?" only if the incidence in terms of factor returns is linked to that in terms of the individuals who appear in the empirical studies. In the first section of Part II, I consider the relation between theories of the personal distribution and the analysis of tax incidence, starting from the classical identification of factor incomes with class interests. The second section of Part II is concerned with the issues of social judgment that arise when we consider the personal distribution of income, including the assessment of progression, its relation to measured inequality, and differences in family composition. In the third section of Part II, I come to the empirical estimates, the relation between microdata and aggregate information, and the move from a snapshot to a life-cycle perspective.

In this review of the issues, I have made no attempt to be comprehensive. I have omitted discussion of many relevant aspects and have said little about those which are well covered elsewhere. There are subjects which I would like to have covered but for which there is no space. These include incidence under monopolistic competition, and the implications of recent developments in the economics of industrial organization. The internal structure of the firm receives no attention; neither do such matters as the type of financing. I do not treat the international or regional aspects of tax incidence, or the implications of incidence for public choice analysis, such as the impact of perceived incidence on the behavior of interest groups.

In focusing on the work of Musgrave and Pechman, this chapter makes particular reference to the United States, but there is a long history of studies in other countries. In the United Kingdom, for example, Jevons prepared a memorandum in 1869 showing the burden of taxation on hypothetical families with different levels of total expenditure, finding that the average tax rate first declines and then increases (Roseveare, 1973). Samuel (1919) assembled more detailed statistics on the taxes paid by families with different levels of income, showing again a U-shaped pattern for the average tax rate, but with tax rates rising much more steeply at high incomes. These studies (for a fuller historical review, see Shoup, 1972) are the forerunners of the official statistics which are now published annually in *Economic Trends* in the United Kingdom (Central Statistical Office, 1988), and which owe a great deal to Nicholson (1964). These official figures for the United Kingdom are less complete than those of Musgrave and Pechman, in that they omit important taxes such as corporation taxes, and do not consider alternative models of incidence.[1] On the other hand, they do cover government spending (again with significant omissions) as well as taxation, and this has been the practice in a number of other countries; see especially the work of Gillespie (1965) for Canada, Bjerke (1964) for Denmark, Reynolds and Smolensky (1976) for the United States, Cazenave and Morrisson (1978) for France, and Franzen et al. (1975) for Sweden.[2] In this chapter, I focus on the tax side of the government budget. I shall not consider the incidence of public spending, but shall treat the question as one of "differential incidence" (Musgrave, 1959a, p. 212).

I. ON INCIDENCE

One of the particular contributions of the empirical studies quoted above has been the examination of a range of assumptions about incidence. Musgrave et al. (1974), for example, make six different assumptions about the incidence of the corporate income tax, five assumptions about the property tax, and two about the employer payroll tax. These assumptions are combined to yield:

most progressive case;
most regressive case;
"benchmark case" allowing for some degree of shifting;
"competitive" case based on the assumptions most appropriate for a competitive market.

In the case of Pechman (1985), there are alternative assumptions about the same range of taxes, leading to eight variants on the calculations, of which one is identified as the least progressive and another as the most progressive.

The Musgrave-Pechman approach of making a range of assumptions has considerable merit. It brings out the sensitivity of results. It is easily explained to a lay audience. At same time, it is a confession of ignorance, and economists have naturally sought to go further. Moreover, Prest (1955), Bird (1980), and others have charged the approach with being internally inconsistent: "calculations of the incidence of direct and indirect taxes are based on conflicting and contradictory assumptions" (Prest, 1955, p. 242). In order to go further, and to assess such a criticism, we need to embed the analysis of tax incidence within an economic model. Indeed, it should be recognized that the description in terms of "alternative incidence assumptions" is shorthand for "alternative assumptions about the underlying economic model." Assumptions about incidence as such have no meaning; they are of interest only if they can be seen to result from a fully specified model of the operation of the economy.

A. General Equilibrium Incidence

A substantial part of Musgrave's *Theory of Public Finance* is indeed concerned with the general equilibrium incidence of taxation. As Musgrave recognized, there had been a number of relevant preceding analyses, including Shephard (1944) and Meade's *Mathematical Supplement to Trade and Welfare* (1955a). The latter indicates the debt of public finance—like other branches of economics—to international trade theory. This debt was clearly acknowledged by Harberger (1962) in his article on the incidence of the corporation income tax, an article that led to the widespread adoption by public finance economists of the two-good two-factor general equilibrium model.[3]

The impact of the Harberger model on the profession reflects the fact that it encompasses the essentials of an equilibrium model, while allowing a convenient representation in terms of either geometry (as in Johnson, 1971) or the "hat calculus" of Jones (1965). The essentials are set out below. On the demand side, I simplify by assuming in Part I that preferences are identical (differences in preferences are introduced in Part II) and that the income elasticities of demand are equal to unity. This means that the relative demands for the two goods, x and y, are independent of the distribution and level of income, depending only on the relative prices of the two goods, p_x/p_y. This relation is shown as a "demand curve" in the top right-hand segment of Figure 2.1. Differentiating logarithmically,

$$(2.1) \qquad \frac{dx}{x} - \frac{dy}{y} = -D \left(\frac{dp_x}{p_x} - \frac{dp_y}{p_y} \right),$$

where D is the sum of the compensated own-price elasticities (see Jones, 1965; Atkinson and Stiglitz, 1980, p. 168).

What does the "supply curve" look like? The two factors, capital and labor, are assumed at this point to be in fixed total supply, given by K and L respectively, but they are perfectly mobile between sectors, and in each case paid their value marginal products (r and w respectively). The output is produced by price-taking firms according to identical constant returns to scale production functions in each sector, with elasticities of substitution σ_x and σ_y respectively. The factor share of labor in sector X is denoted by Θ_{lx}, where $(1-\Theta_{lx}) = \Theta_{kx}$

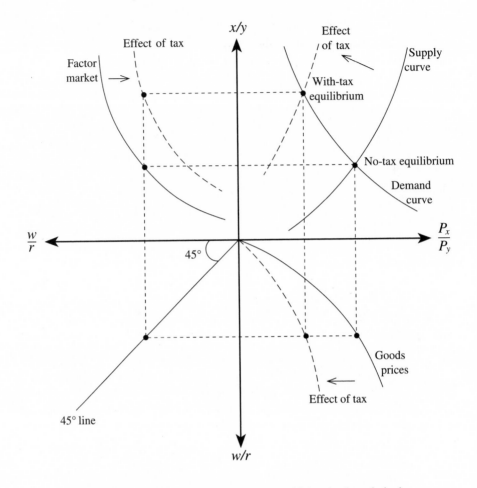

Figure 2.1. Effect of payroll tax on use of labor in the relatively capital-intensive Y-sector.

(and Θ_{ly} and Θ_{ky} are defined correspondingly). From the assumptions made, it follows that the product prices are equal to the marginal (and average) costs, or that

$$(2.2) \qquad \frac{dp_x}{p_x} - \frac{dp_y}{p_y} = \theta \left(\frac{dw}{w} - \frac{dr}{r} \right),$$

where

$$(2.3) \qquad \theta \equiv \theta_{lx}\theta_{ky} - \theta_{ly}\theta_{kx}.$$

Θ is positive if sector X is labor-intensive relative to Y in terms of the factor shares, and is a measure of the relative factor intensities in value terms. The assumption that X is everywhere (that is, for all w/r) relatively labor-intensive underlies the illustration of this relation in the bottom right-hand part of Figure 2.1.

The condition for equilibrium in the factor market is shown in the upper left-hand quadrant in Figure 2.1. Writing the unit cost function in the X-sector as $c_x(r,w)$, with a corresponding definition for the Y-sector, the conditions for full employment of capital and labor are:

(2.4) $\qquad c_{kx}\, x + c_{ky}\, y = K; \quad c_{lx}\, x + c_{ly}\, y = L.$

Differentiating, and making use of the definition of the elasticity of substitution (Atkinson and Stiglitz, 1980, pp. 169–170), and defining

(2.5) $\qquad \lambda_{lx} \equiv c_{lx}x/L$

for the share of labor used in the X-sector, and corresponding expressions λ_{ly}, λ_{kx}, λ_{ky}, we arrive at the following relationship between the shares of output and the factor prices:

(2.6) $\qquad \lambda \left(\dfrac{dx}{x} - \dfrac{dy}{y} \right) = (a_x\sigma_x + a_y\sigma_y) \left(\dfrac{dw}{w} - \dfrac{dr}{r} \right),$

where

(2.7) $\qquad \lambda \equiv \lambda_{lx}\lambda_{ky} - \lambda_{ly}\lambda_{kx}$

is an alternative measure of factor intensity, based on physical quantities rather than on value terms, and a_x, a_y depend on Θ_{ij} and λ_{ij}.[4]

Combining (2.2) and (2.6), we arrive at a "supply curve":

(2.8) $\qquad \lambda\theta \left(\dfrac{dx}{x} - \dfrac{dy}{y} \right) = (a_x\sigma_x + a_y\sigma_y) \left(\dfrac{dp_x}{p_x} - \dfrac{dp_y}{p_y} \right).$

The slope depends on the product $\lambda\Theta$. Looking ahead to the situation where we introduce distortionary taxes, I write w_x for the wage in the X-sector, and define w_y, r_x, and r_y correspondingly. We may then calculate that Θ is proportional to

(2.9) $\qquad \dfrac{w_x/w_y}{r_x/r_y}\lambda_{lx}\lambda_{ky} - \lambda_{ly}\lambda_{kx}.$

It follows that in a world where there are no taxes or other distortions, the ranking according to λ is the same as that according to Θ. This means that in Figure 2.1 the curve in the top left-hand diagram has the slope indicated, and that the supply curve slopes upward. There is a unique equilibrium. One special case is that in which there are fixed coefficients of production, so that the terms c_{lx}, and so forth do not change with w/r. There is then at most one ratio of x/y which gives a full employment equilibrium, and the supply curve is simply a straight line.[5]

B. The Employer Payroll Tax

To illustrate the analysis, I take the case of the employer's payroll tax. Payroll taxes represent a major and growing revenue source in many OECD countries. For example, in the United States their share in the federal tax system has risen from 9 percent in 1950 to 22 percent in 1970 and 40 percent in 1986 (Musgrave and Musgrave, 1989, p. 439).

The employer payroll tax is also one whose incidence has been regarded as uncertain. Whereas Musgrave et al. (1974) in all cases assume that the *employee* portion of the payroll tax is borne by the employee, they make alternative assumptions about the *employer* tax: either that it is shifted forward to consumers in general, or that it is borne by employees. The first of these assumptions implies that the incidence of the tax differs, depending on whether it is paid by the employer or the employee. In the case of Pechman (1985), the alternative is that half (rather than all) of the employer portion is shifted forward in higher prices. The latter corresponds to his least progressive case. In the United Kingdom, the official estimates were initially based on the assumption that the employers' contributions are borne by labor, but this has been replaced by the assumption that they are passed forward to consumers in higher prices (O'Higgins, 1980, p. 39). This variety of assumptions reflects the uncertainty about the tax's incidence. Break phrased it this way: "As the most rapidly growing source of federal government revenues during the postwar period, payroll taxes have drawn the attention of both the public and experts. A major uncertainty . . . has been the incidence of the portion of the tax paid by employers. Is it simply what it says it is, as many workers may believe, or do employers shift it to some other group, as most economists have concluded? And if it is shifted, do the burdens fall mainly on consumers in higher prices or on workers in the form of lower money wage rates?" (Break, 1974, p. 168). The Harberger model may be used to throw light on the incidence of the payroll tax, as in the study by Brittain (1972). Suppose that the tax is introduced at the same time that a proportional tax on all income is reduced, the total government revenue remaining unchanged, so that we are examining the differential incidence of the payroll tax and a proportional income tax. If the employer payroll tax is a *general factor tax*, falling on labor in all uses, then under the assumptions of the model there is no doubt that the differential incidence is on labor. If the payroll tax changes the cost of labor to the employer from w to wT, where $T > 1$, then the pretax wage has to adjust. In contrast, a proportional tax on all incomes requires a proportionate reduction in all incomes—a result that does not carry over to models of variable factor supply, as I shall show below.

The Harberger model was designed to analyze a *partial factor tax*, and there is a case for treating the social security payroll tax as falling on only one sector of the economy, so that there is a covered and an uncovered sector. Those employments not covered may include those in temporary work, those working less than a specified number of hours, those below a specified earnings threshold, and those in the black economy. Another interpretation is that of the uncovered sector as household production (see Boskin, 1972, 1975; Break, 1974, p. 169). Or the social security scheme may be operated by trade unions, in which case there will be differential coverage, as analyzed by Holmlund and Lundborg (1989).

The effect of such a partial tax in the Y-sector, T_{ly}, is examined by Brittain (1972, pp. 33–35) for the special case in which the production functions are identical in the two sectors and are of the Cobb-Douglas form, and in which the demand functions are also Cobb-Douglas. He shows that in this case the tax is again borne fully by labor. More generally (Atkinson and Stiglitz, 1980, p. 179) the tax adds to equation (2.2) a term

(2.10a)
$$-\theta_{ly} \frac{dT_{ly}}{T_{ly}}$$

and to equation (2.6) a term

(2.10b)
$$+a_y \sigma_y \frac{dT_{ly}}{T_{ly}}$$

If the covered sector is relatively capital-intensive, then the effect of the introduction of the partial factor tax is that shown by the dashed lines in Figure 2.1, where the product-price curve in the bottom right-hand quadrant shifts to the left and the factor market equilibrium curve shifts upward. As a result, the supply curve shifts upward, and the output of the covered sector contracts relative to that of the uncovered sector. This contraction increases the demand for labor, tending to offset the factor substitution within the covered sector, and the equilibrium w/r ratio may rise or fall (in the case shown in Figure 2.1, the effects exactly balance). Solving for the change in w/r,

(2.11) $$\left(\frac{dw}{w} - \frac{dr}{r}\right)(\theta\lambda D + a_x\sigma_x + a_y\sigma_y) = (\lambda\theta_{ly}D - a_y\sigma_y)\frac{dT_{ly}}{T_{ly}}.$$

A rise in w/r is more likely (other things being equal) the larger the degree of substitution on the demand side (D) and the smaller the elasticity of substitution in production in the covered sector (σ_y). Even where w/r falls, labor may bear less than the full burden of the tax, in the sense that the change in net wage income is less than the tax revenue.[6]

It is evident that there is a wide range of possible outcomes, depending on the values taken by the key parameters such as the elasticities of substitution in production and consumption. These are parameters whose empirical magnitude is difficult to assess. It is at this point that researchers often terminate their theoretical analyses and resort to numerical calculations. These vary in complexity, from those made originally by Harberger to the highly elaborate applied general equilibrium models of today.[7] There can be little doubt that these latter models have contributed a great deal; at the same time, they should not be regarded as a black box. Implicit in the calculations are answers to the questions about empirical magnitudes that we find so puzzling when posed explicitly. In my view, the computable general equilibrium models should be used in parallel with simple analytical models, as exemplified by Devarajan, Fullerton, and Musgrave (1980).

The lessons that may be learned from simple analytical models are illustrated by considering the implications of the fact that a finite tax causes a distortion in the economy. As noted earlier, and as investigated in the international trade literature (Jones, 1971; Magee, 1976), the existence of distortions may cause the supply curve to cease to be everywhere upward-sloping. This is illustrated in Figure 2.2 for the special case where the production function in the uncovered sector is Cobb-Douglas and that in the covered sector has fixed coefficients,[8] c_{ly} and c_{ky} per unit of output, where the covered sector is more capital-intensive than the overall factor availability:

(2.12) $$\frac{c_{ky}}{c_{ly}} > \frac{K}{L}.$$

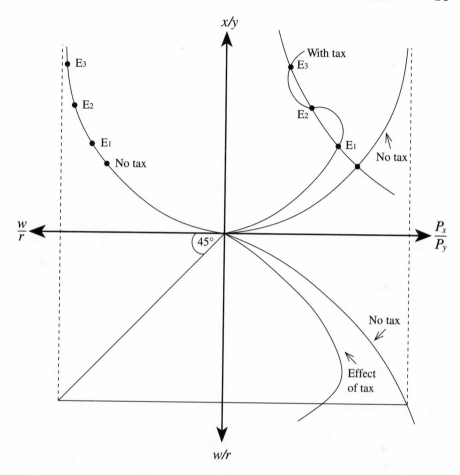

Figure 2.2. Example of effect of payroll tax on Y-sector and multiple equilibria.

It follows that the factor intensity measured in value terms cannot everywhere be one-signed, since Θ positive requires that

(2.13) $$\frac{\theta_{lx}}{\theta_{kx}} - \frac{wT_{ly}c_{ly}}{rc_{ky}} > 0$$

(allowing for the payroll tax in Y). The left-hand side is positive for sufficiently small w/r, but afterward negative, as shown in Figure 2.2 for the case of no tax ($T_{ly} = 1$). The factor demands in the X-sector are

$$L_x = \theta_{lx}(w/r)^{-\theta_{kx}} \cdot x$$

and

(2.14) $K_x = \theta_{kx}(w/r)^{\theta_{lx}} \cdot x,$

giving an equilibrium condition

(2.15) $\dfrac{x}{y} = \dfrac{(Lc_{ky} - Kc_{ly})}{[k\theta_{lx}(w/r)^{-\theta_{kx}} - L\theta_{kx}(w/r)^{\theta_{lx}}]}.$

Assumption (2.12) ensures that the top is positive; from the denominator we can see that there is an asymptote as shown, delimiting a finite range of w/r.

In the absence of taxes ($T_{ly} = 1$), the permissible range of factor prices derived from the factor marketclearing condition excludes the turning point in the price curve, and the supply curve is well behaved. For sufficiently small taxes, this continues to be the case, and we can draw standard conclusions: with the fixed-coefficient assumption, the payroll tax does not affect the factor mix in the covered sector, and the tax operates like an excise. The fact that the Y-sector is, for these values of w/r, capital-intensive means that the wage rate rises. As T_{ly} increases, however, the supply curve begins to bend back, as shown in Figure 2.2. If the demand is sufficiently price elastic, then, as shown, there are multiple equilibria. Corresponding to a specific level of the tax rate, there is more than one equilibrium, each of which has different distributional consequences: at E_3 the w/r ratio is higher than at E_1.

The problem of nonuniqueness of the momentary equilibrium is a matter of considerable concern in the theoretical literature on two-sector growth models (see, for example, Hahn, 1965; Dixit, 1976a, ch. 6), although this does not treat the case of a distorted economy. The typical response has been to make assumptions that ensure uniqueness, but this route is not open here, since it is the tax rate which is responsible for the problem. We must therefore face the question as to which equilibrium is attained. If we specify an out-of-equilibrium adjustment process, then it may be that the equilibrium E_2 can be ruled out on grounds of local instability (Neary, 1978; Atkinson and Stiglitz, 1980, pp. 183–187). The same line of argument may allow us to determine the equilibrium from the historical path of tax rates: for example, if T_{ly} has been increased steadily from zero, then the economy may be at E_1, but in the absence of some argument of this type, it cannot be ruled out that the economy is at E_3. If the demand curve is sufficiently elastic, then the equilibrium E_3 becomes one of complete specialization in the production of X.[9] There is in this case a "prohibitive" level of T_{lx}. In such a situation, there would be a distributional impact of a tax that raises no revenue.

The habit of thinking in terms of a single supply and demand intersection dies hard, and the simple analytical model serves to keep the possibility of nonuniqueness firmly in mind. The importance in numerical applications has yet to be fully understood. Experience suggests that nonuniqueness is not encountered, and Kehoe and Whalley (1985) have demonstrated uniqueness for two applied general equilibrium models. However, the method requires a decomposability property that may be quite limiting. This is likely to be an important area for further research.

C. Definition of Sectors

The application of the Harberger model to the payroll tax raises a number of issues, particularly concerning the interpretation of the model and the underlying assumptions. The first concerns the *definition of sectors*. The Harberger model directs our attention, on the one hand, to intersector differences in policy, and, on the other, to differences in the economic characteristics of sectors (such as factor intensity). We must therefore ask how far the sectoral division corresponds to an important economic reality.

In Harberger's original formulation, the distinction was between the corporate and noncorporate sectors. On the policy side, this is clearly the relevant distinction for the corporate income tax. What is more debatable is the relation with identifiable industries. Harberger recognized that it may "be questioned on the ground that the economy cannot be reasonably be divided into a set of industries which are overwhelmingly 'corporate,' and another set which is overwhelmingly non-corporate" (1962, p. 216), but went on to claim that "this objection has little validity, at least in the case of the United States" (1962, p. 216). He argued that agriculture, real estate, and miscellaneous repair services account for the great majority of noncorporate capital and contain little corporate activity. This has been questioned by Gravelle and Kotlikoff (1989). But even if one does not enter into the question of empirical validity, it still seems relevant to ask about the theoretical basis for the distinction. In particular, what are the economic factors leading one set of activities to be carried out by corporate businesses? This question is addressed by King (1988, 1989) and by Gravelle and Kotlikoff (1989). The latter allow for corporate and noncorporate production in both sectors, modeling the choice between working as a corporate manager or as an entrepreneur. King (1988 and 1989) is concerned with the life-cycle of firms, treating new firms as the embodiment of new ideas, where the investor has the choice between setting up on his or her own and selling the idea to an existing company. This analysis, which is related to that on contracts and ownership rights in firms (for example, Hart and Moore, 1988), seems an interesting line for future development.

The corporate/noncorporate division is one of several which may be relevant. We may, for example, want to follow the two-sector growth literature and identify one sector as producing capital goods and the other as producing consumer goods. The distinction on which I focus here, however, is that implied by the idea of a dual labor market. The idea of labor market segmentation has a long history in institutional labor economics and has been popular among radical economists, but it has recently begun to attract mainstream attention.

The dual labor market formulation has been advanced by Doeringer and Piore (1971), who see the economy as having a favored high-wage primary sector and a low-wage secondary sector. In the primary sector, there is stable employment, internal promotion possibilities, provision of training, and work typically involving skill or the exercise of responsibility. In the secondary sector, jobs are typically unskilled, the work involves little training or prospect of promotion, and there is casual attachment between firms and workers. According to Bulow and Summers, "a typical example of a primary-sector employer is a large manufacturing establishment, while small service firms such as fast food outlets typify the secondary sector" (1986, p. 380). This should be understood as a stylization. In practice, there may be secondary-type jobs within large manufacturing firms, and some small service sector employers may provide training and prospects.

One of the important contributions of the recent literature is to seek to explain the persistence of a wage differential, for otherwise identical workers, as a result of the characteristics of the two sectors. Particular weight has been given to the efficiency wage explanation. In the version developed by Shapiro and Stiglitz (1984), Bulow and Summers (1986), and others, this is related to the costs of supervision in the two sectors. In the secondary sector, jobs are relatively easily supervised, whereas jobs in the primary sector require some degree of responsibility and initiative. Supervision is costly, and primary-sector firms pay a wage premium in order to induce effort with only intermittent monitoring. If Y is the primary sector and X the secondary sector, then a wage differential $w_y > w_x$ can persist in equilibrium. Suppose that the cost of effort is e, and that there is an exogenous probability q of being monitored. The primary-sector worker is assumed to weigh the certainty of $(w_y - e)$ if he puts in effort against the probability $(1 - q)$ of w_y plus the probability q of being fired and earning $(w_x - e)$ in the secondary sector. (It is assumed for convenience that workers are risk-neutral and consider only income in a single period.) The wage premium necessary to just induce effort is[10]

$$(2.16) \qquad w_y = w_x + e\,\frac{1 - q}{q}.$$

In reality a particular industrial sector may contain both primary and secondary jobs; nonetheless, the dual labor market model provides a sectoral distinction with an evident economic rationale, the implications of which seem worth pursuing. Moreover, the secondary sector has a number of features which mean that it is less likely to be covered by the payroll tax, including relatively short-term or casual employment, and illegal employment. In what follows, this is represented in extreme form by assuming that the payroll tax falls only on the primary (Y) sector.

D. Unemployment and Labor Market Frictions

In the dual labor market model, there is the question of the ease of mobility between the sectors. A geographical interpretation of the Harberger model has been given by McLure (1969), where one of the two factors is not mobile between the sectors.[11] In the case of labor, such frictions may result from barriers to migration, as in the model of a developing dual economy by Harris and Todaro (1970). This model has been combined with that of efficiency wages (Stiglitz, 1982a) and has been applied to a developed country, where there are barriers to movement between the secondary and primary sectors and where recruitment to the primary sector is from a pool of unemployed workers seeking jobs. As described by McDonald and Solow, "secondary employment may be regarded as a kind of stigma that bars access to the primary sector. To the extent that secondary workers are regarded by primary market employers as 'inferior' or 'unreliable,' some gesture of separation from the secondary market may increase the chance of being offered a primary-sector job" (1985, pp. 1124–1125). This leads to a queue of workers waiting for jobs in the primary (Y) sector. An equilibrium explanation of unemployment is thus introduced into the model.

The consequences of these frictions for the analysis of tax incidence can be seen if one modifies the earlier Harberger model to allow for efficiency wages and for a queue of workers waiting for jobs in the primary sector.[12] The probability of getting a job in the primary sector is the ratio, V/U, of the number of vacancies to the number of unemployed competing for them. Workers can move freely between unemployment and secondary-sector employment. The wage paid by the latter, w_x, is then compared with the expected value of a wage, w_y, in the primary sector with probability V/U or continued unemployment with probability $(1 - V/U)$. In order for there to be indifference between secondary employment and unemployment, we must have

$$(2.17) \qquad w_x = \frac{V}{U} w_y + \left(1 - \frac{V}{U}\right) e,$$

where e is the value of the effort expended at work and hence the net benefit when a worker is unemployed (at this point, we are taking no account of unemployment insurance). It is assumed that a randomly selected fraction g of those with jobs in the primary sector are made redundant at the start of the period for exogenous reasons, and that an equal number of vacancies is created, so that the rate of success is

$$(2.18) \qquad \frac{V}{U} = \frac{gL_y}{L - L_x - L_y}.$$

The production technology is assumed to exhibit fixed coefficients in both sectors, the primary (Y) sector being taken to be relatively capital-intensive. Using (2.16) to eliminate w_y, the resulting goods-price relationship is shown in the bottom right-hand quadrant of Figure 2.3, where the profit rate r is taken as the numeraire.[13] From the factor market equations, and using (2.18), we can solve for x/y in terms of U/V:[14]

$$(2.19) \qquad \frac{x}{y} = \frac{[Lc_{ky} - Kc_{ly}(1 + gU/V)]}{(Kc_{lx} - Lc_{kx})}.$$

We now have a use for the bottom left-hand quadrant, which shows the relation (2.17) between U/V and w_x, again using (2.16).

From this model with frictional unemployment and efficiency wages, we can see the impact of a payroll tax on the covered (Y) sector. Again the assumption of fixed coefficients means that the factor mix is unaffected. The queue condition is unaffected. The only relationship which is shifted is that for goods prices in the bottom right-hand quadrant. From Figure 2.3 we see that the new equilibrium shifts production toward the uncovered sector, with a rise in the wage rate in both sectors (the wage premium is unaffected). The new findings concern

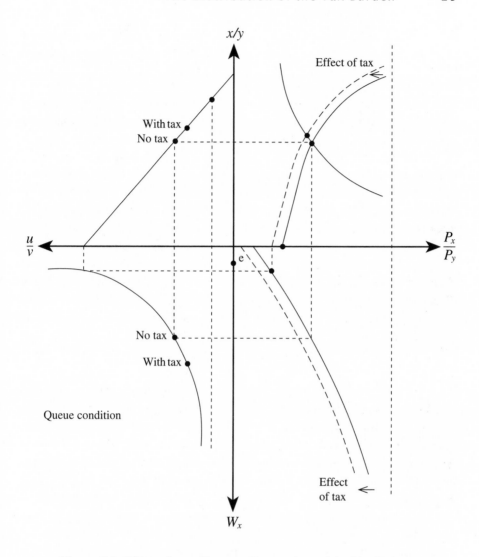

Figure 2.3. Effect of payroll tax on Y-sector in model with efficiency
wages and unemployment queue.

the equilibrium level of unemployment. The effect of the tax is to reduce
U/V and to reduce employment in the Y sector (and hence V). So, with the
assumptions made (which may well be questioned), the use of the payroll tax
in place of a general income tax would reduce unemployment.[15]

The model just described takes a step toward incorporating into the Harberger framework some of the recent developments in labor economics. A second form of equilibrium unemployment is that arising from the frictions in matching jobs to workers (see, for example, Diamond, 1982a; Pissarides, 1979; and Blanchard and Diamond, 1989). Primary-sector jobs become productive or unproductive according to some exogenous process. When a job switches from being unproductive to being productive, a vacancy is announced and there is a matching process of vacancies and unemployed workers. Even if the number of vacancies equals the number of unemployed, the frictions in matching mean that it is less than completely successful. There is again equilibrium unemployment. The implications of matching within the Harberger model have been explored by Davidson et al. (1988), who interpret the two factors as two different types of labor (rather than labor and capital). They emphasize the fact that frictions lead the supply curve to bend backward, especially when the primary sector is small.

The explanation of unemployment in equilibrium terms does not mean that unemployment may not arise as a disequilibrium phenomenon. Where markets do not clear, agents are rationed with regard to factor supplies and commodity demands. The modification of general equilibrium tax incidence to this type of situation has been examined by Dixit (1976b) and by Atkinson and Stiglitz (1980, pp. 222–225), but it is intrinsically difficult. There appears to have been relatively little contact between the literature on disequilibrium macroeconomics and public finance (although for an example of a computational general equilibrium model with unemployment associated with a fixed real wage, see Kehoe and Serra-Puche, 1983).

Finally, most accounts of the employer payroll tax recognize that the incidence may be different if we allow for imperfect competition. It is often suggested that this may rationalize a difference in incidence between employer and employee contributions. For example: "In the short run, a change in the employer contribution will not be reflected in the wage rate simply because wage contracts extend over several years or for other reasons have an adjustment lag . . . But even in the longer run, the competitive market outcome may not apply where market imperfections prevail. Unions may be unwilling to accept a wage cut because the employer contribution is increased, while being willing to absorb an increase in the employer contribution without demanding a wage hike. Employers may find an increase in their tax an occasion for raising administered prices" (Musgrave and Musgrave, 1989, p. 442). The difficulty (one not avoided in this quotation) seems to be in explaining how differences in incidence may arise as an *equilibrium* phenomenon. The impact of a union wage differential in one sector has been examined by Johnson and Mieszkowski

(1970). The effects of unionization are represented by a wage premium, but this clearly needs to be related to the underlying economic determinants. For this purpose, it may be promising to draw on recent work on union structure and objectives, on bargaining models, and on insider-outsider relations (see, for example, Hill, 1984; Carruth and Oswald, 1987; and Lindbeck and Snower, 1988, pp. 246–249).

E. Endogenous Factor Supply and Growth of the Economy

In discussing factor supplies—until now assumed fixed—I shall concentrate on the case of a single good, leaving to one side the complexities which arise in a two-sector model. This means that if the labor supply responds to the real wage rate, there is no problem of defining an appropriate price index to deflate money wages. Let us, for example, write

(2.20) $L = L_0 w^h,$

where w is the real wage rate (the product price being taken as the numeraire) and h is the (constant) elasticity of labor supply (income effects being ignored). Such a model was used by Feldstein (1974b) to analyze the payroll tax, which is now a general factor tax on labor. From his results, we may see that in the case of an infinitesimal tax, with the supply of capital fixed, the ratio of labor's net loss to the tax revenue is

(2.21) $$\frac{1}{1 + (1 - \theta_l)h/\sigma},$$

where Θ_l is the share of labor in aggregate output and σ is the aggregate elasticity of substitution (assumed nonzero). The key element is the elasticity of labor supply relative to the elasticity of substitution. This points up how central conclusions about tax incidence depend on parameters whose magnitudes have generated a great deal of controversy. With $\Theta_l = 2/3$, values of h of 0.15 and σ of 1.5 would imply that labor largely (97 percent) bears the burden, whereas $h = 0.5$ and σ of 1/3 imply that the burden is shared in proportion to the original shares, as with a tax that reduces all incomes proportionately.

This simple model also serves to show that a proportional income tax does not necessarily have a proportional impact on all incomes. A proportional income tax would be partly shifted by labor (as with the payroll tax), but it would be borne fully by capital (on the assumption of fixed supply). This brings out the importance of clarifying the basis for comparison in differential incidence—whether it is a comparison with an alternative *form of taxation* or with an alternative *outcome*.

As we saw earlier, this kind of analysis is more likely to produce qualitative rather than quantitative conclusions. This is well illustrated by the second part of Feldstein's analysis, which examines the effect of the payroll tax on the steady state of a growing economy, where the quantity of capital is fixed at any instant but grows over time, depending on the rate of saving. The key relation is that in terms of the proportionate growth rate of capital per man $(k = K/L)$

$$(2.22) \qquad \frac{dk}{dt} = s(r)f(k) - nk,$$

where $s(r)$ is the saving rate, assumed to depend on the rate of interest, $f(k)$ is output per head, and n is the (constant) rate of population growth. In a competitive economy, r depends only on k, and the condition for steady-state growth $(dk/dt = 0)$ implies that k must solve $s[r(k)] f(k) = nk$. Feldstein deduces that a payroll tax which leaves unchanged the savings rate has no effect on the steady-state capital intensity and hence on the gross wage. Thus, even if labor supply is a function of the net wage rate, there is no long-run shifting of the payroll tax. As Feldstein emphasizes, this result relates to the long run, and we need to consider more carefully the intervening dynamics—a point to which I shall return.

The tax may affect the savings rate via the distribution of income between wages and profits, as in the "classical" accumulation model put forward by Kaldor (1956) and others, where there is a higher propensity to save out of profits than out of wages. In the limiting case, all savings derive from capital income. A full assessment of this approach requires examination of the corporate structure of the economy. A more popular model, with the reverse implications, is that of life-cycle savings. In such a model, savings derive not from capital income but from wage income, as people save for their retirement, whereas the retired members of the population with capital tend to dissave. This may be seen most clearly in the overlapping generations model of Samuelson (1958) and Diamond (1965, 1970), where there are two generations alive in any discrete period. The growth of capital per head is then

$$(2.23) \qquad k_{t+1} - k_t = \frac{sw_t}{1 + n} - k_t.$$

In other words, the capital stock in the next period (the time scale is now naturally discrete) is made up of the savings out of wages, sw_t, of the working population (deflated by $1 + n$ to allow for the population growth) minus the dissaving of the elderly, who use up their capital stock. The savings rate of the working generation is assumed to be derived from maximization of a two-period utility function. A third kind of model is that which emphasizes savings for bequest purposes. In a model of (nonoverlapping) generations, the amount passed on by generation t is a proportion s of the output generated by the capital inherited

$$(2.24) \qquad k_{t+1} = \frac{s}{1 + n} f(k_t),$$

where the factor $(1 + n)$ allows for population growth. The proportion s may depend on the current w and r, or be forward-looking to the future wage and rate of return of the next generation.

If taxes reduce the savings rate, then this may lead to a fall in the steady-state capital per head, and hence in the (w/r) ratio. It is also possible that taxation changes the *qualitative* behavior of the economy, a possibility that has not received the attention it warrants. To illustrate this, let us suppose that the savings rate in (2.24) declines from s^0 to s_0 as the amount of capital inherited increases according to

$$(2.25) \qquad s = \max[s^0(1 - k), s_0].$$

If the production function is $f(k) = k^\beta$, the capital stock evolves according to

$$(2.26a) \qquad k_{t+1} = \frac{s^0}{1 + n} (1 - k)k^\beta, \text{ where } k < (1 - s_0/s^0);$$

$$(2.26b) \qquad k_{t+1} = \frac{s_0}{1 + n} k^\beta, \text{ where } k \geq (1 - s_0/s^0).$$

It is assumed that taxation has the effect of reducing the parameters s_0 and s^0 proportionately. This model is similar to that used by Day (1982) in his analysis of irregular growth cycles, on which I draw below.

The dynamic behavior of the capital stock is shown in Figures 2.4 and 2.5. The assumption about the savings rate means that the right-hand side of (2.26a) reaches a maximum where

$$(2.27) \qquad k = k_m = \frac{\beta}{1 + \beta}.$$

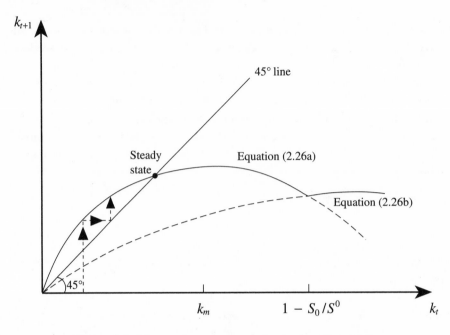

Figure 2.4. Monotonic convergence to steady-state growth.

This value is independent of s. What changes with s is the location of the curve in relation to the 45° line. For s sufficiently small, the maximum of the curve occurs below the 45° line and the economy converges monotonically (once it is to the left of k_m) to the steady state; see Figure 2.4. This is the case examined in most of the public finance literature, and a fall in savings leads to a reduction in the steady-state capital labor ratio and hence in the wage rate. With a higher initial savings rate, the maximum occurs above the 45° line and we may have a stable two-period cycle, as shown in Figure 2.5. There will be alternating periods of (relatively) high wages / low rate of return and low wages / high rate of return. In this situation, a tax which reduces the savings propensity still reduces the average value of k and hence the wage rate, but—what is more important—it may change qualitatively the behavior of the economy. The regime may be converted from one with cycles to one with a monotonic convergence to steady state. A further possibility is that there exists no (weakly) stable cycle, and that the behavior is chaotic.[16] In this case, again, the imposition of a tax that reduces the savings propensity may change the qualitative properties of the dynamic behavior.

The rate of growth attained (on average in the case of cycles) in these econo-

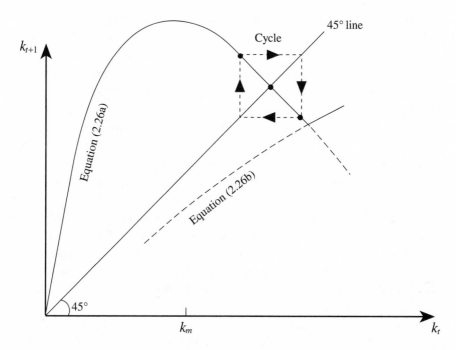

Figure 2.5. Higher savings rate: two-period cycle.

mies is assumed to be exogenous, but the endogeneity of technical progress raises the issue of the effect of taxation on long-run growth performance. In the recent rediscovery of growth theory, Romer (1986), for example, has emphasized the role of positive externalities generating increasing returns in the aggregate. King and Robson (1989) introduce a nonlinear technical progress function, combined with stochastic shocks (which may be due to tax changes). They emphasize the role of history, including past tax policy, in affecting both the level of current output and the equilibrium rate of growth. The endogeneity of technical progress, and the way in which it is affected by taxation, is a subject which is likely to attract increasing attention.

F. Concluding Remarks on the Theory of Incidence

The purpose of this theoretical discussion of incidence is to illuminate what lies behind empirical assessments of the distribution of the tax burden and to identify considerations that would not otherwise come to mind.

The first of these is illustrated by the ambiguity which underlies the concept of differential incidence used in the empirical studies. As Kay (1990) notes, there is a difference between an accounting exercise, in which a conventional standard of reference is applied, and a genuine attempt to measure the difference between two equilibrium situations. The empirical investigators have suggested that their concern is with the latter. Pechman, for example, sets out to show "how the distribution of disposable income . . . differed from what the distribution would have been if all tax revenues had come from a proportional income tax with the same yields" (1985, p. 3). But he does not analyze the impact of a proportional income tax. He is implicitly assuming that a proportional income tax would impose a proportional tax burden, whereas we have seen that, with variable factor supply, a proportionate income tax would not necessarily have this effect. In fact, the comparison is with a tax that reduces all incomes proportionately (as in Musgrave et al., 1974, p. 275). It is an alternative that is being considered, not an alternative *tax*. In contrast, if we are really comparing two equilibria, then we need to examine explicitly the incidence of the alternative tax.

The second consideration is illustrated by the examples which have shown how changes in taxation may change the equilibrium of the economy in a qualitative way. The deep-rooted tendency to think in terms of a single supply/demand intersection means that all too often public finance analysis ignores the possibility that there may be multiple equilibria corresponding to a particular tax regime; the oversight is ironic, since it is the existence of taxes that may well be responsible for the nonuniqueness. The focus on the comparative dynamics of a stable steady state tends to divert attention from the possibility that changes in taxation may induce a change in the mode of behavior of the economy—a possibility that has been more widely appreciated in the macroeconomics literature.

II. FROM FACTOR RETURNS TO PERSONAL INCOMES

My account of incidence in Part I was principally concerned with the effects of taxation on factor returns: the wage rate and the rate of return. I now consider the relation between the functional and personal distributions. This is necessary not only to make the connection with empirical studies of the incidence on families, but also to examine the implications of the tax code itself. The payroll tax, for instance, has an upper ceiling, whose consequences depend on the distribution of earnings within the working population.

If we assume that all capital income accrues to one class of society, and that the other class consists of wage earners, then we have the direct "classical" relationship between factor and personal distributions of income. As Musgrave has described it, "For classical economists, this scheme was doubly attractive. For one thing, it was an analytically convenient grouping, the pricing of various factors being subject to different principles. For another, it was a socially relevant grouping, as the division of society into capitalists, landlords, and workers gave a fair picture of social stratification in the England of the early nineteenth century" (1959a, p. 223). Today, this is scarcely adequate. Not only does the classical model fail to explain the distribution of factor incomes *within* classes (for example the size distribution of wages), but it is evident that we can no longer draw such a sharp division. As Musgrave went on to say, "the social significance of distribution by factor shares has declined . . . Incomes from various factors, especially labor broadly defined, accrue to recipients at high and low points in the income scale, and there is a growing tendency for people to receive incomes from a variety of sources. Thus the focus of the distribution problem has shifted to a size distribution of total income independent of its source" (1959a, p. 223). As a result, we need to study as such the personal distribution of incomes, and this is my subject here.

A. Theories of Personal Distribution and Tax Incidence

In the standard version of the Harberger model, all individuals are identical; but there have been a number of analyses of a two-class model, distinguishing between two classes in the population, $i = 1,2$, according to their shares in factor incomes and their demand patterns (for example, Meade, 1955a; Mieszkowski, 1967).

Suppose that group i spends a fraction s_i of its income on good X (and that utility functions for each group continue to be homothetic), and that the share of capital income in the total income of group i is given by z_i. It can then be shown that equation (2.1) becomes

$$(2.28) \qquad \frac{dx}{x} - \frac{dy}{y} = -D\left(\frac{dp_x}{p_x} - \frac{dp_y}{p_y}\right)$$

$$= -Q(s_1 - s_2)(z_1 - z_2)\left(\frac{dw}{w} - \frac{dr}{r}\right),$$

where Q is the product of the shares in total income of the two groups divided by the product of the shares of the two goods in total spending. Substituting for $(dw/w - dr/r)$ from the pricing equation (2.2), we see that there is now a real possibility that the demand curve may not be everywhere downward-sloping, and that there may on this account be multiple equilibria: for example, where there are fixed coefficients of production so that the supply curve is horizontal. In the two-sector growth literature, particular attention is given to the "class" version, where for capitalists $z_1 = 1$ and for workers $z_2 = 0$. In that case, if the capitalists spend more of their income on the capital-intensive good than do the workers, then multiple equilibria may emerge.[17]

Of particular interest here is the effect of factor price and product price changes on group 1 relative to group 2. Measured in terms of the change in lump-sum income required to maintain utility (Atkinson and Stiglitz, 1980, p. 191), this is

$$(2.29) \qquad (z_1 - z_2) \left(\frac{dr}{r} - \frac{dw}{w} \right) - (s_1 - s_2) \left(\frac{dp_x}{p_x} - \frac{dp_y}{p_y} \right).$$

This provides a formalization of the distinction made by Musgrave between the "sources" and "uses" sides of the account: "One set of effects stems from the 'income-sources' side, where tax policy may change the family unit's [income]. Another set of effects stems from the 'income-uses' side, where tax policy may affect the real value of disposable income by raising or lowering the prices of goods on which the family's income is spent" (1964, p. 195). In the case of the payroll tax, there may be an effect on the uses side, as well as on the sources side. The price of the product produced in the covered sector rises in relative terms, and the impact depends on the relative propensities to spend on this good. (See Hoyt and Smolensky, 1989, for a two-class numerical example.)

If we are to go beyond a simple two-class distribution, then we have to enrich the model. The relevant literature on the distribution of personal income is wide and disparate, reflecting the range of elements which could be incorporated. In describing the functions of the Distribution Branch, Musgrave, in *The Theory of Public Finance*, referred to the distribution of income as the result of "a number of factors including the laws of inheritance, the distribution of innate talents, the availability of educational opportunities, social mobility, and the structure of markets" (1959a, p. 17). To include all of these, even in a schematic way, in a model of the personal distribution of income is highly demanding, and it is not surprising that much of the literature focuses on one or two elements to the exclusion of others. Nonetheless, we can identify the following broad types of model:

a. where individuals differ according to an innate income-earning characteristic, distributed in some specified way across the population,
b. where individuals are identical ex ante, and indifferent with regard to income-relevant decisions, but there are differences in ex post outcomes,
c. where individuals receive, from their parents or others, a transferable income-earning advantage.

These categories are neither exclusive nor exhaustive. The traditional stochastic process theories, for example, could be classified under any of the three headings.

The first type of model is that which underlies the optimum income tax literature stemming from Mirrlees (1971), where there is an exogenously specified distribution of wage rates per hour. Gravelle and Kotlikoff (1989), in their model of entrepreneurship, assume a distribution of productivity. In models of efficiency wages, such as that of Drazen (1986), a distribution of productivities has been posited to provide a rationale for employers paying a wage premium to induce higher-quality workers to apply for jobs. Suppose that, in the spirit of the dual labor market approach, there are two sectors: a secondary sector in which workers are paid according to their productivity, and a primary sector in which employers, in the absence of full information on productivity, pay a uniform wage. If the latter are nonetheless able to apply an (imperfect) screening procedure, so that the probability of acceptance rises with ability, then we may observe both high-skilled and low-skilled workers in the secondary sector, the former not applying for jobs and the latter applying for jobs but being rejected. In such a case, the effect on the personal distribution of income of changes in the relative wages in the two sectors may not be unambiguous.

The second type of model is illustrated by the earlier dual labor market model. Everyone is ex ante identical but there are ex post differences between those who get a primary-sector job, those in the secondary sector, and those who are unemployed.

The third type of model is illustrated by that of Stiglitz (1969a), where individuals inherit material wealth from their parents and save out of the income from this wealth, and out of their earnings, to pass on a bequest to their children (assumed to be equally divided). In Atkinson (1980) and Atkinson and Stiglitz

(1980), this is combined with the intergenerational transmission of earnings advantage, both by genetic endowment and by family background (including the financing of education). At any point in time, the distribution depends on the past history, but in a linear version of the model (for example, with a constant savings rate), it may be shown that the distribution converges, providing that there is regression toward the mean and that the rate of growth of "old" capital is less than the rate of growth of population. This latter condition is in turn ensured by the convergence of the aggregate capital-labor ratio; in the linear model, the latter follows a path which is independent of the distribution and governed by a difference equation similar to (2.24).[18]

In the model just described, the inequality in the long-run equilibrium arises on account of the distribution of random terms affecting earning capacity and bequests; it is, however, possible that this type of model generates inequality independently of such "exogenous" sources. The replacement of the assumption of equal division by the opposite extreme of primogeniture in the model of Stiglitz (1969a) can generate a long-run Pareto Type II distribution even where there are no random influences on incomes. In this case, individual wealth holdings grow without limit, but they represent smaller proportions of a growing population.

This brief description has identified models which incorporate some of the mechanisms listed by Musgrave (1959a, p. 17), including inheritance, innate ability, and education. What is needed, in my view, is to combine these (largely household oriented) models with a richer treatment of the production side of the economy. Earlier, I made reference to endogenous technical progress and the link with the creation of new enterprises. At the level of the individual, this may be associated with the generation of new wealth. The connection between the size distribution of firms and the personal distribution is one which needs to be explored more fully.

B. Social Judgments

In discussing the results of the Harberger model, the factor price ratio w/r provides a convenient summary measure of the distributional impact; but once we turn to the personal distribution, the implications of a tax change are less easily summarized.

First of all, the standard tool employed in empirical studies is the Lorenz curve, and the literature on the measurement of inequality has established the relationship between the Lorenz dominance criterion (where one curve lies uniformly above another) and preference according to a social welfare function defined over incomes, where this function has the properties of being non-decreasing and s-concave (see, for example, Shorrocks, 1983). This provides an explicit justification in terms of the economics of welfare for what would otherwise be a purely statistical procedure.

Second, the notion of Lorenz dominance has been extended to allow for differences in mean incomes. This is very relevant to the comparisons of tax systems, since different equal-yield taxes may have different effects on aggregate income once we allow for behavioral readjustments. In general, this requires the use of an equivalent income measure—as in equation (2.29)—which allows for these adjustments; see King (1983). Here, for convenience of exposition, I assume that the behavioral response takes the form of the isoelastic labor supply function (2.20), which can be derived from an indirect utility function with the following least concave representation (as used in Atkinson and Bourguignon, 1990):

$$(2.30) \qquad V[w(1 - t), G] = \left(\frac{L_0}{1 + h}\right) [w(1 - t)]^{1+h} + G,$$

where t is the marginal rate of income tax and G is a lump-sum grant. The social welfare function is assumed to be defined in terms of units of utility represented in this way.[19] Suppose that we consider a purely redistributive tax, so that the revenue constraint requires

$$(2.31) \qquad G = t(1 - t)^h L_0 \int_0^1 w^{1+h} dF(w),$$

where it is assumed that individuals differ only in their wage rates and that these are distributed according to the cumulative distribution function $F(w)$. Substituting from this, it may be calculated that the mean value of indirect utility is

$$(2.32) \qquad (1 + ht)(1 - t)^h$$

times the mean value in the absence of taxation. The latter is relevant, since the equal-yield proportional tax (with $G = 0$) is zero, so that this is the standard for comparison. It may be verified that the mean is reduced by $t > 0$.

How do we compare these two situations with different mean values? A standard Lorenz curve would simply ignore the latter difference, which does not seem satisfactory. The solution proposed by Shorrocks (1983) is to construct the "generalized Lorenz curve," which is the standard curve multiplied by mean income. The condition for dominance is then that the cumulative total income accruing to the bottom x percent of the population should always be greater (or equal). Where the mean is reduced, as by the progressive tax in this example, then the dominance condition cannot be satisfied; see Figure 2.6.

It seems, therefore, that studies of tax incidence are likely to involve crossing (generalized) Lorenz curves. What can we do? If the intersection, like that in Figure 2.6, is close to the top of the distribution, we may seek "restricted dominance," requiring only that the curve be superior up to, say, the ninety-fifth percentile (Atkinson and Bourguignon, 1990). On the other hand, in reality the curves may cross lower down (or several times). The figures of Pechman quoted at the beginning of this chapter suggest that this may be the case.

We may thus have to resort to summary measures of inequality. One of the

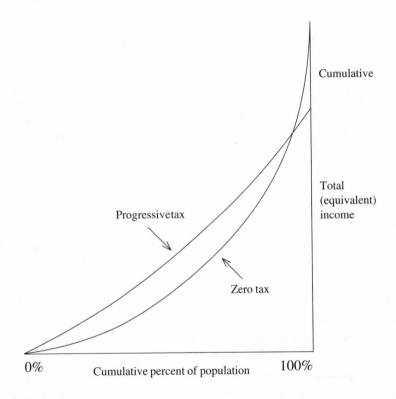

Figure 2.6. Effect of progressive linear tax on distribution of equivalent income.

changes since 1959 is that use is now made of explicit parameters of inequality aversion, as with the ε introduced in Atkinson (1970). In the form comparable with the generalized Lorenz curve, we have the equally distributed equivalent income:

$$(2.33) \qquad Y_{ede} = \frac{1}{N}\left[\sum_i y_i^{1-\varepsilon}\right]^{1/(1-\varepsilon)}$$

where y_i denotes the income of household i and N is the total number of households. The parameter ε can be calibrated using the "leaky bucket" experiment of Okun (1975), with higher values denoting greater degrees of aversion to inequality.

The standard Lorenz approach has also been generalized to allow for situations where tax units differ in relevant respects other than income, such as family size. In the empirical studies of Pechman (1985), it is not evident how he treated such differences, but it appears that he classified families according to their total income irrespective of the family size. Other researchers apply "adult equivalence scales," but there is considerable variation in the scales employed. Buhmann et al. (1988) summarize these differences in terms of a power function of family size, S^e, so that $e = 1$ corresponds to a per capita calculation and $e = 0$ to no adjustment being made. They find that equivalence scales derived from subjective evaluations tend to be quite low, equivalent to values of e ranging from 0.12 to 0.36; that for those based on observed differences in consumer spending, the values of e range from 0.23 to 0.57; that for those used to assess the adequacy of benefit programs, the values of e range from 0.35 to 0.67; and that for those developed for statistical purposes, the values of e are quite high (from 0.70 to 0.84).

As with differences in judgments about vertical inequality, we may seek to apply dominance criteria to compare distributions of income by family size, and the two-dimensional analogue of the Lorenz curve is described in Atkinson and Bourguignon (1987). Alternatively, we may follow the approach of Buhmann et al. (1988) and parameterize the differences. We may then find that a particular tax change reduces inequality for values of ε and e that lie in a particular region. Figure 2.7 shows the case where the actual tax favors the lowest income groups but not those in the middle, and favors large families but not those of an average size. It is preferred to a proportional tax by those who are relatively inequality averse and who would apply a relatively high equivalence

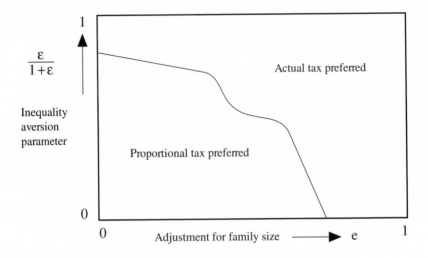

Figure 2.7. Different social judgments with respect to inequality aversion
and the adjustment for family size.

scale. (The vertical axis shows the inequality aversion parameter, normalized
to lie between 0 and 1, so that 1 corresponds to $\varepsilon \to \infty$, or the Rawlsian case;
the horizontal axis shows different treatments of families of different sizes.)

This approach illustrates a general trend in recent years toward explicit recognition of differences in social judgments and toward devising criteria which
identify common ground.

C. Microdata and Distributional Studies

In his review of tax incidence studies twenty years ago, Shoup (1972) distinguished between "the typical-family technique [and] the total-tax-bill technique. The typical-family technique uses the tax law, but no tax collection data.
Given a family's consumption and income levels and patterns, the tax rates can
be applied, with appropriate assumptions about incidence . . . to yield a tax bill
for that family . . . In contrast, the total-tax-bill technique uses tax collection
data and does not require information on tax rates, tax bases, and the like"
(1972, p. 3). The first of these (the typical-family technique) was that used in
early studies in the United Kingdom, such as those of Jevons and Samuel, and
it is still employed frequently at the time of tax changes, so that the effect of
annual finance bills is shown in terms of a series of hypothetical families. But

it cannot adequately capture the diversity of experience found in the real world. This is true even when it is applied to a range of permutations of the typical family. For example, the tables circulated regularly by the United Kingdom Department of Social Security contain a wide variety of family types, but even a generous interpretation does not suggest that more than 4 percent of actual families could be said to fall into the categories considered (Atkinson, King, and Sutherland, 1983).

The second approach (the total-tax-bill technique) is illustrated by the study of Musgrave et al. (1974), which allocated taxes to ten income brackets, using a variety of allocative series. This made use of information from representative sample surveys, such as the Current Population Survey, and of the Brookings MERGE file (see below). The same approach has in effect been used in the empirical implementation of the Harberger model in studies of applied general equilibrium. In these models a link is made in terms of composite family groups, typically classified according to income. These groups receive income from different sources in different proportions and demand goods/supply factors according to estimated demand and supply functions. In the model of Ballard et al. (1985), for example, there are twelve such household groups, defined according to ranges of gross income from below $3,000 dollars (in 1973) to above $25,000. The table given by Shoven and Whalley (1984, p. 1025) suggests that this is not atypical, although Pigott and Whalley (1985) have as many as one hundred socioeconomic household groups.

These studies make use of sample survey data, but do not directly use the microdata themselves. The figures are averages for income groups, or other cross-classifications, and are thus open to the criticism that they "ignore the fact that the estimated variations in fiscal burdens and benefits are often greater *within* income classes than between them" (Bird, 1980, p. 79). For example, there may be, within a particular income group, some workers who are covered by social security payroll tax and others who are not covered. If this is not fully reflected in wage differentials, then there will be differences in tax burdens within the income group, and the averaged figures are misleading. Likewise, there may be taste differences with regard to spending on goods subject to high excises, with the burden being greater on smokers and drinkers.

For this reason, a third technique based on individual microdata was introduced by Nicholson (1964) in the United Kingdom and by Pechman and Okner (1974) in the United States. As the latter explain, "the estimates are based on a microunit data file for a representative sample of seventy-two thousand families (referred to as the MERGE file); when properly weighted, the sample accounts for the estimated total income received by household units in 1966'' (Pechman and Okner, 1974, p. 2). In the same way, Nicholson (1964) employed the microdata of the United Kingdom Family Expenditure Survey, and this is the basis for the current official estimates of the distribution of the tax burden. The use of such microdata means that we can take full account of the variation between individuals which is not captured by the kind of cross-classification applied in earlier studies.

Access to microdata has made a significant contribution to public finance research of all kinds in the past two decades. The decisions by official bodies to make these data available were enlightened and have made a significant contribution to more ''open'' government. At the same time, we have become increasingly aware of the problems which arise in the use of such data.

The first example of such a problem concerns the extent to which the variation recorded in the data is genuine rather than merely random noise. Consider the consumption of alcoholic drink, used in allocating the substantial excises on this item of spending. Individual consumption varies to an extent that cannot be explained by observable characteristics; there is considerable diversity of tastes. At the same time, part of the observed variation in an expenditure survey is attributable to recording error, transitory variations in the timing of spending, and other factors which are more noise than signal. We cannot treat all the diversity as arising from individual fixed effects.[20] Some balance is necessary between the ''raw'' microdata and the high degree of averaging practiced in earlier studies. This is worthy of further attention.

The second problem with the use of microdata concerns the grossing-up of the survey data to give estimates for the population as a whole. The quotation from Pechman and Okner refers to the samples being ''properly weighted,'' and this can be very necessary if there is differential nonresponse in the survey. In the United Kingdom, experiments with the Family Expenditure Survey for 1982 showed that applying a uniform grossing-up factor yields a total for the number of children which is more than one-fourth higher than the total known from administrative statistics, reflecting the higher response rate among families with children (Atkinson et al., 1988).

The third, related example concerns the consistency with aggregate data. The applied general equilibrium literature has attached considerable importance to the calibration of models to a benchmark equilibrium data set constructed from national accounts and other government sources (Shoven and Whalley, 1984). In the same way the MERGE file has been made consistent with the national income aggregates, since there are significant discrepancies for self-employment income, interest, rent, and transfer payments. The same problem arises with certain items of expenditure: "Comparisons between the known total yield from the duties on tobacco and drink with the yield implied in the average figures of recorded expenditure show that, as a whole, people fail to record about half their expenditure on drink and about a quarter of their expenditure on tobacco" (Nicholson, 1964, p. 15). As a result, proportionate adjustments are made to recorded spending.[21] For both income and expenditure, it would be desirable to see a fuller investigation of the sensitivity of the estimates to the pattern of allocation; and the results might better be presented in the form of a range rather than a single value.

Finally, there are the problems in merging data from several sources: the MERGE file combined data from the U.S. Internal Revenue Service file of individual federal income tax returns with a base household survey of the U.S. population (for 1975, the Survey of Income and Education). This gave rise to a literature concerned, on the one hand, with the statistical properties of estimates obtained from matched samples (for example, Sims, 1972), and, on the other, with the more practical problems of matching (for example, Okner, 1972; Ruggles and Ruggles, 1974). What seems to be needed is a full analysis of the consequences of such matching *for the particular purpose* of estimating the distribution of tax burdens. If the results are, for instance, to be presented in terms of some summary measure of inequality, we can say the following about its sensitivity to the assumptions made in matching: "the right question is not the quality of the match itself, but rather the correct use and interpretation of statistics derived from the matched sample" (Kadane, 1975, p. 10). The availability of individual tax burdens has the advantage of allowing examination of the factors responsible for variation in the burden. In this connection, it would be interesting to see wider application of multivariate analysis to individual tax burdens, as in Pechman and Okner (1974, App. D). One important example is the variation with age and family status, and this brings us to the question of the individual life-cycle. A number of critics have argued that the "snapshot" of a single year, including people at all stages of the life-cycle, presents a misleading picture of the lifetime incidence: "Failure to distinguish between lifetime and annual incidence overstates the degree of inequality in tax burdens between groups, suggesting that progressive taxes are more progressive and regressive taxes more regressive than a lifetime analysis would suggest" (Poterba, 1989, p. 329). That this may be so is indicated by the calculations of Davies et al. (1984) for a Canadian cohort. The essential point may be seen in terms of the "sources" and "uses" equation (2.29). The cutting edge of differential impact comes from differences in the ratio of wage and capital income, on the one hand, and of differences in spending patterns, on the other. Viewed over the lifetime, rather than simply for a single year, these differences will be smaller. For example, to the extent that differences in capital income are due to older people's having saved for retirement, this will wash out on a lifetime assessment.

The exploration of lifetime tax incidence will undoubtedly be a major area for research with the increased availability of longitudinal data. This will, however, bring its own problems. One is the welfare significance to be attached to the distribution of a single cohort when there are large intercohort inequalities. This applies not just to differences such as those between ''war babies'' and ''babyboomers'' but also to differences between groups close in age. Levy (1988a) cites the example of someone who repeated two years at school: ''I graduated college in 1932. In 1932 you couldn't find a job. The boys who got out in 1930 had a much easier time and by '32 they were far enough up the ladder to hang on'' (p. 213).

III. OUTLOOK FOR FUTURE RESEARCH

One of the important achievements of modern public finance has been to bring to bear the tools of economic analysis, as illustrated here by the application of general equilibrium analysis—both theoretical and applied—to the problem of tax incidence. It seems to me that this promises considerable scope for research in the future. I have, for instance, discussed some of the developments in the analysis of the labor market which seem particularly relevant to public finance. The same applies to those in industrial organization: to date, there appears to have been little application of new theories of imperfect competition to public finance questions. It is striking, for example, how little reference there is to the impact of taxation in Tirole's *Theory of Industrial Organization* (1988). I have also referred to the dynamics of the economy, and the relation with theories of endogenous growth is an obvious field to explore.

A second important development has been the incorporation of the subject of public finance into the mainstream of economics. The potential of taxes and transfers, and their limitations, need to be an integral part of the design of an economic system, not added as an afterthought. For this reason, I expect to see more interaction between public finance and the field traditionally called ''comparative economic systems.'' What, for example, is the relation between corporate taxation and privatization?

In the past decade there has been widespread cynicism concerning the functioning of government, and quite a number of governments have been ideologically committed to reducing the role of the state. It seems essential that the public finance economist should, irrespective of political fashion, retain a balanced view of the potential and limitations of the state. Rereading Musgrave's *Theory of Public Finance,* I was struck with the force and contemporary relevance of the following passage from the preface: "Intelligent and civilized conduct of government and the delineation of its responsibilities are at the heart of democracy. Indeed, the conduct of government is the testing ground of social ethics and civilized living. Intelligent conduct of government requires an understanding of the economic relations involved; and the economist, by aiding in this understanding, may hope to contribute to a better society" (1959a, p. vi). This seems an appropriate manifesto for public finance in the 1990s.

COMMENTS ON CHAPTER 2 BY ─────────────────────────

James M. Poterba

Significant advances in the last two decades, in both economic theory and in the empirical analysis of household and firm-level data sets, have yielded a new generation of models which can form the basis for incidence analysis. In chapter 2, Anthony Atkinson outlines where incidence analysis has been in the last three decades. He also suggests a number of directions for future research. I shall outline six lines of inquiry that seem especially promising today.

First, incidence analysis must grapple more effectively with imperfectly competitive labor and product markets. Allowing for such imperfections can significantly affect standard results, as three simple examples illustrate. First, in the labor market, "efficiency wage" models suggest that some workers may be paid more than their marginal product because firms need to impose a heavy penalty if workers are caught shirking. Current jobholders in such industries are not indifferent to policies that redistribute employment between high-wage and other sectors, and, contrary to standard models, the sectoral allocation of employment affects social welfare. Jeremy Bulow and Lawrence Summers (1986) provide illustrative analyses and demonstrate that some distortion of the competitive equilibrium can be Pareto-improving.

Second, recent empirical work on imperfect information and the theory of firm behavior suggests new insight on the burden of corporate taxes. This work indicates that many firms face "liquidity constraints," which render the cost of capital for internally financed projects lower than that for externally funded ones. This suggests that tax reforms which raise *average* corporate tax rates, even if they do not affect marginal tax burdens on new investment, may affect the firm's investment plan and hence the level of economic activity. Such average tax rate effects are not present in standard models, which predict that tax reforms that do not affect the marginal cost of funds have only redistributive effects.

Third, in product markets, many recent studies in applied macroeconomics suggest that firms face adjustment or "menu" costs to changing prices. If so, then the most basic tenet of applied incidence analysis—that it does not matter whether a tax is collected from the buyer or the seller—may be wrong. One study, which I coauthored with Julio Rotemberg and Lawrence Summers

(1986), modeled the shift from income taxes to sales taxes in a setting with price rigidities. Our findings suggest potentially important short-run effects on real output. Although building complete models that incorporate many of these effects is difficult, the power of computational general equilibrium algorithms is sufficient to incorporate nominal rigidities and still obtain tractable results.

A fourth major area for future incidence research concerns international factor migration. Already, open-economy models are supplanting simpler closed-economy models for analyzing capital tax burdens. Interregional and international labor migration could also be incorporated into these models. Just as important, however, is the need for empirical research to calibrate these new models. Although researchers in public finance and international economics are nearly unanimous in rejecting the closed-economy view as being inappropriate for industrial nations, there is far less agreement on the extent of capital market integration. Recognizing international factor mobility also raises new questions about the distribution of tax revenue across jurisdictions. For example, in a string of recent court cases the U.S. government has alleged that Japanese auto firms use transfer pricing to reduce their U.S. tax liability while inflating their domestic profits and hence Japanese tax liability. The growing importance of multinational business offers governments a new revenue option: taxing foreign governments. Domestic tax policies can be modified in ways that encourage firms to shift income across jurisdictions, yielding revenue with no changes in real firm behavior.

Models of international factor mobility can be combined with market imperfections such as those described above to yield intriguing interaction effects. If a foreign government provides subsidies to its firms in an ''efficiency wage'' industry, for example, the resulting shift in employment from one country to the other induces an important rent transfer. These effects are larger than the efficiency effects which appear in standard competitive models, and can rival the redistributive effects typically studied in incidence analysis.

A fifth direction for research concerns incidence analysis as the economy moves from one steady state to another. There have been great strides in dynamic economic modeling since many of the traditional incidence models were developed. Some of the basic insights of these models, such as the importance of avoiding reforms which provide windfalls to ''old capital'' or other preexisting assets, are widely accepted among academics even though they have yet to percolate into the policy process. More generally, since changes in asset prices are often the principal short-run incidence effects of tax and expenditure policies, more explicit recognition of these effects will improve the power of economic models to determine who really bears the tax burden. Computational general equilibrium models have, with rare exceptions, ignored these effects in evaluating the incidence of tax changes.

A final important avenue for new research concerns the burdens of taxes and expenditure programs in a lifetime context. The last two decades have witnessed an explosion of research using household-level data to model the distribution of taxes and expenditures across individuals in a given year. Although labor economists are increasingly directing their efforts to panel data sets which provide rich information on individual income and employment histories, the static perspective remains dominant in public finance. Nevertheless, for many public policies ranging from social insurance to capital income taxes, there are important and predictable variations over the life cycle in a household's recipiency or tax-paying status. Work by James Davies, France St. Hilaire, and John Whalley (1984), as well as my own paper on the distributional burden of excise taxes, (1989), suggests the potential influence of this approach in analyzing actual tax instruments. Advances in this area are more likely to depend upon realistic computer models than upon simple theoretical analyses, but the recent improvements in computational power combined with the availability of panel data sets are certain to make this a promising research field.

Incidence analysis is in many ways the centerpiece of public finance. While policymakers display varying interest in economists' prescriptions regarding what government *should* do, there is perennial demand for studies of who gains and loses from government policies. The next three decades will generate a great deal of interesting work on these issues.

COMMENTS ON CHAPTER 2 BY ————————————————————————

Frank Levy

In chapter 2, Anthony Atkinson shows both how far we have come and how far we have to go in understanding the true distribution of the tax burden. In the second part, he discusses the relationship between theories of tax incidence and the distribution of personal income, relationships we must understand in order to make better incidence estimates.

Two of the questions he addresses are of particular interest. The first involves the sources of observed income inequality. The second involves society's judgment as to the appropriate shape of the income distribution. Atkinson notes that theoretical developments in these two (related) areas have been more tentative than in incidence theory per se. This should not suprise us because, as I will argue, each area presents a rapidly moving target. In the United States, both the sources of income inequality and the sentiments in favor of redistribution have changed substantially since Musgrave addressed these issues in *The Theory of Public Finance* (1959). Yet our descriptions of inequality—its appropriate measurement and its appropriate remedies—are only slowly recognizing this fact. To illustrate this situation, I will discuss both questions as they currently apply to the United States.

SOURCES OF INEQUALITY

To appreciate the changing sources of family income inequality, we need only compare the family income distribution's bottom quintiles in 1949 and 1987. In terms of commonly used inequality measures, the two situations are quite similar. The quintile share of family income was 4.5 percent in the earlier year and 4.6 percent in the latter one. The Gini coefficient for the total family income distribution was in the range of .38 for each year.

But when we look at the demographic composition of the quintiles, sharp differences emerge (see table below).

In both 1949 and 1987, about one-fourth of the bottom quintile was made up of elderly families whom we do not expect to work. Despite this constant

Composition of the lowest quintile of the family income distribution (in percent).

	1949 (7.6 million families)	1987 (13 million families)
Share of all family income received by quintile	4.5	4.6
All families with a head older than 65	26	25
Female-headed families with head 65 or younger	10	37
Husband-wife families with head 65 or younger:		
Who live on farms	26	2
Who do not live on farms	38	36
Totals	100	100
Addendum: proportion of families with no earner	23	44

Sources: U.S. Department of Commerce, Bureau of the Census, 1952, 1975, 1989.

proportion of elderly families, the proportion of families in the quintile with no earner rose from .23 in the earlier year to .44 in the later one. The reduction in labor supply corresponds to a second change: the proportion of families headed by nonelderly farm residents fell from .26 of the 1949 quintile to only .02 in 1987, while the proportion of families headed by unmarried women (excluding the elderly) rose from .10 to .37.[1]

One could argue that the census does not adequately measure farm incomes and that some farm families were thus misclassified. But within the context of the census, we can say that a significant number of people in the 1949 bottom quintile were in the quintile because they had, in today's language, "bad jobs"—agricultural jobs with low cash earnings. At the same time, jobs with higher earnings were available, and most of these families (or their children) had the requisite human capital to hold them. Migration to urban areas could easily involve a tripling of cash income which, in census terms, could have raised a family into the distribution's second quintile.

In 1987, by contrast, the "carrier" of bottom-quintile status was more complex. The proximate cause was female headship, which helps explain the lack of labor force participation. But an increasing body of research suggests that low-income, female household heads also have low levels of human capital. Some of this association borders on tautology—for example, having a child as a teenager is often associated with noncompletion of high school. But low-income female heads also score poorly on apparently more basic measures of human capital, such as the Armed Forces Qualification Tests.[2]

The level of human capital in the lowest quintile is important because, so far as one can tell, the association between human capital and earnings is growing. In the last five years, a number of authors have demonstrated a substantial increase in the rate of return to education (Levy, 1988; Murphy and Welch, 1988; Bound and Johnson, 1989). Some portion of this increase is artificial—a reflection of the trade deficit and the resulting slack demand for less highly educated men.[3] But in the terms of Roy's model of the earnings distribution (Roy, 1951), it appears that occupations are becoming more like hunting and less like fishing.[4] Correspondingly, weak labor supply in the bottom quintile partially reflects a low economic return to work.

In sum, standard inequality measures of 1949 and 1987 suggest a similar basis (or nonbasis) for redistribution. But a closer look suggests that the first distribution is describing something like a dual labor market world (for example, Doeringer and Piore, 1971; Harris and Todaro, 1970), while the second distribution is describing a world based on an individual differences model in the spirit of Mirrlees (1971) and Gravelle and Kotlikoff (1989). The result, I suspect, is a widening of the distribution of lifetime incomes with a corresponding decline in the progressivity of lifetime incidence (Davies et al., 1984), with this caveat: individual productivities can be altered, at least to a degree, by investments in human capital.

How should the tax transfer system respond to these developments? The answer, of course, depends on what we were trying to do in the first place. Early in *The Theory of Public Finance,* Musgrave lays out some possible answers to this question in describing the duties of the Distribution Branch: "Democratic thinking, based on the postulate of man's individual worth, seems to establish a presumption in favor of equality, both political and economic. But equality applied to economic matters can be interpreted in different ways, and the choice among different interpretations is a matter of value judgment. To some, equality may imply actual equality in economic welfare at any given time; to others, it may imply the quite different concept of equality of opportunity; and still others may interpret equality in terms of maximum welfare to all members of society" (p. 19).

Putting aside the question of who pays the bill (to which I will return in a moment), the U.S. social welfare function seems to emphasize equality of opportunity. Broad support for a guaranteed minimum standard of living exists only insofar as recipients are clearly working to the maximum of their capacities. Musgrave continues: "If the criterion of equality of opportunity is accepted, we are still faced with a number of different interpretations. Equality of opportunity can be taken to mean equal educational facilities or allocation of jobs on the basis of competitive performance rather than connections. Above all, the idea of equal opportunity involves mobility between various positions in the income scale" (pp. 19–20). Mobility among positions on the income scale can arise through either of two mechanisms: mobility within the income distribution, or mass mobility via economic growth in which the whole distribution is moving up the income scale. The second mechanism raises a final difference between 1949 and 1987. The year 1949 was near the beginning of a twenty-six-year period in which median family income doubled in real terms. Even if cross-sectional measures of inequality had been increasing (which they weren't), successive years would have represented unambiguous improvements in the generalized Lorenz curve comparison of Shorrocks (1983). The poor would have been getting richer while the rich would have been getting richer faster. The pressure for government action would have been correspondingly reduced. More recently, however, the combination of slow income growth and increasing inequality means that 1987 fails to dominate many of the last seventeen years in either a strict or a generalized Lorenz comparison. The result is not mass mobility but rather something more like Hirschman's "Tunnel Effect" (1973): Two lanes of traffic, headed in the same direction, are stalled in a tunnel. One lane begins to move. The other lane hopes that it will move soon, too. But as time passes and the second lane remains stalled, resentment begins to set in. Thus, the pressure for action is there and the question remains: What do we do?

The answer, I believe, involves emphasizing tax transfer programs with two main features. First, they should increase incentives for labor supply at the bottom of the income distribution. Second, they should facilitate the acquisition of human capital both among current workers and among their children.

THE SOCIALLY DESIRED SHAPE OF
THE INCOME DISTRIBUTION

How will the Distribution Branch generate support for such programs? In 1985, Assar Lindbeck wrote an article in which, in passing, he outlined three motivations for broad-scale redistribution:

1. The Grace-of-God motivation, which underlies social insurance. Here, the taxpayer is ameliorating a state which he may, or surely will, occupy in the future.
2. Altruism. Here, the taxpayer applies moral reasoning to ameliorate a state with which he has no possible connection.
3. Enlightened self-interest, in which the taxpayer is ameliorating a state not because he expects to occupy it but because those who do occupy it generate externalities which affect him.

The Grace-of-God motivation is, as we know, alive and well. Over the last sixteen years, median family income for all families has risen by about 5 percent in real terms. But median family income for elderly families has risen by about 30 percent, a tribute to increased Social Security benefits (including indexation) and to better private pension coverage.[5] But for reasons well understood by Tiebout, the Grace-of-God motivation does not automatically translate into support for better inner-city education, much less into increased support for poor parents.

Pure altruism can provide support for either of these programs. But as I and others have noted, altruism in the United States seems to reach high levels only during periods of rapid income growth (Levy, 1985). Not suprisingly, then, politicians act as if they believe that altruism is now at low levels. If there are any who doubt this, I refer them to the *Los Angeles Times* of April 24, 1990,[6] which reports congressional fear of a backlash among families with incomes of $70,000–$90,000, over loss of their child care tax credit (Redburn, 1990). The loss came from a redesigned credit which focused larger benefits on lower-income families. But even in this climate, the same Congress is working on expanded versions of the Earned Income Tax Credit. They believe that aid to the working poor is seen as something quite different from "welfare," particularly when it is posed in the terms used by David Ellwood: any family with a year-round, full-time earner should at least have a poverty-line income (Ellwood, 1988). One can argue that an expansion of the Earned Income Tax Credit raises the return to low levels of education and thus lowers the incentive to acquire additional human capital. But the tax credit also raises the incentive for labor force participation, without which human capital acquisition is a moot question.

This leaves the motivation of enlightened self-interest. Here, too, the Distribution Branch may find some support. In the past two years the public opinion polls have demonstrated a growing awareness of the nation's weakened competitive position.[7] The competitiveness debate has involved much discussion of labor force quality, usually in the context of the "mismatch hypothesis," which projects a severe shortage of skilled labor. The calls for educational reform that arise from this "mismatch" are historically unique because they encompass the education of all children—not just, for example, the education of more scientists from the upper strata of children, as occurred after the Soviets launched *Sputnik* in 1957.[8] Thus, concerns about the economy's future may permit additional investment in the creation of human capital which would otherwise have been impossible.[9]

3

Public Sector Dynamics

Since Richard Musgrave's published his *Theory of Public Finance* in 1959, there has been considerable research on topics relating to fiscal policy in a dynamic setting. Taking Musgrave's *Theory* as a starting point, this chapter reviews the scholarly developments in public sector dynamics that have occurred in the past three decades.

Dynamic issues are those in which time occupies a serious role that cannot be eliminated through the convention of Arrow-Debreu markets; the role of the public sector is a relevant subject whenever governments become, or ought to become, involved in altering market outcomes. Naturally included are questions of investment, saving, growth, and risk taking, all of which have figured prominently in fiscal analysis, but also other central topics such as tax incidence. My discussion here is organized around subjects that have a dynamic aspect and that have been important in the literature, either since 1959 or historically, but I make no claim to comprehensiveness; my choice of topics is based in large part on personal interest. A very helpful guide to the development of this literature during the first part of the post-1959 period is provided in Break's comprehensive survey (1974), to which I will often refer.

My analysis begins with a review of the literature on the public debt. An important branch of research in itself, the study of national debt, of its determinants and effects, also provides a useful starting point because it touches on the central issues I will be dealing with later in the chapter. These include the relationship between current and future fiscal actions, which is important in studying the transition from one tax base to another (Part II); the impact of fiscal policy on capital accumulation, discussed in Part III; the generational effects of fiscal policies, a key element in the measurement of tax incidence (Part IV); and the difficulties of adopting and enforcing fiscal policies in a realistic political environment (Part V).

I. THE PUBLIC DEBT

The Theory of Public Finance reflected the thinking of its time in analyzing the role of budget size and budget deficits from the perspective of the Keynesian objective of stabilization of aggregate economic activity. In the years since, the literature on the public debt has moved away from the Keynesian paradigm. In general, Musgrave's classic division of the functions of government into three "branches," respectively encompassing allocation, distribution, and stabilization activities, has largely been replaced by one with only the first two branches; stabilization policy has come to be viewed more as one aspect of government intervention to alleviate market failure. A natural consequence is that much of the subsequent research on the public debt explored the implications of a more neoclassical approach. More recently, there has been a move toward trying to understand debt policy as the result of the political process.

One may think of literature on the public debt as addressing four questions: Does public debt have any effect? What effects does it have? How is it determined, politically? And how is it measured? Obviously, these questions are related. If debt has no effect, it is unimportant how the level of debt is determined. But if debt is difficult to measure, how can we know what its effects are?

A. The Ricardian Equivalence Proposition

There is probably no fiscal policy issue on which there has been more controversy in the recent literature than the "Ricardian equivalence" proposition. As developed by Barro (1974), the proposition states that government debt will not be perceived as net wealth by taxpayers, because the future taxes needed to finance payments to debtholders will be viewed as an equal, offsetting liability. Hence, individuals will offset government dissaving (that is, debt creation) with private saving.

The implications of the Ricardian equivalence proposition are quite strong. It suggests that pay-as-you-go social security schemes that transfer significant resources from younger to older generations should have no impact on national saving, for the older generations will simply offset these transfers by leaving more to their children. Without any effect on saving, deficits should have no impact on capital accumulation or interest rates. Indeed, the Ricardian equivalence proposition has even been used by politicians, perhaps somewhat cynically, in dismissing the economic significance of large fiscal deficits.

Barro's paper demonstrated that such results could hold even for taxpayers with finite lives, so long as these agents were altruistic, caring not only about their own future tax payments but also about those of their heirs. Since then, economists have sought to determine the theoretical conditions under which Ricardian equivalence would hold and have conducted empirical tests of the hypothesis.

As its name suggests, this proposition has historical roots, and it is accorded due notice in *The Theory of Public Finance* in language that is not at all dated: "In a perfect market system, with rational taxpayer behavior and a pure credit market, it will be equally advantageous for the government to use tax or loan finance. If the taxpayer wishes to spread his burden, he may secure a tax or consumer loan and thus obtain command over resources that otherwise would have gone into capital formation. The outcome will be similar to that of public loan finance, the only difference being that private rather than public debt is issued" (p. 559). But the passage continues: "In the real world, where credit facilities are not available on equal terms to all taxpayers, this equality does not apply. Public loan finance may then be thought of as a means of enabling individual taxpayers to secure tax credit at equal terms. By placing payment on a pay-as-you-use basis, loan finance remains a significant instrument of policy, even though it does not increase the total availability of resources." Musgrave then turns to the remaining issue of the intergenerational burden of deficit finance, without really countenancing the possibility of its being undone by offsetting bequest behavior.

There are several possible interpretations of the much greater subsequent preoccupation with Ricardian equivalence. One is the profession's general movement toward rigorous demonstration of results that might have been implicitly accepted in the past. A vast literature has focused on which types of altruism suffice and on the types of taxes for which Ricardian equivalence would or would not hold.[1]

For example, we have learned that Barro made too strong an assumption when he posited a type of altruism which transformed the problem of a sequence of overlapping generations into that of an infinite horizon family. What is crucial is an unbroken intergenerational link. Even if bequests generate spillover benefits for others in society (Warr and Wright, 1981), the level of bequests (though perhaps generally lower because of this externality) will change to off-set movements in the level of debt. Furthermore, the link of altruism need not be as direct as the one between parent and child; all that is necessary is an unbroken link between the current saver and the ultimate taxpayer, even if the link is quite circuitous (Bagwell and Bernheim, 1988). On the other hand, if future taxes are imposed on risky activities and act as insurance, they are not equivalent to taxes today, which provide no such insurance (Barsky et al., 1986).

Although increasing professional rigor may have contributed to the recent interest in Ricardian equivalence, a related explanation is the growing willing-ness of economists to accept very extreme propositions until they are unambigu-ously refuted empirically. This is rarely an easy task, regardless of the hypothe-sis or its merits. Tests of some implications of the Ricardian equivalence proposition, such as the absence of a relationship between interest rates and public debt, have failed to reject the hypothesis (for example, Evans, 1987). But a recent test of a much more specific prediction of the Ricardian equivalence proposition, that the consumption levels of different generations of a family will respond together to shocks to the income of any given family member (Altonji et al., 1989), clearly rejects the hypothesis.

In summary, the finding of this literature to date is that Ricardian equivalence can hold under a variety of conditions satisfied by at least some part of the population, but that its empirical importance remains to be demonstrated. This uncertainty will undoubtedly sustain Ricardian equivalence research for years to come, and the results will be helpful in addressing questions of long-run incidence. For questions of fiscal policy relating to the short-run impact of defi-cits, however, the intergenerational aspect of the Ricardian equivalence proposi-tion is not especially relevant.

As emphasized in the quote from *The Theory of Public Finance,* Ricardian equivalence fails if there are capital market imperfections. Indeed, as an a priori matter, the wealth effects of deficits on consumption in a pure life-cycle model without bequests but with perfect capital markets are very small (Auerbach and Kotlikoff, 1987; Poterba and Summers, 1987); the distinction between a very long horizon (without bequests) and an infinite horizon is slight, insofar as cur-rent consumption behavior is concerned. Any important impact of fiscal deficits on short-run behavior must come from other factors, such as credit market im-perfections and liquidity constraints. The nature of these credit market imperfec-tions, however, must be carefully specified. For example, one can argue that future tax liabilities financed by current deficits will reduce the amount that liquidity-constrained households can borrow, thereby negating the potential liquidity the debt might provide to constrained households (Hayashi, 1987); but the future tax burden need not fall on those presently constrained. The recent literature attempting to characterize the nature of credit market imperfections therefore promises to be quite relevant to understanding the short-run effects of deficits.[2]

B. Crowding Out and Maturity Structure

In addition to its focus on the wealth effects of the level of national debt, the traditional Keynesian analysis of deficit finance emphasized the importance of the deficit's liquidity and maturity structure in determining the extent of aggregate stimulus and crowding out. The foregoing discussion of Ricardian equivalence highlights this relationship between wealth effects and liquidity.

While the Keynesian approach continued to be refined in the years after 1959 (for example, Tobin, 1962; B. Friedman, 1978), there have also been corollaries of the Ricardian equivalence proposition that have challenged the ability of open-market operations to effect real changes without a concomitant change in the underlying pattern of real government activity (Chamley and Polemarchakis, 1984). More recently, the issue of maturity structure has arisen in a different context (explored more fully below), having to do with the government's commitment to a stated policy and the problem of dynamic inconsistency.

According to the literature on crowding out, one cannot view a current deficit in isolation from other aspects of fiscal policy when considering its effects. Current taxes and spending provide an incomplete description of current fiscal policy. Future fiscal actions are tied to current ones by the government's intertemporal budget constraint, so that a reduction in taxes today implies compensatory fiscal actions in the future (Blinder and Solow, 1974). The effects of current deficits therefore depend on the path of future actions with which they are associated. Even in a strictly neoclassical model (without money), one can generate a wide variety of economic responses to deficit increases, including short-run crowding *in* of private investment, by varying the future levels and types of compensating tax increases (Auerbach and Kotlikoff, 1987).

C. The Positive Theory of Debt

Research on the determination of the public debt has been spurred by both theoretical and political developments. The Ricardian equivalence proposition has provided additional insight into the deficit policy that a benevolent social planner might wish to follow, while recent fiscal policy actions have made the model of fiscal determination by a benevolent social planner seem particularly inappropriate.

If the Ricardian equivalence proposition holds, two important potential explanations for why governments borrow are made invalid. First, it cannot be maintained that deficit financing is a vehicle for spreading the burden of expenditures across generations. Second, it cannot be that the debt serves to alter the level of aggregate economic activity. This helps explain the recent focus on other theories, in order to explain the observed growth in the public debt.

Even if government debt cannot smooth the *burden* of taxation, a benevolent government can still use debt to smooth tax *rates*. A lesson from the theory of optimal taxation that developed during the post-1959 period (for example, Diamond and Mirrlees, 1971) is that, under restrictive conditions about household preferences, the desire to minimize the deadweight loss of taxation implies that tax rates on different consumption goods should be equal. Viewed in a dynamic context, this implies that the tax rate on consumption—or, with additional assumptions, the tax rate on labor income—should be constant over time. With the introduction of uncertainty, this translates into a prediction that labor income taxes should not be *expected* to change (that is, they should follow a random walk), and that debt policy should be driven by this pattern of tax rate selection (Barro, 1979). This approach also has implications for the relationship among different taxes, including the implicit inflation tax and taxes on capital income taxes (Mankiw, 1987; Judd, 1989; Chari et al., 1990).

The tax-smoothing and burden-smoothing hypotheses are, of course, related. For a given tax structure, one cannot change tax rates without altering the level of taxation, and this theory has little to say about changes in the degree of tax progressivity that would break the connection. However, as the events of the 1980s have demonstrated, the model of the benevolent social planner seems particularly inappropriate for characterizing public debt policy. The large U.S. budget deficits of the 1980s seem to correspond much better to a model of budget determination by competing political interests. Here, one may distinguish arguments relating to different tastes for public spending *within* generations from struggles *among* generations regarding the allocation of the fiscal burden.

Within generations, individuals may prefer different levels and patterns of government spending. Those in office may choose current government spending, but the electoral process makes their future ability to do so uncertain. Debt policy, however, provides a tool for constraining the behavior of future governments that may have different preferences for public spending.

The argument that one can reduce spending by running deficits is not a new one. It was proposed quite succinctly by Milton Friedman (1962) and was often cited by policymakers as an explanation for deficit policy in the 1980s. Recent contributions have provided a theoretical model for such a view, founded on the idea that a government can run deficits in order to abridge the power of future governments to tax (Persson and Svensson, 1989; Tabellini and Alesina, 1990). The intuition is that, by increasing the fraction of future budgets that must be devoted to debt service, the government reduces the feasible size of future primary (that is, excluding interest) deficits and, given the limitation on its ability or desire to tax, of future spending as well. Whether this strategy "works" is an important empirical question.

The relative political strength of different generations may also play a role in allocating the fiscal burden. Perhaps the best case to consider in exploring this issue is the pay-as-you-go social security system, since the intergenerational transfers of this program are so clear. The young pay taxes to finance the benefits received by the old, with the prospect of receiving future transfers from subsequent generations. Although the young may be better off if the system is eliminated, the net benefit they receive if the system is maintained grows as they age. Hence, the political power of the young, the middle-aged, and the elderly, determined in part by existing social institutions, will influence the level and even the existence of the social security system (Sjoblom, 1985; Kotlikoff, et al., 1988).[3]

Debt policy as an element of strategy has also characterized the burgeoning literature on developing-country indebtedness and the role of default,[4] which I shall not attempt to discuss here. Clearly, however, the direction of research has moved away from describing the behavior of a single social planner to that of agents with conflicting interests who behave strategically. As a characterization of reality, this approach holds promise.

D. The Measurement of Debt

How should one measure the deficit? I have already mentioned the distinction between full and primary deficits, which exclude interest payments. In *The Theory of Public Finance*, Musgrave discussed the use of capital budgeting for public projects and the traditional notion that debt should be matched to capital spending to ensure the matching of fiscal burdens and public services. He also noted the need to adjust deficits in order for the level of economic activity to obtain a measure of fiscal stimulus. Although full-employment deficits are still regularly calculated, their inadequacy even within the Keynesian framework was noted long ago (for example, Blinder and Solow, 1974). The absence of a capital budget, and other accounting problems with reported deficits, have led to several careful attempts to measure the deficit "correctly" (for example, Buiter, 1983; Eisner and Pieper, 1984).

But there is a much more fundamental problem with reported debt and deficits as measures of fiscal thrust or burden shifting. Put simply, for countries such as the United States, the national debt is largely internal debt, a country's obligation to itself. Once one subtracts external debt, which is an obligation of the country as a whole, one is left with a net "debt" of zero; the phrase often used to make this point is "We owe it to ourselves." That is, the present value of the stock of debt equals the present value of the future primary surpluses needed to service it.[5] It is customary to think of the level of internal debt as a meaningful indicator of the intergenerational distribution of the fiscal burden, but it should be immediately obvious that one will have difficulty using a single number as a measure of the distribution of the fiscal burden across several generations of individuals.

Pay-as-you-go social security may illustrate this point best. The current U.S. budget shows the Social Security pension system to be running huge surpluses, measured as they are on a cash-flow basis. Yet these surpluses are being generated to pay for future benefits already being accrued. If one converted the Social Security system of accounting from a cash basis to an accrual basis, the measured debt and deficits would change markedly (see Kotlikoff, 1986) without there being any change in the intergenerational burden of the system. The national debt would still equal the present value of future primary surpluses, but each would be different in magnitude; there would be offsetting adjustments to current and future deficits without any net impact on the intergenerational distribution of the tax burden.

This example suggests a close analogy to the private sector, where, for example, the accounting treatment of unfunded pension liabilities has been an important issue. The key difference is that we can observe the value of a traded company's liabilities, or at least the public's estimate of them, in its market value.[6] Changes in accounting treatment that do not alter a company's perceived liabilities will not alter its market value. But we do not have such market values for future government claims and liabilities, except in cases where these claims and liabilities involve transactions with private firms and are capitalized in the values of these firms.[7]

The inability of *any* deficit accounting rule to produce an unambiguous measure of intergenerational burden shifting has several interesting implications. First, it casts doubt on tests of Ricardian equivalence based on reported debt measures. Since quite different levels of measured national debt can be consistent with the same underlying intergenerational fiscal burden, they can also be associated with the same levels of consumption, macroeconomic activity, and interest rates, even if Ricardian equivalence does not hold. Second, particularly if strict Ricardian equivalence does not hold, the ambiguity of deficit accounting suggests that it would be useful to derive estimates of the intergenerational fiscal burden and determine the relationship between such measures and reported deficits.[8] Finally, it would be interesting to study changes in government accounting conventions, particularly in reaction to deficit reduction and balanced-budget measures such as the Gramm-Rudman-Hollings legislation recently in force in the United States. Although annual deficit measures may convey considerable information about changes in the distribution of the fiscal burden if the tax structure and accounting conventions are stable over time, it is certainly possible to make the deficit entirely meaningless.

II. SAVINGS AND THE CHOICE OF TAX BASE

Let us now look at the normative and positive effects of the taxation of saving, including the pitfalls of extending optimal tax theory to the intertemporal context and the empirical difficulties that have been encountered in measuring the impact of tax policy on saving.

The normative issues of the taxation of saving are often framed by a discussion of the choice of tax base between income and consumption expenditures. In his posthumous presidential presentation to the American Economic Association, Joseph Pechman (1990) reiterated his long-standing support for a comprehensive, progressive income tax. Yet Pechman also conceded at the start that academic support for alternatives to the income tax had grown: "At one time, support for the expenditure tax was confined to a few members of our profession . . . Today, it is fair to say that many, if not most, economists favor the expenditure tax or a flat rate income tax" (p. 1).

Some who favor a comprehensive expenditure tax do so largely on administrative grounds (for example, Bradford, 1986). In the economics literature, however, most of the discussion of the relative merits of consumption and income taxes has focused on two issues: the impact on economic efficiency and capital formation of changes in the tax treatment of saving, and the distributional effects of a change in the tax base. The issue of *intragenerational* distribution, which concerned such early proponents of the expenditure tax as Kaldor (1955) as well as many opponents who view consumption taxes as regressive, has occupied a less important place in the recent literature.

A. Optimal Taxation and the Consumption Tax

In the sense that it involves time, dynamics played a part even in some of the traditional support for a consumption tax. For example, Fisher (1939) argued that, viewed from a lifetime perspective, the income tax was unfair because it taxed unconsumed labor income twice—once when earned and again when producing interest income. But Musgrave criticized this position in *The Theory of Public Finance:* "The only meaningful way in which the terms *double taxation* or *undertaxation* can be used in connection with equity is to indicate discrimination for or against particular taxpayers in terms of a given index of equality. It is this index that must be decided upon *first* to prove that double taxation or undertaxation occurs, rather than the reverse order. By the same token, the concept of double taxation as *taxing a thing more than once* is fallacious. If three taxes on product X add up to an ad valorem rate which is less than that of a single rate on Y, X is undertaxed, not double-taxed" (p. 163). Indeed, the subsequent literature did move toward analyzing consumption and income taxes in terms of their effective tax rates on different commodities, in this case consumption at different dates.

As discussed in the *Theory of Public Finance* (chapter 12), one can view the consumption/saving decision as a current consumption / future consumption choice. In a simple two-period model with first-period labor earnings, we can write the lifetime budget constraint as:

(3.1)
$$\frac{1}{w} C_1 + \frac{1}{w(1 + r)} C_2 = L,$$

where w is the wage rate, r is the interest rate, C_i is period i's consumption, and L is labor supply. So long as labor supply is not fixed, it is a second-best problem of optimal taxation to determine the appropriate relative burden from taxation in the two periods. But if conditions are such that one would wish to tax first- and second-period consumption at the same rate, this implies that a consumption tax, which in this case is equivalent to a tax on labor income, is to be preferred to a tax on capital and labor income—which would raise the relative price of second-period consumption.

Adding a heterogeneous population and progressive taxation to this simple model reveals that there are relatively weak conditions under which a progressive labor income tax alone, equivalent to a progressive tax on lifetime consumption, is optimal (Atkinson and Stiglitz, 1976). Such theoretical results led to arguments for the consumption tax based on efficiency grounds (for example, Feldstein, 1978; Boskin, 1978).

B. Transition to a Consumption Tax

The foregoing results based on the taxation of a single individual or generation of individuals appear initially to be at odds with the finding that the tax structure appropriate for maximizing steady-state utility or a discounted sum of present and future generations' utilities depends not only on efficiency concerns but also on "Golden Rule" considerations based on the relationship between the economy's interest and growth rates (Auerbach, 1979a; Atkinson and Sandmo, 1980). The results are consistent, however, and their differences tell us much about the distinction between tax *design* and tax *reform*.

This distinction has many dimensions, some of which have been discussed in Feldstein (1976). In the present context, the relevant point (as discussed in Auerbach and Kotlikoff, 1987) is that changes in tax structure affect different generations differently. Although a labor income tax and a consumption tax collecting a given amount of revenue in present value from a single generation may be equivalent, the same two tax bases, applied at a given *date* to different generations, have quite different effects.

First, by taxing consumption out of previously accumulated wealth, the consumption tax is a more efficient tax, equivalent to a tax on labor income *plus* a capital levy.[9] Second, because the ownership of capital is very much related to age, the consumption tax imposes more of the fiscal burden on older current generations and less on the young and on future generations than does a labor income tax. Thus, a shift from labor income taxation to consumption taxation would, efficiency considerations aside, represent a transfer from the old to the young, like a fiscal surplus or the elimination of a pay-as-you-go social security scheme. In a *dynamically* efficient overlapping-generations economy, this will raise steady-state utility (Diamond, 1965), but through intergenerational transfers, *not* through a reduction in deadweight loss.

Calculations reported in Auerbach and Kotlikoff (1987) suggest a sizable difference between the long-run welfare effects of moving from an income tax to a consumption tax and these of moving from an income tax to a labor income tax. Whereas moving to a consumption tax would increase welfare in the long run, moving to a tax on labor income would reduce welfare. More than half of this difference is attributable to differences in intergenerational burdens, rather than to efficiency. Even with such intergenerational transfers excluded, however, a consumption tax increases long-run welfare while a labor income tax reduces it. The gap that remains is attributable to the greater efficiency of the consumption tax due to its inclusion of an implicit capital levy. Neither of these differences (in intergenerational transfers or economic efficiency) appears in the single-generation comparison of the two tax bases.

C. Fiscal Policy and Saving

The importance of considering transitions explicitly can be illustrated using the example of the Individual Retirement Account (IRA), a vehicle introduced for most households in the United States in 1981. Under the scheme, households could deduct contributions to such accounts, which would then be taxable when withdrawn after retirement. The scheme appears to have the key characteristic of a consumption tax, but is implemented under an income tax (through a deduction for new saving). Indeed, many people believed that IRAs had moved the United States closer to a consumption tax.

Yet, as it actually worked, the IRA system allowed the transfer of previously accumulated funds into the accounts, thus eliminating the capital levy component of the consumption tax. Moreover, because interest on borrowed funds remained tax deductible, one could obtain a refund for the capital levy even if one had no capital! Finally, because there was a ceiling on contributions, the availability of the IRA amounted to a lump-sum transfer to the many who were constrained at the ceiling.

How much IRAs have influenced saving in the United States remains controversial,[10] and this illustrates a more general problem of finding the "right" model with which to evaluate the effect of taxes or tax changes on saving behavior. In *The Theory of Public Finance,* Musgrave was agnostic on this point, considering the effects of taxation on saving in several models (pp. 260–268). Subsequently, however, most of the theoretical analysis of various tax bases and schemes has assumed the life-cycle model of saving, with or without bequests. Within this model, it has been difficult to find any responsiveness of saving to the after-tax interest rate. In his 1974 survey, Break concluded that "empirical estimates of this pure substitution effect are sufficiently rare, and those that exist sufficiently small, to justify its classification, for most purposes, in the second-order-of-importance category" (p. 192). Since the arrival of

Euler-equation estimation techniques, empirical estimates of the degree of inter-temporal substitution are now less rare, but they have not gotten much larger. In one recent study, Hall (1988) finds an intertemporal substitution elasticity near zero, for example.

The problem may lie with the pure life-cycle / permanent-income hypothesis. As already indicated, many papers have found considerable excess sensitivity of consumption to predictable movements in contemporaneous income, sug-gesting the presence of liquidity constraints. There is also cross-country evi-dence showing a strong positive relation between growth rates and saving rates that appears to be inconsistent with the life-cycle model (Carroll and Summers, 1989). Finally, there remains a separate controversy over whether business sav-ing is, in itself, important, or whether private households "pierce the corporate veil" and eliminate any influence of business saving on national saving.[11]

Knowing how to model saving behavior is crucial in the design of tax policy, as was already clear in 1959. However, most of the sophisticated theoretical analysis to date assumes a model of saving for which the evidence does not offer great support. Alternative models would suggest different responses to particular changes in taxation and, of equal importance, would also lead to different welfare conclusions. Finding the right model empirically, as well as exploring this model's theoretical implications for the design of tax policy, should be an important item on the public finance research agenda.

III. INVESTMENT INCENTIVES AND RISK TAKING

Saving and investment are closely related, and in some cases it is arbitrary whether one thinks of a tax as operating on the supply (saving) or the demand (investment) side of the market for funds. Thus, the literature on investment has tended to focus on those tax provisions that affect particular assets or types of investment. Let us consider two such areas of research: the effects of taxation on fixed investment, and investment in risky enterprises.

Musgrave devoted one chapter of *The Theory of Public Finance* to the effects of taxation on investment and risk taking. Despite the intervening years, many of his points, and certainly his choice of topics, are consistent with the approach taken in much of the subsequent literature.

A. Investment Incentives

The accelerated depreciation allowances of the Internal Revenue Code of 1954 were already in place in 1959, and so was the profession's concern with investment incentives. *The Theory of Public Finance* discussed the impact of different depreciation schedules on the "effective tax rate," defined in the subsequent literature (for example, King and Fullerton, 1984) as the percentage difference between gross-of-tax and net-of-tax internal rates of return. Although the nature of "economic depreciation" had not yet been clarified by Samuelson's concise contribution (1964), Musgrave went through Brown's classic demonstration (1948) that the extreme form of accelerated depreciation, immediate expensing of investment, produces a zero effective tax rate. The concluding paragraph of his discussion is particularly relevant, in light of the subsequent literature: "This argument, to be sure, relates to the case of a tax on new investment only. A profits tax (limited to old investment) or a capital levy, are different matters. Where depreciation has been taken in the past, while current profits continue to accrue, the tax involves a loss to the investor and a gain to the Treasury, even though instantaneous depreciation is permitted for new investment" (p. 344). The capital levy that distinguishes investment incentives from tax cuts is similar to the one that appeared above in the comparison of taxes on consumption and labor income. Indeed, taxing business profits while allowing an immediate write-off for investment amounts to a "cash-flow" tax that has the same form as a personal-expenditure tax (Institute for Fiscal Studies, 1978). In the case of the business cash-flow tax, the tax base consists of all distributions to households (gross profits less reinvestment) rather than household consumption itself. If the household reinvests the distribution instead of consuming it, however, there will be no tax paid under the business cash-flow tax, since there will be no net distributions.

That investment incentives were seen to provide greater "bang for the buck" than general tax cuts was another way of putting the point that reductions in taxes on old capital income represent "leakages" which have no direct effects on incentives. The attractiveness of such incentives was supported by the important empirical work on investment theory initiated by Jorgenson in the 1960s (for example, Jorgenson, 1963; Hall and Jorgenson, 1967). As observed by Break (1974), "When the parameters of the basic Jorgenson model are estimated empirically, the effects on gross investment of such tax policies as accelerated depreciation and investment credits turn out to be substantial. To policy makers, always eager to find effective ways of influencing the behavior of the economy, the attractiveness of such findings is obvious. Their usefulness for that purpose, however, is subject to important qualifications" (p. 207). This last caveat notwithstanding, investment incentives, including investment tax credits and accelerated depreciation, remained popular into the 1980s. Tax changes steadily increased the distinction between the tax treatment of old and new capital (Auerbach, 1983a). But the applicability of investment equations for policy analysis came to be criticized on more fundamental grounds which have to do with the validity of the estimated equations.

In his celebrated critique of policy design based on econometric models, Lucas (1976) used the investment credit as an example of the problem of using models estimated in one policy environment to predict the effects of different policy rules. Investors ought to respond not only to the current level of the investment tax credit, but also to its expected levels in the future. For example, if a model relating investment to the contemporaneous investment tax credit is estimated in an environment in which the credit is infrequently changed, one cannot use this model to forecast the effects of an active countercyclical investment tax credit policy. The investment response to a temporary tax credit will be larger than that predicted by a model based on the behavior of investors who view the credit as permanent.

One can consider the sharper investment response to a temporary investment tax credit in terms of the capital levy it implicitly incorporates. Today's new capital is tomorrow's old capital. Removal of the credit sometime amounts to a windfall to capital then in place—a reverse capital levy, the anticipation of which encourages current investment. But it is the *anticipation* of the capital levy that matters, for once it occurs it is a lump-sum tax.

This distinction raises another important point about activist policy which was made during the 1970s: that of dynamic inconsistency. Again using the investment tax credit as an example, Kydland and Prescott (1977) showed that the optimal policy rule for the government was not time consistent: reoptimization at each date produced results different from those of once-and-for-all optimization, because there was an incentive ex post to use an ''unannounced'' investment tax credit to induce a capital levy on investment that had been made in the expectation that such a levy would not be imposed.

Policy analysis of investment incentives remains confused. Until recently, the trend has been away from a direct empirical estimation of the relationship of investment and tax incentives, and toward simulation analysis, in which a combination of estimated and assumed parameters is used to generate predictions of the impact of tax policy (for example, Summers, 1981; Shapiro, 1984). This more recent approach is appealing because it does not involve the estimation of ad hoc models subject to the Lucas critique, but it sidesteps one of the ''important qualifications'' cited by Break in his survey of the earlier literature: the need to know the right structural model of investment behavior.[12]

Questions about the heterogeneity of capital goods, the elasticity of substitution in production, and the imperfection of capital markets and hence the relevance of internal cash flow were all central to the investment literature of the 1960s and early 1970s and the associated analysis of policy. The recent renewal of interest in liquidity constraints has brought cash flow back into the investment equation (Fazzari et al., 1988), but still in the ad hoc form in which it previously appeared. Our ability to analyze policy, given the model of behavior, has outstripped our ability to identify the right model.

B. Taxation and Risk Taking

The basic analysis of the impact of taxation on risk taking goes back to the seminal paper by Domar and Musgrave (1944). It was reviewed in detail in *The Theory of Public Finance,* which also made note of Tobin's important piece (1958). Though the subsequent literature (surveyed in Sandmo, 1985) has made significant refinements to the theory, the basic message has not changed.

By sharing some of the gains and losses from risky projects, an income tax reduces the risk borne by private investors. Through the income tax, therefore, governments can encourage investment in risky projects. The social benefits of such an effect of the tax depend on whether risk is efficiently pooled in private capital markets. The incentives for risk taking depend on whether there is a "loss offset," the "negative" tax payment for negative income for which a symmetric tax system would call but which is generally not provided. Musgrave noted that "the idea of positive loss refunds sounds shocking" (p. 320); and it remains so.

In part, limited loss offsets serve to limit the tax arbitrage possibilities that are present in the tax system (for example, Stiglitz, 1983). Also, as in the distinction between investment incentives and tax rate cuts, one must distinguish between old and new capital when considering the impact of a limited loss offset; a deduction of current losses is just a transfer to existing capital, and may actually *discourage* investment by making new investment taxable at the margin, even if that investment is also provided with a prospective deduction of losses (Auerbach, 1986).

Discussions of taxation and risk taking generally raise the issue of capital gains taxation, because risky projects are typically those with the potential to provide significant capital gains. Through deferral and a lower rate of tax, capital gains have been given favorable tax treatment relative to that of income from other assets. Break's analysis of the potential reasons probably still applies: "Presumably a major justification for this kind of nonneutral tax structure is the fear that full taxation of all gains would unduly impair investor incentives to hold risky assets. These fears, insofar as they are not simply a convenient rationalization for less progressive income taxation in general, are probably more illusory than real'' (p. 201). But the effects of capital gains taxes on risk-taking behavior and the potential social benefits to be derived from such behavior are still not very well understood. One justification for providing a lower capital gains tax rate on risky projects is that loss offsets remain limited. Moreover, there have long been arguments that, through innovation, certain types of risky projects provide social spillover benefits well in excess of the private returns to investors.

This type of externality has formed the basis for the recently renewed interest in growth theory (for example, Romer, 1986), and provides a clear reason for policy intervention. Whether such intervention should take the form of lower taxes on risky activities is less clear. As Stern (1990) argues, "The design of policy is, however, limited not only by our ability to model the processes but also by the empirical knowledge of how ideas are generated and used." An argument similar to those made today to encourage risk taking was made in the past in support of an investment tax credit that applied only to investment in machinery and equipment and not to other types of business investment. This argument is less in fashion now (though it has been revived recently; see DeLong and Summers, 1991), but there has not really been any change in our empirical knowledge about the process of technological innovation.

IV. DYNAMIC TAX INCIDENCE

There are many respects in which tax incidence research has emphasized economic dynamics during the past three decades. First, researchers have paid more attention to lifetime than to annual fiscal burdens. Second, they have continued to focus on the incidence of taxes associated with capital accumulation, notably the corporate tax. Third, they have used growth models to study the long-run incidence of taxes. Finally, they have been devoting much more attention to the analysis of incidence in the transition from the short run to the long run and to the associated question of tax capitalization.

A. Measuring Tax Incidence

The Theory of Public Finance made several influential contributions to tax incidence analysis. One was a clarification of the relationship between the measurement of incidence on the sources (income) side and the uses (expenditures) side. Another was the shift in emphasis from the functional distribution to the size distribution of income (see Chapter 2 above). How one actually measures the distributional incidence of different taxes is an empirical question of significant difficulty, and the work of Musgrave and Pechman looms large on this topic (for example, Musgrave et al., 1974; Pechman, 1985).

What has been referred to as the "Pechman-Musgrave approach" (Devarajan et al., 1980) measures the distribution of tax burdens by income class using tax return data and other information to characterize the income sources and consumption choices of individuals in different income classes, and then applies particular shifting assumptions to allocate taxes to individuals. Aside from the partial equilibrium nature of the shifting assumptions, a particular problem with this approach is its use of one year's income and expenditures to measure the incidence of taxation.

This is hardly an unnoticed problem; Break points out in his survey that lifetime incomes would represent a better measure than annual incomes. The use of annual income and expenditure measures has arisen not from ignorance of the problem, but rather from data and computational limitations, both of which one hopes will be smaller obstacles in the future.

For example, it is commonly concluded that consumption taxes are regressive, because the average propensity to consume rises with income. Since the important postwar empirical work on consumption behavior, however, it has been recognized that a household's consumption may vary less than its income, so a longer-term perspective is clearly warranted. Poterba (1989), using this approach, confirms that consumption taxes appear less regressive when income levels over several years are used to classify households. The Social Security system provides another illustration of the problem. If one estimates the annual income distribution of Social Security benefits and taxes, the system appears far more progressive than it is, since retired persons receiving benefits have lower *current* income than the working population paying for the benefits. Surely a more accurate picture would come from looking at the lifetime burden of the system for individuals in different income classes, but this still involves comparing members of different generations. In an economy not in steady-state equilibrium, one needs to consider redistribution across generations.

B. The Incidence of the Corporate Tax

The corporate tax is but one of many taxes on capital income, but its central role in incidence analysis and the controversy surrounding the conclusions of such analyses make it worthy of special attention. The most significant contribution on this subject was Harberger's two-sector general equilibrium model (1962), which characterized the corporation income tax as a tax on the normal return to capital in one of the model's two sectors.

The elegance of the model and the intuitive nature of its results gave it a central role in the literature for many years. Even after the introduction of sophisticated numerical general equilibrium simulation models, one of the first major studies (Shoven, 1976) was a reconsideration of Harberger's analysis that was less restrictive in many ways but did not alter the basic characterization of the corporate tax as a sector-specific tax on the normal return to capital. Yet this description suffers from many shortcomings.

While *The Theory of Public Finance* noted in general terms the effects of the corporate tax insofar as it taxed normal returns, it devoted further attention to the nature of the income being taxed, including competitive and noncompetitive rents. This concern with the nature of competition in the corporate sector and its relation to incidence was common in the literature around that time, as Break's survey indicates. Indeed, the empirical study by Krzyzaniak and Musgrave (1963) reported results indicating that corporations shifted more than 100 percent of corporate taxes *in the short run,* whereas the Harberger model would have predicted little shifting, regardless of parameter assumptions, because of the short-run immobility of capital.

Unfortunately, this thread of the literature has not flourished, even though in recent years the analysis of imperfect competition has come a long way, particularly in modeling the dynamic interactions of firms. One noteworthy exception is a paper by Davidson and Martin (1985), in which the Harberger model is altered to include a noncompetitive sector. The paper considers the equilibrium of a repeated game in which cheating is punished by permanent reversion to a Nash equilibrium. Even in this model, however, a tax on pure, noncompetitive rents would have the standard result (that is, no impact effect), since both the penalty and the gain from cheating would be scaled down by the same rate of tax. Thus, we are still without a model to justify the Krzyzaniak-Musgrave results.

Even among competitive firms, the corporate tax has different components, whose incidence ought to differ. The tax on inframarginal returns exceeding the normal return to capital is a classic tax on pure rent, borne by the shareholders, whereas a tax on the normal return may be shifted à la Harberger. In his influential paper, Stiglitz (1973) argued that the entire tax base should be inframarginal, since tax factors favor the use of debt finance at the margin. Under this view, returns to marginal investment pass from the corporate sector as tax-deductible interest.[13] However, the presence of significant levels of equity in corporate capital structures appears to contradict this model's prediction. In general, there are few questions in the literature that are still subject to so much dispute and uncertainty as the impact of taxes on corporate financial policy.

Aside from pure rent, there are quasirents on existing capital. As already noted in the discussion of investment incentives above, *The Theory of Public Finance* recognized that when there are investment incentives for new capital alone, the higher taxes on income from old capital have the effect of a capital levy.

Pure rent and quasirents undoubtedly account for a significant part of the corporate tax base. In recent years, prior to 1986, the corporate income tax had very low marginal tax rates, taking account of accelerated depreciation and borrowing; marginal corporate tax rates were essentially zero (Auerbach, 1983a). The incidence of the corporate tax depends on the nature of competition among corporations, the determinants of corporate financial policy, and the structure of investment incentives, as well as on the general equilibrium response to a tax on the normal return to corporate capital. There is little point in considering the incidence of "the" corporate tax; the incidence of some of its important components is still poorly understood.

C. Long-Run Incidence

One might view the Harberger model as applying in the "long run," after the capital stock can adjust and the net rate of return in corporate and noncorporate sectors is equalized.[14] In the "short run," with capital fixed, the entire tax is borne by corporate capital via a reduction in its net rate of return. In the past several years the literature has considered the adjustment process in greater detail, showing how short-run and long-run effects are connected via *capitalization*.

Consider the introduction of a corporate tax of rate τ at time t. If r_{nt} is the net-of-tax marginal product of a unit of capital in the corporate sector at time t and r_t is the rate of return in the noncorporate sector, then $r_{nt} \equiv r_t (1 - \tau)$ in the short run, before capital can adjust, and $r_{nt} \equiv r_t$ in the long run, once full adjustment has occurred. The instant the tax is imposed, the value of a unit of corporate capital will be less than one, but greater than $(1 - \tau)$, reflecting the temporary sectoral difference in after-tax rates of return. To know how long the adjustment process takes, and how much capitalization occurs, requires a concrete behavioral model. A standard model for the purpose is the q-theory of investment. Based on the assumption of convex adjustment costs, it provides an optimal path of the capital stock's gradual adjustment to a new equilibrium. The associated marginal products of capital can be used to measure asset price effects of changes in tax policy (for example, Summers, 1981; Abel, 1982; Auerbach, 1989).

In *The Theory of Public Finance,* Musgrave discussed the capitalization of sector-specific capital income taxes, such as the corporate tax as modeled by Harberger. In addition to focusing on the long-run/short-run distinction, the more recent literature has also identified new contexts in which complete capitalization might be observed, as with a tax on corporate distributions (Auerbach, 1979b; Bradford, 1981; King, 1977). But one would change little in Musgrave's discussion of the problems that capitalization poses for reform of the corporate tax: "These considerations bear on the problem of integrating the corporation tax with the personal income tax . . . It has been pointed out that the inequity of past overtaxation cannot be remedied by repeal, since the benefit would not go to those who suffered the initial loss; rather, it would give windfalls to new owners . . . The basic problem is not solved by pointing to the inequities of transition, which might be avoided or limited by taxing the windfalls to new owners at a special rate of capital-gains taxation" (p. 385). Recent experience has suggested that such taxes on windfalls may not be so easy to implement, in part because of attempts to adopt rules aimed at reducing the problem of dynamic inconsistency. I will return to this topic below.

Taking account of capitalization leads one to distinguish not only among types of corporate income, but also among recipients of this income, in considering the incidence of the corporate tax. Even taxes on the normal return to capital, which may be shifted in the long run, will be partially capitalized upon announcement. The most important distributional effects of a change in corporate taxation may be not between capital and labor or rich and poor, but between generations.

For example, the Tax Reform Act of 1986 shifted the tax burden in the United States from households to business, raising the effective tax rate on marginal corporate investment.[15] In the long run, this might depress the return to capital and be borne by those with capital income. Because of a sharp reduction in the distinction between old and new capital, however, the act's immediate effect should have been to increase corporate values,[16] having a quite different effect on those *currently* receiving capital income.

In the long run, total factor supplies can adjust to changes in after-tax returns. Imposition of the requirements of steady-state growth leads to some unexpected outcomes. For example, consider the growth model proposed by Solow (1956). The condition for balanced long-run growth is:

$$(3.2) \qquad s \cdot f(k) = n \cdot k,$$

where k is the capital-labor ratio (with labor measured in efficiency units), n is the growth rate of augmented labor, and s is the national saving rate (including government saving). Since the returns to labor and capital depend only on k, taxes will alter the before-tax wage-rental ratio only to the extent that the national saving rate is changed. In particular, a tax on labor income that decreases labor supply will be entirely reflected in lower after-tax wages unless the propensities to save out of different forms of income differ (Feldstein, 1974). Of course, in a life-cycle model, these savings propensities will differ (Kotlikoff and Summers, 1987).

Transitions to such long-run results may take a long time, however, and behavior during a transition may be very important. As Break (1974) concluded, "It may be, then, that dynamic incidence models are of only limited policy interest and that future research can best concentrate on the nature and speed of the adjustment process by which the economy moves to a new dynamic steady-state equilibrium whenever a given tax change disturbs the old equilibrium" (p. 173). In the years since, this has been very much the nature of research on incidence. But the focus on perturbations from a steady state has led us away from some of the interesting incidence questions that Musgrave posed in *The Theory of Public Finance,* such as the interaction of the distribution of income and the rate of growth. One would hope that the "new" growth theory, which emphasizes the potential dependence of long-run growth rates on transition paths, will permit a renewed interest in such questions. Some initial attempts have been made in this direction (for example, Barro, 1991; King and Robson, 1989).

V. DYNAMIC INCONSISTENCY AND PUBLIC CHOICE

Thus far, the issue of tax reform's treatment of existing assets has come up in many guises: the difference between a consumption tax and a tax on labor income; investment incentives versus tax cuts; capitalization of tax changes. When we consider tax changes as once-and-for-all changes, we can assess the incidence and efficiency effects of policies that include capital levies. But this begs the question of how such policies are determined and the response of rational agents to the policy process. It also provokes us to consider changes in the policy process to reduce the problems of dynamic inconsistency that might characterize the government's optimal plans.

A. Reducing Dynamic Inconsistency

The dynamic inconsistency of optimal government plans was first modeled formally by Phelps and Pollak (1968), but the idea itself is at least as old as the unannounced capital levy. The problem is that a government acting in the best interests of its constituents may wish to dissemble about its future plans. There are many examples in the literature, including Kydland and Prescott's discussion of investment tax credits (1977), Fischer's discussion of capital income taxation (1980), Barro and Gordon's analysis of inflation and the Phillips curve (1983), and Rogers' comparison of labor and consumption taxes (1987).

How should government respond to this problem? If it allows itself freedom of action in subsequent periods, it may ensure a dynamically consistent but inferior outcome. Although the government would like, from the current perspective, to impose low capital income taxes or inflation rates in the future, it cannot credibly promise to do so. Agents take for granted that the government will make the expedient choice when the time comes, and indeed it has no incentive to do otherwise.

One solution is to use a combination of government instruments to make the optimal policy time-consistent. For example, Lucas and Stokey (1983) show how to use the maturity structure of debt to make taxes on labor income time-consistent in a nonmonetary economy. Given the pattern of interest rates promised on outstanding debt, the government can remove any incentive it would have to deviate from its announced path of labor income taxes after current consumption and labor decisions are made. This result may be extended to monetary economies using two types of debt instruments, indexed and nonindexed, to remove the incentive to use unanticipated inflation as a policy tool (Persson et al., 1987). However, these results rest on the assumption that the interest payments themselves will be paid as promised and that, more generally, the government cannot default on its debt or levy capital income taxes on the interest payments. Thus, the fundamental problem of capital levies remains.

Some help may come from the availability of investment incentives. If, for example, a government cannot help levying a high capital income tax in the future, it can mitigate the effect of this higher-than-optimal tax rate by providing investment incentives in the form of immediate credits or grants (Hansson and

Stuart, 1989). So long as there is some limit on the rate of the capital income tax, government can use investment incentives to limit the capital levy to the initial capital stock.

Rather than seeking a solution based on the careful use of fiscal instruments themselves, alternative approaches have enriched the behavioral model, either by adding additional government tools or by considering other equilibria. In addition to instruments of fiscal policy, government can adjust the costs of changing these instruments. If, for example, government can, through the use of rules, force itself to incur costs when changing its policy, this will lessen the time-consistency problem.

Unfortunately, in this case of rules versus discretion, there are costs as well as benefits associated with the use of rules, even if there is some mechanism for making the rules credible or enforceable. First, it may be difficult to define rules that adequately protect against time-inconsistent behavior; it is difficult to define a "retroactive" policy (Graetz, 1977). Second, the rules may constrain the government from responding to actual outcomes in a stochastic economic environment; for example, it may not be able to institute a capital levy in times of severe fiscal need, or make the transition from an income to a consumption tax after it has discovered, on the basis of definitive economic research, that the latter is superior. Third, policies imposed to enforce the "rules" may themselves be costly, as when governments fail to index against the uncontrollable component of inflation in order to discourage themselves from overusing the component that they do control (Fischer and Summers, 1989). Fourth, by instituting rules that reduce the advantages of deviating from the announced policy, government may distort private behavior. For example, requiring that full compensation be paid when property is taken by eminent domain can lead to overdevelopment of land that is subject to being taken in the future (Blume, Rubinfeld, and Shapiro, 1984). All of these costs relate to the difficulty of defining rules that distinguish finely enough among states of the world, a problem due perhaps in part to the lack of clever design, but also to the inability of private agents to distinguish among states of the world, even ex post.

There is also the possibility of reputational equilibria, in which taxpayers "trust" the government so long as it adheres to its announced policy but cease to do so if it deviates. In this case, the government has the incentive *not to deviate* from the optimal policy, because once it does the economy will revert to the inferior time-consistent path (see Barro and Gordon, 1983; also related literature, such as Rogoff, 1989).[17] As in other contexts, this "solution" to the time-consistency problem is not without its problems, notably the multiplicity of equilibria. It also does not take into account a major reason for policymakers to care about their reputations, namely their desire to remain in office.

B. Modeling Political Behavior

In the *Theory of Public Finance,* Musgrave devoted considerable attention to the role of voting behavior in the revelation of preferences for public goods and the determination of fiscal policy, although he included only brief discussion of the behavior of politicians and bureaucrats who administer fiscal policies. The incentives of bureaucrats and politicians have been a subject of concern for many years (for example, Niskanen, 1975; Brennan and Buchanan, 1980), and more recently there have been several attempts to consider the dynamic effects of the political process on fiscal policy.

One hypothesis growing out of the view of government as an absorbing "Leviathan," a view associated with Buchanan (1977), is that under a progressive tax, government expenditures grow faster than the economy, a perverse result of the "fiscal dividend" of growth.[18] Much of the recent literature has focused on another issue: the interaction of voters and politicians, examined by studying the dynamics of monetary and fiscal policy associated with the election cycle. Nordhaus (1975) modeled the behavior of politicians who seek to ensure their reelection by manipulating the economy. By stimulating the economy just before an election, the controlling party can produce a short-run expansion without an immediate worsening of the inflation rate. The key to politicians' success is the failure of voters to understand the true model of the economy—to understand that they are being tricked.

While the evidence on the economic concerns of voters lends some credibility to such an approach (see Fair, 1978), more recent models of the political business cycle have stressed informational asymmetries. For example, Alesina (1987) considers the reputational monetary policy equilibria in a two-party system in which, first, the party policies differ from each other due to differences in their own preferences and, second, voters are unsure which party will prevail in the election. Since the outcome of each election is uncertain, the election will always be followed by a shock to the inflation rate, no mater which party prevails. In an alternative model, Rogoff (1990) considers signaling equilibria in which politicians differ in their abilities to manage the economy. In order to distinguish themselves before an election from lower-ability types for whom such behavior would be very costly (in terms of their own future utility), high-ability bureaucrats spend more and tax less than they would in a full-information context. This model therefore offers an alternative explanation for why politicians might systematically engage in expansionary policy actions before elections, with different policy implications. Although most people would like to prevent politicians from manipulating voters by inducing socially costly business cycles, restraining fiscal actions that serve as signals may also prevent voters from distinguishing good from bad managers and may thus worsen the performance of the electoral process.

We thus have a number of recent theories of why self-serving governments may run deficits. They may wish to appropriate the spending power of future governments, trick voters who believe in a long-run Phillips curve with a short-run economic expansion, or signal their ability to produce public goods and services efficiently by making it difficult for themselves to do so. These hypotheses still await serious empirical evaluation.

VI. CONCLUSIONS

The literature since 1959 has provided enlightening insights into the incidence and efficiency effects of fiscal policies. We now have a better understanding of the connection between long run and short run and of the distinction between tax design and tax reform. Greater concern with reform relative to design (and concern with associated problems such as dynamic inconsistency) has motivated recent attempts to model the relationship of the political process to the dynamics of government behavior.

By its very nature, the study of dynamic fiscal policy and its determinants is influenced by the fiscal policies actually practiced. It is no coincidence that a considerable part of the literature in recent years has studied the public debt. Therefore, in addition to all the unresolved research questions evident from a review of the literature, one can expect new and interesting ones to arise from chosen fiscal policies and from the new economic problems likely to occur in the years to come.

One such issue likely to generate considerable research is the way in which the coming demographic transition will effect the welfare of different generations and the size and financing methods of the public sector.[19] Another is the openness of economies, and the impact of greater factor mobility on growth and income inequality and fiscal policy coordination. For example, the integration of the European Community in 1992 has many implications for the design of individual countries' fiscal policies and the rules by which these policies should be coordinated. Finally, the attempts by many eastern European countries to make the transition from planned to capitalist economies present considerable challenges not only in the determination of macroeconomic policy but also in the design of tax and expenditure polices, so as to preserve equity in a transition to a more efficient allocation of resources.

COMMENTS ON CHAPTER 3 BY ————————————————————
Don Fullerton

Despite Alan Auerbach's claim that he makes no attempt to be comprehensive, Chapter 3 is remarkable for its comprehensiveness. Auerbach bases his discussion on Richard Musgrave's seminal work *The Theory of Public Finance* (1959). Likewise, I wish to take two important books as the point of departure for my comments—namely, George Break's *Intergovernmental Fiscal Relations in the United States* (1967) and Joseph Pechman's *Federal Tax Reform: The Impossible Dream?* (1974). A major theme of this book that is not developed adequately elsewhere is the necessary tradeoff among the seven goals of a good tax system (vertical equity, horizontal equity, economic efficiency, administrative efficiency, simplicity, certainty, and flexibility). Since the point of this commentary is to discuss avenues of future research, I would suggest another look at some of these tradeoffs.

Consider the tradeoff between vertical equity and economic efficiency. Edgar Browning and William Johnson (1984) and Charles Ballard (1988) have followed a very successful strategy of investigating this tradeoff, and we are by now very familiar with the notion that additional redistribution can be obtained only at the expense of additional welfare cost of taxation. But other tradeoffs remain unexamined.

One such tradeoff is that between horizontal equity and simplicity. To place the same tax on two individuals with the same economic income would require measuring the consumption value to the one individual who receives employer-provided benefits, such as the personal use of a company car and business trips to tropical sites; but attempts at such measurement would make the tax system inordinately complex. In addition, the two individuals may have known fully about the nature of their respective jobs before taking them. Louis Kaplow (1989) points out that it is difficult even to define horizontal equity.

Another example is the tradeoff between flexibility and certainty. The goal of flexibility would suggest that the government be able to adjust tax rates in response to temporary circumstances, but the goal of certainty suggests that taxpayers ought to know well in advance the tax consequences of undertaking each economic activity. What is the cost of having a tax system that changes frequently? Jonathan Skinner (1988) has begun some work along these lines, but much remains to be done.

A final example is the tradeoff between economic efficiency and administrative efficiency. In order to tax different uses of capital at the same rate, economic efficiency would suggest the full taxation of imputed net rents of owner-occupied housing, and perhaps of real accrued capital gains, but considerations of administrative efficiency suggest that such rules would be very difficult to implement. Joel Slemrod (1990) has summarized his initial research on compliance and enforcement—that is, on the measurement of administrative cost.

Another reading of Break and Pechman might raise other questions or other tradeoffs. We have measures of the economic efficiency of taxing imputed net rents, or accrued capital gains, but not of the administrative cost. We have no good measures of how individuals differ in their untaxed employer-provided benefits. We have no idea how tax-induced uncertainty interacts with the inherent uncertainty of alternative investments.

Richard Musgrave and Evsey Domar (1944) did some of the earliest work on the government's ability to tax and share risk. An essential question is whether government can accept risk more cheaply than individuals, or diversify it away in a manner that individuals cannot. It is interesting to think about practical examples where these notions might be made more operational. For example, owner-occupied housing could be treated as a risky asset, one that individuals are unable to diversify. Private markets for sharing that risk may not arise, perhaps because of asymmetric information with adverse selection (only those most risky will sign up for the risk-sharing arrangement), or because of moral hazard (individuals would have less incentive to care for the occupied home). The reason for this market failure may be very similar to the reason that landlords seem inadequately diversified: most investors avoid mutual funds of real estate in favor of owning a particular property in a particular neighborhood where they may have better information. In any case, the market failure suggests a role for government. Simply by taxing the risky component of the return to owner-occupied housing, government can take part of the risk of all homeowners and diversify it away (Berkovec and Fullerton, 1992). It may be difficult in practice to measure the annual imputed net return, since the risky component of this return would be related directly to accrued capital gains, but some of this risk would be shared simply by a tax on realized capital gains if there were perfect loss offset. In other words, the current "rollover" or exemption of owner-occupied housing from capital gains taxation may miss this opportunity to reduce economy-wide risk and increase consumer welfare.

A few other issues in Auerbach's chapter bear further mention. First, the effect of taxes on saving and investment is a much-studied topic upon which there would be some consensus by now. Why do opinions differ so widely? Are the reasons political rather than economic? Perhaps the mainstream of the economics profession now believes that these effects are small—but Auerbach alludes to a controversy about the effects on saving of Individual Retirement Accounts. In his notes, he refers to two papers that find effects to be large and one that finds effects to be small. If others wish to dispute either finding, then more research is needed.

Finally, when Auerbach discusses tax incidence, he makes it sound a bit as if everybody agreed that lifetime measures are conceptually correct but just computationally difficult. These computational difficulties are attacked in a book by Fullerton and Rogers (1993). In any case, I am not sure Joe Pechman would agree. The problem is that in standard life-cycle models, consumption is proportional to lifetime income; so a consumption tax is, by that measure, a proportional tax. Yet Pechman believed that a consumption tax is inherently regressive. Perhaps he would worry about liquidity constraints that make future income a mistaken guide for current ability to pay. Also, most consumption tax proposals tax bequests only at the time of consumption by the heir. Yet if the bequest is planned, and therefore displaces other possible consumption of the decedent, then it is valued as (and should be taxed as) consumption of the decedent. It would then be taxed again at the time of consumption by the heir. Only then is consumption proportional to lifetime income.

COMMENTS ON CHAPTER 3 BY
David Romer

Alan Auerbach's wide-ranging survey is highly informative and unfailingly accurate. Since I have little to add to the analyses of the issues that are addressed in his chapter, I would like to devote my comments to an area of dynamic public finance that he does not cover in detail. Although I am not an expert on public finance, I am familiar with Musgrave's classic three-fold division of the roles of the government budget into the allocative, distributive, and stabilization functions. Since the title of Auerbach's chapter is "Public Sector Dynamics," which certainly suggests stabilization policy and budget deficits, I expected stabilization issues to get at least the usual Musgravian third of the discussion. But the entirety of what the chapter has to say about stabilization is the statement that "stabilization policy has come to be viewed more as one aspect of government intervention to alleviate market failure." I can understand why Auerbach, as a public finance economist, wants to reduce all of macroeconomics to a problem in applied public finance, but I believe it is my role as a macroeconomist to resist this.

My comments will therefore focus on an open question concerning stabilization policy that I view as very important. More generally, I want to suggest that while macroeconomics is not just an area of applied public finance, it should also not be left entirely to macroeconomists. The area where public finance and macroeconomics intersect is important, and there are many significant open questions there.

The specific issue I want to discuss is whether stabilization policy can have large benefits. I will simply assume that fiscal policy has real effects of more or less the usual Keynesian type, for more or less the usual Keynesian reasons. I will make this assumption both because I think it is right and because this is not the place to review the macroeconomic debates of the past three decades.

In the traditional view, there is no doubt that stabilization policy can have large benefits: stabilization policy serves to keep the economy at full employment, and thereby prevents large quantities of resources from being left idle. This traditional view is reflected in economists' nonresearch activities. A large proportion of the efforts of policy economists is devoted to stabilization policy, and a substantial fraction of a standard undergraduate program is devoted to issues of stabilization.

But the natural-rate model of the economy that is commonly used in the study of macroeconomic issues (even if researchers are not completely comfortable with it) suggests that the issue is not so clear. Specifically, if there is a natural rate of unemployment or a trend path of output that is not affected by stabilization policy, then, loosely speaking, stabilization policy can reduce the variance of output but cannot affect its mean. When things are put that way, it is no longer obvious that there are large potential benefits to stabilization policy. Given the usual preoccupation with stabilization, the question of whether there are in fact substantial welfare benefits to be gained is thus quite important.

I would like to suggest four possible ways in which there might be large potential welfare gains from successful stabilization. All four are open areas for work. I discuss them in increasing order, in terms of the extent to which they depart from a textbook natural-rate model.

The first possibility is simply that the natural-rate view is correct but that there are large benefits from reducing the variance of output. As Laurence Ball and I have shown (1989), it is possible to model formally Auerbach's suggestion that stabilization policy can be justified as a type of government intervention to correct a market failure; we also found that it is possible for the benefits from this stabilization to be large, but that you have to work very hard to get this result. Figuring out whether the benefits through this channel are large in practice appears to involve getting straight the gory details of the microeconomic foundations of nominal rigidities. At this point, one possibility that cannot be ruled out is that the traditional story of why aggregate demand shocks have real effects is largely correct, but that the benefits of reducing the size of fluctuations around the natural rate are small.

The second possibility is that the traditional view is right. If the aggregate supply curve is not linear but is more like the old-fashioned inverted *L*-aggregate supply curve, then stabilization policy can prevent recessions without having a large cost in terms of making booms smaller. Here the key question is whether there are in fact asymmetries of this sort. Asymmetries are notoriously difficult to find empirically; but it is hard to know whether this is because the world is approximately symmetric or because our econometric techniques have low power in detecting asymmetries. People who have looked for asymmetries at the macroeconomic level, such as Daniel Sichel (1989), J. Bradford DeLong and Lawrence Summers (1986a), and James Cover (1992), have obtained mixed results.

The third possibility is another channel through which stabilization policy could affect average output. As Allan Meltzer has recently argued, one of the central ideas in Keynes's *General Theory* is that stabilization policy can raise *potential* output by improving the climate for investment (Meltzer, 1988). The idea is that stabilization policy leads to lower uncertainty, that this reduced uncertainty raises investment, and that greater investment in turn increases potential output. I am not very interested in the question of whether this is what Keynes had in mind. But it is clear that one could model the mechanism formally. The key question is whether these effects are quantitatively important in practice; determining the impact of uncertainty on investment, for example, would be a central part of evaluating this story.

The final and most radical possibility is that stabilization policy can affect not just average output but its long-run growth rate. What is needed is a combination of some mechanism through which stabilization policy on average raises output with a mechanism, such as learning-by-doing, through which output movements have very long-lasting effects. By combining these two types of mechanisms, successful stabilization policy could raise the economy's long-run growth rate. This idea, however, is not just open for work but is at this point entirely speculative.

I want to conclude with three additional questions concerning stabilization policy and deficits that are also very important and very much open. The first is the empirical counterpart of the question I have been discussing: Has fiscal policy *in practice* been on net a stabilizing or a destabilizing influence on the economy? This is the kind of question that used to get a great deal of attention but that now receives relatively little (a recent exception is DeLong and Summers, 1986a). But the question is no less important now than it was twenty years ago.

The second additional question is the counterpart for long-run policy of the question that I have been discussing for short-run policy. Rather than asking whether there may be large welfare benefits associated with stabilization policy, one could ask whether there may be large welfare costs associated with a policy of consistently running large budget deficits. In light of U.S. fiscal policy over the past ten years, the reason for asking the question should be obvious. Given the amount of unhappiness that so many economists have expressed about the deficit, it is surprising that this issue has not been the subject of more research. (One exception is Romer, 1988.)

My final question is one that we can hope to answer only after we have answered the three questions that I have posed so far. The question is whether the economics profession has added or subtracted from social welfare by making deficits socially respectable. From about 1936 to about 1980, the profession spent a great deal of energy trying to persuade policymakers and the public that deficits were not necessarily terrible, that they did not represent a moral failing. Given recent U.S. fiscal policy, one has to wonder, in retrospect, whether some of this effort was unwise. Musgrave anticipated this potential problem. In *The Theory of Public Finance* (1959, pp. 522–525), he warned about the possibility that an absence of pressure to reduce budget deficits might lead to a breakdown of fiscal discipline. Thus, as always, what we have to say today was anticipated by those who showed the way.

PART II

PUBLIC GOODS, FEDERALISM

4

Public Goods and the Invisible Hand

The invisible hand is a powerful metaphor, and economists have intermittently hoped that it might guide the provision of public goods as well as private goods. The question is an important one for public finance: if the profit motive can guide the supply of public goods efficiently, and if public goods are not required for redistributive purposes, governments should get out of the business of providing them. In the taxonomy of Musgrave (1959), we could reduce the role of government to its distribution and stabilization functions, with the allocation of goods and services left entirely to private suppliers.

There have been at least three strands of thought regarding profit incentives to provide public goods: Lindahl equilibria, the theory of profit-maximizing local developers, and club theory.[1] In this chapter I discuss the latter two, and comment in the conclusion on the role of Lindahl pricing.

Most public goods are provided by local jurisdictions that are numerous enough to be viewed as "competitive." The literature holds that, because of competition, local provision of public goods may be optimal when local jurisdictions are self-interested or profit-maximizing rather than concerned with social efficiency. The two classic papers that led to such arguments were those of Tiebout (1956) and Buchanan (1965). Tiebout's insight was that consumers will move to local jurisdictions that best reflect their demands for public goods, and jurisdictions that do not serve their constituencies efficiently will not survive. Buchanan's insight was that public goods might be partly "rival" in the sense that a consumer's enjoyment declines with the congestion caused by others, and therefore not all consumers should have access to the same facility. These two features together—mobility plus the optimality of having multiple jurisdictions—suggest that competition among self-interested jurisdictions could lead to efficiency. In this chapter, I will try to evaluate this argument.

Early analyses did not distinguish between "local public goods" and "clubs." In view of the large and growing literature on how capitalization of local expenditure and tax policy affects local decisions, such a distinction now seems useful. By "local public good" I mean a public service provided to residents in a particular geographic area—for example, a city. It is assumed that nonresidents can be excluded from consuming the local public good. To be included, a potential member might have to pay two prices: a rental price to live there and, possibly, jurisdiction-specific head taxes or income taxes. The rental price will reflect both the public services and the local taxes. By a "club" I mean a group of consumers sharing a common facility; each consumer's willingness to pay for admission depends on the facility size as well as on the number and possibly the characteristics of the members. The local public goods model and the club model are related but not identical. In the local public goods model, a resident can reduce the price of living in a jurisdiction by consuming less land or housing. The consumer gets the same public goods (say, quality of schools) whether he lives in an apartment or in a fifteen-room house. In the club model, the admission price is fixed for each consumer.[2]

Although the theory of clubs originally focused on the provision of public goods, it is more generally a theory of how to internalize externalities among agents. Sharing the cost of a public good is just one example of how agents confer externalities on one another. There are many other externalities among agents who coalesce into groups. For example, a firm is a group of complementary workers whose joint productivity depends on the composition of the group. A more frivolous example might be a dinner party or some other social gathering. The conviviality of a social gathering depends on who is present. In Part I, I summarize the theory of clubs and show why the theory of clubs is really just a theory of how to price externalities among agents in groups. The prices for admissions to clubs will be nonanonymous whenever the externalities are nonanonymous as defined below. The other agents within a group are willing to pay a positive or negative amount for a particular agent's participation according to the externalities that the agent confers.

The thrust of the modern literature on clubs is that admissions to clubs are private goods like any others, and that we should therefore expect the market to perform well in the sense of the first welfare theorem: market equilibrium (if it exists) is efficient. I will try to show how club theory relates to the theory of competitive equilibrium for private goods economies and try to illuminate features and results that are special to club economies.

Section A discusses concepts of equilibrium in club economies. Section B discusses the relationship between competitive equilibrium and the core in club economies, as a prelude to discussing comparative statics. The comparative statics are that an increase in the proportion of players of one type will lead to a decrease in the utility that that type of player receives in the core and in competitive equilibrium. Section C discusses nonemptiness of the core and existence of equilibrium, and section D criticizes the theory.

"Efficiency" refers to three aspects of an allocation: the number of jurisdictions or clubs, the partition of the population among them, and the provision of public services to each jurisdiction's residents or to each club's members. In the club model, we assume that profits are driven to zero by the possibility of free entry, and as a consequence equilibrium is efficient in all three senses. In models with space, it is hard to conceptualize free entry unless we heroically assume that land is free and that an entrepreneur could appropriate unoccupied land to start a jurisdiction. Otherwise entry would require an entrepreneur to buy up occupied land and secede from whatever jurisdiction it previously belonged to. The latter notion does not conform to legal institutions as we know them. Therefore my discussion of local public goods in Part II takes land as scarce and takes the division of space into jurisdictions as fixed. Whether the partition of population among jurisdictions and the public services within jurisdictions are efficient will depend on the jurisdictions' decision-making rules. Within Part II, Section A shows that the allocation will be efficient in the second and third senses above if jurisdictions choose the fiscal policies that maximize property values. Section B turns to the question of what we should make of this argument.

I. CLUBS

Following the literature, I shall discuss economies with "types" of agents, $t = 1, \ldots, T$. There are N_t agents of type t, where N_t is a positive integer. An agent of type t has a positive endowment ω_t of the numeraire private good. $\mathbf{N}$ will denote $(N_1, \ldots, N_t)$ and $\boldsymbol{\omega}$ will denote $(\omega_1, \ldots, \omega_T)$. The preferences can be represented by utility functions $\mathbf{U} = (U^1, \ldots, U^T)$, where U^t: $R_+ \times \mathbf{Z}_+^T \times R_+ \to \mathbf{R}$ represents the preferences of an agent of type t. ($\mathbf{Z}_+^T$ is the subset of $\mathbf{R}_+^T$ consisting of vectors of integers.) $U^t[g,\mathbf{n},x_t]$ is the utility achieved when the agent consumes private good in amount x_t and public goods in amount g in a coalition described by the vector of integers $\mathbf{n} = (n_1, \ldots, n_T)$. I will let $\mathbf{x} \in \mathbf{R}_+^T$ refer to $(x_1, \ldots, x_T)$. I assume that U^t increases and is continuous in its last argument, private good. The cost of the public good is represented by a function $C: \mathbf{R}_+ \times \mathbf{Z}_+^T \to \mathbf{R}_+$, where $C(g,\mathbf{n})$ is the cost of providing public good g to a group described by $\mathbf{n}$. (The results do not depend on whether there is one public good or many. For simpler notation I will assume there is one.) We will let the set-valued function W represent the equal-treatment utilities that can be achieved in groups $\mathbf{n}$: for each $\mathbf{n} \in \mathbf{Z}_+^T$, $W(\mathbf{n}) = \{\mathbf{u} \in \mathbf{R}^T \mid \exists \ (g,\mathbf{x})$ $\in \mathbf{R}_+ \times \mathbf{R}_+^T$ such that $\omega \cdot \mathbf{n} \geq C(g,\mathbf{n}) + \mathbf{x} \cdot \mathbf{n}$ and $u_t = U^t[g,\mathbf{n},x_t]$ if $n_t > 0\}$. (If $n_t = 0$, then u_t can be anything.)

Letting k index groups, a set $\{\mathbf{n}^k\}$, $k \in K$, $\mathbf{n}^k \in \mathbf{Z}_+^T$, is a *partition* of the population N if $\Sigma_k \mathbf{n}^k = \mathbf{N}$. An *allocation* is a collection $\{(g^k,\mathbf{n}^k,\mathbf{x}^k) \in \mathbf{R}_+ \times \mathbf{Z}_+^T \times \mathbf{R}_+^T\}$, $k \in K$, such that (i) $\{\mathbf{n}^k\}$ is a partition of the population, and (ii) $\mathbf{x}^k \cdot \mathbf{n}^k + C(g^k,\mathbf{n}^k) \leq \omega \cdot \mathbf{n}^k$, $k \in K$. We will say that an allocation *achieves* equal-treatment utilities $\mathbf{u}$ if $U^t[g^k,\mathbf{n}^k,x_t^k] = u_t$ for all $(g^k,\mathbf{n}^k,x^k)$ and all t, provided $n_t^k > 0$. Equal-treatment utilities $\mathbf{u}$ are *feasible* if there is a partition $\{\mathbf{n}^k\}$ of the player set N such that $\mathbf{u} \in W(\mathbf{n}^k)$ for each k.

The most general interpretation of the model is that an agent of type t cares about the types of agents he shares the public services with, as well as the numbers of those agents; that is, crowding is "nonanonymous." But nonanonymous crowding is not the only interpretation of the model. Following are three special cases of interest:

1. *Club economies with anonymous crowding.* We might want to assume that the agents care only about the number of other agents they share with, and not about their types. Then utility functions and the cost function depend only on $\Sigma_t n_t$ rather than on $\mathbf{n}$.[3]

2. *Coalition production.* Suppose that there are no crowding effects in the utility function and no public goods, but that the utility achieved by an agent of type t depends only on the private good he consumes, x_t. If we suppose $C(g,\mathbf{n}) \leq 0$ and ignore the variable g, we can interpret $C(g,\mathbf{n})$ as the output of a firm with workers $\mathbf{n}$. The constraint in the definition of $W(\mathbf{n})$, $\mathbf{x} \cdot \mathbf{n} \leq \omega \cdot \mathbf{n} - C(g,\mathbf{n})$ means that members cannot consume more than the sum of what they produce and are endowed with.[4]

3. *Pure (nonanonymous) crowding.* There is no public good g and $C \equiv 0$. Agents receive utility directly from interaction with other agents in their group, and the allocation problem is how to group agents efficiently. For example, suppose type-1 agents receive high utility from being grouped with type-2

agents, but type-2 agents dislike type-1 agents. Grouping type 1 and type 2 together might be efficient, but a transfer of money or private good is required in order to get type-2 agents to accept type-1 agents into their group. This transfer can be accomplished through positive or negative prices.[5]

A. Price Systems and Competitive Equilibrium

As always, a competitive equilibrium must have a price for each possible good. Otherwise a profit-maximizing entrepreneur cannot know whether there are un-exploited profit opportunities. The goods in a club economy are the private goods and admissions to clubs. In order to focus on the latter, I have assumed (following the club theory literature) that there is only one private good. The private good will be the numeraire, and a complete price system for the club economy with nonanonymous crowding is $\boldsymbol{\pi} = (\pi^1, \ldots, \pi^T)$, where $\pi^t \colon \mathbf{R}_+ \times \mathbf{Z}_+^T \to \mathbf{R}$. The price $\pi^t(g, \mathbf{n})$ is an admission price for an agent of type t to a "club" that provides services in amount g and has membership described by $\mathbf{n}$. This price can be positive or negative, depending on whether the externalities provided by type t are positive or negative, as we shall see when we characterize equilibrium.

The prices $\boldsymbol{\pi}$ are nonanonymous in that the price depends on the agent's type.[6] In contrast, prices for private goods in competitive equilibrium are typically anonymous: the price of wheat is the same for high demanders and low demanders. Private goods have anonymous prices because the prices are established by the cost of supply—either the marginal cost of production or the willingness to pay of the marginal consumer who supplies a unit. In club economies, the cost of "supplying" an admission to an agent may be nonanonymous. It depends on how much the other members want his participation. If he confers positive externalities on the other members, they may pay him to join. If he imposes a crowding cost, they may require a payment from him.

Thus, in the first special case above (anonymous crowding), equilibrium prices are anonymous. If the cost of "supplying" an additional membership in a club is the crowding cost it imposes on previous members, and if this crowding cost is the same for all potential new members, the equilibrium price can be anonymous. In case 3 (pure crowding), admission prices must generally be nonanonymous, and in case 2 (where prices are wages), wages are also non-anonymous: workers with different skills will receive different wages in equilibrium.

The price system I have defined is complete, in that admission to every conceivable club $(g,\mathbf{n})$ by every conceivable type of agent is priced. Of course, not all conceivable clubs $(g,\mathbf{n})$ will appear in equilibrium, and the price $\pi^t(g,\mathbf{n})$ is irrelevant if $n_t = 0$. An aspect of the price system I would like to emphasize is that public goods are not priced separately from admissions; so long as admissions to groups can be priced, Lindahl prices are unnecessary, even though the price system could be further disaggregated into admission prices and Lindahl prices.[7] The key commodity that is priced in this equilibrium is membership in groups, which governs the formation of groups.

An allocation $\{(g^k,\mathbf{n}^k,\mathbf{x}^k)\}$, $k \in K$, and a price system $\boldsymbol{\pi}$ are a *competitive equilibrium* if conditions 1, 2, and 3 hold:

1. No entry: Taking the admissions prices as fixed, no set of admissions and supply of public goods would earn positive profit:
   $\boldsymbol{\pi}(g,\mathbf{n}) \cdot \mathbf{n} - C(g,\mathbf{n}) \leq 0$, for all $(g,\mathbf{n}) \in \mathbf{R}_+ \times \mathbf{Z}_+^T$, $\mathbf{n} \leq \mathbf{N}$;
2. Clubs in equilibrium make zero profit:
   $\boldsymbol{\pi}(g^k,\mathbf{n}^k) \cdot \mathbf{n}^k - C(g^k,\mathbf{n}^k) = 0$, for all $k \in K$;
3. Consumer maximization: The equilibrium consumption bundle is affordable, and if a consumption bundle is preferred to the equilibrium allocation, it is unaffordable. For each t, if $n_t^k > 0$, $x_t^k = \omega_t - \pi^t(g^k,\mathbf{n}^k)$. If $U^t[g,\mathbf{n},x] > U^t[g^k,\mathbf{n}^k,x_t^k]$ and $n_t > 0$, $n_t^k > 0$, then $x > \omega_t - \pi^t(g,\mathbf{n})$.

Condition 3 implies that all consumers of the same type will achieve the same utility in equilibrium. We will say that the competitive equilibrium *achieves* utilities $\mathbf{u}$ if $u_t = U^t[g^k,\mathbf{n}^k,x_t^k]$ when $n_t^k > 0$.

The main idea behind a price-taking equilibrium is that in order to make optimizing choices, consumers and firms *observe prices* and *choose quantities*. Taking prices as fixed, the consumer chooses the type of club $(g,\mathbf{n})$ to join, and the firm chooses the type of club $(g,\mathbf{n})$ to provide. Although this may seem a logical extension of competitive theory, it is not the concept of equilibrium in most of the club theory literature. The most common notion is a "utility-taking" equilibrium where firms *observe preferences* and *choose prices*.[8] In other equilibrium concepts, consumers are permitted to *cooperate* in forming jurisdictions, in contrast to the premise of price-taking equilibrium, which is that each agent optimizes unilaterally against a price system.[9] Consumers choose unilaterally whether to join a real or hypothetical group according to the price system. In equilibrium, no real or hypothetical group could attract any consumer, whether or not other members of that group would also be attracted. In this sense, consumers optimize unilaterally against a price system.

The next section characterizes competitive (or price-taking) equilibrium, using this definition. In Section D, however, I point out that the competitive hypothesis is less reasonable in club economies than in private goods exchange economies, and offer an alternative.

B. Competitive Equilibrium and the Core

Competitive equilibrium provides utilities in the equal-treatment core of the game [N,W], where W is derived from the club economy [N,U,C,ω] above. Utilities $\mathbf{u} \in \mathbf{R}^T$ are in the *equal-treatment core* of the game [N,W] if the utilities $\mathbf{u}$ are feasible and if there is no $\mathbf{u}' \geq \mathbf{u}$ such that $\mathbf{u}' \in W(\mathbf{n})$, $\mathbf{n} \leq \mathbf{N}$, and $u_t' > u_t$ for some t with $n_t > 0$. The equal-treatment core gives the same utility to each consumer of the same type.[10]

Proposition 4.1 (Appendix)[11] (a) If $\mathbf{u}$ is in the equal-treatment core, an allocation $\{(g^k, \mathbf{n}^k, \mathbf{x}^k)\}$ that achieves utilities $\mathbf{u}$, together with the suitable prices $\boldsymbol{\pi}$, is a competitive equilibrium. (b) Utilities achieved in competitive equilibrium are in the equal-treatment core.

Because of the coincidence of the equal-treatment core and competitive outcomes, we can study properties of competitive equilibrium by studying the core, and this is why I present Proposition 4.1. More generally, core-competitive equivalence is of interest because the core and competitive equilibrium permit different opportunities for agents to improve their utilities: in the core, agents can cooperate, whereas in competitive equilibrium, firms and consumers optimize unilaterally, taking prices as fixed. No cooperation is permitted. There is no a priori reason to think the outcomes should coincide.

Probably the most intuitive notion in economics is that scarcity leads to high rents. An interpretation here would be that the utility achieved by a type-t player in the core should decrease with the abundance of players of the same type. This conjecture is true, provided the economy is large enough to exhaust blocking opportunities in a sense defined below. Interpreting the result for competitive equilibrium, the admissions prices that an agent of type t must pay to join clubs will increase (or not decrease) with the abundance of type-t players. In the case of firms, the wages earned by a type-t player should decrease with type t's abundance.

For the comparative static result, I need to define a concept called "exhaustion of blocking opportunities." This is a condition that applies to the game [N, W]. We first define the set of blocking opportunities, $\Omega = \cup_{\mathbf{n} \in \mathbf{z}^T} W(\mathbf{n})$. We will let int$\Omega$ denote its interior. The game [N,W] *exhausts blocking opportunities* if for every $\mathbf{u} \in$ intΩ, there exists $\mathbf{n} \leq \mathbf{N}$ such that $\mathbf{u} \in W(\mathbf{n})$. That is, every $\mathbf{u} \in$ intΩ can be achieved in some coalition in the game, although it is not necessarily feasible in the game as a whole.[12] If the core of a game that exhausts blocking opportunities is nonempty, any utility vector in the core must lie in the upper boundary of Ω (see Figure 4.1). Otherwise there is a larger utility vector in intΩ, and there is a coalition in the game that could achieve that utility vector. Such a coalition could block.

Since equal-treatment core utilities must be on the boundary of Ω, the comparative statics I present will follow from how we move along the boundary when there is a change in the relative numbers of players of different types in the game. We shall use points in the T-simplex, $S = \{\mathbf{s} \in \mathbf{R}_+^T | \Sigma_t s_t = 1, s_t$

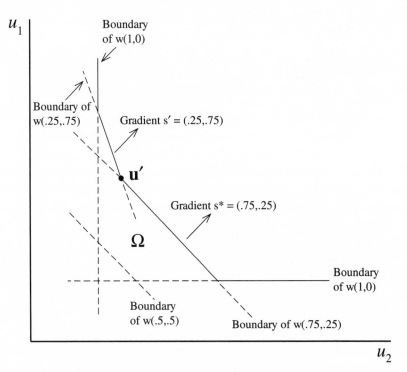

Figure 4.1. The set of blocking opportunities.

rational}, to describe the composition (relative numbers of players) of a game or of a coalition: the composition of a game [N,W] is a point $s \in S$ such that for a suitable integer r, $r\mathbf{s} = \mathbf{N}$. Similarly, the composition of a coalition $\mathbf{n}$ is a point $s \in S$ such that for a suitable integer r, $r\mathbf{s} = \mathbf{n}$. The integer r is the size of the game or the coalition.

We must now address two questions: What additional restrictions on W guarantee that we can compare the utilities in the cores of two games with different compositions, when both exhaust blocking opportunities? What restrictions on W guarantee that blocking opportunities are exhausted for finite games [N,W]?

To associate compositions $\mathbf{s}$ with utility vectors on the boundary of Ω, we need more structure on W. We define $w(\mathbf{s}) = \cup W(r\mathbf{s})$, where the union is over all numbers r for which $r\mathbf{s} \in \mathbf{Z}_+^T$. Then $\Omega = \cup_{s \in S} w(\mathbf{s})$. We notice that if W is homogeneous, $w(\mathbf{s}) = W(r\mathbf{s})$ for all $r\mathbf{s} \in \mathbf{Z}_+^T$, and if utility is transferable, $w(\mathbf{s})$ has a linear boundary with gradient $\mathbf{s}$.[13]

The comparative static result can be seen in Figure 4.1 for two types. When the boundary of $w(\mathbf{s}')$ crosses the boundary of $w(\mathbf{s}^*)$, the boundary that crosses from above has a smaller s_1. Figure 4.1 shows a special case where the boundary of Ω is comprised of the boundaries of $w(\mathbf{s})$ for only four compositions, $(0,1)$, $(.25,.75)$, $(.75,.25)$, $(1,0)$. For other compositions, such as $(.5,.5)$, $w(\mathbf{s})$ does not intersect the boundary of Ω. If the player set $\mathbf{N}$ has composition $(.25,.75)$, then utilities in the core lie on the boundary of $w(.25,.75)$. If the player set $\mathbf{N}$ has composition $(.5,.5)$, then utilities in the core are achieved in a partition of the player set in which half the coalitions have composition $(.25,.75)$ and the other coalitions have composition $(.75,.25)$. The only utility vector in the core is the intersection $\mathbf{u}'$. Thus, since we have moved down the boundary in moving from the game with composition $(.25,.75)$ to the game with composition $(.5,.5)$, the utility of type-1 players has decreased.

If the boundaries of $w(\mathbf{s})$ cross as shown in Figure 4.1, we therefore see that when the composition of the population shifts its weight toward more type-1 players, the utility achieved by type-1 in the core cannot increase and might decrease. The boundaries cross as required when utility is transferable, so that the boundary of $w(\mathbf{s})$ is linear with gradient $\mathbf{s}$.

Proposition 4.2 (Appendix)[14]   Suppose that there are T types of players $t = 1, \ldots, T$, and that utility is transferable. Suppose that $\mathbf{u}$ is in the equal-treatment core of [N,W], that $\mathbf{u}'$ is in the equal-treatment core of [N′,W], and that both games exhaust blocking opportunities. Then $(\mathbf{u} - \mathbf{u}') \cdot (\mathbf{N} - \mathbf{N}') \leq 0$ and $(\mathbf{u} -$

$\mathbf{u}') \cdot (\mathbf{s} - \mathbf{s}') \leq 0$. Suppose further that the proportion of type-1 players is larger in the player set $\mathbf{N}'$ than in $\mathbf{N}$, while the relative numbers of other players are proportionately smaller. That is, $(s_1'/s_1) > 1$, while $(s_t'/s_t) = $ k, $t = 2, \ldots , T$, for some k < 1. Then $u_1 \geq u_1'$.

As a result of Proposition 4.1, which says that the equal-treatment core and competitive equilibrium coincide, we can interpret this comparative static result for competitive equilibrium. Suppose that the game $[\mathbf{N},\mathbf{W}]$ derived from the club economy $[\mathbf{N},U,C,\omega]$ has transferable utility[15] and exhausts blocking opportunities. Then if the number of type-t players increases, the admissions prices paid by type-t players in competitive equilibrium, π^t, will not decrease and may increase.

I turn now to the second question: What kinds of games exhaust blocking opportunities? First, holding the composition of a coalition fixed, if a finite game exhausts blocking opportunities, per capita payoffs cannot increase without bound as the size of a coalition increases. If the economy had "pure public goods," no game of any size would exhaust blocking opportunities. Enlarging the population would always enlarge the set of feasible utilities, since a larger group of people, each sacrificing the same amount of private goods, could produce more public goods. An infinitely large player set might be able to provide unbounded per capita utility. The club theory literature, beginning with Buchanan (1965), assumes that the benefits of sharing a public good are eventually outweighed by crowding costs, and that therefore per capita payoffs are bounded. More specifically, for each composition $\mathbf{s}$, there is an optimal size, say $r^*(\mathbf{s}) < r^{**}$, such that the set of utilities $W(r^*(\mathbf{s})\mathbf{s})$ contains $W(r\mathbf{s})$ for all $r\mathbf{s} \in \mathbf{Z}_+^T$. For $r > r^*(\mathbf{s})$, the set of feasible utilities might be diminished by crowding. For $r < r^*(\mathbf{s})$, the set of feasible utilities is diminished because the cost of the public good is shared by too few people. Large enough games that satisfy such scale assumptions exhaust blocking opportunities.[16]

Second, a *finite* game will not exhaust blocking opportunities unless Ω is the union of $w(\mathbf{s})$ for a finite number of compositions $\mathbf{s}$. A finite game $\mathbf{N}$ contains a finite number of possible coalitions with a finite number of compositions, so if all compositions $\mathbf{s} \in S$ are required to achieve the utility vectors in Ω, a finite game will not suffice. While it is not difficult to find conditions under which finite games exhaust blocking opportunities, these conditions exclude, for example, games derived from private goods exchange economies. To solve this problem, Engl and Scotchmer (1992) introduce the notion that a game "approximately" exhausts blocking opportunities, and, using this definition, show a slightly weaker version of monotonicity and of the comparative static results which apply to the epsilon core defined below, as well as to the core.[17]

The result that the equal-treatment utility received by type t declines with the abundance of type t is perhaps most compelling in the "pure externalities" interpretation of club economies (special case 3) or in the production interpretation (special case 2), in which agents confer externalities by their intrinsic characteristics, rather than by contributing to public goods. In the case of anonymous crowding (special case 1), the result holds only trivially: for club economies with anonymous crowding that exhaust blocking opportunities, the utility achieved by each type of player in the core is invariant to the composition of players. In Figure 4.1, the boundary of Ω is the "L" formed by the vertical and horizontal lines that bound $w(0,1)$ and $w(1,0)$. If both types of players are represented in the population, the utility vector in the core of any game that exhausts blocking opportunities is represented by the intersection of these two lines.

C. Approximate Cores and Approximate Equilibria

What we have described is a coalition structure game, where problems of existence, or nonemptiness of the core, often arise.[18] This is easily seen when crowding is anonymous and when all players have the same preferences. The argument is similar when crowding is nonanonymous. The discussion that follows is heuristic and omits many technical aspects. For ease of graphical exposition, it also assumes that utility is transferable and that people are homogeneous.

We shall let u^* refer to $\max\{U[g,n,\omega - [C(g,n)/n]] \mid (g,n) \in \mathbf{R}_+ \times \mathbf{Z}_+\}$, and shall let n^* represent the smallest number of members that can achieve this maximum per capita utility. If the population size is not an integer multiple of n^*, it may be impossible to partition the population into groups of size n^*, and if so it is impossible to achieve per capita utility u^* or total utility nu^* for the entire economy of size n. We will define a function $\mu: \mathbf{R}_+ \to \mathbf{R}_+$ which will describe a lower bound on the maximum total utility available to n people. The value $\mu(n)$ is constructed as follows. Partition the club economy of n people into the maximum number of groups of size n^*, and then distribute all the private good so everyone in the game achieves the same utility. Members of the remainder group, which has fewer members than n^*, will consume more private good than the others, since they are in an inefficiently small group. Let $\mu(n)$ be the total utility achieved by the economy of n people in this allocation, which is no greater than nu^*.

Since the number of clubs of size n^* can be large if the population size N is large, and since the remainder group is smaller than n^*, the transfer from each member of a size-n^* group to each member of the remainder group can be small if the population size n is large. Therefore the difference between $\mu(n)/n$ and u^* can also be small; see Figure 4.2.

If the population is larger than n^*, then the core must provide each player with utility u^*, represented by the slope of the line in Figure 4.2. If any player receives less utility than u^*, he can propose a coalition that has n^* members and improves his own utility while leaving none of the others worse off. Thus, if the population size is larger than n^* and is not an integer multiple of n^*, the core may be empty.

But suppose there are costs of coalition formation. Players will not form a new coalition unless the gains to doing so are large enough to cover this cost. This idea motivated the notion of ε-cores, formulated by Shapley and Shubik (1966). A payoff u is in the equal-treatment weak ε-core if no coalition can

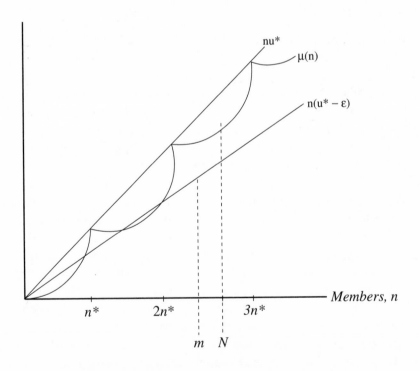

Figure 4.2. Club size, total utility and the ε-Core.

achieve per capita utility greater than u when each member must pay a cost ε to form the coalition. Wooders (for example, 1980, 1983) has applied this idea to many club contexts to show that for large enough populations the ε-core is nonempty.[19] Figure 4.2 exposits the basic idea in the case of one type of consumer.

Figure 4.2 shows that, for any $\varepsilon > 0$, the ε-core is nonempty for a large enough population, and ε can be as small as we like. For each ε, we can find a large enough population size m so that, first, $\mu(N)/N \geq u^* - \varepsilon$ for $N > m$, and, second, no coalition could block when giving up ε per member, since $(\mu(n) - \varepsilon n)/n \leq u^* - \varepsilon$ for all $n > 0$. Thus, for any $\varepsilon > 0$, the utility $u^* - \varepsilon$ is in the weak ε-core for a large enough population N. Further, ε can be chosen as small as we like by choosing m large.

The foregoing arguments apply to the case of anonymous crowding (or a homogeneous population), but also apply when crowding is nonanonymous— for example, in special case 2, where a "club" is a firm whose output depends on the number and composition of its employees. Suppose, for instance, that the complementarities are very strong, so that the workers get positive output only in groups with equal numbers of workers of all types. Then n^* is the size of firm that maximizes output per capita among firms with equal proportions.

We can now ask if our argument above for core/competitive equivalence extends in a natural way to the ε-core and a natural concept of ε-competitive equilibrium. We want to define ε-competitive equilibrium in a way that permits us to interpret each group that shares a public good as a firm. Then firms would be numerous, and it might be reasonable to think of each one as a price taker. The allocation constructed above achieves an equal-treatment utility u in the ε-core by dividing the economy into groups of size n^* and asking each of those members to contribute something to a "remainder group." But firms in competitive equilibrium cannot be forced to make transfers to other firms, so it would be unconvincing to interpret each group in that allocation as a firm in competitive equilibrium. One way to define ε-competitive equilibrium so as to avoid this problem is to retain the same concept of competitive equilibrium as in Section B but only to require optimization (the third condition) for "most" consumers, excluding those in the "remainder group," who are a small fraction, say ε, of the population. Then prices defined as in Proposition 4.1 are competitive prices. Each firm in equilibrium has size n^*, and no (g,n) provides positive profit. All consumers in ε-competitive equilibrium achieve utility u^* except the remainder group, whose size relative to the population would be at most ε.[20]

Another approach to existence of equilibrium is to consider Nash equilibrium instead of price-taking behavior, as discussed in two of my papers (1985a, 1985b), which are mentioned below.

D. A Criticism of Price Taking and Discussion of Other Equilibrium Notions

The price-taking equilibrium described above can be criticized on at least two grounds. First, the "quality" of a membership $(g,\mathbf{n})$ cannot really be "chosen" by the profit-maximizing entrepreneur the way one might choose the color of an automobile, since each member represented by $\mathbf{n}$ must agree to join. Second, the "optimal" size n^* of Figure 4.2 represents an indivisibility in the economy. If the population is partitioned into clubs of sizes n^*, a finite economy will inevitably have a finite number of clubs (firms) in equilibrium, and these will likely not be price takers.

A more reasonable equilibrium concept might be one in which entrepreneur j chooses the facility size g^j and the price of admission p^j, and consumers distribute themselves among clubs so that, conditional on the strategies $\{(p^j,g^j)\}$, no consumer could increase utility by switching. The game has two stages. In the first stage the clubs simultaneously choose $\{(p^j,g^j)\}$; in the second stage the consumers distribute themselves. The utility achieved by a consumer in a club depends on how many other members it has and who they are. Clubs anticipate the distribution of consumers in the second stage when choosing their strategies in the first stage.

This equilibrium notion is very similar to price competition, except that the congestion quality of each club is endogenous to the prices, and therefore each club's demand is not "infinitely elastic" with respect to price (Scotchmer, 1985a, 1985b). If one club lowers its price while keeping its public goods fixed, it will attract more members, but it will not attract the whole population because congestion sets in and reduces the attractiveness of the club.

For the case of anonymous crowding, I showed (1985a, 1985b) that admission prices in such an equilibrium will typically be higher than the "competitive" prices in a finite economy, but that facilities will be efficiently provided to members. Since firms earn rents, there will be an excessive incentive to enter, and the number of clubs in equilibrium will typically be too large. As the economy is enlarged, however, the equilibrium prices and club sizes converge to the competitive ones. For a sufficiently large economy, equilibrium in pure strategies exists.

This alternative equilibrium notion has not been investigated for the case of nonanonymous crowding.

II. LOCAL PUBLIC GOODS

When public goods are provided by jurisdictions whose boundaries are defined by boundaries in geographical space, consumers "join" the club by paying to reside on land in the jurisdiction. The allocation of land cannot be disentangled from the partition of consumers among jurisdictions. As explained in the introduction to this chapter, I shall assume that when jurisdictions are fixed in geographical space, there is no mechanism to redraw the boundaries and thus no mechanism for entry. There is another strand of literature which assumes that land (sometimes called "islands") is a free good and that a "developer" can occupy an island whenever he can build a profitable development on it.

Whether or not entry is possible, the basic "developer" model concludes that we do not need to worry about efficient provision of local public goods because, whether or not the number of developments is endogenous, profit-motivated land developers will develop communities that provide public goods efficiently.[21] The basic model assumes that the developer can partition a development into lots and then sell off the lots for a price that reflects the public services, the lot size, and the congestion imposed by the number of residents. Provided that communities are "small," local developers will provide public goods efficiently, and the population will be distributed efficiently. This is usually argued by pointing out that there is a division into lots, admission prices (land prices and/or taxes), and public goods that satisfy the first-order conditions for efficiency.

Even assuming that jurisdictions are "small," the standard "developer" model can be criticized as being much too centralized. The developer decides everything, including the provision of public services and the number of residents that the jurisdiction will have. In the following section I therefore explore to what extent the "developer" is inessential. As a foundation for embellishing the model, I discuss in detail the case in which public goods are "pure" within the jurisdiction (in that the cost of providing them does not depend on the number of residents) and there are no externalities of crowding other than those captured in the scarcity of land. Even if the jurisdiction manager has no direct control over the land price, lot sizes, or number of residents, he will provide public goods efficiently, provided that his objective is to maximize property values, because he realizes that property values capitalize the fiscal services of the jurisdiction. An equilibrium among jurisdictions, when jurisdictions are fixed and land use is decentralized, will be efficient in that there is no repartition of residents among jurisdictions or any revision of public services that will be a Pareto improvement.

As in the "first welfare theorem" of competitive equilibrium theory, the argument does not rely on first-order conditions and convexity. At the end of Section A, I discuss how the argument should be modified if there are crowding costs either in utility or in costs of providing public services. In Section B, I criticize this theory and contrast it with alternative theories.

A. Efficiency and Property Values

Following the literature in urban economics, let us suppose that there is a finite number of types of consumers, $t = 1, \ldots, T$, and that a consumer of type t has a utility function $U^t: \mathbf{R}^3_+ \to \mathbf{R}$, where $U^t[g,s,x]$ represents his utility when he consumes public services in amount g, space in amount s, and private good in amount x.[22] We assume that U^t is strictly increasing in its second and third arguments. A consumer of type t has initial endowment of private goods y_t and income Y_t, which includes a share of rental income.[23] There are N_t consumers of type t, and N^j_t will represent the number of such consumers in jurisdiction j. I will let $\mathbf{N}^j = (N^j_1, \ldots, N^j_T)$ and $\mathbf{N} = (N_1, \ldots, N_T)$. Suppose that the public goods in jurisdiction j are g^j, provided at cost $c(g^j)$, and that the amount of land in jurisdiction j is A^j. We will let x^j_t and s^j_t represent the private-good consumption and land consumption of a consumer of type t who resides in jurisdiction j. An *allocation* is a collection of vectors, $\{(g^j, s^j_t, N^j_t, x^j_t)\}_{j=1\ldots J, t=1\ldots T}$ in $\mathbf{R}^4_+$ such that $\Sigma_t N^j_t s^j_t = A^j$, $\Sigma_j \mathbf{N}^j = \mathbf{N}$, and the allocation is *feasible* if $\Sigma_t y_t N_t = \Sigma_{j,t} N^j_t x^j_t + \Sigma_j c(g^j)$.[24] In an allocation, all land and consumers are accounted for. If the allocation is feasible, the consumption of private good and the cost of the public good do not exceed the available resources. We say that an allocation *achieves* utilities $\{u_t\}$ if $U^t[g^j, s^j_t, x^j_t] = u_t$ for all t and j such that $N^j_t > 0$.

To decide whether to increase public services, the local authorities must predict the effect on property values. This requires a complete price system—that is, a land price for every possible provision of public goods g (whether or not any jurisdiction provides that level of public goods in equilibrium). We will let p: $\mathbf{R}_+ \to \mathbf{R}_+$ represent land prices, where $p(g)$ is the unit price of land when a jurisdiction provides public goods in amount g. Each jurisdiction is a price taker in that it believes the capitalization function p is unaffected by its own public services. Prices are linear in land consumption, but might be nonlinear in g. As in the previous section, I have formulated the competitive hypothesis as a price-taking hypothesis, although it is often formulated in this literature as a "utility-taking" hypothesis.

A local public goods equilibrium (LPGE) is a feasible allocation $\{(g^j, s_t^j, N_t^j, x_t^j)\}_{j=1...J, t=1...T}$ and land prices p such that conditions 1–3 are satisfied:

1. Each consumer can afford his or her consumption bundle: for each t and j, if $N_t^j > 0$, then $s_t^j p(g^j) + x_t^j \leq Y_t$.
2. No consumer can achieve more utility by living in another (real or hypothetical) jurisdiction or by consuming a different amount of land: if (g,s,x) is preferred by a consumer of type t to (g^j, s_t^j, x_t^j), where $N_t^j > 0$, then $p(g)s + x > Y_t$.
3. No jurisdiction can increase property values by providing a different level of local public goods, when it knows that the public goods will be capitalized: for each j, and for all $g \in \mathbf{R}_+$, $A^j p(g^j) - c(g^j) \geq A^j p(g) - c(g)$.

The value $A^j p(g) - c(g)$ is the net rental value of land in jurisdiction j if the costs of public goods are taxed away from landowners through property taxes. Thus, by maximizing $A^j p(g) - c(g)$, the jurisdiction acts on behalf of landowners.

Condition 2 implies that if consumers of type t reside in two different jurisdictions in equilibrium, then the utility received in both must be the same—say, u_t.

Lemma Let $\mathbf{u} = \{u_t\}$ be the utilities achieved by an LPGE, and let p represent the equilibrium land prices. Then

(a) Land prices p satisfy the following condition:

(4.1)
$$p(g) \geq \max_t \sup_{s>0} \frac{Y_t - m^t(g,s,u_t)}{s} \text{ for all } g \in \mathbf{R}_+,$$

where m^t is an expenditure function implicitly defined by $U^t[g,s,m] = u_t$ for $s > 0$.[25]

(b) If consumers of type t occupy land in jurisdiction j in equilibrium (that is, if $N_t^j > 0$ and $s_t^j > 0$), then $p(g^j) = [Y_t - m^t(g^j, s_t^j, u_t)] / s_t^j = -\partial m^t(g^j, s_t^j, u_t)] / \partial s$.

Proof. (a) Suppose not. Then for some t and some s, we would have $p(g)s + m^t(g,s,u_t) < Y_t$, which would imply that a consumer of type t could achieve more utility than u_t, since $x^t > m^t(g,s,u_t)$ is affordable. This is a contradiction. (b) If $p(g^j) > [Y_t - m^t(g^j, s_t^j, u_t)] / s_t^j$, then type t could not achieve utility u_t, since $m^t(g^j, s_t^j, u_t)$ is not affordable, a contradiction. The last equality follows from characterizing the maximum of (4.1). ■

The equilibrium land prices described by the above lemma are commonly called a "bid rent function,"[26] and have two interpretations: Equation (4.1) says that the price in a jurisdiction capitalizes the value of public goods, in the sense that the price equals the maximum of consumers' willingnesses to pay per unit of land to live there. Willingness to pay is defined such that it preserves the consumer's equilibrium utility level. Part (b) says that the occupant of land is the highest bidder, and that the price of land in each jurisdiction allocates space according to the familiar rule that the ratio of land price to the price of the private good is equal to the marginal rate of substitution.

The following proposition, which asserts that an LPGE is efficient, does not comment on existence. An immediate problem with existence which is solved by a continuum of consumers is that for each jurisdiction j, we must have $A^j = \Sigma_t N_t^j s_t^j$, where s_t^j is an optimizing lot size. This will usually not be exactly satisfied when N_t^j is an integer.

Proposition 4.3 An LPGE is efficient in the sense that any other allocation that achieves the equilibrium utilities **u** uses more resources.

Proof. Let $\{(g^{j*}, N_t^{j*}, s_t^{j*}, x_t^{j*})\}$ be the feasible allocation associated with the LPGE that achieves utilities **u**, and let p* be the equilibrium land prices. The following inequalities show that any other allocation $\{(g^j, N_t^j, s_t^j, m^t(g^j, s_t^j, u_t))\}$ uses at least as much resources as the LPGE. In (4.2), the first inequality follows from part (a) of the above lemma and from the fact that $\Sigma_t N_t^j s_t^j = A^j$.[27] The second inequality is condition (3) in the definition of LPGE, and the equality follows from part (b) of the lemma.

$$(4.2) \quad \sum_{j,t} (N_p^j s_t^j) \left[\frac{Y_t - m^t(g^j, s_t^j, u_t)}{s_t^j} \right] - \sum_j c(g^j)$$

$$\leq \sum_j [A^j p^*(g^j) - c(g^j)] \leq \sum_j [A^j p^*(g^{j*}) - c(g^{j*})]$$

$$= \sum_{j,t} (N_t^{j*} s_t^{j*}) \left[\frac{Y_t - m^t(g^{j*}, s_t^{j*}, u_t)}{s_t^{j*}} \right] - \sum_j c(g^{j*}).$$

Since $\Sigma_{j,t} N_t^j Y_t = \Sigma_{j,t} N_t^{j*} Y_t$, we can subtract out the terms involving Y_t. Hence:

$$(4.3) \qquad \sum_{j,t} N_t^j m'(g^j, s_t^j, u_t) + \sum_j c(g^j) \geq \sum_{j,t} N_t^{j*} m'(g^{j*}, s_t^{j*}, u_t) + \sum_j c(g^j).$$

Thus, the resources consumed in the LPGE are no greater than the resources which would have to be consumed in any other allocation that achieved utilities **u**. ∎

In equilibrium, consumers might sort themselves among jurisdictions according to their preferences for public goods. The variable g can be interpreted as a vector, and we could imagine that jurisdictions differ in the public goods they provide in equilibrium, and therefore differ in the consumers they attract.

The only crowding costs in this simple model arise because a large population drives up the price of land. One could modify the model by introducing other congestion effects—for example, utility might decline with the number of residents, or the cost of providing g might increase with the number of residents. A similar argument to the one just presented would apply, provided that a variable representing crowding is introduced to the utility function or cost function and that each jurisdiction can choose the number of residents directly as a developer would—say, by zoning or by dividing up the land into lots.

But, again, the "developer" model is much too centralized. The most viable means to limit a jurisdiction's population or to encourage population growth is to impose jurisdiction-specific taxes or subsidies. We should therefore ask whether, if taxes are the only means to govern immigration, jurisdictions will still achieve an efficient allocation in aggregate—that is, an efficient distribution of population as well as efficient provision of public goods within jurisdictions.

If crowding presents a negative externality, either because residents dislike congestion or because the cost of public goods increases with the number of residents, the jurisdiction will try to limit immigration by imposing a head tax (or local income tax)—say, τ^j. Conditional on $\{(g^j, s_t^j)\}$, the values of the first and fourth expressions in (4.3) do not change with the head tax.[28] The tax discourages immigration, however, since the value s that maximizes $[Y_t - m'(g^j, s, u_t) - \tau^j] / s$ increases with τ^j (with the appropriate convexity assumption). The head tax discourages immigration and reduces the price of land in the jurisdiction, which encourages each resident to consume more land. Thus, the head tax allows the jurisdiction to reduce the equilibrium population. But the jurisdiction cannot control the population exactly using the local head tax unless the demand for land is continuous in price. Thus, the conclusion that head taxes and public goods are sufficient policy instruments to achieve efficiency may require convexity of preferences.

These arguments do not require Lindahl pricing, and neither did the arguments for clubs. As long as there is an admission price of any sort, Lindahl prices for units of the public goods themselves are unnecessary.

B. Interpretations and Criticisms

The above line of reasoning does not explain the number of jurisdictions. We need an additional mechanism to partition the space into jurisdictions efficiently, and this is not given by the model. For the competitive hypothesis to be justified, we would want the number of jurisdictions to be large. There are many reasons the efficient number of jurisdictions might be large. It might be costly for residents to travel great distances to to visit a centralized public facility; average costs of supplying the public good might increase very rapidly; and there might be congestion costs in the supply of public goods or in their consumption, as mentioned above.

An unsatisfying aspect of the price-taking formulation of the results in Section A is that jurisdictions must know the capitalized price of land at all fiscal policies g or (g,τ). If we had, for example, a symmetric equilibrium in which all jurisdictions provided the same fiscal services, the complete price system would not be observable. The problem of "predicting" the land price that would capitalize fiscal policies would require the jurisdiction to observe preferences, which is precisely what a price-taking equilibrium seeks to avoid. Of course the problem of knowing the prices of unsold goods in a price-taking equilibrium is not unique to this context. In a private-goods economy, some goods are typically not traded. Without observable market prices, how does a firm know whether these goods would be profitable?

Of course, for the price-taking assumption of the previous section to be *justified*, there must be many jurisdictions. Each jurisdiction must think that citizens' utilities will not change when it changes its provision of public goods, and therefore that the land price will change according to (4.1). Such a belief is justified only if the jurisdiction is very small relative to the rest of the world. To be concrete, suppose that there were only one jurisdiction (for example, the federal government) and that preferences were given by $U[g,s,u] = x + h(g) + f(s)$. The jurisdiction's population is fixed, and the only reasonable belief is that the price of land satisfies $f'(A/N) = p^*$, where A is the area and N is the population. The constant price p* is not a competitive equilibrium, since consumers prefer a jurisdiction with many public goods and landowners prefer none. A price system satisfying (4.1) would be a competitive equilibrium, but the manager of the single jurisdiction could not reasonably believe those prices would prevail at different g, since consumers' utility is not fixed by the possibility of moving elsewhere.

In a previous paper (1986), I investigated the level of public services that will be provided in the intermediate case in which jurisdictions are not perfectly competitive but there is more than one jurisdiction. If a jurisdiction unilaterally improves its fiscal services, there will be utility effects elsewhere. As residents immigrate to the improved jurisdiction, their emigration from other jurisdictions depresses the demand (and price) of land there, leaving the remaining residents better off. In this work, I assumed as above that each jurisdiction wanted to maximize its aggregate property value net of costs of public goods, that the jurisdiction had no direct control over the size of population or land prices, and that the jurisdictions would achieve a Nash equilibrium in "fiscal policies" (public services and taxes). As a result of the utility effects, if the public services are funded through property taxes, jurisdictions will underprovide public goods in equilibrium. But if the jurisdiction can also use jurisdiction-specific head taxes, which have incentive effects, efficiency is restored.

The conditions required for a price-taking equilibrium to exist have not been explored. I have already pointed out the need for a continuum of consumers. Another impediment might be multiple public goods, as shown by the following example.[29]

Suppose there are two jurisdictions, m and s, each with land mass equal to one, and two types of consumers (in equal numbers), M and S, where type-M people want a museum and type-S people want a sports complex. The museum and sports complex cost the same amount. The land prices p_m and p_s must be equal, since the jurisdictions must make the same "profit" in equilibrium. Consumers of one type cannot occupy both jurisdictions, because all such consumers must receive the same utility in equilibrium. Thus, the consumers must be segregated. But then equilibrium might not exist, since equilibrium would require that each consumer's demand for land in each jurisdiction must be the same to ensure that everyone would have a place to live and that there would be no land left over.

To my knowledge, existence of equilibrium has not been investigated. At a minimum, existence would seem to require more continuity in the aggregate demand for land in each jurisdiction than the above example exhibits.

Public policies that serve the interests of property owners might be unappealing to citizens concerned with equity. But so are private policies that maximize the wealth of shareholders in ordinary competitive theory. The elegance of the invisible hand in both cases is that efficiency follows from self-interested behavior. Nevertheless, the invisible hand might be small comfort to those who believe that redistribution of endowments is impossible and that the most feasible form of redistribution is through provision of public services. I should therefore mention other decision rules that local jurisdictions might follow.

A natural alternative is for the jurisdiction manager to be concerned with residents rather than landowners. But then the objective function is not well defined. Whenever the local services are increased or decreased, there will be immigration to or emigration from the jurisdiction. Whose preferences count? Those of the residents who were present before the change, or those of the residents who are present after? A natural way to incorporate the residents' preferences in public decisions is to let them vote. Unfortunately, voting can lead to inefficiencies even when consumers cannot move around, and can get worse when consumers vote with their feet as well as with their ballots (see Inman, 1987).

Another possibility that has been too little discussed is that the hand behind local public expenditures is visible rather than invisible—that is, public-expenditure decisions are made according to a cost-benefit calculation. If the local analyst adds up the costs and benefits in the way we are taught in graduate school—by including the willingnesses to pay of all affected parties inside and outside the jurisdiction and ignoring transfers such as increased tax revenues and changes in property value—then, by definition, public projects will be built only if they are (potentially) Pareto-improving.

The three special problems that arise in cost-benefit analysis at the local level are that (1) transfers of money or revenue from nonmembers of the jurisdiction to members are likely to be counted as benefits even though they are transfers from an aggregate social perspective; (2) real benefits to nonresidents are likely to be excluded; and (3) policy interventions induce immigration or emigration, so that it is unclear whose benefits and costs count. Siting a baseball stadium is a good example of the first problem. During the 1980s, the city of San Francisco considered whether it should build a new stadium for the Giants. Advocates argued, on the basis of increased city revenues and local commerce, that the city should build the stadium. Advocates overlooked the fact that these increases displace revenues and commerce that would alternatively accrue elsewhere.

Abating pollution is an example of the second problem. Local pollution usually has spillover effects on residents elsewhere. In deciding whether pollution controls should be imposed on local businesses, local authorities are likely to undercount benefits. Cost-benefit analysis (or any other decentralized mechanism for choosing public goods, including the one above) can work well only if all benefits accrue within the jurisdiction.

A subtler version of problem 1 is linked with problem 2, and occurs when a potential project would induce immigration. Consider, for example, an improvement in local schools. Immigration has two effects. First, immigrants become beneficiaries of the improved public goods, and, second, the migration will coincide with increased rental prices in the improved jurisdiction, and possibly with a decrease in rental prices elsewhere. The increased utility from lower rental prices outside the jurisdiction is "real" rather than only a transfer, because it alters consumption of space and housing (see Scotchmer, 1990 for further discussion of this problem).

The "classical" technique of adding up the costs and benefits of consumers everywhere and ignoring transfers will not be politically viable at the local level. A local analyst who accounts for impacts on nonresidents as well as on residents, and who ignores pecuniary impacts on residents such as transfers to landowners through capitalization, will have trouble explaining the cost-benefit analysis to the local constituency. After all, why should members of the local constituency care about effects beyond the jurisdiction's boundary? And shouldn't they be pleased to receive transfers from nonresidents, either through tax revenues or through property values? One would like to find a cost-benefit calculus that depends only on local impacts but that leads to efficient decisions in aggregate. To my knowledge, this question has not been investigated.

III. CONCLUSION

We might summarize these investigations by saying that profit incentives are moderately effective in providing "club" goods but might be less effective in providing "local public goods." In the latter case, profit must be interpreted as wealth of landowners, and the objective of making property owners richer can be politically unviable. In addition, there is the thorny problem of how to divide geographical space into jurisdictions.

Nowhere have we needed Lindahl prices. Lindahl pricing was an attempt to understand public goods as private goods by establishing personalized prices for consuming them. The notion was that, although public goods are nonrival in the sense that one person's enjoyment does not impede another's, a consumer can nevertheless be excluded if he or she refuses to pay. Thus, we can let each person's unit price be his or her willingness to pay for the marginal unit of public services at an efficient allocation. Then the sum of personal prices equals the marginal cost of the last unit. If each person's willingness to pay decreases and the marginal cost of supply increases with the level of public services provided, the public services will be provided efficiently. If public services were underprovided, the marginal unit would be profitable. If they were overprovided, the marginal unit would be unprofitable.

Even for pure public goods, Lindahl pricing has never been thought a viable way to elicit supply, primarily because consumers have an incentive to misrepresent their preferences so as to pay a low unit price for public goods. Furthermore, the public good may be indivisible (a bridge), so that competition among many suppliers, each providing part of it, would be hard to interpret. This is especially true if the marginal cost of providing units is not constant, so there is a problem of allocating the cost among many suppliers. In the context exposited here, Lindahl prices are unnecessary whether or not preferences are observable, so long as a "lump-sum" price (a land price or an admission price) can be charged; we need competition "among" jurisdictions, but not competition "within" jurisdictions in providing public goods.

But Lindahl prices raise the question of what must be known to achieve equilibrium in the above models. In club economies with nonanonymous crowding, we assume that types are observable. Otherwise, crowding effects would have to be anonymous. In club economies with anonymous crowding, prices can be anonymous, just as in private goods exchange economies. The complete price system can be characterized by the cost function.

In perfectly competitive local public goods economies, the local jurisdiction needs to know the price or capitalization function, which might not be observable. If all jurisdictions provide the same public services in equilibrium, there is no price dispersion to observe. In order to know the capitalization function in that case, a local jurisdiction must know preferences. Although this is unsatisfactory, we notice that a similar problem arises in private goods exchange economies, where firms have no way of knowing the "demand price" of an untraded good.

Nash equilibria among a finite number of clubs or jurisdictions have not been studied for the case of heterogeneous tastes or nonanonymous crowding. A logical assumption on what is observable would be that each player (club, jurisdiction) knows the distribution of tastes but cannot identify the tastes of any individual. In such contexts it is unclear when equilibria in pure strategies would exist or how close they would be to efficient. These are open questions.

APPENDIX

Proof of Proposition 4.1. (a) Let $\mathbf{u}$ be in the equal-treatment core. For each $(g,\mathbf{n})$ we will construct prices $\mathbf{\Pi}(g,\mathbf{n}) = (\Pi^1(g,\mathbf{n}), \ldots, \Pi^T(g,\mathbf{n}))$, and from these prices we will construct equilibrium prices $\boldsymbol{\pi}$. If $U^t[g,\mathbf{n},0] \leq u_t < \lim_{x \to \infty} U^t[g,\mathbf{n},x]$ and $n_t > 0$, then by continuity there exists $x \geq 0$ such that $U^t[g,\mathbf{n},x] = u_t$. For this x, let $\Pi^t(g,\mathbf{n}) = \omega_t - x$. If $U^t[g,\mathbf{n},0] > u_t$, let $\Pi^t(g,\mathbf{n}) = \omega_t$. If $n_t > 0$ and $U^t[g,\mathbf{n},x] < u_t$ for all $x \geq 0$, let $\Pi^t(g,\mathbf{n}) = -2\boldsymbol{\omega}\cdot\mathbf{n}$. If $n_t = 0$, let $\Pi^t(g,\mathbf{n}) = \omega_t$. (The latter price is irrelevant.) We have constructed $\mathbf{\Pi}$ so that $\mathbf{\Pi}(g,\mathbf{n}) \leq \boldsymbol{\omega}$.

For each $(g,\mathbf{n})$, and for a nonnegative value $\varepsilon(g,\mathbf{n})$ characterized below, we will let $\boldsymbol{\pi}(g,\mathbf{n}) = \mathbf{\Pi}(g,\mathbf{n}) + \varepsilon(g,\mathbf{n})\,\mathbf{1}$ where $\mathbf{1}$ is a T-vector of ones. We will let $\varepsilon(g,\mathbf{n}) = 0$ if $U^t[g,\mathbf{n},\omega_t - \Pi^t(g,\mathbf{n})] = u_t$ for all t for whom $n_t > 0$. Otherwise we will choose $\varepsilon(g,\mathbf{n})$ to be a small positive number. We will show that prices $\boldsymbol{\pi}$ and the core allocation are a competitive equilibrium.

Condition 3 of the definition of competitive equilibrium is satisfied by construction of the prices $\boldsymbol{\pi}$. There is no club $(g,\mathbf{n})$ that would provide any member more utility than he gets in the core, and the core allocation achieves the core utilities. If $U^t[g,\mathbf{n},x] \geq U^t[g,\mathbf{n},0] > u_t$ and $n_t > 0$, we have chosen $\pi^t(g,\mathbf{n}) = \omega_t + \varepsilon(g,\mathbf{n}) > \omega_t$, so that an agent of type t cannot afford such a club. If $U^t[g,\mathbf{n},x] < u_t$ for all $x \geq 0$, then the club $(g,\mathbf{n})$ cannot provide the core utility u_t irrespective of the price of admission. In the remaining case, for some $x \geq 0$, $U^t[g,\mathbf{n},x] = u_t$ and $U^t[g,\mathbf{n},\omega_t - \pi^t(g,\mathbf{n})] \leq U^t[g,\mathbf{n},\omega_t - \Pi^t(g,\mathbf{n})] = u_t$. Since the core allocation achieves $\mathbf{u}$, we have that $\varepsilon(g^k,\mathbf{n}^k) = 0$, $\boldsymbol{\pi}(g^k,\mathbf{n}^k) = \mathbf{\Pi}(g^k,\mathbf{n}^k)$ and $U^t[g^k,\mathbf{n}^k,\omega_t - \pi^t(g^k,\mathbf{n}^k)] = u_t$ if $n_t^k > 0$.

Thus we only need to check conditions 1 and 2.

We first consider potential clubs $(g,\mathbf{n})$ for which there exists t such that $n_t > 0$ (which means $n_t \geq 1$) and $U^t[g,\mathbf{n},\omega_t - \Pi^t(g,\mathbf{n})] < u_t$, which occurs only when $\Pi^t(g,\mathbf{n}) = -2\boldsymbol{\omega}\cdot\mathbf{n}$. We must check condition 1: such a club would provide nonpositive profit. Recalling that $\boldsymbol{\pi}(g,\mathbf{n}) \leq \boldsymbol{\omega} + \varepsilon(g,\mathbf{n})\,\mathbf{1}$, and letting $|\mathbf{n}| = \Sigma_t n_t$, we have $\mathbf{n}\cdot\boldsymbol{\pi}(g,\mathbf{n}) - C(g,\mathbf{n}) = n_t[-2\boldsymbol{\omega}\cdot\mathbf{n} + \varepsilon(g,\mathbf{n})] + \Sigma_{i \neq t} n_i\,\pi^i(g,\mathbf{n}) - C(g,\mathbf{n}) \leq n_t[-2\boldsymbol{\omega}\cdot\mathbf{n} + \varepsilon(g,\mathbf{n})] + \Sigma_{i \neq t} n_i\,[\omega_i + \varepsilon(g,\mathbf{n})] - C(g,\mathbf{n}) \leq -2\boldsymbol{\omega}\cdot\mathbf{n} + \boldsymbol{\omega}\cdot\mathbf{n} + |\mathbf{n}|\varepsilon(g,\mathbf{n}) - C(g,\mathbf{n}) \leq -\boldsymbol{\omega}\cdot\mathbf{n} + |\mathbf{n}|\varepsilon(g,\mathbf{n}) - C(g,\mathbf{n})$, which is negative for $\varepsilon(g,\mathbf{n})$ sufficiently small.

We now consider the remaining potential clubs $(g,\mathbf{n})$ such that for all t with $n_t > 0$, $U^t[g,\mathbf{n},\omega_t - \Pi^t(g,\mathbf{n})] \geq u_t$. The clubs in the core allocation belong to this group. To show that condition 1 holds for the equilibrium prices $\boldsymbol{\pi}$, we first show that for $\mathbf{n} \leq \mathbf{N}$, $\mathbf{n}\cdot\Pi(g,\mathbf{n}) - C(g,\mathbf{n}) \leq 0$ with strict inequality if $U^t[g,\mathbf{n},0] > u_t$ and $n_t > 0$ for any t. If the inequality did not hold, then $\mathbf{n}\cdot[\boldsymbol{\omega} - \Pi(g,\mathbf{n})] + C(g,\mathbf{n}) < \mathbf{n}\cdot\boldsymbol{\omega}$, which means that a coalition $\mathbf{n} \leq \mathbf{N}$ could achieve more utility than $\mathbf{u}$ by providing public goods g and private goods $\mathbf{x} > \boldsymbol{\omega} - \Pi(g,\mathbf{n})$. This contradicts the premise that $\mathbf{u}$ is in the core. Now suppose that $n_t > 0$ and $U^t[g,\mathbf{n},0] > u_t$ and suppose that $\mathbf{n}\cdot\Pi(g,\mathbf{n}) - C(g,\mathbf{n}) = 0$, or that $\mathbf{n}\cdot[\boldsymbol{\omega} - \Pi(g,\mathbf{n})] + C(g,\mathbf{n}) = \boldsymbol{\omega}\cdot\mathbf{n}$. Then the coalition $\mathbf{n}$ could provide at least as much utility as $\mathbf{u}$, and strictly more to types t for whom $U^t[g,\mathbf{n},0] > u_t$, by providing public goods g and private goods $\mathbf{x} = \boldsymbol{\omega} - \Pi(g,\mathbf{n})$. Again this contradicts the premise that $\mathbf{u}$ is in the core. We now show that condition 1 holds for the prices $\boldsymbol{\pi}$ if $\varepsilon(g,\mathbf{n})$ is sufficiently small. If $U^t[g,\mathbf{n},\omega_t - \Pi^t(g,\mathbf{n})] = u_t$ for all t for whom $n_t > 0$, then condition 1 is satisfied because $\varepsilon(g,\mathbf{n}) = 0$ and $\mathbf{n}\cdot\boldsymbol{\pi}(g,\mathbf{n}) - C(g,\mathbf{n}) = \mathbf{n}\cdot\Pi(g,\mathbf{n}) - C(g,\mathbf{n}) \leq 0$. For the case that there exists t with $n_t > 0$ and $U^t[g,\mathbf{n},\omega_t - \Pi^t(g,\mathbf{n})] = U^t[g,\mathbf{n},0] > u_t$, we have shown that $\mathbf{n}\cdot\Pi(g,\mathbf{n}) - C(g,\mathbf{n}) < 0$. By choosing $\varepsilon(g,\mathbf{n})$ sufficiently small, we can ensure that $\mathbf{n}\cdot\boldsymbol{\pi}(g,\mathbf{n}) - C(g,\mathbf{n}) = \mathbf{n}\cdot[\Pi(g,\mathbf{n}) + \varepsilon(g,\mathbf{n})] - C(g,\mathbf{n}) < 0$.

Finally we show condition 2: that under the price system π, a club $(g^k,\mathbf{n}^k)$ in the core allocation provides zero profit. We know from the previous paragraph that it cannot provide positive profit. Since $(g^k,\mathbf{n}^k,\mathbf{x}^k)$ is part of the core allocation, $U^t[g^k,\mathbf{n}^k,x_t^k] = u_t$ if $n_t^k > 0$, and therefore $\boldsymbol{\pi}(g^k,\mathbf{n}^k) = \Pi(\mathbf{n}^k,\mathbf{x}^k)$. If condition 2 were not satisfied, then $\mathbf{n}^k\cdot\boldsymbol{\pi}(g^k,\mathbf{n}^k) - C(g^k,\mathbf{n}^k) < 0$, which would imply that $\mathbf{n}^k \cdot \mathbf{x}^k + C(g^k,\mathbf{n}^k) = \mathbf{n}^k\cdot[\boldsymbol{\omega} - \boldsymbol{\pi}(g^k,\mathbf{n}^k)] + C(g^k,\mathbf{n}^k) > \mathbf{n}^k\cdot\boldsymbol{\omega}$, which contradicts the premise that $(\mathbf{n}^k,\mathbf{x}^k)$ was a club in the core allocation.

(b) Let $\mathbf{u}$ be the utilities achieved in competitive equilibrium. Suppose those utilities are not in the core. Then there exists $(g,\mathbf{n},\mathbf{x})$ such that $\mathbf{x}\cdot\mathbf{n} + C(g,\mathbf{n}) \leq \boldsymbol{\omega}\cdot\mathbf{n}$, $\mathbf{n} \leq \mathbf{N}$ and $U^t[g,\mathbf{n},x_t] \geq u_t$ for all t such that $n_t > 0$, with strict inequality for some such t. But by condition 3 and monotonicity we have that if $n_t > 0$, $\omega_t - \pi^t(g,\mathbf{n}) \leq x_t$, with strict inequality for at least one such t. But then $[\boldsymbol{\omega} - \boldsymbol{\pi}(g,\mathbf{n})]\cdot\mathbf{n} + C(g,\mathbf{n}) < \mathbf{x}\cdot\mathbf{n} + C(g,\mathbf{n}) \leq \boldsymbol{\omega}\cdot\mathbf{n}$, which implies that $\boldsymbol{\pi}(g,\mathbf{n})\cdot\mathbf{n} - C(g,\mathbf{n}) > 0$, in contradiction to condition 1. ∎

Proof of Proposition 4.2. Let $\{\mathbf{n}^j\}$, $j \in J$, and $\{\mathbf{n}^k\}$, $k \in K$, be partitions of the player sets $\mathbf{N}'$ and $\mathbf{N}$ for which $\mathbf{u}' \in W(\mathbf{n}^j)$, $j \in J$, and $\mathbf{u} \in W(\mathbf{n}^k)$, $k \in K$. The results will follow from the two inequalities: (i) $\mathbf{u}'\cdot\mathbf{n}^k \geq \mathbf{u}\cdot\mathbf{n}^k$ for each $\mathbf{n}^k$

in the partition $\{\mathbf{n}^k\}$, and (ii) $\mathbf{u}\cdot\mathbf{n}^j \geq \mathbf{u}'\cdot\mathbf{n}^j$ for each $\mathbf{n}^j$ in the partition $\{\mathbf{n}^j\}$. To see why the first inequality holds, recall that since utility is transferable, there is a number $V(\mathbf{n}^k) \in \mathbf{R}_+$ such that $\mathbf{u} \in W(\mathbf{n}^k)$ if and only if $\mathbf{u}\cdot\mathbf{n}^k \leq V(\mathbf{n}^k)$, and if $\mathbf{u}$ is in the core of $[\mathbf{N},W]$, $\mathbf{u}\cdot\mathbf{n}^k = V(\mathbf{n}^k)$. If $\mathbf{u}'\cdot\mathbf{n}^k, < \mathbf{u}\cdot\mathbf{n}^k$, then $\mathbf{u}'\cdot\mathbf{n}^k < V(\mathbf{n}^k)$, which means that $\mathbf{u}'$ is in the interior of $W(\mathbf{n}^k)$ and therefore in the interior of Ω. Therefore the game $[\mathbf{N}',W]$ contains a coalition that could achieve a utility vector greater than $\mathbf{u}'$, and that coalition could block. A similar argument shows the second inequality.

To complete the argument, we must sum the first inequality over k and the second inequality over j, which yields (iii) $(\mathbf{u}' - \mathbf{u})\cdot\mathbf{N} \geq 0$ and (iv) $(\mathbf{u} - \mathbf{u}')\cdot\mathbf{N}' \geq 0$. Together these imply that $(\mathbf{u} - \mathbf{u}')\cdot(\mathbf{N} - \mathbf{N}') \leq 0$ and $(\mathbf{u} - \mathbf{u}')\cdot(\mathbf{s} - \mathbf{s}') \leq 0$.

The conditions on $\mathbf{s}$ and $\mathbf{s}'$ imply that $N_t' = dN_t, t = 2, \ldots, T$, for an appropriate $d > 0$, and $N_1' > dN_1$. Hence $N_1' = d(N_1 + \delta|\mathbf{N}|)$ for an appropriate $\delta > 0$. Dividing the inequalities (iii) and (iv) by $|\mathbf{N}|$ and $d|\mathbf{N}|$ respectively, we have $(\mathbf{u}' - \mathbf{u})\cdot\mathbf{s} \geq 0$ and $(\mathbf{u} - \mathbf{u}')\cdot(s_1 + \delta, s_2, \ldots, s_T) \geq 0$. Adding these inequalities, we see that $(u_1 - u_1')\delta \geq 0$. The result follows. ∎

Daniel L. Rubinfeld

The chapter by Suzanne Scotchmer provides an excellent background for some-one who wishes to study the economics of the local public sector. Scotchmer's focus is the development of a set of sufficient conditions under which multiple jurisdictions or clubs will operate efficiently. The resulting model serves as a useful straw man, for it makes clear the rather restrictive set of conditions under which economic efficiency can be ensured. In these comments, I will pursue Scotchmer's development a bit further, by stressing the limitations of the decentralization argument. At issue is the importance of interjurisdictional externalities in an economic world in which limited information and legal and political constraints are the norm rather than the exception.

Local officials may pursue any number of objectives; if they are property value maximizers and if other strong conditions hold, efficiency can be achieved. But if we assume that officials are concerned with maximizing the benefits to their constituents net of the costs that they bear, efficiency may not be possible.

DECENTRALIZATION: YES OR NO?

There is much to be said for the decentralization of the provision of public goods and services. Decentralization allows individuals a variety of bundles to choose among, as well as two means of expressing preferences: voting within a jurisdiction, and migrating between jurisdictions. Decentralization has another advantage: it may limit the ability of public officials to use their political (and economic) power to enrich themselves at the expense of their constituents. The advantages of decentralization correspond to the advantages of the competitive market system; to the extent that there is competition, we would expect decentralized outcomes to be economically efficient.

But a model in which public goods and services are provided in multiple jurisdictions is not equivalent to the model of the perfectly competitive economy. The unhappy consequence is that decentralization does not ensure efficiency. This leaves the political economist with a difficult choice. Should she advocate a decentralized fiscal economy without the first-best welfare theorems, or should she urge centralization, which introduces a new set of political complications and a new set of potential inefficiencies?

DISTINGUISHING BETWEEN CLUB MODELS AND LOCAL PUBLIC GOOD MODELS

Scotchmer distinguishes club models and local public goods models by defining the former to apply to shared facilities, with admissions fees used to exclude those who do not pay their fair share. The role of space in club models is either nonexistent or relatively unimportant. Models with public goods, on the other hand, cannot assess admissions fees directly, and must rely on other indirect devices (taxes, zoning, and so on) to restrict entry. Space is an important component of club models; it is the capitalization of public goods and taxes into the land (space) prices that achieves a decentralized equilibrium. This distinction is not always made in the literature, but it does allow for a useful contrast.

The efficiency properties of the two models should be distinguished. Scotchmer shows, under a fairly broad set of assumptions, that a competitive equilibrium *in the club model with entry* generates a fully efficient outcome which is in the core. The admission fee serves as a competitive price. However, competition among local jurisdictions may not lead to an efficient outcome, since entry is difficult.

EFFICIENCY?

The case for efficiency depends crucially on two assumptions: first, either there is no space, or, if there is space, it can be partitioned into jurisdictions; and, second, decision makers maximize profit or the aggregate value of the land. Under these assumptions, the entry and exit of profit-maximizing club owners (or the appropriate partitioning of land) will lead to an equilibrium with an efficient number of clubs. This equilibrium will be efficient because all externalities are internalized—that is, all the effects of the movement of an individual from one club to another and all the benefits of public goods can be accounted for by admission fees and land prices.

There are two important reasons we should not believe the efficiency conclusion. The first concerns spillovers. When the number of jurisdictions is fixed, any efficiency claims are only second best; they do not consider improvements that can be made if the world is repartitioned into new jurisdictions. A good example is the historically determined boundaries of states in the United States.

These boundaries cut across important air and water sheds, creating political externalities among states. However, if we were to begin anew and redefine a set of jurisdictions that included water and air sheds, we could better allow for the internalization of important environmental externalities. Alternatively, there may be taxes and other instruments that can internalize these externalities and improve economic efficiency without redrawing jurisdictional boundaries.

The second argument against efficiency is that managers are not likely to maximize either property values or profit. With more complex objectives, these managers can be expected to drive the economy to allocate resources inefficiently.

In what follows I comment on each of these two sources of inefficiency.

FIXED JURISDICTIONS, LIMITED SPACE, AND SPILLOVERS

Assume that there are a finite number of profit-maximizing jurisdictions, defined geographically. (Annexation, repartitioning, and so on are not feasible.) Jurisdictions have a limited number of tax instruments (for instance, the property tax) and generally cannot assess admissions fees. In such a model the existence of equilibrium is problematic. Suppose, for example, that there are two groups of individuals, high-income and low-income, that jurisdictions supply a public good for which demand is income elastic, and that this public good is paid for by a flat-rate property tax. In addition, suppose the demand for property is positively correlated with the demand for the public good. As a consequence, individuals will enjoy different (marginal) benefits from consuming the public good, and will face different marginal costs (the larger the consumption of property, the greater the cost of public goods). In this situation, jurisdictions cannot assess admissions fees to each group that equate the marginal benefit received from the public good (to the jurisdiction) to the marginal cost.

Now consider as a possible equilibrium an arrangement in which some jurisdictions contain all low-income individuals, while others contain all high-income individuals. In fact, this cannot be an equilibrium because low-income individuals will find it advantageous to move to the high-income communities (they get a lot more of the public good, at very little, if any, increased cost), but the high-income individuals may not want low-income immigrants (if the marginal cost of providing more of the public good outweighs the additional tax revenue generated). Correspondingly, high-income individuals will not want to locate in low-income communities, because they will receive less of the public good then they desire, with very little savings in taxes. The net result is what I would term a "Groucho Marx disequilibrium": if there is a low-income jurisdiction that wants high-income members, the high-income individuals won't want to join, whereas anyone with a low income who wants to join the high-income jurisdiction won't be welcome as a member.[1]

But suppose that an equilibrium does exist. That equilibrium is likely to involve extensive externalities between jurisdictions. One obvious source of externalities is spillovers, involving the environment or public services. But externalities are also created when the optimizing behavior of one jurisdiction creates price effects that distort the economic choices of other jurisdictions. A few examples might prove useful.

Suppose that public goods are financed by property taxes. When an individual moves from jurisdiction A to jurisdiction B, she raises the marginal cost of that public good in A (to a taxpayer in A) and lowers the marginal cost in B, creating incentives that may cause jurisdictions to compete for members inefficiently.[2] Another way to see this point is to realize than when jurisdictions use non-lump-sum taxes to differing levels of public goods, tax rates are likely to vary substantially. Migration will have different effects on different jurisdictions, creating distortions that reduce economic welfare.[3]

The fact that there are a finite number of jurisdictions adds a third source of difficulties for the public goods model. Because the number of jurisdictions is finite, each jurisdiction has a small degree of market power, and, as a result, policy changes in one jurisdiction can have important effects on other jurisdictions. One interesting example is a proposal to apply severance taxes on coal in the western United States. These taxes would reduce the output of coal and drive up the price paid by nonresident consumers of coal resources. As a result, distortions would be felt throughout the entire U.S. economy.[4]

As a theoretical matter, these inefficiencies can be remedied if one is allowed to choose from a sufficiently large set of possible policy instruments. For example, admissions fees for private clubs are considered appropriate, so that congestion and other externalities within a club can be efficiently priced. However, there are legal, constitutional, and political limitations on the use of taxes, fees, and other instruments to regulate the migration of individuals. Thus, while it has been suggested that fiscal zoning can be used to turn the property tax into a pure benefits tax, thereby allowing the Tiebout model to generate efficient outcomes, the politics of zoning makes it clear that zoning has not been used in this manner.[5] Similarly, limiting the eligibility of individuals to receive certain public sector benefits can improve economic efficiency; but in cases such as welfare, limiting eligibility has been ruled unconstitutional by the U.S. Supreme Court.[6]

THE INEFFICIENCIES OF LOCAL COST-BENEFIT ANALYSES

As Scotchmer's paper points out, there are a number of reasons that cost-benefit analyses undertaken by local public officials are likely to be inconsistent with the achievement of global efficiency. Local cost-benefit analyses focus only on local benefits and costs, usually include transfers, and often omit real external effects. This raises an intriguing question that seems open to further research. Are there special cases (or general principles) in which the biases associated with local cost-benefit analysis can be removed or corrected by a national social planner? A few examples should give a flavor of what I have in mind.

In a paper written about ten years ago, Paul Courant and I considered the welfare effects of a capital tax applied in one jurisdiction in a system of numerous jurisdictions.[7] Using a highly stylized example, we showed that as much as one-third of the total deadweight loss of the tax could be felt outside the taxing jurisdiction. Tax policy in Berkeley or Peoria can matter to the rest of the world. Knowing that these effects can be important, and that their magnitude depends crucially on certain parameters (involving the marginal productivity of capital, and the elasticity of substitution between land and capital), it would be interesting to ask whether a national "tax" on the use of capital could improve the efficiency of local cost-benefit analyses.

It is also interesting to note that in one form of the local public goods model, a change in one jurisdiction's fiscal policy is likely to increase welfare if there is an increased migration into the jurisdiction and decrease welfare is there is outmigration.[8] (The same would not be true if we were examining a Nash equilibrium.) This suggests that information (properly corrected and controlled) about the pattern of migration, tied to a migration tax or subsidy, could improve economic efficiency as well.

A related set of issues would arise were we to view the problem in the context of a Nash equilibrium in which all jurisdictions are simultaneously and independently making choices about taxes and public goods. We know, for example, that AFDC (Aid to Families with Dependent Children) is likely to be underprovided by many states, since high levels of benefits encourage individuals to move, thereby increasing the marginal cost of the program to constituents. A new Nash equilibrium with better efficiency properties could be achieved, however, if an appropriate system of federal grants or subsidies can be designed. The general point is not new, but relatively few efforts at program design have been tied directly to the kinds of cost-benefit analyses that local politicians are likely to undertake.

5

Federalism and Government Finance

Much of the analysis in public finance takes place in an institutional vacuum. The study of the incidence of various taxes or the provision of a public good often (and for good reason) is of a general and formal character that possesses little institutional content. The public sector in the real world, however, consists of a set of institutions—and spending and tax programs are enacted and function within this context.

A fundamental institutional dimension of the public sector is a "layering" of governments. The modern nation-state has a central government that addresses matters of national concern. But it also has other "levels" of government: regional, state, or provincial public bodies, and local government units with fiscal responsibilities for their own geographically defined jurisdictions. And this "federal structure" of the public sector opens up a whole new set of important and fascinating issues for public finance: the proper allocation of fiscal functions among the different levels of government; the most effective assignment of revenue responsibilities and specific tax instruments to the various levels; the role of intergovernmental financial transfers between levels of government; and the vertical assignment of regulatory responsibilities.

This chapter is a survey of work on these issues—a survey of so-called fiscal federalism. Over the past three decades, since the publication of Richard Musgrave's monumental volume *The Theory of Public Finance* (1959), there has emerged a large body of research exploring a whole range of important issues in multilevel public finance. My purpose here is to provide an overview and some reflections on this body of work, with special attention to the challenging research agenda that remains.

I shall begin with a brief review of the division of fiscal functions among levels of government, using Musgrave's insightful prescription (1965) as a point of departure.

In Part II, on the so-called tax-assignment problem, the issue will be whether certain forms of taxation are better suited for use at particular levels of government—or whether anything goes.

In Part III we will examine intergovernmental grants, a distinctive fiscal instrument of major and growing importance in the twentieth century. The development both of the theory of intergovernmental grants and of their use as a policy instrument is an intriguing and curious one—and there are some quite fundamental matters that are still not well understood.

Researchers have devoted the most attention, as measured in terms of numbers of published papers in the field, to the topic of local finance and the Tiebout model, the subject of Part IV. A fundamental debate is still going on concerning the efficiency properties of ''Tiebout behavior'' in the context of existing local fiscal structure.

Parts V and VI address two more recent issues in the literature. The first, ''regulatory federalism,'' concerns the locus of regulatory authority in a federal system. The question here is whether the setting of such things as standards for environmental quality should be centralized in a national regulatory authority or delegated to regional or local agencies. The final part turns to an issue of public choice and fiscal federalism: the effect of the vertical structure of the public sector—namely, its degree of centralization—on the growth and size of the government sector as a whole. Here we will examine the claim that increased centralization enhances the monopoly powers of the state and leads to an expanded public budget (Brennan and Buchanan, 1980). I will conclude with some reflections on centralizing and decentralizing forces in the public sector.

Throughout this chapter, I will be using the term ''fiscal federalism'' to refer to a public sector with two or more levels of decision making. Such a definition is far more inclusive than a narrow political definition that would encompass only systems with formal federal constitutions. From an economic perspective, virtually any public sector is federal in character, in that fiscal decisions are made, de facto, at different levels. The issue is really one of the degree of centralization. At the same time, I don't want to be misunderstood on this matter. This general point emphatically does not mean that the presence of a federal constitution is of no economic moment: constitutional structure surely matters for the way in which the public sector functions. The point more simply is that *fiscal* federalism addresses a particular aspect of the public sector: its vertical structure. It explores those issues that arise in the fiscal relationships among public decision makers at different levels of government.

I. THE DIVISION OF FISCAL FUNCTIONS AMONG LEVELS OF GOVERNMENT

As Tocqueville observed more than a century ago, "The federal system was created with the intention of combining the different advantages which result from the magnitude and the littleness of nations." From a fiscal perspective, we can understand Tocqueville's basic point as suggesting that the presence of several levels of government offers an opportunity to centralize decision making on those economic matters where national policies are needed and to allow "local" fiscal choice where it is most advantageous.

Musgrave introduced some substance to this general supposition by sketching out a proposed assignment of functions. Drawing on his tripartite division of functions for the public sector, he concluded his brief treatment of fiscal federalism (1959a, pp. 179–183) with the statement: "The heart of fiscal federalism thus lies in the proposition that the policies of the Allocation Branch should be permitted to differ between states, depending on the preferences of their citizens. The objectives of the Distribution and Stabilization Branches, however, require primary responsibility at the central level" (pp. 181–182).

Musgrave's rough guidelines for the assignment of functions, although the subject of considerable attention and some dispute in the subsequent literature, retain much of their validity. Macroeconomic management for stabilization purposes—although the subject of wide ranging and fundamental controversy—must (to the extent it is pursued at all) be largely centralized. The management of the supply of money and credit is nearly everywhere the responsibility of a central monetary authority. On the budgetary side, there is limited scope for decentralized management of demand because of the openness of small local economies. The stimulative effects of local tax cuts, for example, would tend to flow out of the local economy as the bulk of any new spending is directed to goods produced elsewhere.

Edward Gramlich (1987b) contends that decentralized government has some role in countercyclical policy. In particular, macroeconomic "shocks" (such as the rapid rise in energy prices) often have a very different impact on various regions of a country. Decentralized governments can address the particular conditions of their ''local'' economies; the central government will find such geographical discrimination difficult, with its broader instruments for the management of aggregate demand. In addition, decentralized agencies can make some contribution to an effective countercyclical policy through the use of ''rainy day'' (or stabilization) funds. State and local governments can accumulate revenues during good times and then draw on these funds during recessions, so as to stabilize spending and tax rates over the course of the business cycle. But the scope for decentralized stabilization policy seems quite limited, so that the primary responsibility for this function must rest with the central government.

Likewise, there exist real constraints on decentralized redistributive policies. A local government, for example, which undertakes an aggressive policy to redistribute income from wealthy households to poorer ones runs the uncomfortable risk of attracting low-income individuals and of chasing away the well-to-do. There is some evidence gathered in the United States suggesting that such mobility of the poor exists to some extent and that it has discouraged the adoption of decentralized measures to assist the poor (see Brown and Oates, 1987). In addition, Ladd and Doolittle (1982) suggest that support of low-income households is, to some extent, a national ''public good.'' This is not an easy proposition to establish empirically. But even in its absence, the potential mobility of the poor creates a standard sort of externality that is likely to result in the underprovision of assistance to low-income families within a wholly decentralized system (Brown and Oates, 1987).

This point should not be exaggerated, however. There is certainly some capacity for decentralized support of the poor. Pauly (1973) has argued persuasively that there is typically much greater concern in a community for the local indigent than for the poor elsewhere. This leads to an efficiency argument for localized poor relief.

What emerges from all this is a case for some sharing of the Distribution Function. David King argues (1984, p. 36) that there should be ''a basic national redistribution policy, and that subcentral authorities should be allowed to alter the degree of distribution in their areas within specified limits.'' At any rate, there does seem to be an important (if not exclusive) role for the central government in the Distribution Branch.

Musgrave is surely correct when he says that ''the heart of fiscal federalism'' is to be found in the Allocation Branch. It is in the tailoring of outputs of local public goods to the particular tastes and circumstances of different jurisdictions that the real gains from decentralization are to be realized. This takes its sharpest form in the Tiebout model of local finance, where individuals ''shop'' among jurisdictions offering alternative levels of outputs of local public goods. As Tiebout (1956) and the subsequent literature show, for the "perfect" case, such shopping behavior leads to an outcome that realizes the potential gains from decentralization to the full extent; the local public sector does fully as well as the private sector in allowing each individual to select the most efficient level of consumption of each good. As Tiebout put it: "Just as the consumer may be visualized as walking to a private market to buy his goods, the prices of which are set, we place him in the position of walking to a community where the prices (taxes) of community services are set. Both trips take the consumer to market . . . Spatial mobility provides the local-public-goods counterpart to the private market's shopping trip" (p. 422). So long as the taxes individuals must pay reflect accurately the marginal cost of extending the local services to the new resident, the outcome will be Pareto-efficient, just as it is in the private sector.

The mobility of consumers, while certainly enhancing the scope for allocative gains from decentralized choice, is by no means necessary for the case for the decentralized provision of local (or regional) public goods. Even in the complete absence of mobility, there will still, in general, exist welfare gains from varying local outputs with local tastes and costs. The tailoring of outputs to local circumstances will, in general, produce higher levels of well-being than a centralized decision to provide some uniform level of output across all jurisdictions (see Oates, 1972, p. 35, on the Decentralization Theorem). And such gains do not depend upon any mobility across jurisdictional boundaries.[1]

The potential gains from decentralized choice can be quite large.[2] But the actual realization of these gains in the context of more realistic fiscal institutions is a matter of some contention. We shall return to this issue in the discussions of local finance and interjurisdictional competition.

II. THE TAX-ASSIGNMENT PROBLEM

In addition to assigning the responsibility for different expenditure functions to the appropriate levels of government, there is the matter of revenue instruments. The issue here is the vertical structure of the revenue system. Are certain tax instruments, for example, better suited for use by the central government and others more appropriate at the local government level? Or, alternatively, is this simply a matter of administrative convenience?

A cursory examination of vertical revenue structure across countries reveals wide diversity. Nearly all major forms of taxation are employed at central, state or province, and local levels somewhere in the world. This does not imply, however, that the tax-assignment problem is a vacuous issue. An improper vertical alignment of tax instruments may come at considerable cost to society, in both efficiency and equity terms.

For a systematic treatment of this issue, we can turn (once again) to Musgrave (1983). In a short paper that provides a useful point of departure for the analysis of this problem, Musgrave put forth a set of general guidelines for the assignment of revenue instruments to different levels of government. He suggested the following "principles" for tax assignment:

1. Highly progressive taxes, especially for redistributional purposes, should be centralized. For the reasons discussed in the preceding section, such taxes are to be avoided at decentralized levels of government because of the perverse incentives they create for migration among jurisdictions. A personal income tax with a strongly progressive rate structure should thus be reserved for the central government.

2. In general, lower-level governments should eschew taxes (at least nonbenefit taxes) on highly mobile tax bases.[3] Such taxes can distort the locational pattern of economic activity. Decentralized governments are better advised to employ taxes on relatively immobile tax bases (such as land).

3. The central government should exercise primary taxing authority over those tax bases that are distributed across jurisdictions in a highly unequal fashion. Taxes on deposits of natural resources, in particular, should be centralized to avoid geographical inequities and to prevent allocative distortions that can result from the "local" taxation of such resources.

4. While user taxes and fees have much to commend them at all levels of government as benefit taxes, they are an especially appealing revenue instrument at the most decentralized levels of government. They create, in principle, no potentially distorting incentives for movements among jurisdictions. In the context of the Tiebout model of local finance, for example, such taxes promote efficient decisions by mobile consumers.

The revenue system also has important implications for fiscal decision making. For instance, taxes which are largely exported to residents of other jurisdictions effectively reduce the tax-price to locals of public programs—and, in this way, may encourage excessive public expenditure on local services (McLure, 1967). Roger Gordon (1983) has explored this general set of issues in an optimal taxation framework and finds numerous channels through which local taxes generate externalities and the associated inefficiencies when local decision makers seek to maximize the well-being of their own residents. In the vertical design of tax structure, it is thus important to be aware of the ways in which the use of particular taxes can create perverse signals for fiscal choices. User, or benefit, taxes again get excellent marks on efficiency grounds: they not only tend to provide the proper incentives for location decisions but also give the right cost signals to residents for the determination of levels of local services.

The discussion points to a general prescription for vertical tax structure. It suggests, in brief, that the central government is in the most advantageous position to employ progressive redistributive taxes (on personal income or, perhaps, expenditure), whereas highly decentralized levels of government should seek out relatively immobile tax bases (such as local real estate) or should rely on user charges. Intermediate-level governments such as states or provinces obviously have more room to maneuver than small local governments; there is more scope here for the use of income and sales taxes—though potential mobility is still operative to some degree as a constraint on tax policy.

Although the vertical structure of revenue systems worldwide displays considerable variation, it appears to be far from random. There are some general patterns. And the normative perspective emerging from the foregoing discussion possesses some explanatory power. We do, in fact, find that many countries rely heavily on progressive income taxation at the central level. Local governments, in contrast, often place a primary reliance on property taxation (where at least the land portion of the tax base is immobile). Local use of charges for certain public services is also quite common. A more systematic study of the extent of similarities in vertical tax structure and their correspondence to this normative framework would be very useful.

The next step for research on the tax assignment problem brings us to the important, but more difficult, issue of the magnitude of the distortions from deviations from this prescription. It is a fairly straightforward matter to catalogue the potential forms that tax-induced distortions can take. But it is much harder to assess the approximate size of these distortions. It may well be the case that the distortions discussed in this section tend, in practice, to be rather minor—that the actual magnitude of the welfare losses is small.

There is little evidence on this important question. In one recent study, Timothy Goodspeed (1989) explores the use of redistributive taxes at the local level. Making use of a general equilibrium model of a metropolitan area, Goodspeed compares the efficiency and redistributive properties of local income taxation relative to a system of local head taxes. He finds that local governments in his model can employ progressive income taxes to accomplish some significant income redistribution with only quite modest efficiency losses. The Goodspeed study is purely a general equilibrium exercise with no direct empirical content; nevertheless, it certainly suggests the possibility that we have exaggerated the extent of the constraint on the local use of ability-to-pay taxation. There is a real need for some careful empirical work to provide us with a better sense of the magnitudes we are dealing with here.

In a somewhat similar vein, Peter Mieszkowski (1983) has examined the distortions from the decentralized taxation of natural resources. In particular, Mieszkowski and Toder (1983) estimate that the efficiency losses resulting from distorted location decisions under the decentralized taxation of energy resources in the United States amount to roughly 4 percent of energy revenues. The estimates are hedged with a number of important qualifications, but again one comes away with the sense that the distortions may not be of great moment. There are, of course, some important equity arguments (as well as an efficiency argument) for the centralization of such tax bases.

In sum, we have some general prescriptions for the assignment of revenue instruments to different levels of government. But we badly need a better empirical sense of just what is at stake here.

III. INTERGOVERNMENTAL GRANTS AND REVENUE SHARING

In a system of governments, there is an extra degree of freedom in the budget constraint, in the sense that budgetary balance (inclusive of any debt issues) is not required at each level—or unit—of government. Revenues at one level of government, for example, can fall short of spending, if the difference is made up by transfers from other levels of government. The use of such intergovernmental transfers—or grants—has become a prominent feature of modern fiscal federalism. In the United States, for instance, the state and local government sector received about $120 billion in grants from the federal government in 1989—accounting for roughly 16 percent of state and local receipts. Local government in the United States is yet more dependent on intergovernmental transfers with grants from state to local governments constituting approximately one-third of local revenues. These fractions are even larger in some other countries.

Economists provided, early on, a normative framework for the structuring of a system of intergovernmental grants. George Break (1967), in a major Brookings study of intergovernmental fiscal relations, set forth a systematic view of the grant system.[4] This perspective called for a set of open-ended matching grants to decentralized governments for programs that involved external benefits to other jurisdictions. Following the standard prescription for Pigouvian subsidies to individual decision makers, the argument here was that the appropriate matching terms would induce state or local governments to "internalize" the benefits provided to residents of other jurisdictions into the "local" decision calculus. The second class of intergovernmental grants consists of unconditional grants; the case for such transfers with no strings attached rests in part on equity grounds, in that "equalizing grants" with more generous sums going to poorer jurisdictions would promote society's redistributional goals.

Break advanced a second, and more intriguing, rationale for unconditional grants. His argument concerned a general tendency toward underspending on the part of state and local government. Fearing adverse effects on business investment and economic growth, state and local officials (so the argument goes) are reluctant to increase tax rates or introduce new taxes. In short, an atmosphere of "tax competition" leads to suboptimal state and local budgets. Unconditional grants, from this perspective, provide a needed supplement to state and local revenues on purely efficiency grounds, a supplement that would result in a substantial increase in state and local spending.

This line of argument was further buttressed by Walter Heller and Joseph Pechman, who, in the 1960s, pressed the case for revenue sharing by the federal government with state and local governments. The basic premise for the proposed Heller-Pechman plan was that a highly income-elastic federal revenue system generated large and "automatic" increments each year to federal revenues—increments that were larger than needed for federal government programs and that would tend to throw the federal budget into surplus and exert a "fiscal drag" on the macroeconomy. In contrast, expenditure "needs" were growing rapidly at the state and local levels, where they tended to outstrip the more modest growth in revenues from a relatively income-inelastic state and local revenue system. The cure for this problem was revenue sharing, which would effectively link the rapidly growing sources of revenues at the federal level with rapidly growing expenditure needs at state and local levels.

All this sounds rather curious now, in these days of huge federal deficits. But things were quite different then. I remember Pechman presenting a seminar at Princeton in the late 1960s at which he argued persuasively on behalf of the revenue-sharing proposal. He stressed that the additional funds would provide a much needed stimulus to state and local spending. In fact, I can still recall him citing a Brookings estimate from a not fully identified source that "approximately 52 cents of every revenue-sharing dollar" would be directed into additional public expenditure.

I raise this historical episode not just for a glimpse into fiscal history. There

are, in fact, some central issues at stake here that go to the heart of intergovernmental fiscal relations. These issues involve the effects of intergovernmental
grants on public expenditure and Break's concern with tax competition.

There is something quite disturbing about Pechman's claim that 52 cents of
every dollar of unconditional grants will be spent by state and local government.
Unconditional grants (assuming that they are truly unconditional—that is, lump
sum—in character) should have only income effects on the recipient's budgetary behavior. As David Bradford and I (1971) showed formally, unconditional
grants to a community should, for a wide class of collective choice rules, have
effects on spending that are identical to those of an increase in private disposable income. Given the shares of state and local government spending in national income, it is hard to believe that desired spending at the margin on state
and local services is more than, say, 10 to 15 cents per dollar of additional
income. Pechman's estimate is obviously much in excess of this—and later
work tends to support Pechman on this matter. According to Gramlich's widely
cited survey (1977) of research on intergovernmental grants, existing empirical
work indicates that typically something like 40 to 50 cents of such grant dollars
manifest themselves in additional public spending.

This phenomenon is well known in the literature as the "flypaper effect,"
to indicate that "money sticks where it hits." Taken at face value, the flypaper
effect has some rather damning implications for the functioning of democratic
institutions. It suggests that the representatives of the populace in state and local
government do not follow, in budgetary terms at least, the will of the electorate.
The flypaper effect, for example, appears wholly at odds with the prediction
of the median-voter model, a model of responsive government. Instead, flypaper
behavior points to the presence of Niskanen sorts of politicians who seek to
expand the public budget for their own purposes beyond levels desired by the
citizenry. It suggests that political competition is insufficient to provide needed
fiscal discipline.

The public finance literature has, predictably, not stopped here. In fact, this
phenomenon has given birth to a vast number of papers that respond in widely
differing ways to this empirical "challenge" to existing theory.[5] The responses
are basically of three different kinds:

1. Some claim that the flypaper effect is fundamentally a "mirage" of one
form or another. These researchers argue that grant programs have been misunderstood and modeled incorrectly—and that if things are done properly, the
flypaper effect will disappear (or at least take on a much reduced magnitude).

2. A second line of response is to admit the existence of the flypaper effect,

but to provide a framework in which it is fully consistent with the behavior of responsive government—with, say, the median-voter model.

3. The third class of papers, in a public choice spirit, essentially takes the existence of the flypaper effect as a refutation of responsive public sector agents. These papers present models of a Niskanen sort in which, through various mechanisms, officials ''overspend'' grant funds relative to what their constituents would truly wish.

I shall not attempt here an exhaustive survey of this literature, but it is of interest to get the flavor from selected papers for these three ways of dealing with the flypaper effect. The first set of papers contends that the ''measured'' flypaper effect is the result (largely at least) of analytical and econometric imprecision. One error of this type is to treat certain grants mistakenly as lump sum in character. In this vein, Howard Chernick (1979) argues that in choosing recipients for various project grants (that are funded with what are in appearance closed-ended lump-sum funds), granting agencies favor those projects where the recipient agrees to spend the largest amount of its own funds. Such procedures effectively convert an apparently lump-sum grant into one with implicit matching provisions. It would certainly not be surprising to find a large expenditure effect for such programs.

Taking an alternative but related tack, Robert Moffitt (1984) contends that measured flypaper effects can result from misspecifications that involve contemporaneous correlation between the disturbance term and the price and income variables in an OLS equation. In a careful study of the AFDC program, Moffitt makes use of an econometric technique that accounts for nonconvexities in the program; he does not find a flypaper effect. Bruce Hamilton (1983) argues along a different line that, because of omitted variables, the propensity to spend from private income is understated by expenditure studies relative to the propensity to spend from grants received from higher-level governments. The basic claim in this set of papers is that, with proper analysis and estimation procedures, we will not find (much of) a flypaper effect.

The second class of responses does not contest the existence of the flypaper effect, but finds that it is fully consistent with responsive government—that it is consistent with the maximization of a representative consumer's utility. Jonathan Hamilton (1986) offers an interesting explanation of the flypaper effect along these lines. In Hamilton's model, local governments must resort to distortionary taxation to raise their own revenues—so that there is an added cost, a deadweight loss, associated with locally raised funds. Grant funds are free of any such cost. It is less expensive, in a sense, for a community to spend grant funds on local services than to raise local taxes to fund these services. A larger fraction of an increment to grant funds will thus be directed into local government spending than of private income. In Hamilton's model, then, an observed flypaper effect emerges that is fully consistent with, say, a median-voter model.

The third general approach to the issue turns to various public choice models involving budget-maximizing bureaucrats, fiscal illusion, and agenda manipulation that produce a flypaper effect as their predicted outcome. It is to be emphasized that budget-enlarging propensities by public agents are not in themselves sufficient to generate overspending. Effective political competition can prevent such outcomes. There must be further elements present that create the capacity for bureaucrats to indulge these propensities. Some of the papers in this class introduce a kind of fiscal illusion (Courant et al., 1979; Oates, 1979) through which local agencies can "hide" grant funds to some extent—and use them to induce the electorate to believe that the marginal cost of public services is lower than it really is. Alternatively, Filimon et al. (1982) make use of the Romer-Rosenthal framework (1979) under which local officials have certain agenda-setting prerogatives because of existing "reversion" provisions (that is, voters support higher budgets than they prefer because the alternative "reversion" budget is yet more distasteful). It is not hard to show that models in this spirit can generate flypaper effects, as local agencies manipulate grant funds in ways that allow large chunks of them to flow into an expanded public budget.

These are just a few selections from what has become a large literature on the flypaper effect. The real problem at this juncture is trying to discriminate among the various approaches to explaining this empirical finding. There is a real need to devise empirical tests that can systematically distinguish among them.

One further aspect of the flypaper effect has gone largely unnoticed and seems to me quite intriguing: a potential asymmetry. I was struck in a recent paper by Gramlich (1987b) with his observation concerning the response of state and local government to the fiscal retrenchment under the Reagan administration during the 1980s. This retrenchment involved large cutbacks in a wide range of federal grant programs to state and local government. Gramlich observed that state and local governments responded to these cutbacks by picking up most of the slack: they increased their own taxes and largely replaced the lost grant funds so as to maintain levels of existing programs.[6] If this is so, it implies a basic asymmetry in the response to intergovernmental grants. It suggests that while state and local government spending responds vigorously to the receipt of grants, it is relatively insensitive to the loss of grants. Does money stick where it hits—but come unstuck without leaving a gaping hole behind? This merits some study.

Finally, there is the matter of the impact of normative grant theory on actual grant policy. As discussed earlier, through the efforts of Break and others, public finance economists have developed a systematic normative theory of intergovernmental grants. It is of interest to see how well existing grant systems correspond to the economist's "model."

We look first for a set of matching grants where spillover benefits are present. Examining the federal grant system in the United States, we initially do find some programs that can be understood in these terms: matching grants for interstate highways, municipal waste treatment plants, and other projects involving external benefits. On closer examination, however, these grant programs do not correspond at all well to the theoretical precepts. Most of them have had very high federal matching rates—80 to 90 percent. It is impossible to believe that external benefits are large enough to warrant such generous matching terms (Oates, 1980; Gramlich, 1985a). Moreover, these programs often cut off at specified, modest levels so that they are actually closed-end matching programs from the perspective of potential recipients. And, as theory makes clear, closed-end matching grants are, in principle, no different from unconditional grants once the cutoff point is reached. Federal grants for allocative purposes do not, in fact, resemble their theoretical counterparts very well.

More generally, Robert Inman (1988) finds in a careful and recent study that the economic theory of intergovernmental grants cannot provide a very satisfactory explanation of the structure of U.S. grant programs; he finds that a basically political model does a much better job of explaining the U.S. system of federal grants. Even for federal grant programs whose primary objective is fiscal equalization, Holcombe and Zardkoohi (1981) find that various political variables have far more explanatory power than the economic variables that represent the stated goals of the program. Some state aid programs may do better in this respect. John Yinger and Helen Ladd (1989), for example, find that state assistance to central cities has been focused on the cities with the greatest need.

At any rate, it appears that intergovernmental grant systems do not mirror very accurately the economist's principles for the design of such systems. While this may be dismaying, it does have a positive aspect: it suggests that careful analysis and reform of the grant system may yield large returns in terms of a more effective realization of society's allocative and distributive goals.

IV. LOCAL FINANCE

There now exists an enormous theoretical and empirical literature on local finance. A systematic survey and assessment of this entire body of research is well beyond the scope of this paper.[7] Instead, I wish to explore two central and intriguing issues in the literature. They relate to the relevance of the Tiebout model to the functioning of the local public sector.

As Musgrave emphasized, decentralized finance assumes its greatest importance in the Allocation Branch. And the Tiebout model in its pure form embodies the full thrust of Musgrave's contention. As noted earlier, the Tiebout world is one in which individual households "shop" among communities and select, as a place to reside, the community that provides the fiscal package best suited to their tastes. The appealing efficiency properties of the model are dependent on a range of heroic assumptions, several of which have been investigated in the literature. To take one important example, Tiebout assumes that all income takes the form of dividend income. This assumption is much stronger than it need be; the idea here is simply to break any necessary link between the jurisdiction of residence and the jurisdiction in which one works. If, in contrast to Tiebout, one requires individuals to work and reside in the same jurisdiction (this might be better described as a "regional model"), then the nice efficiency properties of the model are largely lost (see Flatters, Henderson, and Mieszkowski, 1974; and Stiglitz, 1977). It is certainly arguable, however, that the Tiebout assumption is the better one for the analysis of local finance in a metropolitan setting with a multiplicity of small municipalities.

I wish, however, to examine two other issues. The first has to do with the way in which local governments finance public services: the local revenue system. And the second concerns the nature of the production functions for local services, a matter addressed in several recent papers.

The original Tiebout paper is quite remarkable in many respects, one of which is the vague way in which several critical matters are treated. The issue of how communities finance their services is little discussed; the term "tax" appears hardly at all in the entire paper. It was left to the subsequent literature to work all this out in a more careful way. What is clear is that the efficiency properties of the model depend critically on the use of marginal-cost pricing.

Tiebout communities must charge residents a price or ''tax'' equal to the cost of extending the local service to an additional resident. Assuming constant costs along the population dimension, this suggests an equal head tax on all residents so that individuals end up buying local services in much the same way as they purchase private goods: they pay a price equal to marginal cost. Tiebout financing thus becomes a form of benefit taxation.

Now, it is true that local governments rely to some extent on user charges to finance certain local services. But the great bulk of own revenues for most local governments comes from local property taxes. This raises a serious problem. On first inspection, at least, local property taxation bears little resemblance to the marginal-cost pricing assumed in the Tiebout model. In fact, it is not hard to show that the tax discourages the consumption of housing and by linking housing consumption to the tax bill also distorts decisions concerning local public service consumption (Oates, 1972, ch. 4; Hamilton, 1976). It would thus appear that the system of finance required for the efficient operation of a Tiebout system is, in practice, largely lacking—and with it goes, to some extent at least, the efficiency case for a system of local finance with fiscally mobile households.[8]

In an ingenious paper, Bruce Hamilton (1975) tried to save the day. Hamilton showed that the introduction of a system of ''fiscal'' zoning ordinances into the model (under which local governments effectively specify a minimum consumption level of housing) converts the local property tax back into a pure benefit tax, and thereby restores the efficiency properties of the mobility model. The zoning constraint effectively divorces the housing consumption decision from the selection of a level of local public goods consumption and eliminates the distortion in these choices.

The Hamilton model, however, involves some strong assumptions. And we have been left with the perplexing and, as yet, largely unresolved issue of which model provides the better description of the operation of the local sector. On the one hand, we have the ''new view'' of the property tax, championed by Peter Mieszkowski and George Zodrow (1989), which sees the tax as distorting; under this view, the ''average'' burden of the tax across the country falls on owners of capital, and local differentials function like ''excise taxes'' with a complicated pattern of incidence. The Mieszkowski-Zodrow argument thus calls into question the efficiency properties of our system of local finance.

On the other hand, there is the Hamilton-Fischel view that the local property tax approximates a benefit tax, with its salutary implications for the efficient functioning of the local sector. Hamilton and Fischel base their case on the widespread use of zoning measures throughout the United States and their sense that these measures typically constitute binding constraints on local fiscal and housing decisions of the sort envisioned in the earlier Hamilton model.

The evidence bearing on this basic issue is indirect and fragmentary. There is, for example, a considerable body of econometric work that finds substantial capitalization of fiscal differentials across communities.[9] One's first inclination (as in Oates 1969) is to take this finding as empirical support for the Tiebout model. If individuals shop among communities, we might expect to find them bidding up the value of residences in communities offering more attractive fiscal packages, consisting of high levels of services at relatively low tax rates.

Further scrutiny, however, has suggested that the implications of capitalization are far more restricted. In fact, in a pure Tiebout equilibrium, it can be argued that there should be no capitalization at all (Edel and Sclar, 1974). At any rate, as is now clear (see Mieszkowski and Zodrow, 1989), capitalization can legitimately be taken as evidence that individuals shop among communities and pay more for houses in fiscally advantaged jurisdictions—but it does not tell us anything about whether the "supply side" of the Tiebout world is functioning as envisioned in the model. Some capitalization is, in fact, consistent with both the benefit view and the new view of local property taxation, so that this finding does not help us to distinguish between these two basic hypotheses.

There are some bits of evidence that one can take as favorable to the Hamilton-Fischel position. A necessary condition for the reasonably efficient operation of the Tiebout mechanism is a wide range of choice among communities. A study by Fischel (1981) of U.S. metropolitan areas suggests that this condition is probably satisfied: most urban areas in the United States provide a wide range of residential choice for individuals who work (or who for other reasons reside) in the area.

The presence of "Tiebout sorting" in the local sector would manifest itself in tendencies toward homogeneous community composition. Tiebout homogeneity takes the form of (roughly) equal demands for local services—demands which are not directly observable. But assuming that demand varies systematically with such things as family income and housing demand, we should expect to find in a Tiebout world that the variation in income and in housing consumption is significantly less within communities than across communities. Casual empiricism suggests that this is indeed true, as do two systematic studies of the matter (Hamilton, Mills, and Puryear, 1975; Eberts and Gronberg, 1981).[10] This is not, however, a very strong test. Tendencies toward homogeneity are surely consistent with other sorts of models of local fiscal behavior.

It would be useful to have some more direct evidence on fiscal zoning measures—on their pervasiveness and on whether or not they seem typically to constitute binding constraints on local decisions. To support their sense that such ordinances are generally not binding, Mieszkowski and Zodrow (1989) cite the Houston case, where they claim that the vast majority of houses exceed (by a large margin) the size constraint imposed by existing ordinances. But some students of zoning take issue with this claim. Fischel (1990), for example, notes that "virtually every law professor who specializes in land use regards fiscal zoning as a serious constraint" (p. 3). Moreover, the simple presence of heterogeneity does not undermine the Tiebout-Hamilton model. So long as the supply of undeveloped land is fixed and is itself subject to ordinances that prevent adverse fiscal impacts, the property tax will function as a benefit tax. As Hamilton (1976) showed, capitalization will effectively eliminate intracommunity transfers on existing developed parcels and thereby "accommodate" existing heterogeneity.

In sum, we badly need more systematic and carefully assembled evidence on this basic issue. As things stand, it is impossible to reject either the new view or the benefits view in favor of the other. And this is an important matter: the two views have fundamentally different implications both for the efficient functioning of the local public sector and for the incidence of local property taxes.

There is a second troublesome issue that I would like to raise briefly. One of the many assumptions of the Tiebout model is that communities possess identical production functions for local services. This might seem a reasonable and relatively innocuous assumption; we are accustomed to assuming, for private sector production, that firms have identical production functions. But this assumption is far less compelling in the public sector, and this has bothered me for some time now (Bradford, Malt, and Oates, 1969; Oates, 1977, 1981). Although communities may have similar access to purchased inputs and to the provision of "directly produced" services such as police patrols and school classes, they have much less control over the levels of "final services" such as the degree of safety in the community or the quality of the local school system. The point here is that the level of final services (and this is what consumers presumably care about) depends not only on budgetary inputs but on the composition of the community.[11] Two communities with identical levels of inputs per capita may have very different levels of final outputs, if, for example, their populations differ in the propensity to engage in illegal activities or possess differing levels of motivation and ability to learn in school.

This raises some thorny problems for local finance. Several recent papers have explored this matter, and three of them, in particular, have examined the implications for efficient community formation (Brueckner and Lee, 1989; de Bartolome, 1990; Schwab and Oates, 1991). The simplest approach (followed in all three papers) is to assume that there exist two kinds of people with differing effects on "productivity" in local services, and that the cost of providing a specific level of local outputs depends upon their proportions in the local population (as well as on levels of purchased inputs). There may easily exist certain gains in production from the "mixing" of the two types of people (for example, the presence of good students may, over certain ranges, raise the performance of weaker students), which creates a case in terms of cost savings for some local heterogeneity in the population. Optimal community composition in such a setting can involve a tradeoff between the gains from homogeneity in consumption (à la Tiebout) against the cost savings associated with heterogeneity in production.

The interesting issue here is how equilibrium outcomes in a mobility setting compare with the optima. This is a complicated problem that can involve troublesome nonconvexities. Brueckner and Lee (1989) show that in a club-theoretic framework, a community developer can achieve an efficient outcome by employing differential pricing: the "entrance fee" must be higher for the class of individuals that has the less favorable effect on "community productivity" for local services.

The difficulty is that such price discrimination is typically not feasible in a public setting. Schwab and Oates (1990) note that such pricing would typically involve a "super-regressive" tax system in which lower-income families are charged higher local taxes (in absolute amount) than are higher-income families. One way to address the problem is through a second-best measure consisting of a system of equalizing grants that make communities more willing to accept lower-income households. This, interestingly, is a pure efficiency argument in support of equalizing grants to local governments.

These are simply two of several major and interesting issues in the local finance literature. Decentralized finance has compelling efficiency-enhancing potential, but there are a number of complications that need to be better understood.

V. REGULATORY FEDERALISM

Although regulatory policy may appear to lie outside the province of an essay on fiscal federalism, the two are, in important ways, intimately related. Let us look now at the centralization of regulatory activity, since the analysis of fiscal issues in a federal structure has much to contribute to our understanding of regulatory federalism. For purposes of concreteness, I shall place the discussion in the context of environmental policy. As should be obvious, however, issues in environmental federalism have direct relevance to regulatory issues in other areas.

To begin with, there is a striking and intriguing anomaly in U.S. environmental policy. Under the 1970 Amendments to the Clean Air Act, the U.S. Congress directed the Environmental Protection Agency to set uniform standards for air quality on a nationwide basis. The EPA responded by establishing such standards: maximum permissible concentrations of key air pollutants that are to be met at *every* point in the country. Two years later, Congress enacted a set of Amendments to the Clean Water Act. Here, Congress instructed the states to set their own standards for water quality and to develop programs to achieve those standards. The contrasting approaches pose a basic question: Should we set national standards applicable to all areas in the nation, or should we adopt a more decentralized approach to standard setting that would allow state or local agencies to determine specific standards for their own jurisdictions?

On the first cut, basic economic principles seem to provide a straightforward and simple answer to this question: standards should vary among jurisdictions according to local circumstances. The argument here is essentially the same as that for the decentralized provision of any public good. Since for many pollutants, the benefits and costs of environmental management are regional or local in character, the optimal level of control is likely to vary from one jurisdiction to another. A first-best outcome will clearly involve the setting of standards such that the marginal benefits from pollution control equal marginal abatement costs on a jurisdiction-by-jurisdiction basis (Peltzman and Tideman, 1972). This proposition is subject to the important and obvious qualification that it applies to those pollutants whose effects are localized; where emissions travel across boundaries (as in the case of acid rain deposition), wholly decentralized solutions are obviously inappropriate, for the usual sorts of reasons.

But where the benefits and costs of regulatory programs are "local" in nature, a decentralized approach appears to be in order. This simple prescription, however, may overlook certain political realities in local fiscal and environmental decision making. John Cumberland (1981), for example, has argued that in their eagerness to attract new business investment to create jobs and income, local decision makers are likely to relax environmental standards excessively. This argument is obviously a close cousin to George Break's concern over the effects of tax competition among state and local governments. As Break (1967) put it: "The trouble is that state and local governments have been engaged for some time in an increasingly active competition among themselves for new business . . . In such an environment government officials do not lightly propose increases in their own tax rates that go much beyond those prevailing in nearby states or in any area with similar natural attractions for industry . . . Active tax competition, in short, tends to produce either a generally low level of state-local tax effort or a state-local tax structure with strong regressive features" (pp. 23–24).

This issue of interjurisdictional competition has received increased attention in recent years, following the devolution of fiscal and regulatory responsibility during the Reagan administration. John Shannon, of the Advisory Commission on Intergovernmental Relations, suggests that we have entered a new era of "Fend-for-Yourself Federalism." From this perspective, the basic Break-Cumberland argument is that central intervention is needed to "save state and local governments from themselves."

This is not an easy argument to assess; but it is clearly an important one, for it goes to the very core of the case for a decentralized fiscal system. Until recently at least, there was little systematic theory addressing this issue—and very little evidence aside from informal and anecdotal reports.

In two papers, Robert Schwab and I (Oates and Schwab, 1988, 1989) constructed a set of models that explore the properties of interjurisdictional competition. In these models "local" decision makers set the values of various policy parameters involving both local tax rates on capital and environmental standards. The setting of these parameters involves explicit tradeoffs between local wage income and levels of local public goods and environmental quality, the kinds of tradeoffs that are at the heart of the tax competition argument. For the "base case," these models produce an encouraging finding: local decisions that maximize the welfare of local residents are efficient. Environmental standards in these models are set such that the cost of improved environmental quality at the margin equals the residents' willingness to pay. In short, in our basic models of interjurisdictional competition, local fiscal *and* regulatory decisions yield the right sorts of outcomes. Such competition is, in these models, efficiency-enhancing; it is not a source of distortions in resource allocation.

In the second of the two papers (1989), we extended the basic model to encompass the issue of the well-being of future generations, in response to the expressed concern that purely local decisions in the framework of a mobile society will not take into account the welfare of those yet unborn. An interesting result emerged in our two-period model: we found that local decision makers again make efficient decisions—but this time in a way that incorporates the welfare of future generations. The mechanism that generates this result is the capitalization of environmental damages that manifest themselves in the future. Current residents take into account the interest of future residents because prospective environmental quality is reflected in the present value of land parcels. Although this may not be a surprising finding, there is a mechanism that provides this kind of discipline on *local* choices that is absent at the central level. The usual presumption is that central decision makers are in a better position to take into account the well-being of future generations, but this is not altogether clear.

The results from the basic models thus support fiscal and regulatory decentralization. At the same time, these results are not highly robust. They are hedged by a number of important qualifications. If, for example, local officials behave in a Niskanen fashion and seek to maximize the size of the local budget, they will, in our models, not only set tax rates too high but will also establish excessively lax environmental standards in order to attract more business investment and expand the local tax base. Alternatively, if there are dissident groups in the community with differing interests in economic development and environmental quality, the outcome is no longer likely to be an efficient one (although it can involve too little or too much pollution). Perhaps even more important, if local government is constrained in its choice of tax instruments to a tax on local capital, then, as Zodrow and Mieszkowski (1986) and others have shown, inefficiently low levels of local public goods are the predicted result. Or, in a setting of "imperfect competition" with jurisdictional interactions, Mintz and Tulkens (1986) find that Nash equilibria exhibit some tendency toward underprovision of local services.

I know of no systematic empirical evidence on this matter. But one can't help feeling that we are not on the right course with some of our rigid, national standards for air quality. It is becoming increasingly clear, for example, that the costs of requiring southern California to meet the same standards for air quality as the rest of the nation are exorbitant and unreasonable. Instead of acknowledging the special circumstances of the southern California basin, we have responded by extending the time schedule for compliance; southern California continues to adopt new measures, unjustifiable on any sort of benefit-cost calculation, and with no prospect of ever attaining the standards. The cost of ignoring the case for environmental federalism can be very high.

This may well be true of certain other forms of regulation. The imposition of rigid regional land-use regulations that disregard the distinctive character of local jurisdictions can result in substantial welfare losses. Indeed, as we saw above, local discretion on zoning matters is essential for the efficient functioning of the Tiebout-Hamilton model. Fiscal federalism and regulatory federalism are interrelated in fundamental ways.

VI. A PUBLIC CHOICE ISSUE: DECENTRALIZATION AND THE SIZE OF THE PUBLIC SECTOR

Geoffrey Brennan and James Buchanan (1980) suggested a wholly different perspective on the role of decentralization in the public sector. Their contention is that decentralization can serve as a constraint on the undesired expansion of government.

The twentieth century has been characterized by a rapid growth of the public sector in most of the developed countries. This continued growth has become the source of widespread concern both in the political world and in certain parts of the scholarly community (see, for example, the papers in Forte and Peacock, 1985). Presidents and prime ministers have been elected on platforms committed to programs of budgetary restraint.

In the public choice literature, one finds extensive efforts to understand and describe the process of public sector growth. The Brennan and Buchanan view, a very striking one indeed, is that the public sector can be envisioned as a monolithic agent, a Leviathan, that systematically seeks to maximize its budgetary size, irrespective of the desires of the citizenry. Musgrave (1981), among others, vigorously contested this view. But what is of interest here is Brennan and Buchanan's claim that decentralization is an effective mechanism to control Leviathan's expansive tendencies. The basic argument is that, just as competition in the private sector exercises its disciplinary force, so competition among different units of government at a decentralized level of government can break the monopolistic hold of a large central government. As Brennan and Buchanan put it, such competition within the public sector in the context of the ''interjurisdictional mobility of persons in pursuit of 'fiscal gains' can offer partial or possibly complete substitutes for explicit fiscal constraints on the taxing power'' (1980, p. 124).

This is a not only a very provocative policy recommendation for decentralization of the public sector; it also suggests a hypothesis by which the Leviathan view of government can be put to an empirical test. The logic of the Brennan and Buchanan argument suggests that, other things equal, we should expect to find that the size of the government sector varies inversely with the extent of fiscal decentralization.

The initial empirical study of this hypothesis (Oates, 1985) explored the relationship between decentralization and public sector size for two quite different samples: a cross-sectional sample of forty-three countries and a second cross-sectional sample consisting of the state-local sectors in the United States. In neither case was I able to find any evidence of a significant negative relationship between the extent of fiscal decentralization and the size of government (as measured by tax receipts as a fraction of GNP). The findings, in short, were not consistent with the Leviathan view.

Some subsequent work, however, has muddied the waters a bit.[12] In particular, two studies making use of U.S. county data (Eberts and Gronberg, 1988; Zax, 1989) have found evidence that the presence of more general-purpose local government units is associated with a smaller overall size of the county public sector. It may be that in this smaller geographical setting, the potential mobility of individual households is higher and acts to constrain local government budgetary activity. Even here, however, the results are not uniformly supportive of Leviathan. Forbes and Zampelli (1989) found that the more counties there are in a metropolitan area, other things equal, the larger the metropolitan fisc— just the opposite of what the Leviathan view would suggest.

Cross-sectional studies at an international level consistently fail to find support for Leviathan. The share of the central government in the national fisc does not appear to be systematically related to the size of the public sector. James Heil (1991), in a follow-up study to mine, employed two different international data sources with more recent figures and likewise found no relationship between the fiscal share of the central government and the size of the public sector.

The evidence is not wholly clear. But there is not enough unambiguous support available to make a convincing case that decentralization in itself constrains government size. *If* we want smaller government, then other measures are probably in order.

VII. PATTERNS AND TRENDS IN FISCAL CENTRALIZATION

In an almost tautological sense, it is clear that fiscal federalism is here to stay. A public sector in which fiscal decision making is wholly centralized or, alternatively, wholly decentralized is virtually inconceivable. What we observe is a kind of tension between forces promoting fiscal centralization and those encouraging greater decentralization in the government sector. The balance seems to shift from one period to the next.

The tendency over the first half of the twentieth century was overwhelmingly in the direction of increased centralization. In the United States, for example, the central government's share of total public expenditure grew from about 35 percent in 1902 to 72 percent in 1952; over this same period, local governments' share fell from 55 percent to 15 percent. This led some observers to see centralization as the natural course of evolution of the public sector over time. Late in the nineteenth century, Tocqueville had, in fact, predicted just this; his forecast was that "in the democratic ages which are opening upon us . . . centralization will be the natural government." In the twentieth century, we find a corollary in "Bryce's Law"—the contention that "federalism is simply a transitory step on the way to governmental unity" (McWhinney, 1965, p. 105). The argument, in essence, was that a public sector with a heavy reliance on decentralized fiscal choice does not constitute an equilibrium; it will move over time in the direction of growing centralization.

But such pronouncements were premature. The trend in the second half of the century has been, if anything, in the other direction: the state and local sector now exhibits a larger fiscal share than it did in 1952. Similar tendencies reveal themselves in most other industrialized countries. A better description seems to be one of a shifting balance, with the vertical structure of the public sector responding over time to the differing sorts of demands made upon it.

There are some striking differences in patterns of vertical fiscal structure across countries. The most dramatic and pervasive is the marked divergence in the degree of decentralization between the economically advanced and the developing countries. In one recent study of fiscal centralization involving samples of countries at different stages of economic development (Oates, 1985), the mean central-government share of public expenditure was 89 percent for the sample of developing countries and 65 percent for the sample of industrialized nations. A dominant feature of the public sector of most developing countries is a relatively small role for local government, with heavy reliance on the central government both for the collection and disbursement of public revenues. Substantial fiscal decentralization seems to go along with more advanced economic status.

Among the industrialized countries, fiscal federalism has exhibited some intriguing forms of innovation over the course of the twentieth century. In several countries, the evolution of the public sector has been in the direction of a more complex and highly specialized set of fiscal units. In the United States, for instance, there has been a striking rise in the number of "special districts." These are single-function entities (primarily at the local-government level) that now provide a diverse set of services including highways, hospitals, libraries, sewers, housing, fire protection, and others.

New *levels* of government have emerged to address the growing demands on the public sector. Metropolitan government has come into being in the United Kingdom, Canada, the United States, and other countries in an effort to coordinate fiscal decision making between central cities and their associated suburban communities. The formation of new levels of government is not limited to lower tiers. In Europe, a new top layer of government is developing in the European Community. It is by no means clear what the ultimate scope of European "central government" will be, but it is certainly striking to watch its evolution alongside the continuing movements for "devolution" of the public sector in many member countries.

The growing complexity of the vertical structure of the public sector seems to render inaccurate and surely incomplete any contentions concerning general trends toward greater centralization or decentralization of government. The evolution of fiscal federalism seems rather to be in the direction of developing a more specialized set of fiscal institutions, to which fiscal responsibilities and instruments are assigned in ways that make the public sector more responsive to the variety of demands placed upon it.

Although economic analysis has much to contribute to our understanding of intergovernmental fiscal relations, I want to emphasize, in conclusion, a perhaps rather obvious point: the "solutions" to federal fiscal problems must depend in important ways on the historical and constitutional character of individual countries. As Richard Bird (1986) has stressed, this national "character" has profound implications for the range of feasible and effective federal policy. It is possible, for example, for a unitary country like Great Britain to redraw local boundaries and redefine local tax instruments on a nationwide basis; in countries with federal constitutions, such redesign of fiscal jurisdictions and institutions is outside the realm of the possible. "Federal finance," as Bird points out, is a quite different matter from multilevel finance in unitary countries.

At the same time, this is surely not to say that all is a matter of individualized politics and that "anything goes." Sound and careful analyses of intergovernmental fiscal structures reveal, all too often, instances where existing institutions and policies simply are not achieving their professed allocative and distributive objectives. Economic analysis, both theoretical and empirical, can make a fundamental contribution to the design of more effective systems of intergovernmental finance—systems in which fiscal functions are located appropriately within the vertical structure of the public sector and in which existing policy instruments are matched effectively with these functions.

Helen F. Ladd

Wallace Oates's choice of topics in his chapter is selective and, not surprisingly, reflects his own interests and contributions. Similarly, my comments are selective and reflect my interests and policy orientation. My remarks focus on two topics: intergovernmental grants and the tax assignment issue.

INTERGOVERNMENTAL GRANTS

Oates alludes to the debate over general revenue sharing, and appropriately so because of Joe Pechman's role with Walter Heller in initiating and developing the revenue sharing proposal. Oates focuses on the theoretical puzzle of the flypaper effect—that is, the empirical observation that money sticks where it hits. But I would like to raise some other issues.

Pechman and Musgrave did not see eye to eye on the merits of general revenue sharing. In a 1970 conference on state and local public finance sponsored by the Federal Reserve Bank, Pechman (1970) supported not only the idea in general but also the administration's new proposal to distribute funds to states on a per capita basis modified by tax effort. Although his own earlier proposal included no pass-through to local governments, by 1970 Pechman had apparently realized the importance of assisting local as well as state governments and had generally come to support the administration's proposal to include a mandatory pass-through. In contrast, Musgrave's paper at that same conference (Musgrave and Polinsky, 1970) was highly skeptical of the revenue-sharing concept. Musgrave believed that revenue sharing was a luxury that was not well designed to meet the two main fiscal problems of state and local governments: first, low capacity relative to need in the low-income states, and, second, large intrastate disparities associated with urban problems and the concentration of poverty. Based on their empirical analysis, Musgrave and Polinsky suggested it might be preferable for the federal government to take over responsibility for welfare than to introduce revenue sharing.

This disagreement between Pechman and Musgrave on the merits of general revenue sharing raises two important policy-relevant issues. The first is whether it makes sense for the federal government to provide aid directly to local governments. The second is, assuming one wants to use aid programs to offset disparities among jurisdictions, how one should measure a jurisdiction's revenue-raising capacity relative to its expenditure needs.

Direct federal aid to cities. Should the federal government bypass the states and provide aid directly to cities? The important conceptual point here is that in the United States, we have three levels of government, not the two that are the basis for much of the conceptual modeling. Thus, we need to think hard about the principles that might guide policy in this regard.

In the 1960s and 1970s, direct federal aid to cities grew tremendously. This growth reflected three different policy strands. First was the desire to empower disadvantaged and minority households in urban areas by providing a host of new federal aid programs in the areas of manpower training, elementary and secondary education, and community development. Second, was the no-strings-attached approach to aid embodied in the general revenue-sharing program. The third policy strand, which emerged during the 1974–1975 recession and which was embodied in a variety of countercyclical aid programs in the mid-1970s, was the belief that intergovernmental grants could be used to help stabilize the national economy and to offset the recession-related fiscal pressures on state and local governments. Starting in 1978 and accelerating during the Reagan years, however, direct federal aid to local governments was cut back dramatically, culminating in the elimination of general revenue sharing in 1986.

In light of the pressing problems in U.S. cities, such as crime, violence, homelessness, AIDS, and drugs, many of which have a fiscal dimension, I believe it is time for public finance economists to reconsider the appropriate fiscal relationship between the federal and local governments. John Yinger and I tried to do that in our recent book, *America's Ailing Cities* (1989), but more work is clearly needed. This research needs to address at least four issues. The first is the basic conceptual rationale for using intergovernmental aid to offset disparities across jurisdictions. Second is an analysis of the relative strengths of the federal government versus the state governments in dealing with the fiscal problems of local governments, an analysis that needs to incorporate significant institutional detail. Third is the need for a better empirical understanding of the interactions between levels of governments—as, for example, the extent to which the state governments offset direct federal aid to cities by cutting back their own aid. And fourth, assuming policymakers choose to offset fiscal disparities, is the question of how to measure those disparities.

Measuring revenue-raising capacity and expenditure need. A major element of Musgrave's 1970 critique of the general revenue-sharing proposal was that it did not target assistance to states or cities with the greatest need relative to their revenue-raising capacity, a fact that he and Polinsky documented with a crude but useful empirical analysis. I certainly do not wish to defend the now-defunct federal general revenue-sharing program. But Musgrave and Polinsky's key point is worth emphasizing: formulas for distributing equalizing aid to state or local governments ought to incorporate variations in expenditure need as well as variations in revenue-raising capacity. Moreover, the observation that disparities are currently much greater across jurisdictions within states than they are across states provides support for state-specific revenue-sharing programs.

With respect to revenue-raising capacity, the standard measures are either the representative tax system developed by the Advisory Commission on Inter-governmental Relations (ACIR) or personal income augmented by tax exporting. The latter measure is conceptually more appealing than the former because of its consistency with consumer theory, but suffers from being difficult to implement.

With respect to the measurement of expenditure need, the challenge is to develop a measure that reflects only cost factors that are outside the control of local officials. In his 1970 paper, Musgrave emphasized the importance of not using actual expenditures as a measure of need and developed a rough measure for each state using work-load figures on the number of poor people and number of students. Twenty years later, the ACIR is finally following his lead and is developing a representative expenditure system for states to complement its representative tax system.

But variation in work loads is not the only determinant of variation in expenditure need. In an influential 1969 paper, Bradford, Malt, and Oates provided a useful conceptual analysis that distinguished between the direct or intermediate outputs of the public sector and the final outputs that are valued by consumers, emphasizing that the costs of the latter depend on the harshness of the environment for providing public services. This insight is now serving as the basis for more sophisticated regression-based approaches to measuring expenditure need that isolate the effects of environmental cost factors on public service costs and hence on expenditure need (see, for example, Bradbury et al., 1984; and Ladd and Yinger, 1989).

State government behavior. A final point about intergovernmental grants relates to my first point about the United States having a three-tiered governmental system. Now that state governments are being asked to play an increasingly important fiscal role, more research on state fiscal behavior would be fruitful. As elaborated by Oates, the theory of local government behavior is quite well developed. In contrast, we have few models of state government behavior. Compared to local governments, state governments are less subject to the discipline of the Tiebout model and tend to be more heterogeneous. Consequently, simple median-voter models are often not appropriate, and more complex political economy models are needed. Craig and Inman (1982, 1986) have done some interesting empirical modeling of education and welfare spending, with state governments fully embedded in a three-tiered governmental system; but more research is needed.

THE TAX ASSIGNMENT PROBLEM

Oates focuses primarily on the normative issue of tax assignment, drawing heavily on the insights of Musgrave. Two recent or upcoming events have renewed interest in both the normative and positive aspects of this issue.

European economic integration. The first is European economic integration, which significantly reduces barriers to mobility across countries within the European community. After integration, each country must worry about the impact of the tax not only on the amount of economic activity but, as is true for U.S. states, also on its location.

As Roger Gordon has shown, a number of challenges arise for the design of European tax institutions. One challenge reflects the absence of a national government in the European Economic Community. The U.S. literature on federalism indicates that redistributive tax or spending programs should be assigned, if possible, to the federal government and that lower levels of government should rely on benefit taxes or taxes on relatively immobile factors. Without a national government in Europe, the best that can be achieved with respect to redistribution on the tax side is the harmonization of taxes across countries. But tax harmonization leaves open the possibility for countries to compete on the benefit side—for example, in terms of the quality of medical care. With respect to the desired benefit taxation for local public goods and services, the value-added tax may represent the best compromise on the grounds that consumption of privately provided goods is closely related to consumption of public goods. For this purpose, tax rates should not be harmonized; instead they should be allowed to vary across countries, in line with preferred levels of services.

My point here is simply that European economic integration represents a new and important motivation for research on fiscal federalism. Our understanding of the U.S. intergovernmental system should provide a rich set of lessons for fiscal federalism in Europe (see, for example, Inman and Rubinfeld, 1991).

The Tax Reform Act of 1986. The federal Tax Reform Act (TRA) of 1986 focused attention on the intergovernmental dimension of tax policy in the United States. In particular, the federal tax proposals inspired a tremendous amount of work on the effects of federal tax deductibility of state and local taxes and spending. A detailed microeconomic study by Gramlich (1985), plus studies based on aggregate data by others, examined the probable impacts on spending of removing deductibility and produced estimates ranging from 1–2 percent to 20 percent or more. The clearest prediction with respect to the final bill, which eliminated deductibility for sales taxes but maintained it for state and local income and property taxes, was that states would shift away from sales taxes in favor of deductible taxes. But this result has not materialized (see Courant and Gramlich, 1990), since states apparently have increased their reliance on sales taxes. This new puzzle has inspired research to find an explanation. Inman (1989, initially in a somewhat different context) focused on the role of distributive politics, and Metcalf (1993) has looked at differential tax exporting. As noted by Courant and Gramlich (1989), the important point for researchers is that the economist's emphasis on price effects seems to be misplaced. More sophisticated political economy models of the state tax decision are needed.

In addition, the Tax Reform Act of 1986 (TRA86) provides opportunities for gaining new insights into old issues such as tax competition and the flypaper effect. For example, the changes associated with TRA86 provide a natural experiment for examining the extent to which states look to neighboring states when setting their income tax rates (the issue of tax competition) and for determining how states responded to the ''windfall'' revenue gains from base broadening at the federal level—the issue of the flypaper effect (see Case, 1993; Quigley and Smolensky, 1993; and Ladd, 1993).

Location distortions of local taxes. Finally, with respect to the tax assignment issue, I would like to quibble with Oates's assertion that little empirical work has been done to measure the behavioral distortions associated with state and local taxes. His statement ignores the large empirical literature on the location decision of firms. Though much of this literature appears to support his suggestion that the distortions may be small, several of the more recent and careful studies are increasingly finding that taxes do matter (see, for example, Helms 1985; Newman and Sullivan, 1988; and Bartik, 1991).

COMMENTS ON CHAPTER 5 BY ————————————————————
Peter Mieszkowski

In his chapter, Wallace Oates presents theoretical discussion, reports on empirical results, and identifies a number of unresolved issues. Since we disagree on very few points, I shall supplement his observations, aiming to fill in some gaps in presentation and to develop linkages among different policy issues and theoretical constructs.

Normative discussions of federal grants have justified open-ended matching grants in terms of spill-ins and spill-outs of public expenditures benefits between communities. Matching grants perform a coordinating function between governments and induce local fiscs to increase their expenditures on education and income redistribution.

Unconditional grants features are sometimes designed to redistribute income from richer areas to poor communities. It is interesting that Oates emphasizes George Break's rationale for unconditional grants—the distortionary effects of fiscal competition between local governments—and virtually ignores the contributions of James Buchanan (1950, 1952), who was the first to develop the "efficiency basis" of federal grants.

Buchanan, writing at a time when the southern states were relatively poor and unindustrialized, emphasized the migration effects induced by economies of scale, including urban agglomerations and varying resource endowments between regions. The essence of Buchanan's argument was that economies of scale in consumption resulting from the concentration of population in high-income industrial regions lead to lower per capita taxes for the finance of nonrival public goods. Also, the taxation of land rents and capital in northern cities provided a distorting fiscal advantage to large, rich regions. Equally productive, or equally situated, individuals in North Carolina and New York would have unequal real incomes, since the New York resident would reap a large fiscal consumer surplus and New York, the rich region, would be overpopulated relative to an optimal distribution of the nation's population. Buchanan advocated federal grants to low-income southern states and emphasized the problems the South had in attracting skilled labor and capital. In some of his work, the grants were designed to restore horizontal equity and were proposed as payments to individuals rather than to groups of individuals. The middle-class engineer residing in North Carolina would receive a federal grant to offset the fiscal disadvantages of residing in the South.

These policies designed to offset the advantages of economies of scale in consumption were controversial. One prominent critic was Richard Musgrave (1961). A concern was that grants to low-income regions would induce the outmigration of residents to growing, high-income regions in western states. Also, the emerging theory of public goods made it clear that individual welfare and fiscally induced migration depend on the marginal benefits and marginal costs of public goods rather than on total benefits and total costs. If state and local governments utilize benefit taxation, the efficiency argument for offsetting federal grants is weakened.

But the analytical literature stimulated by Buchanan's early work has confirmed that fiscal externalities will lead to the overpopulation of rich regions. This work, the regional branch of the Tiebout literature, emphasizes differences in resource endowments between regions and models how these differences and economies of scale lead to large concentrations of population. One important result, as shown by Vernon Henderson (1986), is that decentralized urban development, especially in less developed countries dominated by one or two large cities, will lead to an inefficient system of cities. Migration and investment decisions in the presence of scale economies need to be coordinated by central governments in order to promote the earlier development of secondary cities.

The Buchanan contributions on fiscal grants, with their emphasis on horizontal equity and efficiency, are the basic building blocks of recent Canadian contributions to fiscal federalism and the design of federal grants. Robin Boadway and Frank Flatters (1982), in a wide-ranging contribution, argued that provincial taxes on capital and natural-resource rents lead to horizontal inequities and inefficiency and require offsetting federal grants.

In the United States, in contrast to the situation in Canada and Australia, federal grants are not designed to be equalizing between groups of individuals residing in different regions. Equalization takes place at the level of individuals or narrowly defined groups residing in poor neighborhoods or school districts. Regional income differentials have narrowed considerably over time in the United States, and U.S. political traditions mitigate against federal grants to affect the distribution of the population between regions.

The alternative efficiency justification for unconditional grants—the distorting effects of fiscal competition—was first put forth by George Break in 1967. This point is germane to three parts of Oates's chapter, namely those concerning intergovernmental grants and revenue sharing, local finance, and regulatory federalism. If, as claimed by Bruce Hamilton and William Fischel, local property taxes are perfect benefit taxes, they cannot be the distorting taxes that might be used to explain the "flypaper effect." The models of tax competition that have been developed to support George Break's concerns over the effects of fiscal competition all assume distorting nonbenefit capital taxes to prove that local public goods will be underprovided. This is inconsistent with the Hamilton-Fischel hypothesis of binding zoning and perfect benefit taxation.

As Oates points out, Jonathan Hamilton (1986) was the first to suggest that the marginal propensity to spend on local public goods for federal grants (.45), which is higher than that for own income (.10), does not require models of strategic bureaucratic behavior or voter misperception. Hamilton argued that if local governments use distorting taxes, while from their standpoint federal unconditional grants are nondistorting, the marginal propensity to spend out of grants will be higher than out of own income.

The commonsense explanation for this result is quite straightforward. If at the margin the "cost" of an additional dollar of tax is larger than additional dollar of forgone private consumption (say, two dollars), then a dollar of nondistorting federal grants is more valuable to a community than an additional dollar of ordinary income. Since such grants can be used to decrease taxes, one dollar is in effect worth two dollars. So it appears that the difference in the marginal propensity to spend on public goods out of grants relative to the community's own income is proportional to the magnitude of the tax distortion. The empirical result—that marginal expenditure for unconditional grants is more than four times the marginal expenditure for own income—suggests that only part of the measured flypaper effect can be explained by the distorting effects of taxes, unless it can be demonstrated that the "true" marginal cost of raising local taxes is four times the nominal cost.

David Wildasin (1989) has carried out a theoretical and numerical analysis of the distorting effects of the local property tax. Interjurisdiction capital mobility leads local governments to underspend on public service, since each community overestimates the "true" social cost of public funds. The capital that migrates out of a community in response to an increase in a capital tax is not lost to society as a whole. Wildasin estimates that the social marginal cost of local spending is about 70 percent of the cost perceived by a locality, and that the marginal subsidy rate, in the absence of other federal grants, to a jurisdiction when it raises an extra dollar of own-sources revenue is 40 percent. The subsidy, which internalizes the externality resulting from the mobility of capital, depends on a community's tax rate and the average tax rate in the nation. Wildasin's results indicate that the property tax externalities are quite large and that the exclusive reliance on property tax revenue will lead to substantial amounts of underspending on local public goods. But Wildasin's results support the view that only a small portion of the flypaper effect can be explained by the distorting effects of local taxes.

The local property tax revenues have decreased over time as a proportion of total revenues of local governments in the United States, but they remain 75 percent of own-tax revenues, and the average effective tax has remained constant over the last thirty years. The continuing reliance on this tax might be taken as evidence for the Hamilton-Fischel view that contrary to the results of the models of fiscal competition, binding zoning transforms the tax on capital into a perfect benefit tax. In contrast, Henderson (1991) has argued that, in general, homeowners will not impose property taxes if nondistorting sources of revenue are available. In support of his theoretical work, he presents evidence that over-time property taxes have decreased to 40 percent of locally raised revenue while user fees and other nontax revenues have increased to 50 percent.

Luc Noiset and William Oakland (1992) have developed an original argument for the continued use of the property tax. They assume a metropolitan area where all employment in the central city labor is supplied at a predetermined level of utility and some of the labor resides in residential suburbs. The imposition of a property tax on industrial capital in the central city will be distortionary and will decrease the demand for labor and the size of the metropolitan area. A metropolitan government would not use this tax, but the imposition of a property tax by the central city enables this jurisdiction to export some of the tax burden to suburban landowners.

This work is important as an explanation for the continuing utilization of the property tax, and it emphasizes the spatial concentration of business activity within a metropolitan area. Notwithstanding the efforts of Michelle White (1975a, 1975b) and William Fischel (1975) to generalize Hamilton's results to industrial capital, the benefit view of the property tax is least persuasive for industrial and commercial capital. The requirement of perfect of binding zoning is severe, and in the spatially featureless version of the Tiebout model there are no economies of scale and no clustering of business activity. Urban economics has traditionally explained clustering in terms of transportation nodes related to intercity transportation—that is, the existences of airports, railway stations, ports, and waterways. Also, as shown by the development of clusters of office and shopping centers in the suburbs, intrametropolitan transportation also leads to spatial differentiation. The suburban clusters typically occur at the intersections of high-speed freeways.

I hope the suggestive work of Noiset and Oakland is the first step to integrating the two branches of the Tiebout literature, the regional and the metropolitan. James Buchanan and those who followed him stress economies of scale and ignore commuting within islands or metropolitan areas. On the other hand, Tiebout and Hamilton stress residential choice and intrametropolitan mobility without allowing for a satisfactory specification of income and employment generation that recognize economies of scale and spatial differentiation through transportation nodes.

PART III

TAX POLICY

CHARLES E. MCLURE, JR., AND
GEORGE R. ZODROW

6

The Study and Practice
of Income Tax Policy

Intelligent conduct of government requires an understanding of the economic relations involved; and the economist, by aiding in this understanding, may hope to contribute to a better society.

Richard A. Musgrave, *The Theory of Public Finance*

INTRODUCTION

The period since the publication of Musgrave's *Theory of Public Finance* in 1959 has been an extremely active one in both the study and the practice of tax policy. The increase in theoretical rigor and the application of powerful new methods of empirical analysis are staggering. Major theoretical advances in the economics of taxation include general equilibrium modeling, optimal taxation, growth theory, and the analysis of the effects of taxes on labor supply, savings, risk taking, and investment. In many respects, Musgrave's much-heralded treatise provided the foundation for those developments.

The development of high-speed electronic computers has made possible enormous advances in both econometrics and simulation of economic models. Econometric analysis has progressed from quite rudimentary ordinary least squares estimates of single-equation models based largely on aggregate cross-section or time-series data (often done using mechanical calculators) to extremely sophisticated estimation of simultaneous-equation models, based on thousands of observations of the behavior of individuals, households, and firms.

165

It is now possible to simulate general equilibrium interaction in models containing dozens of commodities and quite general descriptions of consumption and production relationships. The availability of large data bases and the ability to manipulate them electronically also make it possible to undertake detailed analyses of the revenue implications and distributional effects of changes in tax policy.

Important changes in the U.S. income tax occurred in 1962, 1964, 1969, 1976, 1978, 1981, and 1986, and there were many other less important tax acts. At times, public policy—or at least debate on policy—has strongly reflected the state of the art of economic analysis; at other times, it has not. To some extent, the evolution of economic analysis of tax policy has been influenced by the need for policymakers to understand the economic effects of taxes and changes in taxes—for what Musgrave calls an ''understanding of the economic relations involved.'' But often this work has been done after the fact, instead of providing inputs for the tax policy process. To some extent, economic analysis of tax policy has followed its own internal logic. This chapter examines the interplay between economic analysis of tax policy and the federal income tax policies actually enacted and implemented in the United States during the quarter-century leading up to the 1986 act, arguably the most far-reaching reform since the introduction of the income tax in 1913.

To make the chapter manageable, we shall restrict its coverage to domestic aspects of the federal income tax. Thus, it does not deal with the expenditure side of the budget or with such important tax issues as taxation of gifts and bequests, social security, the possibility of an American value-added tax, the property tax, other state and local taxes, or fiscal federalism.[1] In addition, it focuses on basic issues of domestic income taxation, and thus does not consider either international aspects of federal income tax policy or such important but less central issues as the taxation of nonprofit organizations or most issues peculiar to the taxation of particular sectors (for example, insurance, banking, and oil and gas). Moreover, the chapter concentrates primarily on microeconomic issues; it does not deal in any depth with the use of tax, budgetary, or debt management policy to achieve macroeconomic stability.[2] Finally, it is necessarily selective; it focuses primarily on major scientific advances in the theoretical and empirical economics of taxation and on some of the direct applications of those advances to the analysis of tax policy. This last restriction is a severe one. We are forced to devote relatively little attention to much of the vast literature applying economic analysis to tax policy problems, including the multivolume series *Studies of Government Finance* produced under the direction of Joe

Pechman during his tenure as director of the Economic Studies Program at the Brookings Institution. In addition, we say relatively little about the policy work done by tax lawyers, much of which has been extremely influential.

Part I describes the conventional wisdom on tax policy circa 1960, just after publication of Musgrave's *Theory of Public Finance*. Given the continuing significance of this body of thought, this "snapshot" is important to set the stage for what follows. Part II briefly describes the most important developments in academic thinking relevant to the income tax policy of the past twenty-five years. Part III outlines the evolution of income tax policy during the same period. Part IV offers some speculations as to why advances in economic analysis appear in some respects to have influenced policy and in other respects not.[3]

I. ACADEMIC THOUGHT IN 1960

In 1960 much of what was known about the economics of taxation was contained in a single volume, Musgrave's *Theory of Public Finance* (1959a). In addition, a three-volume, 2,382-page *Tax Revision Compendium,* containing 182 papers and giving the views of the leading experts on tax policy, had just been published by the House Ways and Means Committee (1959). In 1961 the Joint Economic Committee brought much of this together in *The Federal Revenue System: Facts and Problems, 1961.* Together these provide a convenient survey of the economics of taxation and the conventional wisdom on appropriate income tax policy at the beginning of the 1960s.[4] In what follows we attempt to give some flavor of the extent and nature of the professional consensus on several key issues of theory and policy that prevailed in 1960. Not surprisingly, the views of "liberal" and "conservative" experts differed on many issues. The consensus view tended to be that of the more numerous liberals. Pechman's *Federal Tax Policy* (1966) distilled much of that liberal consensus.

A. Some Basic Principles

A few basic principles guided much of academic thinking on tax policy in 1960.[5] First, taxation should be economically neutral. This maxim was almost universally interpreted to imply that all goods and services should be taxed at uniform rates. Although the theory of the second best had been around for a few years,[6] and the arguments for differential taxation of whatever is inelastic in supply or demand (to minimize the excess burden of taxation) and for taxing complements to leisure (as a surrogate for taxing leisure itself) were well known,[7] this body of thought did not seem to have much practical significance.

Few researchers were careful in distinguishing between economic distortions, which involve only substitution effects, and incentive effects, which involve both income and substitution effects.[8] Concentration on uncompensated elasticities (for example, of labor supply) may have reflected the residual influence of wartime thinking, when incentives seemed to be of primary importance, as well as a failure to realize fully the welfare implications of distortions.

Second, taxation should also be fair or equitable. Equity was defined in two dimensions, the horizontal and the vertical. Horizontal equity was seen to be a matter of equal treatment of those in similar circumstances, as measured, for example, by income, after taking account of marital status, family size, unusually high medical expenses, and so on. Vertical equity involved the variation in the tax treatment of those in dissimilar circumstances. The idea that tax burdens should be related to some notion of ability to pay generally provided the basis for arguments for progressive taxation to achieve vertical equity, although there were few concrete indications of how progressive the tax system should be. Liberals tended to favor much more progressive taxation than did conservatives, perhaps because they placed greater emphasis on equity than on efficiency.

Finally, taxes should be simple. They should not be overly demanding of resources for compliance and administration. Most tax specialists had little to say about how to achieve this objective.

B. The Tax Base

In 1960 there was almost no disagreement with the tenet that income, rather than consumption, should be the basis for direct taxation;[9] in a chapter on consumption-based taxation, Due (1959, p. 273) referred to "the general acceptance of income as the most suitable measure of economic well-being." This preference seems to have had a largely philosophical basis.[10] Some were dubious about the equity of omitting savings from the tax base.[11] Despite the recent appearance of Kaldor's *An Expenditure Tax* (1955), some seemed implicitly to equate consumption taxation with indirect taxation and therefore with regressive taxation. In addition, it was generally thought that the direct expenditure tax was not administratively feasible.[12] Although it was recognized that the income tax distorted the saving-consumption choice, while a proportional consumption tax did not, this aspect of neutrality was not given high priority.

C. Haig-Simons Income

Once income was chosen as the basis for taxation, it was necessary to have a workable definition of income for tax purposes. Academic opinion was strongly in favor of starting from the Haig-Simons "accretion" definition of income (consumption plus the change in net wealth), but it was not unanimous. Dan Throop Smith, a professor at the Harvard Business School who was deputy secretary of the Treasury under Eisenhower, wrote (1959, p. 1234), "The concept used here clearly rejects the idea that increases in one's wealth, plus consumption . . . , is a reasonable measure of income." Of course, it might be necessary to make compromises with administrative realities, especially by basing taxation on realization rather than on accretion.[13] Yet there were many instances in which the conventional wisdom, at least as reflected in policy positions, was at odds with a reasonable interpretation of Haig-Simons, and other instances in which we now know that not enough attention was paid to problem areas. As we review these issues, it is interesting to note that Musgrave often had a greater appreciation of their complexity than many of his colleagues.

1. INTEGRATION OF THE INCOME TAXES

Opinion was divided on whether to integrate the individual and corporate income taxes. Most tax economists probably favored integration, but others believed that integration was undesirable, unnecessary, or infeasible. Richard Goode (1946; 1951, pp. 214–217), for example, believed strongly that integration was not required or appropriate, in part because corporations are separate entities and should be taxed as such and in part because it was not feasible to raise all federal revenue from the individual income tax. Some observers thought that integration would not be needed if the corporate tax were shifted to consumers or workers.[14] Smith (1961, p. 199) believed that even if the corporate income tax were not shifted, it was needed to assure current taxation of retained corporate earnings. Complete integration, via the partnership approach, was considered to be too complicated to be administratively feasible.

2. CAPITAL GAINS

Much attention was focused on the taxation of capital gains.[15] Though some (for example, Smith, 1959) questioned whether such gains constituted income and should be taxed at all, the predominant view was that realized capital gains should be taxed like other income.[16] Harold Groves (1959, p. 1195) wrote, "the rate discrimination between capital gains and other income . . . has been condemned by most critics who have had a high regard for fairness and neutrality in the tax system." One of the most widely held views among academic economists was the desirability of taxing gains on assets transferred at death via "constructive realization."[17] Conservative economists generally disagreed with these views, supporting preferential treatment of long-term gains, citing, *inter alia,* the problem of bunching of gains, the taxation of fictitious gains in inflationary times, and the need for incentives for saving and investment. Some supported the view that capital gains were not really income.

3. INFLATION ADJUSTMENT IN MEASURING INCOME

Some find it entirely inappropriate to use the Haig-Simons definition of income to determine the tax base if it is calculated without adjustments for inflation. Yet Henry Simons, in his *Federal Tax Reform,* written in 1943 in the context of World War II and published in 1950, wrote derisively about the possibility of inflation adjustment in the measurement of income: "Does anyone really propose that we correct all tax bases for price-level changes?" (p. 136). A few economists, notably George Terborgh (1959), proposed inflation adjustment for depreciation allowances, but the proposal fell on deaf ears, in part because the United States was putting the inflation of the Second World War and the Korean War behind it and moving into a brief period of relative price stability. Moreover, Musgrave (1959a, p. 169) correctly noted "that all assets and liabilities should be adjusted for changes in price levels and that accretion should be measured in real terms. Yet it is hardly possible in practice to carry out all these adjustments . . . Equity may be impaired rather than improved by piecemeal adjustments to allow for price-level changes in selected parts of the system."

4. TAXATION AND INVESTMENT

In contrast to current debates, those of 1960 placed little emphasis on the effects of taxation on saving; virtually all the attention was devoted to taxation and investment.[18] This may reflect the influence of Keynesian thought, in which the lack of investment, and not the lack of saving, was the bogey to be slain.

The debate on the incentive effects of taxes on investment generally distinguished two issues, the tax treatment of depreciable assets and the tax treatment of losses. Domar and Musgrave (1944) demonstrated that an income tax might actually increase investment in risky assets, provided taxation was proportionate and loss offset was complete. This supplied important theoretical underpinnings for carryforward (and carryback) of losses. Whereas complete offset for capital losses would be appropriate in a system based on accrual taxation, it would be inappropriate under a system based on realization, given the taxpayer's discretion in realizing losses but not gains.

In another important paper, E. Cary Brown (1948) showed that a system with expensing or immediate write-off of investment and complete loss offset would eliminate the tax burden on equity-financed investment and thus be neutral. A natural, if incorrect, extrapolation of that result was that acceleration of depreciation allowances would move the system toward neutrality. This view—and the possibility of using tax policy to encourage investment—confronted the conventional wisdom with a dilemma that continues to puzzle policymakers, for it seems to be fundamentally inconsistent with a comprehensive income tax based on the Haig-Simons definition of income. Brown's paper may have been important in providing the policy rationale for the 1954 introduction of accelerated depreciation; this policy also reflected widespread dissatisfaction with the existing provisions for deducting depreciation.[19] By 1962 the need for investment incentives had many advocates among supporters of comprehensive income taxation.

5. TIMING ISSUES

In order to implement the Haig-Simons definition of income, it is necessary to know when changes in net worth occur—in practical terms, when income should be "recognized" for tax purposes and when deductions should be allowed for the costs of earning income. Failure to handle timing issues satisfactorily can create inequities and distortions. Early discussions of timing issues (for example, those on accounting provisions in the *Tax Revision Compendium* and in Hellmuth, 1959) typically focused on differences between commercial or financial accounting and accounting for tax purposes. There was relatively little explicit consideration of how to resolve timing issues in a way that would give the most accurate measure of income, as defined by the Haig-Simons concept. Thus, the inherent complexity of a conceptually satisfactory resolution of timing issues seems not to have been recognized.

6. GLOBAL VERSUS SCHEDULAR TAXATION

The conventional wisdom of 1960 was clearly in favor of a global definition of income, rather than the application of different schedules of rates ("schedular taxation") to particular types of income. This can be seen most dramatically in the widespread condemnation of both the exclusion of income from state and local securities and the preferential treatment of long-term capital gains. Closely related were proposals to close other loopholes, such as those for fringe benefits.

In retrospect, it is clear that implementation of the Haig-Simons definition was seen too much as a simple choice between taxing and not taxing well-specified amounts of income (for example, income from municipal bonds).[20] Too little attention was devoted to the inherent difficulties of implementing the definition (because of timing, inflation adjustment, and other problems) or to their implications. In particular, the possibility that saving and investment incentives might give rise to "tax shelters" (the use of artificial tax losses to offset otherwise taxable income) is notably absent from the discussion. The *Tax Revision Compendium* devotes only two-and-a-half pages to the taxation of partners and partnerships, the usual vehicle for tax shelters. Willis (1959, p. 1707) writes, "Subchapter K of the Internal Revenue Code deals quite comprehensively with the income taxation of partners and partnerships."

7. PERSONAL DEDUCTIONS

Much of the 1960s discussion of income tax policy was concerned with the propriety of various personal deductions, especially those for state and local taxes, home mortgage interest, charitable contributions, and medical expenses. Most academic opinion probably favored ending the deduction for state and local taxes that are not costs of earning income; some favored retaining the deduction for state and local income taxes or replacing deductions with tax credits.[21] In the case of interest deductions on home mortgages, it was recognized that there was no totally satisfactory solution, short of taxing the imputed income from owner-occupied housing.[22] On balance, academic opinion probably favored ending this deduction.

8. INCOME AVERAGING

It has long been recognized that application of progressive rates to fluctuating incomes can produce inequities and that some form of income averaging is desirable, though complicated. Indeed, Vickrey (1939, 1947) proposed a scheme for lifetime averaging, and the *Tax Revision Compendium* contained no fewer than eight papers on fluctuating income and the need for income averaging. The possibility of "bunching" of gains was offered as one justification for the preferential treatment of long-term capital gains.

D. The Tax-Paying Unit

In 1960 the married couple was generally accepted to be the proper tax-paying unit. This was true for two quite different reasons. First, divorce was less common than it is today, and a smaller fraction of wives worked. Under such conditions one might find little fault with Due's statement (1959, p. 155) that "the most logical unit for the application of an income tax is obviously the income-earning and income-spending unit, which in modern society is typically the family." Second, it had been only a dozen years since Congress had given residents of all states the privilege of income splitting, previously enjoyed only by couples in community property states. The resulting discrimination against single taxpayers had begun to gain the attention of the tax policy community,[23] but little thought was given to the disincentive effects of subjecting the earnings of the second worker in a household to a marginal tax rate based on the earnings of the primary worker.[24]

E. Tax Rates

Views toward progressivity in the rate structure were based largely on considerations of income redistribution.[25] Despite what Blum and Kalven (1953) had called the "uneasy case for progressive taxation," most tax economists probably favored substantial progressivity, and, reflecting World War II pressures, the top marginal rate under the federal individual income tax was a staggering 91 percent in 1960. Little concern was expressed about disincentive effects. One observer (Lampman, 1959, p. 2245) remarked: "While there is diversity, the weight of scholarly opinion has shifted somewhat toward the idea that some of the consequences of reducing inequality are more favorable or less unfavorable than they once were generally held to be . . . The propositions that moves toward economic equalization will diminish cultural achievements and slow economic growth have been severely shaken."

The conclusion that labor supply was not particularly sensitive to changes in taxation was based primarily on studies of labor supply which suggested that a wage increase caused a positive substitution effect on labor supply that roughly offset a negative income effect. This evidence was supported by survey results (Break, 1957, 1959; Holland, 1969) suggesting that the labor supply of high-income individuals was not particularly responsive to changes in income taxation. As suggested above, the distortionary effects of income taxation were masked by concentration on the uncompensated elasticity of labor supply.

Of course, there were many who disagreed with Lampman's sanguine assessment. Smith (1961, p. 35) referred to "virtually confiscatory individual tax rates" and asserted that "there has been growing recognition of the perverse effects of very high tax rates, even by those who earlier had supported them as a matter of social policy."

F. Summary

It seems reasonable to say that in 1960 the majority of tax economists active in public policy debates would have accepted the following principles of income tax policy, and the implied changes to the U.S. income tax at that time:

1. Equity demands that the primary sources of taxation should be direct and personal.
2. Income should be the basis of direct taxation.
3. Uniform taxation of a broad base is desirable for both horizontal equity and neutrality reasons.
4. Taxable income should follow the Haig-Simons definition as closely as administratively feasible.
5. Global taxation is appropriate, whereas schedular taxation is not.
6. The family should be the tax-paying unit.
7. Capital gains should be taxed as ordinary income.
8. Investment incentives could be useful under certain circumstances.
9. Inflation adjustment in the measurement of income is not needed.
10. Highly progressive tax rates are appropriate for income distribution reasons.

There was no agreement on the need to integrate the corporate and individual income taxes.

In retrospect, it seems that too little attention was paid to the distortions and disincentives caused by taxation, especially the disincentives caused by high marginal rates. In addition, the apparent belief that global taxation based on the Haig-Simons definition of income could actually be implemented seems somewhat naive, given then-extant and essentially inevitable gaps in the tax base (for example, taxation of capital gains at realization) and what we now know about the difficulty of dealing satisfactorily with income measurement issues, including timing and the potential need for inflation adjustment, and the problems (such as tax shelters) that arise from neglecting them. The neglect of timing issues, the need for inflation adjustment, and tax shelters can easily be explained by the low rates of inflation and low interest rates that had prevailed since the Second World War[26] and the relative novelty of large legislated deviations of taxable income from economic income.

II. THE DEVELOPMENT OF ACADEMIC THINKING, 1960–1985

In this part, we provide a broad but necessarily selective overview of the evolution of recent theoretical and empirical advances in the economics of taxation, focusing on those developments that appear to be the most relevant to the formulation of tax policy. Whenever possible, we cite survey articles that provide a much more comprehensive discussion of the issues being discussed.

Our brief survey is organized by topic. It begins with a variety of positive results on the effects of taxation on economic behavior, and then turns to some normative results from the optimal taxation literature as well as from the ongoing debate regarding the relative merits of direct taxation based on consumption rather than income. We conclude by reviewing the literature on tax expenditures and tax shelters, topics on which the primary contributions have been made by tax lawyers interested in public policy, especially those working in the Office of Tax Policy of the U.S. Treasury Department or on the staffs of the three tax-writing committees of Congress (the Senate Finance Committee, the House Ways and Means Committee, and the Joint Committee on Taxation). In each case, we cover primarily contributions made prior to the passage of the Tax Reform Act of 1986; in a few instances we include references to publications that provide useful commentary on the literature of this period, even if it was published slightly later. This review sets the stage for our discussion in Part IV of the extent to which academic developments have played a significant role in influencing the course of tax policy, especially in the formulation of the 1986 act, an extremely wide-ranging piece of tax reform legislation.

A. Taxation and Labor Supply

Prior to the early 1980s, the conventional wisdom among public finance economists was that labor supply—especially that of prime-age males—was not particularly sensitive to changes in taxation, since changes in net wages appeared to result in roughly offsetting income and substitution effects on labor supply.[27] This conclusion was seriously questioned by Hausman (1981b), who noted that results regarding the relative insensitivity of labor supply to changes in wages do not necessarily imply that a progressive tax system (with increasing marginal tax rates) has similar results. Hausman constructed a model that captured explicitly the convexity of the individual budget constraint under a progressive tax system, and obtained empirical results that were strikingly at odds with the existing literature.[28] In particular, his estimates suggested that the tax system in the United States in 1975 reduced the labor supply of prime age males by 8.2 percent, and that the total excess burden of taxes on labor supply was 28.7 percent of tax revenues.[29]

These rather dramatic results, especially when combined with other studies suggesting that taxes had significant excess burdens,[30] played an important role in academic and policy discussions of the desirability of lower marginal tax rates. However, as will be discussed in Part IV, two recent studies—published several years after passage of the Tax Reform Act of 1986—have raised serious questions regarding Hausman's methodology and results.

B. Taxation and Saving

1. ASSET ACCUMULATION

The effect of taxation on saving—even if the latter term is defined narrowly to include only saving in the form of the accumulation of physical assets—is certainly one of the more contentious issues in public finance.[31] As in the case of labor supply, the effect of a tax increase is theoretically ambiguous in even the simplest model (a two-period life-cycle model with earnings only in the first period and no bequests), because a negative substitution effect on saving is offset by a positive income effect. Early empirical results suggested that saving is largely invariant to changes in net returns.[32]

More recent research calls this result into question. In particular, Summers (1981a) argues that the standard two-period analysis with earnings only in the first period is misleading because it ignores a "human wealth" effect—the increase in the present value of future earnings resulting from the reduction in the discount rate attributable to an increase in the tax rate on capital income.[33] In simulations of a model with individuals having a fifty-year time horizon, Summers argues that including this human wealth effect (in addition to the standard income and substitution effects caused by a change in the rate of return to saving) implies a very large aggregate uncompensated interest elasticity of saving, typically in the range from 1 to 3. Evans (1983) and Starrett (1982) argue that these rather large uncompensated saving elasticities are reduced significantly when alternate parameters and functional forms are used in simulations similar to those performed by Summers. Nevertheless, the magnitude of the aggregate saving response that occurs in the Summers analysis has profound tax policy implications and has provoked a great deal of interest among both academics and policy makers.[34]

Empirical attempts to measure the effects on saving of changes in the rate of return have been plagued by measurement issues, especially of the rate of return variable; results have been quite mixed. Early studies, such as Wright (1969), suggested small and negative effects. In a very influential paper, Boskin (1978a) argued that these studies did not properly account for taxes and inflationary expectations in measuring the real after-tax rate of return. His results suggest a positive aggregate uncompensated saving elasticity in the neighborhood of 0.4. Moreover, Summers (1981a) argued that if Boskin's results are modified to include a rough estimate of the human wealth effect, the aggregate uncompensated saving elasticity increases to around 2, in line with Summers' simulation results noted above. In marked contrast, Howrey and Hymans (1978, 1980) questioned Boskin's data and methods, and the empirical evidence presented by Blinder and Deaton (1985) suggests that interest rates have an insignificant effect on consumption and thus on saving.[35]

2. HUMAN CAPITAL ACCUMULATION
Another dimension of the saving decision that attracted increased interest during this period was the human capital accumulation decision. In particular, Driffill and Rosen (1983) construct a multiperiod life-cycle model in which both labor-leisure and human-physical capital decisions are endogenous. They show that taxes can have important effects on human capital accumulation decisions; indeed, they estimate that tax distortions of human capital decisions account for 60 to 65 percent of the total welfare cost under an income tax.

C. Taxation and Investment

Academic research in determining the effects of taxation on investment has proceeded on a number of fronts. The following discussion focuses on taxation and risk taking, marginal effective tax rate analysis, the idea that the corporate tax is primarily a tax on economic rents and on entrepreneurship, the "new view" of the effects of dividend taxation, and empirical efforts at measuring the effects of taxation on investment.

1. TAXATION AND RISK TAKING
The seminal contribution regarding the effects of taxation on the allocation of an investment portfolio among risky and relatively safe assets is Domar and

Musgrave (1944).[36] They argue that proportional taxation with full loss offset is likely to encourage risk taking, because the government shares proportionately in the gains and losses to risky investment, thus leaving the ''price'' of risk unchanged but lowering the amount of risk borne by the investor for any given portfolio.

Similar results are obtained in an expected utility framework by Tobin (1958), Mossin (1968), and Stiglitz (1969b). Taxation unambiguously increases the share of the portfolio allocated to the risky asset if the rate structure is proportional, if the tax system provides for full loss offset, and if the safe asset bears a certain return of zero. Unfortunately, the effect of taxation on risk taking becomes theoretically ambiguous once any of these critical assumptions is relaxed. For example, if the return to the safe asset and the wealth elasticity of risk taking are positive, taxation may reduce risk taking. Indeed, the effect of taxation is ambiguous even in the absence of loss offsets, since the taxation of only positive returns to investment creates offsetting income and substitution effects on the demand for the risky asset.

Empirical evidence on the effects of taxation on risk taking is fairly sparse. The most commonly cited article is by Feldstein (1976c), who examines a 1962 data base and argues that tax effects are an important determinant of portfolio composition in the United States. In particular, relatively risky common stocks are held predominantly by high-income individuals who face high marginal tax rates but benefit the most from preferential capital gains tax rates. Empirical investigation of the effects of taxation on risk taking is complicated, however, by difficulties in modeling the effects of all the relevant details of the tax system. For example, an accurate modeling of the level of taxation of returns to investment in risky assets in the United States should account for (1) the progressivity of the income tax structure, (2) the absence of inflation adjustment of capital income, (3) limitations on deductions of capital losses against ordinary income, (4) the taxation of capital gains upon realization rather than accrual, (5) the exemption of capital gains transferred at death (and preferential capital gains tax rates prior to 1986), (6) the effects of all other tax preferences for saving and investment, and (7) the gains from being able to structure investment transactions so as to reduce tax liability (Stiglitz 1983).

2. MARGINAL EFFECTIVE TAX RATE ANALYSIS
To measure the net effect of all of the complex provisions of the tax code that affect investment decisions, several investigators, including especially King and Fullerton (1984), building on the cost-of-capital formulations of Jorgenson

(1963) and Hall and Jorgenson (1967), have constructed a framework for measuring the "marginal effective tax rate" (METR) implied by a tax structure.[37] The METR is generally defined as the percentage reduction in the gross return to an investment induced by taxation, taking into account all depreciation deductions, investment tax credits, interest deductions, special income exemptions, and so forth allowed under the tax code over the life of the investment. The METR approach has been quite useful to policy analysts, since it provides a straightforward measure of how the tax system affects a variety of critical investment decisions. These include the extent to which the tax system distorts decisions regarding different types of investments (and thus investment in different business sectors), different methods of finance, and different organizational forms. METR analysis also illustrates how the burden of taxation varies with inflation. Such analyses have, in particular, been relevant to the extent that policymakers have recently become more concerned about eliminating tax preferences (or "investment incentives") for various industries and types of investment in order to "level the playing field," so that investment resources are allocated by market mechanisms rather than by tax policy (Hulten and Klayman, 1988). In addition to King and Fullerton (1984), examples of METR studies include Hulten and Wycoff (1981) and Fullerton and Henderson (1984), who analyze the pattern of tax differentials under the Economic Recovery Tax Act of 1981, and Fullerton (1987), who examines the effects of the Tax Reform Act of 1986.

3. THE CORPORATE TAX AS A TAX ON RENTS
AND ENTREPRENEURSHIP

One standard result of METR analysis is that the business level tax on an investment that is entirely debt-financed is zero if interest expense is deductible, if depreciation for tax purposes equals economic depreciation, and if there is no inflation. This highlights a point emphasized in a provocative article by Stiglitz (1976), who argues that if firms use debt finance to finance marginal investments, the existence of a corporate tax should have no impact on marginal investment decisions. Moreover, this analysis applies to investment financed from retained earnings as well, so long as there is arbitrage at the firm level in the sense that firms use retained earnings to finance new investment only if the after-tax return on such investment exceeds the implicit return that would be earned from retiring debt. Thus, Stiglitz concludes that the corporate tax should be viewed primarily as a tax on economic rents and as a tax on entrepreneurship, since start-up firms typically have no retained earnings and very limited access to debt finance.

4. THE "NEW VIEW" OF DIVIDEND TAXATION

The effects of taxation on the level of investment are further complicated by uncertainty regarding the impact of the taxation of dividends at the individual level. The "traditional view" described by Musgrave (1959a), Break and Pechman (1975), and McLure (1979) is that the U.S. tax system imposes a double tax on the income attributable to equity-financed investment; specifically, such income is taxed first at the corporate level (assuming there are limits to the arbitrage described above, so that firms face a higher cost of capital for equity finance than for debt finance) and then again at the individual level, when earnings are distributed as dividends. Implicit in this view is the assumption that firms distribute earnings because dividends have an inherent value that offsets the additional tax burden incurred by such distributions; for example, dividends paid (1) may provide valuable information regarding current or future profits in situations in which firms have better information than shareholders, or (2) may reduce managerial discretion in situations characterized by principal-agent problems attributable to the separation of ownership and control in the modern corporation.

This view has been questioned by proponents of the "new view" of the effects of dividend taxation (King, 1974, 1977; Andrews, 1974; Auerbach, 1979b, 1983b; Bradford, 1981; and, in an international context, Hartman, 1985).[38] These investigators argue that, in the case of retained earnings finance, taxation of dividends at the individual level has no marginal impact on saving and investment decisions. The rationale underlying this view is that retained earnings are "trapped" within the corporation, in the sense that they can be consumed only if distributed and subjected to the dividend tax. Thus, both the returns to and the opportunity costs of investment financed with retained earnings are reduced proportionately by the taxation of dividends, which in turn implies that dividend taxation has no marginal effects on such investment.

Unfortunately, empirical evidence that might distinguish between the traditional and new views is mixed. Auerbach (1984) finds evidence that investments financed with new share issues generate earnings significantly higher than those attributable to investments financed with retained earnings—a result consistent with the new view implication that new share issues are a relatively high cost source of funds. However, in an examination of U.K. firms over the period 1950–1981, Poterba and Summers (1985) find that dividend taxes and payouts are negatively related, as predicted by the traditional view, and that an investment equation based on the traditional view has greater explanatory power than an equation based on the new view alternative.[39] In addition, Bagwell and Shoven (1989) show that share repurchases and cash mergers and acquisitions have become an increasingly important alternative to dividends as a means of distributing cash to shareholders; this calls into question an essential assumption of most new view models—that firms must use taxable dividends to distribute funds to their owners.[40] Finally, note that empirical investigations of this issue are complicated by the fact that the new view applies only to mature enterprises that fund marginal investments by reducing dividend payments; that is, at any point in time, one could expect each of the two competing views to be relevant for some subset of firms.

5. ECONOMETRIC ESTIMATES

Given the uncertainties noted above, it is probably not surprising that empirical evidence on the importance of tax effects on the level of investment is inconclusive. For example, Feldstein (1982) presents evidence suggesting that taxes are a very important determinant of investment, whereas Chirinko and Eisner (1983) conclude that other factors are far more important than any tax effects. Chirinko (1986, 1987) is especially critical of Feldstein's view that the interaction of inflation and a tax system based on historical costs has had adverse effects on investment. (For a reply, see Feldstein, 1987.)

D. General Equilibrium Modeling

One of the most prolific areas of research in public finance in recent years has been the use of general equilibrium models to examine the economy-wide effects of taxation.[41] Although described in broad terms by Musgrave (1959a) and anticipated in the international trade literature (Meade, 1955a, 1955b), the use of a general equilibrium approach to modeling the effects of taxes began in earnest with the analysis of the corporate income tax by Harberger (1962), who concluded that capital owners were likely to bear the full burden of the tax.[42] The structure of the Harberger model—two sectors, fixed total factor supplies, perfect factor mobility, no initial taxes, a single consumer, and perfect competition—was sufficiently simple that one could solve analytically for the specific effects that determined incidence and the parameters that determined the sign and magnitude of those effects.

Much recent research has been devoted to elaborations and applications of the Harberger model. Early efforts focused on analyzing the incidence effects of altering the basic assumptions of the model, such as perfect factor mobility, a single consumer, and the absence of any initial taxes (McLure, 1970, 1971, 1974; Mieszkowski, 1967; Ballentine and Eris, 1975; Vandendorpe and Friedlaender, 1976).[43] But beginning with the work of Shoven and Whalley (1972), attention has focused on numerical simulations of computable general equilibrium (CGE) models. Although such models do not yield analytical results, they provide a means of numerically evaluating the effects of tax policy changes in a multisector, many-consumer general equilibrium context. Indeed, the level of detail of the analysis is limited only by computational difficulties (which are today becoming less of a constraint) and the availability of reliable data.

Many of the restrictive assumptions of the Harberger model are easily relaxed in a CGE framework. Existing taxes are modeled easily, so that the incidence of reforms can be analyzed. The inclusion of a large number of consumer groups permits analysis of the distributional consequences of tax changes, and the disaggregation of production into a large number of industry groups permits analysis of the effects of differential taxation by sector. For example, the model of the U.S. economy constructed by Ballard, Fullerton, Shoven, and Whalley in 1985 (hereafter, BFSW) includes twelve types of consumers and nineteen industry groups.

In addition, as shown by BFSW, the assumption of a fixed capital stock can be relaxed by assuming that saving in one period augments the capital stock in the following period, and that labor supply decisions in each period can be made endogenous. Goulder, Shoven, and Whalley (1983) examine the implications of relaxing the assumption of a closed economy. Slemrod (1983a) and Galper and Toder (1984) examine the effects of introducing considerations of risk and endogenous financial behavior. Dixit and Stiglitz (1977) and Katz and Rosen (1985) show that the incidence of the corporate tax is altered dramatically if some sectors of the economy are characterized by imperfect competition.

Computable general equilibrium models have been used to examine a host of policy issues. For example, Fullerton, King, Shoven, and Whalley (1980) and Fullerton and Gordon (1983) examine the effects of corporate tax integration in the United States,[44] Fullerton (1982) investigates the possibility that labor income tax reductions might result in an increase in tax revenue, and Devarajan, Fullerton, and Musgrave (1980) analyze the distribution of the tax burden under alternative model formulations. Several studies have focused on the efficiency effects of the tax system or of proposed reforms; these studies show that the excess burdens attributable to the tax system are relatively large. For example,

Ballard, Shoven, and Whalley (1985a) estimate that the marginal excess burden of the U.S. tax system in 1973 ranged from 17 to 57 percent of revenue; Ballard, Shoven, and Whalley (1985b) estimate that the analogous total excess burden ranged from 13 to 24 percent of revenue. The simulations by Fullerton, Shoven, and Whalley (1983) suggest that a movement from an income tax to an expenditure tax with a preference for housing would result in an efficiency gain of 2.0 percent of lifetime resources, defined to include the present value of leisure; this gain increases to 2.7 percent if preferences for housing are eliminated. Because of the nature of the CGE models used, these studies use exact methods of calculating excess burdens, following Rosen (1978) and Hausman (1981a), rather than the earlier linear approximations popularized by Harberger (1964).[45]

In addition, the results of general equilibrium analyses of tax incidence provide an important input into analyses of the distribution of tax burden. In the effort to determine the distribution of the tax burden in the United States, Musgrave, Pechman, and others have used an approach that can be characterized as the quantification of incidence assumptions.[46] That is, incidence assumptions are used to assign tax burdens to various groups such as consumers of various products, workers, owners of capital, and so forth. Then information on consumption patterns, sources of income, and other factors are used to allocate the burdens among income classes, in order to determine the progressivity of the tax system. Pechman and Okner (1974) and Pechman (1985) rely on various results from the literature on general equilibrium analysis in choosing alternative assumptions about the possible incidence of the corporate income tax, the property tax, and the payroll tax; they then test the sensitivity of their estimates of the distribution of the tax burden to variations in incidence assumptions.[47] Note that these analyses all consider annual "snapshot" distributions of tax burdens; more recently, Davies, St-Hilaire, and Whalley (1984) have provided a methodology for computing cumulative tax burdens over the life cycle.

Finally, it should be noted that, despite the many advances in the construction of CGE models, a variety of remaining problems must be addressed before such models can be used with confidence to evaluate the effects of changes in tax policy. These are discussed below in Part IV.

E. Taxation in Growth Theory Models

As noted above, the basic Harberger model is a static one in the sense that total factor supplies are assumed to be fixed. In addition to the BFSW method of introducing dynamics into the model, three other approaches have appeared in the literature.[48]

The first is the introduction of taxes into a Solow-type growth model. In such a model, the steady-state rate of growth is determined exogenously by factors such as the rates of growth of the labor force and of productivity, and thus cannot be affected by taxation. However, reductions in capital intensity imply that capital can shift at least part of the burden of a capital tax to labor. This is in fact what occurs in the growth models constructed by Krzyzaniak (1967) and Feldstein (1974a,1974b). Indeed, in the simplest models in which all saving is done by the capitalists in the economy, a capital tax is fully shifted to labor. More generally, Feldstein's results suggest that the extent of shifting is between one-third and one-half. Feldstein (1974b) also shows that the long-run incidence of a tax on labor income will be invariant with respect to the elasticity of the supply of labor, so long as the tax has no effect on capital intensity.

The second approach to analyzing dynamic incidence is to examine the effects of taxes in an overlapping generations life-cycle model. The results in this case are strongly affected by assumptions regarding the distribution of tax revenues across generations. For example, in a two-period life-cycle model, Diamond (1970) shows that if the revenues from a tax on capital income are distributed to the elderly, capital intensity declines unambiguously and the tax is partially—and perhaps even more than fully—shifted to labor. In contrast, if revenues are distributed to the young, capital intensity increases, since the young save more, capital intensity increases, and wages rise while the return to capital falls. The general point here—that redistribution from the old to the young increases saving—also plays an important role in the papers by Summers (1981a), Auerbach and Kotlikoff (1983b), and Auerbach, Kotlikoff, and Skinner (1983), because the incidence of wage tax and consumption tax reforms reflects large intergenerational redistributions; these redistributions in turn imply that the two tax systems have very different steady-state properties.

Finally, several analyses of dynamic incidence focus on the effects of capital income tax changes on the prices of existing assets in the presence of adjustment costs (Summers, 1981b; Auerbach and Kotlikoff, 1983a). The existence of adjustment costs implies that tax changes will cause owners of different types of assets to experience windfall gains and losses during the transition to a new steady state; these capitalization effects increase with the length of the adjustment period, and may be a more important component of the incidence of a tax change than the long-run effects on net factor returns. This is especially likely to be the case if the reform involves changes in the relative tax treatment of different industries, with the overall level of capital income taxation remaining roughly constant.

Auerbach and Kotlikoff note that the asset price effects implied by capital income tax reforms are sometimes surprising. In particular, the introduction of investment incentives may result in capital losses for the owners of existing assets, since the required level of market returns falls in the new equilibrium in response to the incentives.[49] Another implication of this type of analysis is that tax reforms that have similar long-run effects on marginal effective tax rates may have very different short-run effects. For example, although tax rate reductions and new investment incentives can be structured to have similar long-run impacts, only the former policy will result in a windfall gain to owners of existing assets; this implies that investment incentives have a larger "bang for the buck" in terms of investment stimulated per dollar of revenue forgone.

F. The Optimal Taxation Literature

In the 1960s, analyses of alternative tax structures typically focused on their properties in terms of the criteria of equity, efficiency, and simplicity. Efficiency was generally believed to be roughly equivalent to tax "neutrality"; in addition, although tradeoffs among these three criteria, especially that between efficiency and vertical equity, were certainly recognized, they were not evaluated formally. In contrast, since the publication of the seminal optimal taxation papers by Diamond and Mirrlees (1971a, 1971b) and Mirrlees (1971), a great deal of research activity has been devoted to the analysis of "optimal" tax structures; such structures are designed either to maximize efficiency or to achieve an optimal balance between efficiency and equity objectives, relative to an explicit social welfare function. Below we summarize very briefly the main results in four major areas of optimal taxation: optimal commodity taxation, optimal labor income taxation, the optimal mix between direct and indirect taxes, and the distinction between optimal tax design and optimal tax reform.[50]

1. OPTIMAL COMMODITY TAXATION
The optimal commodity taxation literature has demonstrated that neutrality or equal-rate taxation of all commodities is generally inefficient. Rather, efficiency requires that commodity taxes be structured so that the tax system causes equiproportionate reductions in compensated demands for all commodities (Samuelson, 1951; Diamond and Mirrlees, 1971a, 1971b; Atkinson and Stiglitz, 1972). In the absence of cross-price effects, this condition yields the "Ramsey

rule," which specifies that commodity tax rates should be inversely proportional to demand elasticities (Ramsey, 1927). Although efficiency considerations alone imply that the highest tax rates should be applied to necessities, for which demand is relatively inelastic, this result can be modified to reflect distributional concerns. Specifically, Diamond (1975) derives a "many-person Ramsey rule," in which the efficiency considerations described above are balanced against the requirement that relatively low taxes be applied to commodities consumed disproportionately by the poor (and by individuals with a high propensity to consume relatively heavily taxed goods and thus generate revenue for the government).

2. OPTIMAL LABOR INCOME TAXATION

Although the notion of designing an income tax system to equalize marginal sacrifice dates to Edgeworth (1897), the idea of designing tax policy to maximize a social welfare function that aggregates individual utilities was not formalized until the path-breaking paper by Mirrlees (1971). In addition, Mirrlees was the first to introduce the incentive effects of labor income taxation explicitly into the analysis by allowing the labor-leisure choice to be endogenous; individuals were assumed to have identical utility functions but to differ in their level of productivity. General results in this formulation are rather few. The most striking is that the marginal tax rate on the individual with the very highest income should be zero; the rationale is that a positive marginal tax rate might cause a reduction in labor supply that would reduce the utility of the highest-income individual without raising any revenue. The implications of this result for actual income tax structures are far from clear, however, since the argument applies only for the very highest-income individual; that is, zero may be a rather poor approximation to the optimal tax rate on, say, the top 1 percent of the income distribution.

More attention has focused on the results Mirrlees obtained by assuming specific skill distributions and a Cobb-Douglas individual utility function. Specifically, his results suggest that the tax structure should be approximately linear (with a subsidy to those with low incomes), with marginal tax rates declining somewhat at the highest income levels. In a commonly cited passage, Mirrlees (1971, p. 208) says, "I must confess that I had expected the rigorous analysis of income taxation in the utilitarian manner to provide arguments for high tax rates. It has not done so."

Much subsequent research has focused on examining the extent to which the relative lack of progressivity (apart from that implied by the subsidy to low-income individuals) found by Mirrlees is still optimal under alternative formulations or parameter values.[51] Atkinson (1973) shows that use of the Rawlsian social welfare function (which implies that the tax structure should be chosen to maximize the welfare of the worst-off individual in the society), rather than the simple unweighted sum assumed by Mirrlees, results in a more progressive rate structure; optimal tax rates typically fall in the 30–45 percent range rather than the optimal rate of roughly 20 percent found by Mirrlees.

Stern (1976) argues that the degree of labor supply elasticity implied by the assumption of a Cobb-Douglas utility function is excessive, and that a constant elasticity of substitution formulation with an elasticity of 0.4 (rather than 1.0 as implied by the Cobb-Douglas formulation) is more consistent with the empirical literature on labor supply. He shows that in this case, even with a social welfare function that simply aggregates individual utilities, marginal tax rates may approach 80 percent.

These results suggest that the prescriptions of the optimal taxation literature are rather sensitive both to the nature of the welfare function chosen to represent societal preferences and to the parameter values assumed in the simulations. Although the popular impression seems to be that this literature supports low flat-rate taxes, the above discussion suggests that such an inference may be misplaced (Rosen, 1988a; Haveman, Chapter 9 below).

The optimal taxation approach has also been applied to the issue of the choice of the taxable unit under the income tax. The conventional wisdom in the United States during much of the period since 1960 has been that joint consumption is an essential characteristic of a family environment, so that the family is the appropriate unit for taxation. However, the clear implication of the optimal taxation literature on this issue is that relatively low tax rates should be assessed on family members with relatively elastic labor supplies. The labor supply literature strongly indicates that the labor supply of women—those most likely to be secondary earners in a two-earner family—is far more elastic than that of men. This suggests that low marginal tax rates on secondary earners are desirable (Boskin and Sheshinski, 1983). In marked contrast, joint filing implies that the secondary earner faces first-dollar taxation at the relatively high marginal tax rate of the spouse. The optimal taxation approach thus provides a strong argument for individual filing. In addition, individual filing is supported by those who believe that the tax system should be neutral with respect to the marriage decision (Munnell, 1980).[52]

3. OPTIMAL TAX MIX

The optimal taxation literature has also addressed the issue of the appropriate combination of direct and indirect taxes, especially the question of whether it is desirable to supplement an income tax with differential commodity taxes. Consider first a linear income tax (a lump-sum grant or subsidy coupled with a constant marginal tax rate on all wage income) when individuals differ only with respect to productivity. In this case, differentiated indirect taxes may be desirable to tax goods consumed disproportionately by the rich or to increase the size of the lump-sum subsidy; note, however, that in the latter case it will be desirable to achieve the subsidy increase efficiently—that is, by taxing necessities with low price elasticities of demand. Uniform taxation is desirable only under special circumstances, including the case in which all individuals have identical Stone-Geary utility functions (Atkinson, 1977; Deaton, 1979, 1981; Deaton and Stern, 1985).

A nonlinear income tax obviously provides more flexibility to achieve distributional goals with the income tax. In this case, uniform indirect taxes are optimal, provided that the utility function is characterized by weak separability between labor and all consumption goods; that is, the marginal rates of substitution among all goods must be independent of the amount of leisure (Atkinson and Stiglitz, 1976). Unfortunately, it appears to be rather difficult to determine empirically whether such separability is a reasonable assumption (Deaton, 1987).

The optimal taxation literature has addressed another type of tax mix question: the extent to which taxes on production should be used. Diamond and Mirlees (1971a,1971b) show that production taxes should be avoided entirely, provided that all commodity taxes are set optimally and any economic profits are taxed at a 100 percent rate. Since these two conditions are quite restrictive, the relevance of this result is open to question.[53] In particular, this result does not imply that uniform taxation of capital income—the proverbial "level playing field"—is generally optimal, especially when certain forms of capital, such as that invested in owner-occupied housing, are untaxed (see Feldstein, 1985).

4. OPTIMAL TAX REFORM

Finally, Feldstein (1976a) points out that the optimal taxation literature focuses on tax design rather than on the more policy-relevant issue of the reform of an existing tax system. He argues that initial conditions are important to the extent that irreversible investment decisions are made based on the provisions of the existing tax system; in this case, the implementation of unexpected reforms causes arbitrary and capricious redistributions (as analyzed in the asset price change literature discussed above) that are undesirable from a social standpoint.[54] Although compensation of losers is one means of mitigating this problem, such treatment generally seems politically infeasible (Feldstein, 1976b); the fact that the "windfall recapture tax" proposed by the U.S. Treasury (1985a) failed to win passage reinforces this conclusion (Aaron, 1985; Zodrow, 1988). Alternatively, the redistributions caused by reform can be reduced by altering the timing and implementation of reform. Results in this area are varied, since optimal tax reform policies—which include various combinations of grandfather rules, or postponing, phasing in, or partially enacting reform—depend on the particular reform being enacted as well as the extent to which adjustment costs are large (Zodrow, 1981, 1985, 1986, 1992).

G. The Tax Base Debate: Income versus Consumption

A basic policy issue that has recently received considerable attention in the public finance literature is the question of whether the base of a system of direct taxation should be income or consumption.[55] The traditional view was clear on this issue: the preferred approach was a Haig-Simons tax on a comprehensive measure of income, and the consumption tax option was rejected as unfair or impossible to administer effectively.[56] A reading of the current literature, however, suggests that there is fairly widespread (although certainly not unanimous) support among economists for a consumption tax base.[57] Given the importance of this basic issue, it will be useful to examine the debate in some detail.

Many of the academic arguments in support of a switch to consumption taxation are based on efficiency considerations. Some of these draw on the optimal taxation literature. Unfortunately, an essential characteristic of optimal taxation theory is that it invariably generates results that depend significantly on the particular structure of the model analyzed and its parameter values. Thus, in even the simplest possible case—a partial equilibrium, two-period, life-cycle model with identical individuals and no bequests—the question of the optimal tax base cannot be answered unambiguously.

For example, one can show that consumption taxation (modeled as tax exemption of capital income) is optimal if the individual utility function is weakly separable in consumption and leisure and homothetic in the two consumption goods; an alternative interpretation is that consumption in each of the two periods must be equally complementary with leisure (Sandmo, 1974; Auerbach, 1979c). Although this characterization is not "unreasonable," it is straightforward to show that alternative utility functions imply that an income tax or even a capital income surcharge is optimal. Indeed, Atkinson and Sandmo (1980, p. 282) argue that it is "a misapplication of the optimum tax literature to suggest that it provides a clear-cut answer to the choice between income and consumption bases." Moreover, there is little in the way of econometric evidence that would resolve the issue, especially since the critical parameters include several cross-price elasticities that are typically ignored in empirical studies.

Not surprisingly, the issue is not clarified if more complex models are used. In particular, suppose that the model is extended to consider changes in saving and thus capital intensity in an overlapping generations framework, and that the capital stock in the economy falls below the "golden rule" level. Although these conditions seem to favor consumption taxation, King (1980) shows that— apart from the intertemporal effects noted above—the taxation of capital income under an income tax is desirable because it induces more saving (in order to finance payment of future taxes on capital income) and thus a larger capital stock.[58] The simulation results on this issue are also somewhat ambiguous. The simulations in the paper by Summers (1981a) described above suggest huge welfare gains from implementing a consumption tax—on the order of 11 percent of lifetime income for a movement from an income tax to a consumption tax (7 percent for movement to a wage tax). As noted above, however, subsequent research has questioned the large savings responses of the Summers model, and models with smaller savings responses generally imply that smaller efficiency gains would be obtained from a consumption tax reform in the model. For example, in one version of the Auerbach and Kotlikoff (1987) model— which builds on the work of Auerbach, Kotlikoff, and Skinner (1983)—the implementation of a consumption tax reform results in a steady-state welfare gain of only 2.3 percent of lifetime resources (including the value of leisure), whereas the implementation of a wage tax actually results in a welfare loss of 0.9 percent. Moreover, the simulations of Goulder, Shoven, and Whalley (1983) suggest that any gains from a consumption tax reform might be reduced or eliminated in an open-economy context, because some of the reform-induced increase in saving flows abroad so that domestic investors and the government together receive only the net (after foreign tax) return.

Consumption tax proponents also argue that the tax is preferable to an income tax on equity grounds. They argue that (1) vertical equity goals can be achieved under either tax through the appropriate choice of rate structure, and (2) the consumption tax is preferable on horizontal equity grounds because individuals with equal lifetime endowments bear equal lifetime tax liabilities, whereas under an income tax those who earn early in life, save, and consume late in life bear differentially higher liabilities. However, Zodrow (1990) has shown that the latter result depends to some extent on the simplifying assumptions made in the standard analysis of this issue, and that the horizontal equity issue becomes ambiguous when some of these assumptions, such as constant tax rates and identical tastes for leisure, are relaxed.

Finally, consumption tax proponents also argue that the tax is preferable to the income tax on simplicity grounds. The primary advantages are at the business level, where a host of complex timing and inflation adjustment problems that plague the income tax disappear under a consumption-based business tax of the cash-flow type (Bradford, 1986; McLure, 1988; Aaron, 1990; McLure, Mutti, Thuronyi, and Zodrow, 1990). In addition, individual taxation, as well as business and individual tax integration, would generally be simpler under a consumption tax, especially if the "prepayment" or yield exemption approach were used (Bradford, 1986; McLure and Zodrow, 1990).

H. Tax Expenditures and Tax Shelters

No discussion of academic thought on tax policy during the quarter-century ending with the 1986 act would be complete without explicit mention of two critical concepts: tax expenditures and tax shelters. The first of these has conditioned the debate on tax reform and the second has provided much of the rationale for recent reform. Much of the work on these problems was done by lawyers rather than by economists; much of it can be traced directly or indirectly to the influence of Stanley Surrey.

1. TAX EXPENDITURES

In a 1967 speech, Surrey, then assistant secretary of the Treasury for tax policy, provided the germ of the idea that became known as tax expenditures (quoted in Surrey, 1973, p. 4): "Through deliberate departures from accepted concepts of net income and through various special exemptions, deductions, and credits, our tax system does operate to affect the private economy in ways that are usually accomplished by expenditures—in effect to produce an expenditure system described in tax language . . . We need a full accounting for these effects of the tax system . . . which tax rules are integral to a tax system in order to provide a balanced tax structure and a proper measurement of net income, and which tax rules represent departures from that net income concept and balanced structure to provide relief, assistance, incentive or what you will for a particular group or activity."[59] Developed further, the tax expenditure budget has been included in the annual budget since passage of the Budget Act of 1974. Although Surrey intended that the benchmark for calculating tax expenditures should be based on the Haig-Simons definition, he recognized that the definition would need to be modified in various ways to make its application practical.[60] Thus, the 1974 act refers to a "special" provision that is a "deviation from the normal tax structure."[61]

2. TAX SHELTERS

Tax shelters ordinarily involve the combination of three elements: deferral of tax liability, conversion of ordinary income to preferentially taxed capital gains, and leverage. They allow taxpayers not only to avoid tax on income subject to these benefits, but to use excess deductions (tax losses) to "shelter" income from other sources. Shelters are ordinarily organized as limited partnerships. This allows tax benefits to be combined with limited liability and sold to taxpayers who do not participate actively in the conduct of the business producing the tax losses (see, for example, U.S. Congress, Joint Committee on Taxation, 1975, 1983, 1984).[62]

The problem of deferral goes well beyond acceleration of depreciation allowances, which is perhaps the best-known timing issue. It includes numerous troublesome technical questions of timing, including those raised by original issue discount obligations, premature accruals (for, say, reclaiming strip mines), and capitalization of expenses. The importance of timing issues increases dramatically with interest rates. It is interesting to note that much of the work in the area of the "time value of money," inherently an economic problem, has been done by tax lawyers rather than by economists.[63]

Leverage is important not only because it generates interest deductions, but also because it allows the taxpayer to gain the benefits of deferral and capital gains treatment on more than her own investment. Interest deductions are especially important in inflationary times. Indeed, because United States tax law allows deductions of all nominal interest payments, it is possible for real after-tax interest rates to be negative.[64] The inflation and high interest rates of the 1970s and 1980s increased the attraction of tax shelters.[65]

It seems safe to say that the public policy implications of tax shelters first came to be appreciated during Surrey's tenure as assistant secretary under Presidents Kennedy and Johnson (1961–1968). But a fundamental change occurred between 1968 and the 1986 act. High-income individuals investing via small partnerships, or even as individuals, had long used tax shelters to reduce their taxes. But these shelters had had economic substance and had not been not used in an abusive fashion. Things got out of hand when innovations in financial instruments made it possible to combine the advantages of limited liability and flow-through of losses and market shelters, to reach a wider clientele. With a new group—tax shelter promoters—wanting to feed at the public trough, abusive shelters based on phony assumptions and fraudulent evaluations and having no economic substance appeared. As noted in Part III, the resultant abuses sparked public revulsion that led to the 1986 act. A variety of ways were used to eliminate tax shelters or limit their benefits (aside from eliminating the preferential treatment of capital gains), including elimination of deferral, limitations on the benefits of leverage, other schedular approaches, and the minimum tax.[66] In this there was no effort to distinguish between shelters that had economic substance and those that did not.[67]

I. Summary

The following is a list of views that probably would have been acceptable to the majority of tax economists in 1985:[68]

1. Economic efficiency is valued more highly than vertical equity.
2. Horizontal equity is less important than previously thought, because differences in taxation of income from capital are expected to be reflected in different before-tax returns.
3. The growing complexity of the income tax is a matter of concern.
4. Consumption is more appropriate than income as the basis for direct taxation (that is, it is more efficient, fairer, and simpler to administer).
5. The individual should be the tax-paying unit.
6. The Haig-Simons definition of income is difficult to implement, especially because of timing issues.
7. It may be necessary to tolerate schedular elements if all deviations from the Haig-Simons definition cannot be eliminated.
8. Investment incentives are not necessary or desirable under the consumption-based tax, but many believe they may be desirable under the income tax to stimulate capital formation.
9. Integration of the income taxes is appropriate, but may be needed only for dividends paid on new issues of shares.
10. Inflation adjustment in the measurement of the tax base, which is not

needed under a consumption-based tax, should be considered under an income tax if inflation cannot be contained.

11. Highly progressive tax rates should be avoided.
12. Uniform taxation (of what is taxed) is not necessarily optimal, since not all economic activities, especially leisure, can be taxed, and income from owner-occupied housing may not be taxed for political or administrative reasons.

As in 1960, there are substantial areas of disagreement among the profession on what constitutes good tax policy. It appears, however, that the dominant view has shifted from a philosophy of redistribution and uniform taxation that might be labeled "liberal" to a conservative philosophy that plays down distributional concerns and supports preferential treatment of the income from capital.[69]

III. THE EVOLUTION OF FEDERAL INCOME TAX POLICY, 1960–1986

In this part, we describe some of the key features of the evolution of the federal income tax from 1960 to 1986.[70] Instead of trying to be comprehensive, we focus on issues that illustrate the interaction between academic thinking and public policy. We pay particular attention to the 1986 reforms. In Part IV we consider the extent to which policy was influenced by academic analysis during this period.

A. What Happened

1962. In the effort to "get the nation moving," President John Kennedy proposed, and Congress enacted, an investment tax credit (ITC) for investment in equipment. The ITC has been suspended and reenacted several times since then, generally to promote macroeconomic stability. The original 1962 action reflected the influence of academic opinion (for example, Brown, 1948), as well as other forces.

1964. Before his assassination, Kennedy had proposed a far-reaching program of reforms developed with the assistance of some of the nation's leading tax policy experts—those who had created the consensus described at the end of Part I. This program included rate reduction, a minimum standard deduction (to eliminate tax on low-income households), income averaging, and constructive taxation of capital gains at death. When finally enacted, the 1964 act consisted of little more than reduction of individual income tax rates (the maximum rate fell from 91 to 70 percent), the minimum standard deduction, and income averaging. (The primary corporate rate was reduced from 52 percent to 48 percent.)

1969. At the end of the Kennedy-Johnson years, the Treasury Department left an agenda of needed tax reforms based on the conventional wisdom, as augmented by internal analysis of tax expenditures, tax shelters, and timing issues.[71] These became the basis for the reforms adopted in 1969. The 1969 law included a maximum tax on earned income of 50 percent and the introduction of the ''add-on'' minimum tax on preference income. The latter was adopted in lieu of a proposal to allocate deductions between taxable and nontaxable income. A 20 percent cap was placed on the amount by which the tax paid by a single person could exceed that paid by a married couple with the same taxable income filing a joint return. The previous 25 percent limit on the tax rate applied to long-term capital gains was eliminated; since half of such gains were subject to tax, the maximum rate rose to 35 percent.[72]

In addition, a limitation on the deductibility of ''investment interest'' was introduced to curtail the deduction of interest incurred to finance investments that did not yield current income. This antishelter provision constitutes nearly explicit recognition that it makes no sense to follow the rules of a global income tax that allow full current deduction of expenses (including interest) if other rules allow deferral of the recognition of the income associated with the expenses.[73]

A ''minimum tax'' on ''preference income'' was also enacted in 1969. Though generalization is difficult, it appears that over time the base of the minimum tax has come to represent a concept much closer to Haig-Simons income than does the normal income tax base. Thus, the minimum tax can be interpreted as evidence of congressional schizophrenia: tax preferences are enacted, but their use is limited, in part to prevent the politically unpalatable spectacle of wealthy taxpayers and corporations paying little or no taxes.

1976. In 1976 there was an abortive attempt to reduce the tax advantages of transfer of appreciated property at death. Instead of constructive realization at death, the chosen approach was carryover of the decedent's basis. Opponents of this reform claimed that it was administratively infeasible (inaccurately, in the opinion of several disinterested tax lawyers who reviewed earlier drafts of this chapter); its effective date was postponed, and the provision was eventually repealed before going into effect.

"At-risk" rules were also introduced to prevent taxpayers (in certain circumstances) from taking deductions for expenses in excess of their economic investment in an activity. Indebtedness for which the taxpayer is not personally responsible (nonrecourse loans) are not considered to be at risk.[74]

1978. The Carter administration's proposal for tax reform "stuck more religiously to reform principles than its predecessors in 1964, 1969, and 1976," but "the mood of Congress and the country was shifting rapidly toward lower taxes and away from tax reform . . . Never in the history of the income tax were proposals so out of step with congressional intentions, and never were they so completely defeated" (Witte, 1985, pp. 205, 207). In an attempt to increase capital formation, Congress reduced the inclusion rate for capital gains to 40 percent; this reduced the maximum tax rate on such gains to 28 percent.[75]

1981. The first year of the Reagan presidency saw a dramatic 23 percent reduction in individual tax rates. The top marginal tax rate paid by individuals was cut from 70 percent to 50 percent, ending the distinction between earned and unearned income. This reduced the maximum rate on long-term capital gains to 20 percent. Rate brackets, personal exemptions, and the standard deduction were indexed for inflation, starting in 1985.

A 10 percent deduction was provided for couples filing jointly, for up to $30,000 of the earned income of the spouse with the lower earnings. This reflected in part the concern that taxing these earnings at the marginal rate based on the income of the spouse with the higher earnings creates severe disincentive effects, especially given the econometric evidence that the labor supply of secondary earners is much more elastic than that of primary earners.

The inflation of the 1970s, combined with a tax system that made no allowance for inflation in the calculation of depreciation allowances, had been detrimental to investment in business plant and equipment (see Feldstein and Summers, 1979; Hendershott and Hu, 1983). The 1981 response was not inflation adjustment, but the highly Accelerated Cost Recovery System of depreciation (ACRS), combined with restoration of the ITC. This policy did not reflect academic opinion; it was the result of a "bidding war" in which Republicans and Democrats vied to see who could be more generous in their proposals for investment incentives.[76] It resulted in zero or negative METRs on the income from many assets and opened the way for tax shelters. While ACRS greatly simplified compliance for many ordinary taxpayers (both small businesses and large corporations), it also added to complexity by creating opportunities for both legitimate and bogus tax shelters.[77]

1986. The most far-reaching reform of the U.S. income tax in its seventy-year history was completed in 1986.[78] Many have attributed the success of the 1984–1986 effort at tax reform to the "ground rules" under which the political debate was conducted—namely, that tax reform should be both revenue neutral and distributionally neutral. If rates were to be reduced significantly, it would be necessary to broaden the base by a corresponding amount. Moreover, those individuals and industries that paid taxes would be pitted against those that did not; it would not be possible to pit rich and poor against each other, as in the past.

The ITC was repealed, depreciation was decelerated, and the deductions for personal interest (that which was not supported by a mortgage to purchase or improve the home of the taxpayer) and for state and local sales taxes were eliminated. Both income averaging and the partial deduction for the earned income of secondary earners were eliminated, to simplify individual tax filing. Individual income tax rates were again reduced, to a marginal rate of only 28 percent on those with the highest incomes.[79] Personal exemptions, standard deductions, and the earned income credit were increased, effectively removing those below the poverty level from the income tax roles. The distinction between realized long-term capital gains and ordinary income was eliminated (for most purposes).[80]

The primary corporate tax rate was reduced to 34 percent. The alternative minimum tax, which had replaced the "add-on" minimum tax in 1983, was strengthened and extended to corporations. One of the more bizarre developments was the decision to base the minimum tax temporarily on the book income of corporations, as reported to shareholders.[81] Several of the other anti-shelter provisions had a strong schedular flavor (limits on deductions for "passive-activity losses"—losses incurred in activities in which the taxpayer has no active role, tighter limits on deduction of investment interest, and so on). Although criticized for their complexity and lack of conceptual foundations, these rules, especially the limits on passive-activity losses, have essentially killed the tax shelter industry (see Koppelman, 1989).

The 1986 act addressed many timing issues. Whereas previous laws had contained an assortment of rules governing what had to be capitalized and what could be deducted currently, the new law contained uniform provisions for cost capitalization. Among expenses that must be capitalized are certain interest payments, general and administrative expenses, pensions, and fringe benefits. Inventories and assets constructed by the taxpayer were affected by these changes. Income from long-term contracts must be taxed in part according to the percentage of completion, instead of on a completed contract basis. Rules for recognizing income from installment sales and governing the use of the cash method of accounting were also changed.

The 1986 act may be almost as significant for what it omitted as for what it included.[82] In particular, the Treasury Department's 1984 proposals to President Reagan, sometimes referred to as Treasury I, were considerably more comprehensive in their coverage. They called for the taxation of employee fringe benefits in excess of a floor, elimination of deductions for all state and local taxes, inflation adjustment of the measurement of income from business and capital, a 50 percent deduction for all dividends paid, and—reflecting proposals that would have eliminated most of the building blocks of tax shelters—elimination of the alternative minimum tax. They did not contain a proposal for the elimination of the deduction for interest on home mortgages—the only area President Reagan had ruled off-limits during the period before release of Treasury I.[83] In addition, no attempt was made to tax capital gains on an accrual basis or when they were transferred at death, and the treatment of retirement savings remained closer to that prescribed by a consumption-based direct tax than by an income tax.

Many of these unsuccessful proposals, like some of the successful ones, were based on old ideas—ideas that formed part of the conventional wisdom in 1960. These included elimination of deductions for state and local income and property taxes, taxation of fringe benefits, and taxation of indexed capital gains as ordinary income. The proposals for inflation adjustment approximated the theoretically correct response to the fear that inflation would continue to distort the measurement of income from business and capital. The 1986 act's taxation of capital gains as ordinary income, without adjustment of basis for inflation, was seen by the authors of Treasury I as a mixed blessing.

The Treasury I proposal to provide a corporate deduction for dividends paid had an interesting history.[84] Those in the Office of Tax Policy who were responsible for preparing the tax reform proposals for Treasury Secretary Donald Regan's consideration had difficulty deciding whether to propose a dividend deduction or a system of imputation credits of the type used in Europe—and indeed performed several flip-flops on the issue in their meetings with Regan. They eventually chose the dividend-paid deduction on simplicity grounds. One characteristic of this approach, which had been thought to be a fatal liability, automatic provision of relief to foreign shareholders (McLure, 1975b, 1979), became an asset because it would have helped attract foreign investment to finance the U.S. budget and trade deficits. Regan and his advisers also considered the desirability and feasibility of limiting dividend relief to dividends on new shares, before rejecting the proposal because of fears of complexity and abuse.

B. Summary

This brief review reveals several interesting patterns. First, 1960s vintage academic thinking on tax policy was quite influential at both the beginning and the end of the period, especially in the tax reforms of 1969 and 1986. Among the marked early triumphs of the conventional wisdom were the introduction of the ITC, income averaging, and reduction of the preferential treatment accorded long-term capital gains, including the failed attempt at carryover of basis. The alternative minimum tax is a schizophrenic "backstop" provision that can be interpreted as an admission of defeat for the "global taxation" philosophy of the conventional wisdom.

The basic philosophy of Treasury I was consistent with this earlier conventional wisdom. There was, however, far greater recognition of the importance of timing issues, the harm done by high marginal tax rates, and the need for integration and for inflation adjustment in the measurement of income. The 1986 act reflected the first two of these concerns, as well as more traditional components of the conventional wisdom. The 1986 act also exhibited greater willingness to tolerate schedular elements, especially where there were no satisfactory solutions to problems of income definition. Much of this, notably the attention to timing issues and tax shelters, as well as the use of the concept of tax expenditures to make the case for tax reform, reflected the influence of work begun under Stanley Surrey at the Treasury Department during the 1960s. The 1986 act was a clear repudiation of the modern view that consumption is preferable to income as the basis for direct taxation.

Between 1969 and 1986, policy was shaped less by the 1960s view and more by the newer conventional wisdom, but at times (for example, in the extremely generous treatment of depreciable assets in the 1981 act) it seemed to follow no rational course. The radical rate reduction that began in 1981 and culminated in the 1986 act reflected the view that the disincentive and distortionary effects of high rates outweigh any social benefits from their redistributive effects. Although advocacy of a consumption-based direct tax may have contributed to the extremely generous treatment of depreciable assets under the 1981 act, this view proved to have no staying power.

IV. THE INTERACTION OF ANALYSIS AND POLICY

In several important respects, the debate leading up to the Tax Reform Act of 1986 reflected current academic thought on tax policy, as outlined in Part II. This was especially true of the support for lower marginal tax rates for both individuals and corporations on incentive and efficiency grounds.[85] As Slemrod (1990, p. 166) notes, "a key message of the optimal progressivity literature, that high marginal rates may not be appropriate, even for egalitarian social welfare functions, has apparently won the day."[86] Nevertheless, most of the debate reflected the more traditional arguments that we have characterized as the 1960s consensus view; certainly that view was far more influential than the current conventional wisdom in the development of the 1986 reform. Indeed, in his 1988 Richard T. Ely lecture to the American Economic Association, Henry Aaron (1989, pp. 9–10) made the following observation: "The remarkable characteristic of the debate leading up to the Tax Reform Act of 1986 was how much the old concepts of equity and how little recent advances in normative tax theory were invoked not only among politicians but also among economists . . . Theorists have transformed scholarly discussion about taxation, but the resulting scholarly literature has had remarkably little effect on political debate . . . The old-time religion . . . although in theoretical shambles, . . . remains the source of almost the only principles cited in debates on tax policy."

Aaron offers several possible explanations for this phenomenon.[87] First, he suggests that the traditional principles are less prone "to manipulation and distortion in the rough and tumble of the political process." They may lead to the most sustainable, if not the largest, increases in welfare. Second, the theoretical underpinnings and empirical support for certain propositions "are too diffuse to justify action." Models are based on "strong and dubious assumptions." He concludes, "In such a world, the generalists who make our tax laws desert simple rules at their—and our—peril, because if they do so, they become sitting ducks for ex parte research, well-paid advocates, and just plain deception." The remainder of our comments are devoted to fleshing out Aaron's observations. For expositional convenience we distinguish, somewhat artificially, between analytical issues and political considerations.

A. Analytical Issues

1. THE COMPLEXITY OF RECENT ANALYSIS

In 1960 much of what was being said by the academic tax policy community was accessible to the layman. Even if some strands of the argument were difficult to follow, there was nothing very difficult about such key issues as whether to tax long-term capital gains as ordinary income, whether to end the exclusions for many fringe benefits and interest on municipal bonds, or whether to eliminate the deductions for state and local taxes and home mortgage interest. While one might agree or disagree with any particular proposition, one probably would not find them strange or hard to comprehend. This situation has changed dramatically. The propositions being advanced by those in the forefront of theoretical work in tax policy are by no means obvious to those not trained in mathematical economics, and it is often difficult to choose between competing (and often highly contradictory) positions without some understanding of the mathematical arguments or econometric issues underlying them. Moreover, some of the results of the theory of optimal taxation would probably strike members of Congress as strange, if not bizarre; the notion that the marginal tax rate paid by the person with the highest income should be zero is one example.

Of course, not all the recent thinking on tax policy is so esoteric that policymakers cannot understand it. Much of what has been written about the choice between income and consumption as the tax base is rather straightforward. But much depends on particular assumptions. This is where Aaron's comment about sensitivity to specification comes into play.

2. LACK OF CONSENSUS

In earlier years, there was remarkable unanimity regarding the appropriate federal tax policy, as virtually all the leading public finance specialists had long-standing records of supporting a comprehensive Haig-Simons income tax. In particular, the primary alternative—a consumption-based direct tax—had received little serious discussion. It was widely perceived to be both unfair and unworkable; even those who did not reject it on equity grounds had thought it infeasible. In addition, some of the problems that currently are the focus of policy discussions, including especially the timing and inflation adjustment problems that arise when one attempts to measure real economic income accurately, were either not recognized or largely ignored. There was general agreement that the incentive effects of taxation on labor supply and saving were fairly small, so that quite progressive tax rates, which were widely viewed as desirable on equity grounds, had fairly small efficiency costs. As a result, public finance economists could generally speak with one voice when advising policymakers. Moreover, as noted above, the arguments they used to support their positions were easily understandable by politicians, their notions of horizontal and vertical equity were appealing to most citizens, and their recommendations appeared to be generally consistent with administrative simplicity. Indeed, since efficiency notions were often interpreted to mean uniform taxation, they were fairly easy to explain to policymakers and the public.

In recent years, this consensus has evaporated. Many—but not all—public finance economists support basing direct taxation on consumption rather than income, and argue that a consumption-based direct tax is more efficient, fairer, and simpler to administer than an income tax. There is much greater concern about the incentive effects of taxation, and less agreement about the desirability of the redistribution implied by a steeply progressive tax structure. Moreover, a whole new school of thought, led by James Buchanan, has challenged the basic premises of both traditional and more modern public finance theorists.[88] This school argues that the primary goal of those in government is to maximize revenue, and that the best tax structure is one that limits the resulting tendency toward overexpansion of government (for example, see Brennan and Buchanan, 1980). This view condones the use of taxes that many would consider ''bad'' because they are unpopular. Thus, the tax policy prescriptions of this school of thought and the optimal taxation school are often diametrically opposite.[89]

In addition, despite the many significant academic advances that have occurred in public finance in recent years, we have not yet obtained definitive answers to a large number of both positive and normative questions regarding tax policy, including especially the incidence and other effects of the corporate income tax and the effects of dividend taxation at the individual level. Since in many cases public finance economists cannot agree on a single answer to various tax policy questions, policymakers are relatively free to base decisions on concerns other than those typically addressed in the academic literature.

3. INSTABILITY OF THE CONVENTIONAL WISDOM

In addition, the conventional wisdom of public finance economists has changed considerably—often in ways that could be described as cyclical. For example, with respect to the effect of taxation on labor supply, the early view was that labor supply was largely unaffected by taxes. Hausman's results then suggested that a progressive tax system has large labor supply effects and large excess burdens. However, more recent results suggest that the previous view may have been more nearly correct. Triest (1990) uses the same data set as does Hausman but for a different year (1983 rather than 1975) and uses similar estimating techniques, but finds much smaller tax effects on labor supply (a reduction for prime-age males of 2.6 percent rather than 8.2 percent). MaCurdy, Green, and Paarsch (1990) argue that Hausman's estimation technique inappropriately constrains individual behavior at kink points on a piece-wise linear budget constraint, and show that a less restrictive estimation procedure results in very small effects of taxation on labor supply. Such dramatic fluctuations in the conventional wisdom about the effects of taxation may be inevitable, but they must be disconcerting to the policymaker who, for example, advocated lower marginal tax rates in 1986 partially on the strength of Hausman's oft-cited results.

A similar story can be told for saving. The conventional wisdom of "Denison's Law" was contradicted by the empirical results presented by Boskin (1978a) and the implications of the theoretical model constructed by Summers (1981a), which in turn are inconsistent with the recent work of Hall (1988) that suggests an intertemporal elasticity of substitution of approximately zero, as well as with the conclusion of Skinner and Feenberg (1990) that the after-tax interest rate has little effect on aggregate saving. Similarly, opinion has fluctuated on the use of investment incentives. Indeed, the emphasis on a "level playing field" for investment choices that provided much of the impetus for the 1986 reforms has recently been challenged by the finding of de Long and Summers (1991) that investment in machinery and equipment generates huge positive social externalities by increasing technological advancement and growth. Presumably such variance in the conventional wisdom makes policymakers extremely reluctant to base decisions on the current state of the art in public finance. It also may lead to a feeling that virtually any policy can be supported by a selective reading of the existing public finance literature, especially since there is so much uncertainty regarding the values of several key parameters.

4. LITTLE EMPHASIS ON DISTRIBUTION AND ADMINISTRATIVE COSTS

An important reason that the results of much recent academic research have had only a minimal impact on policy deliberations is that the underlying models often either ignore or deal only peripherally with two issues that are of the utmost importance to most policymakers: administrative concerns and distributional or "equity" issues. (The recent work on administrative costs by Slemrod, 1990, is an exception to this generalization.) Steuerle (1992, p. 82) has argued that in the recent literature, "issues of fairness, efficiency, and administration, were disdained as institutional, structural, and micro issues not worthy of attention."[90] This is in marked contrast to much of earlier research (see, for example, the work on the distribution of tax burdens cited above). Musgrave (1982, p. 25) has commented: "While my generation of tax economists has placed much emphasis on equity, the younger generation is now stressing efficiency. This change . . . may reflect the fact that efficiency considerations are more amenable to the exercise of technical tools, a practice that brings rewards to the young professional but may not be most helpful to a balanced view of reform."

It is worth noting that the Treasury I proposal to eliminate the partial exemption of capital gains was motivated in large part by the complexity of such a policy: "The sharp distinction . . . between capital gains and ordinary income has been the source of substantial complexity. Application of different rates . . . inevitably creates disputes . . . and encourages taxpayers to recharacterize their income . . . A significant body of law . . . has developed. Its principles are complicated in concept and application . . . The . . . resources consumed . . . are substantial, yet there is little confidence that the results derived in particular cases are even roughly consistent" (U.S. Department of the Treasury, 1984, vol. 3, p. 181).[91] Theoretical results are likely to have a significant impact on policymakers and thus on tax policy only if the models underlying the results deal explicitly with distributional and administrative considerations.[92]

5. PROBLEMS WITH USING CGE MODELS TO GUIDE POLICY

There are still many problems with using computable general equilibrium models as a reliable indicator of the effects of tax policy. Perhaps the most critical need is for more reliable estimates of parameter values, especially the labor supply and saving elasticities discussed above. Moreover, many econometricians object to the fact that the benchmark equilibrium in computable general equilibrium models is typically established by "calibrating" the model to be consistent with data taken from various sources for a single year; they would prefer that the models be estimated rather than calibrated to fit to a single data point. The METR literature suggests that greater disaggregation of the production sector is desirable in CGE models, since the effective tax rates facing various industries—and indeed, various investments and methods of finance within a particular industry—differ considerably when all details of the tax system are taken into account. The theoretically appropriate way to deal with various taxes, especially the corporate income tax and the taxation of dividends at the individual level, is far from clear. The treatment of the foreign sector in most models is quite primitive. Even the most complicated models ignore many important aspects of tax policy. Finally, the data used to calibrate the models are often far from reliable.

6. PROBLEMS WITH USING OPTIMAL TAXATION
THEORY TO GUIDE POLICY

Although the theory of optimal taxation is very useful in identifying the parameters whose values are critical to resolving certain policy issues, there appears to be relatively little conclusive empirical information regarding these parameters. Moreover, as Slemrod notes (1990, p. 167), "many of the critical issues lie outside the usual domain of optimal taxation theory." He identifies simplification, tax shelters, and problems induced by inflation as issues figuring heavily in the debate on the 1986 act that lie outside the optimal taxation domain. This suggests that optimal taxation theory will not be successful in resolving critical tax issues to the satisfaction of most policymakers; this in turn deprives officials of the benefit of unassailable economic arguments that could be used to counter the pleadings of special interest groups.

Similarly, optimal taxation theory is useful in identifying important relationships between variables that are not intuitively obvious or indeed counterintuitive. Nevertheless, since these relationships are almost always theoretically ambiguous, the main effect of the theory may be to reinforce the belief that even simple theoretical models are often unable to provide unambiguous guidance to policymakers, thus again depriving officials of any principled economic defense against special pleading.

Finally the theory's prescriptions for differential taxation could lead to serious abuse in the real world. Tax differentials would not necessarily be based on theoretical considerations or on serious and unbiased econometric analysis. More likely they would reflect the political influence of special interest groups, which could employ "hired guns" to produce countless studies demonstrating that their industries qualified for preferential tax treatment.[93]

B. Political Considerations

Of course, as suggested above, tax policy may in many cases reflect political considerations rather than economic arguments. Economic models do not capture these effects, which are important in a democracy.

1. TAX SHELTERS AND THE PERCEPTION OF EQUITY

Beyond the obvious impact of special interest groups, public perceptions may play a critical role in the formulation of specific policies. For example, public disgust stimulated by evidence that many wealthy individuals and profitable corporations were paying no taxes was clearly an important factor explaining some of the 1969 reforms and the many antishelter provisions of the 1986 act.

Three episodes illustrate the power of evidence that the wealthy pay no taxes. First, in 1969, following the lead of the Treasury Department, the House Ways and Means Committee (1969) reported that 154 taxpayers with adjustable gross income in excess of $200,000 had paid no income tax in 1966.

Second, the depreciation allowances and investment tax credit enacted in 1981 were so generous that many corporations could not utilize them fully and took advantage of provisions for "safe-harbor leasing" to transfer the tax benefits to those who could use them—often tax shelter partnerships. This allowed many profitable corporations to eliminate or "zero-out" their tax liability and created a public outcry.[94] Safe-harbor leasing was repealed in 1982.

Third, the proliferation of tax shelters following the 1981 act allowed many wealthy taxpayers to avoid taxes and created what might be called the "cocktail party problem" ("I don't pay any taxes. What? You do?") In an effort to determine the importance of shelters, the Treasury Department (1985b) calculated 1983 tax liabilities of those with high "total positive income," or TPI (that is, income disregarding business and investment losses, as well as deductions for retirement savings and the exclusion of 60 percent of long-term capital gains). It reported that 11 percent of returns with TPI in excess of $1 million paid virtually no income tax (that is, less than 5 percent of TPI). Steuerle (1992, p. 91) has suggested that the primary difference between the 1980s and earlier efforts at tax reform was "concern over the widespread pattern of tax evasion, legal and otherwise, generated by the tax shelter industry."

As indicated earlier, tax shelters are built on arbitrage. One of the objectives of the 1986 act was to end tax shelters, by reducing opportunities for arbitrage and by other means. Slemrod (1990, p. 174) notes, "The problem of tax arbitrage suggests that the rate of tax on capital income is not as important as uniformity with respect to the financial structure, intermediation process, and the identity of the wealth owner.'' Many commentators, whose support of consumption-based direct taxes is apparently based on analysis of investments financed entirely with equity, fail to appreciate this point when they favor investment incentives in a world of debt finance.

2. THE TAX LEGISLATIVE PROCESS

A final important cause of the decline in the influence of academic analysis—and the increased vulnerability to the partisan interests Aaron identifies—may be the way tax legislation is enacted.[95] At one time, the tax legislative process was an orderly one. The House was jealous of its constitutional prerogative of initiating revenue legislation. When asked to do so, the administration would propose a well-considered package of proposals, often put together with the assistance of academic advisers. In extreme cases, the proposals would include draft legislation. Once legislation reached Capitol Hill, it would be considered in closed sessions by legislative committees headed by powerful chairmen who could control what changes would and would not be considered. The party system was also stronger, so that party discipline could be used to stave off maverick attacks on tax packages, as did the Senate rule limiting floor amendments. Under these conditions, it was much more likely that legislation would reflect the majority views of the tax policy community.

All this has changed. Legislation may now only nominally originate in the House. Administration proposals are put together in a much more haphazard manner, and therefore often lack coherence. Even worse, the way legislation is considered by Congress has greatly deteriorated. As Eustice (1989, p. 14) notes, "Congress often acts with intemperate speed on particular tax bills, while seldom, if ever, returning to the scene of the crime to repair the damage caused by hastily drafted legislation."

The chairmen of the tax-writing committees no longer hold the power they once did, and there is substantially less party discipline.[96] Well-financed lobbyists representing special interests are much more important than before. Because of ''good government'' laws, legislation is considered in open sessions, under the close scrutiny of lobbyists who are able to determine unambiguously whether their efforts to influence various members of Congress have been successful.[97]

The tax-writing committees now have much stronger staffs than previously, breaking the near monopoly of the Treasury Department. At times these staffs help advance the conventional wisdom of the day. But they can also serve partisan efforts of Republicans or Democrats or the particular interests of influential constituents.

Congress is not the only new locus of sophisticated staff work. Several of the large accounting firms have created groups made up of former staff members from the Treasury or Congress and devoted to the analysis of the effects (on revenues, resource allocation, and income distribution) of tax proposals. This breaking of the Treasury-Congress monopoly on data and economic modeling has provided lobbyists with potent weapons in fighting their causes.

As a result of these changes, maverick proposals and crazy laws are the order of the day. In such an environment, it is little wonder that the consensus view has become less important and the views of particular individuals and interest groups more important.[98]

Another political development deserves attention: the fact that in recent years Congress and the White House have been dominated by different political parties. In the early part of our historical review, both the executive and legislative branches were in the hands of the Democrats, the party most sympathetic to the conventional wisdom of the day. This may help explain the 1964 act and even the 1969 act; though the latter was passed in the early days of the Nixon administration, it was put together and gained unstoppable momentum during the Johnson administration. The lack of such a congruence helps explain why George Bush was unable to gain passage of a lower capital gains rate—a policy that probably is not favored by a majority of tax professionals.[99]

3. THE SPECIAL CASE OF THE 1986 ACT

In a book published only in 1985, Witte wrote (pp. 379, 380) about the prospects for "a major tax reform along standard comprehensive tax base lines": *"There is nothing, absolutely nothing in the history or politics of the income tax that indicates that any of these schemes have the slightest hope of being enacted in the forms proposed."* This echoed the title of a book published a decade earlier by Break and Pechman: *Tax Reform: The Impossible Dream?* (1975). Yet in 1986 "one headline in the *Washington Post* told the whole story: THE IMPOSSIBLE BECAME THE INEVITABLE and the dream of America's fair share tax plan became a reality" (Birnbaum and Murray, 1987, p. 285).

The propositions advanced thus far do not fully explain the Tax Reform Act of 1986. For further insights we must draw on other developments.[100] One was the appearance on the American scene of a popular president who despised high tax rates. It appears not to be much of an overstatement to say that, for Ronald Reagan, tax reform *was* rate reduction.

A second important contributory explanation of the nature of the 1986 act was the end of fiscal dividends. During much of the period from the end of World War II until the late 1970s, incipient surpluses were created by the decline in the fraction of national output devoted to defense spending, the inflation-induced reduction in the burden of interest on the national debt, the maturation of the social security system, and the increased tax revenues generated by the interaction of a progressive rate schedule and both real economic growth and inflation. These "fiscal dividends" made it possible for Congress to enact tax laws that lost revenue and made the system worse, rather than better. As Steuerle (1992, p. 80) says, "the availability of easy money was a source of funds for deform, as well as reform." The end of "easy money," which was reflected in the tax reform debate in the criterion of revenue neutrality, meant that the achievement of Reagan's goal of rate reduction required true tax reform.[101]

In the legislative arena the setting of the agenda can be crucial; this was clearly true in the case of the 1986 act. Interpretations of the agenda of tax reform by two participants in the process of formulating Treasury I are worth quoting in this regard. Charles McLure, the Deputy Assistant Secretary of the Treasury who had primary responsibility for the development of the tax reform proposals that became Treasury I, has said (1985, p. 32), "The overriding objective of Treasury I was to tax, as nearly as possible, *all real economic* income more uniformly and consistently and at lower rates." Eugene Steuerle, who was the economic coordinator of the Project for Fundamental Tax Reform, has written (1992, p. 103), "The goal of each module would be to discover *ways in which the current system departed from a comprehensive income tax*" (emphasis added). This agenda provides at least a partial explanation of why, in the words of Conlan et al. (1990, p. 243), "the initial Treasury I plan was an astonishingly pure expression of expert views. Although never formally proposed as legislation, it—rather than existing law—set the standard against which subsequent proposals were measured." This agenda, while never consciously accepted, was never fully abandoned.

PART IV

OPTIMAL TAXATION
AND EXTENSIONS

7

Optimal Taxation and Government Finance

In his *Theory of Public Finance* (1959), Musgrave shaped his subject, and our subject, in terms of the three objectives of policy: allocation, distribution, and stabilization. Economic government was analyzed in terms of three branches of the imaginary fiscal department, dealing with these three groups of objectives. More than two hundred pages of the book were devoted to the study of stabilization, which we would now call macroeconomic policy. In a much more recent text, Atkinson and Stiglitz's *Lectures on Public Economics* (1980), macroeconomic policy is excluded. Specialization has increased, and public economics, even public finance, is taken to refer to allocation and distribution. Stabilization is left to the macroeconomists and their textbooks. It is interesting, though, that the most recent major text on macroeconomics, the one by Blanchard and Fischer (1989), devotes a single, concluding chapter to monetary and fiscal policy issues.

This bifurcation of public finance is not mere subdivision and specialization as the organism expands. It reflects developments in economists' ways of thinking about different aspects of public finance that may not be easily reconciled. A key issue is the basis for judgment, the treatment of objectives in analyzing economic policy. As Musgrave asserted, "There is no simple set of principles, no uniform rule of normative behavior that may be applied to the conduct of public economy. Rather we are confronted with a number of separate, though interrelated, functions that require distinct solutions" (1959, p. 5). He went on to deal with a multiplicity of objectives, analyzing each aspect of public finance in terms of those objectives that seemed most apposite—merit wants, utilities, inflation, and the aggregate level of activity.

The purist welfare-economics approach to public economics cannot easily accept this pluralist method. That is one reason macroeconomics appears to play so little part in optimal tax theory, which nevertheless purports to be (potentially, one must say) a complete analysis of policy. It is interesting to see how Blanchard and Fischer deal with this issue of objectives: "Evaluating the full-fledged social welfare function, which is likely to depend on the utilities of current and prospective members of society, under alternative policies, rapidly becomes analytically untractable. Thus we often have to rely on a simpler objective function, a *macro welfare function,* defined directly over a few macroeconomic variables such as output, unemployment, inflation, or the current account" (Blanchard and Fischer, 1989, p. 568). They then proceed to discuss policy issues in terms of a quadratic loss function, whose arguments are the rate of inflation and the level of output. As has often been remarked, it is difficult to find a basis for the numerical specification of such a loss function (other than impressions of the relative importance politicians assign to inflation and aggregate activity); and the procedure ignores serious issues of measurement and principle: What price index matters? Is it the rate of inflation or fluctuations in the rate of inflation that matters? What kinds of unemployment matter, and how much? It is much easier to ask such questions than to establish a framework for analyzing them systematically.

There have been notable analyses of what may be regarded as macroeconomic questions, using an optimal tax framework—by Phelps, and by Lucas and Stokey, for example. The main macroeconomic aggregates can, after all, be seen as manifestations of general microeconomic equilibrium. It is customary to view the effects of unanticipated inflation as a tax on money; and unemployment can be modeled as the outcome of preferences for leisure, influenced by the tax / subsidy / social insurance system. But it better represents the current state of public finance to contrast general equilibrium optimal tax theory using a microeconomic welfare function, with analyses of fiscal and monetary policy based on some kind of tradeoff between macroeconomic variables that do not easily relate to microeconomic categories.

At a relatively crude level, it is interesting that inflation, or at least inflation at more than a few percentage points per year, is widely regarded (particularly by noneconomists) as highly undesirable, although it is difficult to make a precise case for this judgment. Presumably the social cost of inflation cannot be fully derived from the kind of welfare function that is used in microeconomic analyses of policy. At least there is little in the way of highly articulated models connecting microeconomic welfare functions and the costs of inflation (or unemployment, for that matter). The pain of disappointed anticipations and costly money is only part of what is supposed to constitute the undesirability of inflation (although there are still many quite long-term contracts denominated in money). It is believed, rather, that political effects—unreasoned dislike by people at large, or panic and painful reactions by public authorities—are in some sense costly, in ways that are difficult to compare with microeconomic costs and benefits but that may be substantial all the same.

These general remarks are not a preface to an integrated treatment of the issues of macroeconomic finance within a general theory of public finance. This chapter simply looks at two issues that arise in government budgetary decisions, and looks at them from the standpoint of optimal tax theory—a thoroughly microeconomic way of analyzing public policy. These are issues in macroeconomics that microeconomic techniques can fairly easily address. Neither involves the price level. Only the first touches on large-scale imbalances between supply and demand. The first topic is the central issue of budget balance: the choice of policy variables when there is uncertainty about the effects of taxes and the costs of expenditure programs. The second is the question of assessing the cost of funds raised through taxes, for public expenditure projects.

I. BUDGET BALANCE AND OPTIMAL TAXES

A fully articulated theory of optimal taxes in a general equilibrium model may be taken to be a theory of all policy, leaving no room for a macroeconomic theory of policy. In this part, I want to explore some of the limitations of that view. In brief, the argument is that setting optimal taxes and expenditure plans, according to the ideas of optimal tax theory, will, under certain circumstances, lead to disequilibrium. The relationship between the disequilibrium and actual outcomes and the way it is influenced by policies are not readily analyzed by the techniques of welfare economics. It may be best to analyze these policy issues in ways that are quite different from the welfare-function method, just as particular numerical methods (in mathematics, physics, and engineering) are not selected by finding the method that maximizes some well specified objective function.

First, we need a model—the standard general equilibrium model with taxes. We consider an economy in which all taxes and subsidies are proportional to the consumption or supply of various commodities, except that there is also a uniform head tax or subsidy. It is well known that such a tax system is incentive-compatible, since it requires for its operation only information that is generated by ordinary economic behavior. Though in reality there is scope for further refinement of the tax system (by having some nonlinear taxes, and by discriminating on the basis of unchangeable observable characteristics), these possibilities will be ignored in order to keep the structure of the model as simple as possible. Also for the sake of simplicity, assume there are no private-sector pure profits, at least in equilibrium. This amounts to supposing that there are no economies of scale—untrue of course, but some model other than perfect competition would be needed if we allowed for economies of scale—and that all possible sources of decreasing returns have become tradeable assets, and can be subject to taxation.

We shall consider policy issues for this economy, judging the policies by their impact on a measure of welfare, which is taken to be a sum of the utilities of individual households. The policy questions could be discussed with a more general or different form of welfare function. The additive form keeps the conditions for optimality somewhat simpler. Whether it is a reasonable form has been much discussed. On the whole, I find it so.

We shall be dealing with public expenditure, and must take account explicitly of the way that public expenditures affect utility. Specifically, let us treat all public expenditures as public goods, affecting (possibly) every household's utility. The following notation will be used: household h's utility is $v(q,b,z)$, where q = the vector of consumer prices, b = lump-sum income, and z = the vector of public goods. Household's net demands are $x^h(q,b,z)$. *Aggregate* production possibilities are described by an equation $F(y,z) = 0$ in terms of an aggregate net production vector y, available for private consumption, and z. There are constant returns to scale. This way of putting things leaves the production technology for public goods implicit, but simplifies the notation. All functions are assumed to be differentiable.

Provided that competitive conditions prevail, we can describe optimal policy for this economy fairly easily: this is the first task of optimal tax theory.[1] The general idea is that producers face prices $p = q - t$, where t is the vector of tax rates; and that choosing tax rates optimally is equivalent to choosing q optimally. We can therefore say that an equilibrium with optimal taxes satisfies

(7.1) $$q,b,z \max \sum_h v^h(q,b,z), \text{ subject to } F\left(\sum_h x^h x(q,b,z), z\right) = 0.$$

This statement does not involve producer prices or tax rates explicitly. In competitive equilibrium, producer prices will be proportional to the derivatives of F. Optimal q and b are determined only up to multiplication by a positive constant, and the same is true of p. There are therefore many equivalent systems of optimal tax rates t, corresponding to different consumer and producer price levels.

When we go on to obtain first-order conditions for optimal taxes and expenditure levels, we should allow for the possibility of corner solutions, with some consumer prices being zero, but that does not seem to be an important possibility in the standard model with complete markets. It will be assumed that the optimum is not a corner solution. One expects that, realistically, the optimal b will be positive. The variable b corresponds to the effect of income-tax deductible allowances in real-world tax systems.

The first-order conditions for optimality can be written[2]

(7.2a)
$$\frac{\sum_h v_b^h x_h}{\sum_h v_b^h} = \frac{p \cdot \sum_h x_q^h}{p \cdot \sum_h x_b^h},$$

where p are producer prices, proportional to the derivatives of F with respect to y; and

(7.2b)
$$\frac{\sum_h v_b^h m_h}{\sum_h v_b^h} = \frac{p \cdot \sum_h x_z^h + r}{p \cdot \sum_h x_b^h},$$

where m_h is the vector of marginal rates of substitution between the public goods and income for household h, and r is the vector of producer prices for public goods. The terms p and r can of course be thought of as marginal costs in terms of some arbitrary unit of account.

Conditions (7.2b) will be used intensively in Part II. Conditions (7.2a) are one form of the conditions for optimal taxation. They are, as written, highly implicit, and various other forms of the conditions have been given over the years—notably the covariance form proposed by Diamond (1975), which emphasizes the covariance between demands and marginal utilities, already apparent in the product form of the left-hand side of (7.2a).

The left-hand side of (7.2a) is naturally interpreted as a welfare-weighted average of demands. The right-hand side is equal to the derivative of the general lump-sum subsidy b with respect to tax rates, holding government net tax revenue (and producer prices) constant. To show this, one uses the consumer budget constraint, and introduces tax rates explicitly as $t = q - p$. One particularly appealing form for the conditions comes fairly directly from (7.2a),[3] using consumer budget constraints, which imply $q \cdot x_q^h = x_h$ and $q \cdot x_b^h = 1$, and can be written in a more summary notation:

$$(7.2c) \qquad t \cdot (\overline{x}_q + \overline{x}_b x^*) = x^* - \overline{x},$$

where x^* is the welfare-weighted average of demands and $\overline{x}$ is the unweighted average of demands. The matrix post-multiplying t is singular: and that is right, because optimal t is indeterminate. The taxes can be made determinate by selecting a particular commodity arbitrarily as untaxed numeraire. Despite the indeterminacy, (7.2c) gives the right flavor: the level of tax rates tends to be inversely proportional to certain modified demand elasticities, and directly proportional to the relative unimportance of the commodity to those who have high welfare weights (at the optimum).

These first-order conditions for q, b, and z at least provide us with a way of organizing our ideas about the various considerations that influence optimal policy levels, and can sometimes be made to tell us something about magnitudes. Part II will provide an illustration of the use of these conditions to deal with particular policy questions. Macroeconomic considerations are trivial in the model as set out. Government budget balance (over all time in an intertemporal version of the model) is implied by equality of supply and demand in all markets. This aspect becomes more interesting when we recognize that there is in reality uncertainty about demand and supply conditions, with policy variables set ex ante—that is, before the state of nature is fully known.[4] Uncertainty can be incorporated into the model by having x_h and F depend on the state of nature s, and assuming that there is uncertainty about s when policy variables are chosen (and announced).

In reality, of course, there is a time dimension to demand and supply, and policy variables can change over time, responding to changing information as well as predicted changes in the economy. However that may be, if the government calculates optimal policy variables from (7.1), or a generalization of it allowing for intertemporal developments, and then implements the calculated policy variables, the outcome will be random; and indeed there may not be an equilibrium, in which case the outcome is not described by the model as we have set it out. Randomness would not in itself seem to pose any great difficulties for an optimizing approach. Indeed, there is a literature on the desirability of tax smoothing that has the government budget surplus or deficit, and tax rates, vary over time in response to changing circumstances. Existence of equilibrium is more of a problem.

It is worth examining this more closely. What happens depends on whether or not there are elements in the tax system that are indexed to prices. Suppose first that the tax system is wholly unindexed. That is not at all realistic, of course. On the basis of an optimizing calculation, the government sets specific taxes t, so that consumer prices and producer prices must be related by $q = p + t$. The variables z and b are also set as specific numbers. Suppose these were calculated to be consistent with equilibrium when demand functions and production possibilities took some particular form. Now we ask whether, when these functions have changed, there is an equilibrium with markets clearing— that is, whether there are prices p such that

$$(7.3) \qquad \sum_h x^h(p + t,b,z) = y \text{ maximizes } p \cdot y, \text{ subject to } F(y,z) = 0.$$

There are here as many equations as there are commodities, and as many un-knowns as commodities (namely the producer prices), but that does not guaran-tee the existence of equilibrium. There is no general existence theorem available for a system of equations like this, describing an economy with given specific taxes. The simplest case, of a two-good model, shows that there can be a prob-lem with existence. For given tax rates, we find that public expenditure plans z can be too large for equilibrium to be possible.

Let us call the two commodities consumption and labor, and denote them by c and l. Production possibilities are $c + z = l$. Suppose the government tries to implement the optimum with a tax t on purchases of consumption. If there is to be equilibrium with H consumers, producer prices for the two goods must be equal (I take it that there must be some production). Let the prices be (p,p). The budget constraint for each consumer takes the form

$$(7.4) \qquad (p + t)c = py + b.$$

As p varies from very small to very large, the consumers' aggregate choice of (L,L) follows a curve connecting $(Hb/t,0)$, the choice when $p = 0$, to, say, (C',L'), the choice when the budget constraint is $c = y$, corresponding to

$p = \infty$ (see Figure 7.1). If z is large enough, the curve will not cut the production frontier.

In this example, we find that fluctuations in the underlying state of the economy could make the planned level of the public good so large as to be infeasible—not technically infeasible, but such that no possible prices could bring about an equilibrium with that level of the public good. In other states, there would be an equilibrium. The price level would have to vary to bring it about. In some states of nature, the required price changes would be large. Price stickiness is then likely to be important. A macroeconomist would recognize the importance of allowing for price stickiness in assessing the impact of policies. The point is that in some states of nature the impact of price stickiness may be considerable, and disequilibrium the right conclusion.

Even if fluctuations were sufficiently small that an equilibrium would always

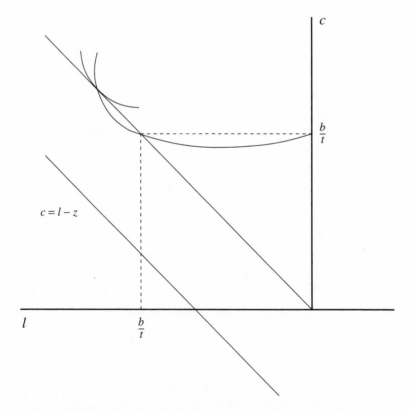

Figure 7.1. Choice of consumption and labor supply.

exist, the optimal taxation problem is incorrectly formulated if we take it to have the form (7.1) with the v^h replaced by their expected values. To get the correct formulation, denote the state of nature by s. The government should choose t, z, and b to maximize

$$(7.5) \qquad \sum_h \mathbf{E}[v^h(p(s) + t,b,z,s)],$$

$$\text{subject to } F\left(\sum_h x^h(p(s) + t,z,s),z,s\right) = 0 \text{ for all } s.$$

($\mathbf{E}$ is the expectation operator, averaged over states s.) The multiple resource constraints would be handled by state-dependent shadow prices. These can be interpreted as shadow prices on government revenue in different states of nature; but they do make the tax rules less transparent.

Formulation (7.3) has made an illegitimate assumption in supposing that equilibrium will always exist. Nonexistence is even more likely when taxes are indexed to prices. The value of labor–income tax allowances, for example, is proportional to wage rates, and sales taxes and property taxes are proportional to the corresponding prices. The extreme case is when all taxes are proportional to prices. In that case, we can write

$$(7.6) \qquad q = Tp, \, b = \beta p_0,$$

where T is a diagonal matrix of proportional tax rates, β is a scalar, and p is some appropriate price. Equilibrium requires that

$$(7.7) \qquad \sum_h x^h(Tp,\beta p_0,z) = y \text{ maximize } p \cdot y, \text{ subject to } F(y,z) = 0.$$

Now both consumer demands and producer supplies are homogeneous of degree 0 in producer prices p. With n commodities, there are in effect $n - 1$ degrees of freedom, and the Walras Law is not available to make sure that the nth market clears when all the others clear.

In this model, we can expect that, if one of the policy variables, say β, or the level of z, could vary ex post, equilibrium would be possible. An assumption of that kind was made in a paper by Diamond and myself (1974) on shadow pricing for public sector decisions in an economy where tax rates, not being optimal, were largely fixed: we assumed rather arbitrarily that government policy variables had just enough flexibility to ensure that equilibrium was always possible. That is making the economy march to the modeler's convenience. It is tempting to say that this nonequilibrium problem is a reason for not having fully indexed tax systems; but we have seen that even without indexing, there may be existence problems, though of a weaker kind.

An alternative view of the matter is that we have here found, lurking in the microeconomic optimal tax model, some aspects of the macroeconomic problems of adjustment and stabilization; and that welfare maximization is not a satisfactory way of analyzing the policy issues in this context. What we want are means of adjustment that will bring the economy rapidly to equilibrium, without serious side effects. It appears to be difficult to compare different budgetary adjustment processes on the basis of their impact on a welfare function like the one used above.

Compare what is at issue with the business of selecting a numerical algorithm to solve an equation. In choosing such an algorithm, we base our selection not on an optimizing analysis but on a number of desirable properties, such as rapid convergence, applicability to a wide range of functional forms, and so on. Although we want to make a rational choice, we are unable to formulate the choice problem as an optimization; we fall back on considering multiple objectives, and not measuring them very precisely either.

When policies are set ex ante, and disequilibrium ensues, the actual outcome is the result of adjustments whose welfare cost is hard to assess. There could be automatic stabilizers in the tax system, taking up some of the strain. The question that arises is whether automatic stabilizers would be better than leaving the system to adjust: in cases where disequilibrium cannot be removed without change in the policy parameters, one must assume that automatic stabilizers would be an improvement. Then we want to know which taxes and expenditures should be adjusted ex post, and in response to what observations. Properties like rapid convergence and robustness to variations in behavior and technology are, plausibly, more important than the effect on welfare in the steady-state outcome for a particular model. In effect, we want a kind of analysis that would be complementary to the microeconomic analysis used in most of the tax literature.

II. THE COST OF GOVERNMENT FINANCE

The second topic to be addressed is a more straightforward one. It is the question whether there is a good general argument against public expenditure on the grounds of the distortionary cost necessarily involved in financing the expenditures by tax revenues. Several notable papers have addressed the issue. Until recently, the literature suggested that the argument is valid on the whole, though not completely general.[5] It deserves further consideration. It is a question concerning the broad balance of public activity, to which nevertheless the techniques of microeconomics can be directly applied.

Pigou long ago claimed that the existence of distortionary taxes, which he recognized as essential and whose necessity is a central feature of optimal tax theory, was a reason for not "carrying public expenditures as far" as would be done if the simple rule equating marginal cost to marginal benefit of consumers were applied. This issue was carefully treated by Atkinson and Stern (1974), following an earlier examination of the question by Dasgupta and Stiglitz (1971), who had seen that Pigou's claim was not necessarily correct in an optimal tax framework. It is still generally held that the existence of distortion is a reason for imposing a premium on the cost of public funds when considering possible public expenditures, and therefore for lower levels of public expenditure than would have been optimal in a first-best world.[6] Indeed, Atkinson and Stern's analysis gave some support for the view, since they show that, in an interesting local sense, the optimal level of public goods is less in the second-best than in the first-best.[7]

Atkinson and Stern study a Ramsey economy, where consumers are identical and there is no lump-sum tax. The issue really needs to be considered in the context of a multiperson economy, with a uniform lump-sum subsidy or tax chosen optimally alongside commodity taxes. It is true that in actual economies, there is nothing that corresponds exactly to a uniform lump-sum subsidy, but personal tax allowances are not dissimilar in effect for those not on the lowest incomes, and welfare payments apply to many on the lowest incomes. The existence of these taxes and subsidies must considerably modify the intuitive Pigouvian argument, since it is not necessary to raise revenue for additional public expenditure by distortionary taxation: if desirable, it can be done by reducing the uniform lump-sum subsidy. Indeed, one can argue that the existence of a nondistortionary tax allows the cost of raising revenue to be assessed entirely by that yardstick, since on the margin all sources are equally good. I shall show how it is possible to interpret the conditions for optimal public good provision in that way. But that is not the whole story, for the structure of second-best taxation certainly does affect the value to people of public expenditures.

There are two ways of approaching the issue. One is to interpret the first-order conditions for optimality in such a way that one can see to what extent the rule for pricing public goods may differ from the first-best (Samuelson) rule for the optimal provision of public goods. When we do that, it will be seen that aggregating private marginal evaluations of the public good does not necessarily overstate the marginal value of the public good when the distortionary effects of financing are properly allowed for.[8] The other way of addressing the issue tries to compare the second-best optimal level of public good provision with the first-best. I shall state and prove a proposition somewhat analogous to the Atkinson-Stern proposition for the Ramsey economy. One implication is that, in the many-person case, the second-best optimal level of provision can easily be greater than the first-best level.

Recall the rule for optimal provision of a public good in a first-best world. Samuelson showed that it is a necessary condition for optimality that the marginal cost of the public good be equal to the sum of individuals' marginal rates of substitution of the public good for the numeraire. In terms of our notation, that means

$$(7.8) \qquad r = \sum_h m,$$

provided that the producer-price level is such that q (which must be proportional to p) is equal to p. Notice particularly that the formula needs the assumption that consumer and producer price levels are the same. Of course when there are no taxes, that is inevitable. But if there were perfectly neutral taxes, levied at the same proportional rate on every commodity (amounting to subsidies on goods sold by households), the real equilibrium would be the same, but condition (7.8) would no longer hold. We would recover (7.8) by insisting that public good prices and marginal rates of substitution should be measured in terms of the same numeraire.

When tax rates vary from commodity to commodity—as they must if revenue is to be raised—it is tempting to take as numeraire something that is not taxed; but there is no reason why that choice would make aggregate marginal rates of substitution equal to public good marginal costs. To see precisely what is required, we want to compare (7.8) with some form of the first-order condition for optimal public good provision in the second-best world. The condition stated above as (7.2b) is equivalent to

$$(7.9) \qquad (1 - t \cdot \bar{x}_b)Hm^* = -Ht \cdot \bar{x}_z + r,$$

where m^* is the welfare-weighted average marginal rate of substitution in the consumer population, H is the number of consumers, and, as before, $\bar{x}$ is average consumer demand, so that $t \cdot \bar{x}_b$ and $t \cdot \bar{x}_z$ are the effects of lump-sum income and public good expenditure on commodity tax revenue per head. It is not immediately clear how one can compare (7.8) and (7.9), though they can both be thought of as equations for r. For more convenient comparison, write (7.9) as

$$(7.10) \qquad r = Hm^* - Ht \cdot (\bar{x}_b m^* - \bar{x}_z).$$

The first term in (7.10) corresponds naturally to the aggregate of marginal rates of substitution in (7.8): it is the welfare-weighted aggregate. What can we say about the other term? Notice that (7.8) holds only when producer and consumer price levels are in a particular relation to each other (namely, equality), whereas (7.10) is valid independently of these price levels. This suggests that the second term in (7.10), involving tax rates which vary with the relative consumer and producer price levels, is there only to allow for a possible difference in price levels. Indeed, it could well be zero.

On the whole, one would expect the elements of the vector $\bar{x}_{bm}^* - \bar{x}_z$ to be positive. If, for example, demands are independent of the level of public good provision, $\bar{x}_z = 0$; if goods and services are normal, $\bar{x}_b$ is a positive vector; and if the public goods are desired, m^* is positive, too. Therefore, when taxes are primarily on consumer goods, and the elements of t are therefore mainly positive, the second term in (7.10) would make r less than welfare-weighted aggregate marginal rates of substitution. In effect, marginal rates of substitution would be higher because of the higher consumer price level, and we should adjust for that before comparing r with marginal costs in producer price terms. In the opposite case, with tax revenue primarily from taxation of factors (such as the income tax), the opposite conclusion would hold: in that case, most of the components of the vector t would be negative, corresponding to taxation of commodities supplied by households.

Indeed, one can say that (7.9) expresses the simple idea that, when we ask consumers (or guess on their behalf) what some public expenditure would be worth to them "in cash," we should adjust the answer to allow for consumer prices being higher (or lower) than producer prices because of taxes, and the price indexes should use as weights income-marginal expenditure shares. The other term on the right of the equation simply allows for direct tax revenue effects of changing public expenditure. It would not be right to make any further adjustment to allow for "distortion."

In a recent paper, Mervyn King (1986) derives an equation equivalent to (7.9), but analyzes it into parts, one of which he calls the Pigou term, which he claims reflects the distortion from raising extra revenue. I believe this is a misinterpretation. Since it is possible to write the conditions in the form (7.9), we can see that distortion really plays no part in assessing marginal benefits.

King does derive the price-level adjustment principle I have just described for the special case of a linear income tax system in an economy where the public good is neither a complement nor a substitute for leisure.

These first-order conditions do not tell the whole story. It is still possible that the real outcome of optimal policies when the government must use distortionary taxes to raise revenue will have lower levels of public good provision than would an economy with perfect lump-sum taxation. I do not know how to give anything like a full answer to that question, but it is possible to throw some light on it by looking for an approximate answer, in a certain sense.

To start with, we know that in an economy without inequality, in which all consumers are identical and in which a uniform lump-sum subsidy is available as a policy tool, the first-best and second-best optima coincide. It should be possible to find out how the optimal levels of public good provision vary as the degree of inequality varies, at least for small inequality. To keep matters reasonably simple, suppose that there is only one kind of public good. Denoting optimal public good provision in the first-best and second-best cases by z_1 and z_2 respectively, we let them depend upon a parameter α that describes the degree of underlying inequality in the economy, with $\alpha = 0$ meaning identical consumers. We have $z_1(0) = z_2(0)$. We try to calculate the derivatives with respect to α at $\alpha = 0$. If we find that $z_1'(0) > z_2'(0)$, it will follow that $z_1(\alpha) > z_2(\alpha)$, at least for all sufficiently small α.

This approach attempts to make the desired comparison between optima in distorted and undistorted economies for at least some economies—namely, those that have a small degree of underlying inequality—when we do not know how to make the comparison for all economies. It turns out that the result is ambiguous. That ambiguity is perhaps the most interesting feature of the result, for it shows that, contrary to the intuitions I have been discussing, there is no general presumption that the existence of distortions is a reason for adding a premium to the apparent cost of public expenditures.

This conclusion supports the argument that, on the margin, we may think of public expenditures as being financed by any particular tax—for example, the general lump-sum subsidy, which is not distortionary. Although it is optimal to have distortionary taxation, this is for distributional reasons, and does not imply that marginal increases in the public expenditure requirement would or should increase rather than decrease "aggregate distortion." But it turns out that, even in economies with small underlying inequality, the conditions for either sign of the comparison are not readily interpreted. It would seem that no simple intuitive principle is available.

A slight change of notation is convenient. Individuals in the model are indexed by a variable n and have indirect utility functions $v(q,b,z,n)$. The variable n is distributed in the population with mean μ and variance α. The variable v is taken to be strictly concave in b and z. The idea is that we can find approximations to the first-best and second-best levels of public expenditure z when α is small. To do this, we suppose that the distribution of individual characteristics n is parametrized by α. So long as the density of the distribution depends nicely on α, the precise distribution does not matter.

The remainder of this section is devoted to proving the following result:

Proposition.   Assume that the utility of a public good is additively separable from the utility of private goods. Then, for a small degree of underlying inequality, the optimal level of provision for the public good is greater under optimal second-best taxation than in the first-best, if

$$\frac{v_{bbn}}{v_{bn}} > \frac{1}{2}\frac{v_{bbb}}{v_{bb}}$$

In the opposite case, the second-best level is less. Note that the condition given is equivalent to requiring that $-v_{bb}/v_{bn}^2$ be a decreasing function of b for given n.

Given z, taxes are chosen optimally. That includes lump-sum taxation, whether uniform in the second-best case or perfectly discriminating in the first-best. Total utility resulting is $W(z,\alpha)$. The first-order condition for optimal z is then $W_z(z,\alpha) = 0$, from which we deduce

(7.11) $$W_{zz}(z,0)\frac{dz}{d\alpha}\bigg|_{\alpha=0} = -W_{z\alpha}(z,0).$$

This is true both for the first-best economy and for the second-best economy. $W(z,0)$—maximized utility when everyone has $n = \mu$—is the same in the first-best and the second-best, since discriminating lump-sum taxation is not required. Therefore, $W_{zz}(z,0)$ is the same in the two cases. By our concavity assumption, it is negative. Thus, (7.11) implies that $z_1 - z_2$, the difference between public good supply in the first-best and second-best cases, is an increasing function of α at $\alpha = 0$ if and only if $W_{z\alpha}$ is greater for the first-best economy than for the second-best. To prove the proposition, we shall calculate $W_{z\alpha}(z,0)$ for these two cases.

The strong simplifying assumption that utility is separable between public and private goods is needed to get a manageable expression for $W_{z\alpha}(z,0)$ in the first-best case. The analysis for the second-best case does not need the simplification. With additive separability, we can write average utility in the population as $\mathbf{E}v(q,b,n) + g(z)$, where $\mathbf{E}$ is the expectation operator for the random variable n, and where net demands per person are $\mathbf{E}x(q,b,n)$, independent of z. Since there is only one public good, we may as well take its producer price to be 1. We shall measure it per capita, so that the resource constraint can be written (locally) as $p\mathbf{E}x(q,b,n) + z = 0$.

Consider the optimum with uniform lump-sum taxation. We have

(7.12) $$W(z,\alpha) = \max_{q,b} \ [\mathbf{E}v(q,b,n) + g(z) \mid p \cdot \mathbf{E}x(q,b,n) + z = 0].$$

Introduce a Lagrange multiplier λ for the constraint, so that at the optimum

(7.13) $$\mathbf{E}v_b = \lambda p \cdot \mathbf{E}x_b$$

(we shall not need the first-order conditions for q), and

(7.14) $$W_z(z,\alpha) = g'(z) - \lambda,$$

λ, q, and b all depend on α and z. When $\alpha = 0$, $q = p$ and $b = -z$ are the values that maximize (7.12); for, with identical consumers, public spending can be financed optimally by a lump-sum tax. The variables q and b are determined only up to multiplication by a positive scalar. As α varies, choose particular maximizing $q = q(\alpha)$ and $b = b(\alpha)$ so that they are differentiable functions of α.

From (7.14), $W_{z\alpha}(z,0) = -\lambda_\alpha'(z,0)$. The derivative of λ can be calculated using (7.13). To do this, we need to obtain the derivatives of $\mathbf{E}v_b$ and $p \cdot \mathbf{E}x_b$ with respect to α, evaluated at $\alpha = 0$.

To calculate the derivatives, we can use the general proposition that, for any nice function f,

$$\mathbf{E}f(\alpha,n) \cong f(0,\mu) + f_\alpha(0,\mu)\alpha + \frac{1}{2}f_{nn}(0,\mu)\alpha,$$

and consequently

$$\frac{d}{d\alpha} \mathbf{E}f(\alpha,n)\bigg|_{\alpha=0} = f_\alpha(0,\mu) + \frac{1}{2}f_{nn}(0,\mu).$$

The derivative of $\mathbf{E}v_b$ at $\alpha = 0$ is calculated by setting $f(\alpha,n)$ equal to $v_b(q(\alpha),$

$b(\alpha),n$), and using the facts, already noted, that $q(0) = p$ and $b(0) = -z$. We immediately obtain

(7.15)
$$v_{bq}(p,-z,\mu) \cdot q'(0) + v_{bb}(p,-z,\mu)b'(0) + \frac{1}{2} v_{bnn}(p,-z,\mu).$$

Since $v_q = -v_b x$, we have $v_{bq} = -v_{bb}x - v_b x_b$, and the first two terms in (7.15) can be written

$$v_{bb}[b' - x \cdot q'] - v_b x_b \cdot q'.$$

This expression simplifies further, since we can show that $b' = x \cdot q'$. To do so, we use the fact, implied by the resource constraint, that $p \cdot \mathbf{E}x$ is constant as α varies. Differentiating, we have

$$p \cdot x_q(p,-z,\mu) \cdot q'(0) + p \cdot x_b(p,-z,\mu) \cdot b' + \frac{1}{2} p \cdot x_{nn}(p,-z,\mu) = 0.$$

The coefficient of q' is $-x$, the coefficient of b' is 1, and the last term is 0— all because of the budget constraint $p \cdot x(p,b,n) = b$. Consequently, $b' - x \cdot q' = 0$, as claimed. We then have the following expression for the desired derivative:

(7.16)
$$\left. \frac{d}{d\alpha} \mathbf{E}v_b \right|_{\alpha=0} = -v_b x_b \cdot q'(0) + \frac{1}{2} v_{bnn}.$$

We also need to calculate the derivative of $p \cdot \mathbf{E}x$ with respect to α. Using the same method, this time with $f(\alpha,n) = p \cdot x_b(q(\alpha),b(\alpha),n)$, the derivative is found to be

(7.17)
$$p \cdot x_{bq}(p,-z,\mu) \cdot q'(0) + p \cdot x_{bb}(p,-z,\mu)b'(0) + \frac{1}{2} p \cdot x_{bnn}(p,-z,\mu).$$

This expression simplifies, since the identity $p \cdot x_b(p,b,n) = 1$ yields, on differentiation, $p \cdot x_{bp} = -x_b, p \cdot x_{bb} = 0, p \cdot x_{bnn} = 0$. Therefore,

(7.18)
$$\left. \frac{d}{d\alpha} p \cdot \mathbf{E}x_b \right|_{\alpha=0} = -x_b \cdot q'(0).$$

We can now use (7.16) and (7.18) in differentiating equation (7.13):

(7.19)
$$\frac{1}{2} v_{bnn} - v_b x_b \cdot q' = -\lambda x_b \cdot q' + \lambda',$$

where we have used the fact that $p \cdot \mathbf{E}x_b = p \cdot x_b(p,-z,\mu) = 1$ at $\alpha = 0$. Note finally that $\lambda = v_b$, and we have the result

$$(7.20) \qquad W_{z\alpha}(z,0) = -\frac{1}{2} v_{bnn}(p,-z,\mu) \text{ for the second best.}$$

Surprisingly, the formula for this cross-derivative is more complicated for the first-best economy. In that case, lump-sum income is a function $b(n)$ of individual characteristics, and is chosen in such a way that marginal utility is the same for everyone. Define a function $B(n,\lambda)$ by the equation

$$(7.21) \qquad v_b(p,B(n,\lambda),n) = \lambda.$$

The resource constraint requires that

$$(7.22) \qquad \mathbf{E}B(n,\lambda) + z = 0.$$

For the same reason as before, we need to evaluate the derivative of λ with respect to α at $\alpha = 0$. Differentiating (7.22) yields

$$(7.23) \qquad B_\lambda(\mu,\lambda(0))\lambda'(0) + \frac{1}{2} B_{nn}(\mu,\lambda(0)) = 0.$$

From (7.21), $B_\lambda = 1/v_{bb}$; and $v_{bb}B_n + v_{bn} = 0$, so that $v_{bb}B_{nn} + v_{bbb}B_n^2 + 2v_{bbn}B_n + v_{bnn} = 0$. Multiplying (7.23) by v_{bb}, we obtain the desired result: for the first-best economy,

$$(7.24) \qquad W_{z\alpha}(z,0) = -\frac{1}{2} v_{bnn}(p,-z,\mu) - v_{bbn}B_n - \frac{1}{2} v_{bbb}B_n^2,$$

where $B_n = -v_{bn}/v_{bb}$. Comparing (7.20) and (7.24), and using (7.11), we deduce that optimal z is larger in the second-best case if

$$v_{bbn}B_n + \frac{1}{2} v_{bbb}B_n^2 > 0.$$

Rewriting this condition somewhat, dividing by the negative number $B_n^2 v_{bb}$, leads to the condition given in the proposition. Optimal public good provision is greater in the second-best case than in the first-best if

$$(7.25) \qquad \frac{v_{bbn}}{v_{bn}} > \frac{1}{2} \frac{v_{bbb}}{v_{bb}}.$$

We have assumed that $v_{bb} < 0$. Notice that B_n is the rate of increase of lump-sum income in a first-best equilibrium. If n were the individual wage rate, and labor supply were normal, B would be negative—that is, it is reasonable to assume that $v_{bn} < 0$. The two third derivatives in (7.25) are not readily signed, though most utility functions used satisfy $v_{bbb} > 0$. I conclude that the comparison is ambiguous.

Condition (7.25) can be expressed in terms of a familiar object, the coefficient of absolute inequality aversion ("inequality" seems a better qualifier than "risk" in this context), $A = -(v_{bb}/v_b)$. The derivatives of A with respect to b and n can be written

$$A_b = A^2 + A \frac{v_{bbb}}{v_{bb}}, \quad A_n = -\frac{v_{bn}}{v_b}\left[A + \frac{v_{bbn}}{v_{bn}}\right].$$

We may reasonably expect that A is a decreasing function of both n and b. As noted already, $v_{bn} < 0$. Making these assumptions, straightforward substitutions transform (7.25) into

(7.26) $2 \dfrac{v_b}{v_{bn}} A_n + A + \dfrac{A_b}{A} < 0.$

The first two terms are positive, the third negative. Optimal public expenditure is higher in the second-best case if $-A_b/A$ is relatively large: for example, if A is small.

It is disappointing, but not surprising, that one should not be able to find a really simple, easily checked criterion for lower public expenditure in a second-best economy. The main lesson of the analysis is that we cannot easily tell which way the balance goes. The useful result, though more superficial, is the first-order condition for optimality of public good provision. Will someone now estimate relative consumer and producer price levels, using the income-marginal expenditure weights, and (a more challenging problem) the effect of public expenditures on tax revenues?

8

Integrating Allocation and Stabilization Budgets

The approach to integrating stabilization and allocation budgets that is used in this chapter arises directly from Musgrave's classic *Theory of Public Finance* (1959a). The *Theory* begins with the now familiar conceptualization of government activities which postulates separate budgets for the Allocation, Distribution, and Stabilization branches. As Musgrave makes clear, this division is useful because it organizes the subject conceptually, not because it is generally true that decisions in each of these areas can be simply decentralized. In applying the conceptualization, Musgrave proceeds, in part, on the basis that in analyzing one branch, one can assume that the other branches are successful in carrying out their tasks. This division not only provided a good way to think clearly about individual policies; it supplied a framework for building the then relatively new second-best approach in a consistent manner. My own work on optimal taxation grew directly out of the general equilibrium formulation in the *Theory*, contributing to the integration of the Allocation and Distribution branches. In this chapter, I address the way in which development of the micro foundations of macro can lead to a similar integration of the Stabilization and Allocation branches. I present pieces and parts of this integration, partly in terms of simple models to illustrate the possibility of sustained formal development. I first focus on real models and then extend the analysis to consider inflation.

As Break and Pechman wrote in their influential book (1975), ''Regardless of whether one tends to favor passive neutrality or active optimization as the proper goal of a good tax system, the nature and size of its effects on the allocation of resources are important aspects of its performance'' (p. 8). This chapter builds on the conceptions of Musgrave, Break, and Pechman in pointing to promising directions for research.

I. LOOKING BACK: OPTIMAL TAXATION

From the perspective underlying separable budgets, there is no tradeoff between equity and efficiency; the government has sufficient powers to set the distribution of income as desired, without distorting any private decisions. This conclusion is obviously wrong. The relevant problem is to formulate a model which generates insights into how the balance between equity and efficiency should be struck. Several ingredients are required. Either as an assumption or as an implication of more basic assumptions, it should be impossible in the model to change the income distribution without affecting marginal decisions. The model needs to be a general equilibrium model. It needs to be analytically tractable. At the outset, the model should have many of the properties of familiar models, so that one can appreciate the implications of new assumptions.

In the 1960s, the natural way to fit these criteria was to preserve the competitive general equilibrium model, but to drop the ability to set lump-sum taxes and transfers separately person by person. A poll tax (uniform lump-sum tax) is obviously feasible. But while a poll tax destroys the link between the need for government revenue and the efficiency of private markets, it does not eliminate the necessity of an equity-efficiency tradeoff. To operate on income distribution, the poll tax, presumably in the form of a poll subsidy, needs to be combined with distorting taxes to finance the subsidy. (One can imagine models, I admit, where the income distribution question is primarily related to certain goods—for example, medical services—so that one uses a poll tax to subsidize medical care.) This combination of assumptions—competitive general equilibrium, no individual lump-sum taxes, poll taxes, and distorting taxes, whether linear or nonlinear—immediately leads to a model in which it is impossible to get whatever equity and efficiency combination one wants and in which, with a social welfare function added, the efficiency-equity tradeoff can be optimized.[1]

In this tradeoff, the cost of distorting markets is compared with the gain from redistributing income.[2] In the 1960s, the latter appeared straightforward, or at least familiar, whereas the former did not. The former required evaluating the distortionary impact of revenue raising in terms that could be compared with marginal redistribution gains. The simplest model for describing the cost of revenue generation by distorting taxation was (and is) a one-consumer model.

And so the route to understanding the equity-efficiency tradeoff was through the minimization of distortion in a one-consumer economy. This route—or detour, if you will—had unfortunate implications for its reception; it was attacked for ignoring income distribution. Yet the route seemed to me to be the best way (and at the time seemed to be the only way) to make sense of the limits on income redistribution. The purpose of this historical discourse is not to defend past work, but to emphasize the parallelism in the discussion of stabilization that follows.

II. LOOKING AHEAD: OPTIMAL STABILIZATION

To pursue the analogy for stabilization of the optimal taxation approach to distribution, let us start from the same obvious point. Just as it is impossible to redistribute income perfectly, it is impossible to stabilize an economy perfectly. No one knows how to do it. Perhaps this is due to inadequate tools. Perhaps, however, it is only a failure of research to date. It was easy to see which assumption needed dropping from competitive general equilibrium theory to have an interesting second-best income distribution problem; it seems hard to find a similar strategy for stabilization. We want a stabilization problem that represents a tradeoff, for that is what we actually confront.[3] Macroeconomists pose the tradeoff between unemployment and inflation.[4] I would like to pose the tradeoff between efficiency and stabilization, whatever that may mean. I have in mind three different types of circumstances. One is a prolonged period of low output, the second is a large identifiable shock, and the third is demand uncertainty. In other words, I will consider three different public finance questions that arise in these three different contexts. These different contexts make clear that our notion of stabilization covers a wide variety of problems.

It is a natural research strategy to proceed in two steps—to ask first whether a question can be posed in a totally real model, and then to present a model with nominal values, to include the important issues that surround inflation. This may seem awkward, but it differs little from approaching income distribution via a one-consumer model. I propose to consider some examples of what one might mean by incorporating stabilization and efficiency in a single real model (ignoring income distribution). Then I will consider inflation.

A. Prolonged Low Output

Let's begin with an intriguing idea presented by Robert Haveman and John Krutilla (1967).[5] Consider a government investment which will use, directly and indirectly, quantities of labor spread over time. Some of the labor will be drawn from other employment; some from unemployment. The mix of sources will vary with the aggregate unemployment rate (and the location and choice of project). The correct shadow value of labor for cost-benefit analysis should reflect this mix of sources, and so should vary with the (forecasted) state of the economy as the project is built. Haveman and Krutilla provided some sample calculations based on alternative assumptions of the relation of the mix of sources to the unemployment rate and the relative shadow value of an unemployed worker. This paper has always seemed to me to point in the right direction. Of course, it is only a piece of an integrated model. It says that if one is stabilizing an economy imperfectly, then there are implications for allocation rules. Why or how the economy is imperfectly stabilized or how public production affects the use of other stabilization tools is not modeled. As a corollary, the shadow values of employed and unemployed labor are not generated internally.

I do not know of any model which will simultaneously explain why employment rates remain at low levels for extended periods of time either nationally or locally (the United States in the 1930s, Europe in the 1980s) and which will generate the needed shadow values and response derivatives. As a suggestion of how part of the model can be crafted, consider an extension of my work on search equilibrium (1982a).[6] Since this model is a partial equilibrium steady-state model of the labor market, I am not considering the use of public projects to counter the typical business cycle. Rather, I am considering how the average level of unemployment should affect project evaluation, and how project evaluation might be evaluated for extended periods of high unemployment. The supplies of workers and jobs are taken as given. I do not model the animal spirits or forecasts that lead to one level of job creation rather than another. A steady-state search model has an equilibrium unemployment rate which will respond to the creation of government jobs.[7] Thus, the optimal response of public good production (in public jobs) to the level of private job creation (taken as given, possibly after optimal stabilization) can be analyzed. It would be straightforward to replace the given level of private jobs by a given relationship between the level of private jobs and the level of public jobs. Then one would analyze the optimal response of public good production to shifts in this relationship. If one identifies public jobs with public goods, the allocation of jobs between public and private sectors includes an efficiency question. There is no significance in the assumption that public jobs produce public goods; a similar analysis could be done if public sector jobs produced a different private good or were simply less efficient ways to produce the same output.

Let us denote the supply of labor by L, the number of private and public jobs by K and K^*, and the number of filled jobs by E and E^*. When filled, a private job generates a flow of y units of private consumption good. When filled, a public job generates a flow of y^* units of public good. For convenience, we will ignore income distribution and assume that consumption is equalized per capita. We will also assume additivity in the instantaneous utility function and the same level of disutility whether working or searching, giving a flow of utility per person of $u(yE/L) + u^*(y^*E^*)$. Instantaneous utility is discounted at the rate r. Filled jobs exogenously break up with a separation rate s (viewed as a Poisson parameter). A matching technology generates $M(E,E^*,L,K,K^*)$ and $M^*(E,E^*,L,K,K^*)$ newly filled public and private jobs.[8] This labor market will have a steady-state equilibrium which satisfies

$$(8.1) \qquad sE = M(E,E^*,L,K,K^*)$$
$$sE^* = M^*(E,E^*,L,K,K^*).$$

Thus, social welfare of consumption can be written as:

$$(8.2) \qquad W(E,E^*,L,K,K^*) = \int_0^\infty e^{-rt}[u(yE(t)/L) + u^*(y^*E^*(t))]dt$$
$$dE(t)/dt = -sE(t) + M(E(t),E^*(t),L,K,K^*)$$
$$dE^*(t)/dt = -sE^*(t) + M^*(E(t),E^*(t),L,K,K^*)$$
$$E(0) = E$$
$$E^*(0) = E^*.$$

That is, we assume that the initial position of the economy has the steady-state employment levels.

Let us now assume that the investment to create a public job costs C in additive disutility.[9] Thus, the first-order condition for the optimal provision of public goods balances this cost C against the present discounted value of the induced change in public and private consumption. We are interested in how this balance varies with K. Calculating the derivative of the social welfare of consumption with respect to the creation of another public sector job starting at a steady state, we have the first-order condition (see Diamond, 1980):

$$(8.3) \qquad C = \partial W/\partial K^*$$
$$= r^{-1}(u'y/L, u^{*\prime}y^*)[(r + s)\mathbf{I} - \partial \mathbf{M}]^{-1}(\partial M/\partial K^*, \partial M^*/\partial K^*)',$$

where $\mathbf{I}$ is the identity matrix and $\partial \mathbf{M}$ is the matrix of derivatives of M and M^* with respect to E and E^*. To see how the optimal number of public jobs varies with the number of private jobs, we calculate (8.3). In doing this, we must treat E and E^* as endogenous variables given by (8.1).

The shape of the optimal tradeoff will depend on both the curvature in the utility functions and the nature of the matching functions. If utility functions were linear with equal coefficients on both types of employment and if jobs entered symmetrically in producing employment, then the optimal tradeoff between public and private jobs would be one-for-one, since welfare could be written in terms of their sum. For example, this would be the case if job matches were allocated in proportion to vacancies and vacancies entered symmetrically in producing matches:

(8.4) $$M = [(K - E)/(K + K^* - E - E^*)]f(E + E^*,L,K + K^*)$$
$$M^* = [(K^* - E^*)/(K + K^* - E - E^*)]f(E + E^*,L,K + K^*),$$

where f is an aggregate matching function.

In contrast with this case, let us consider logarithmic utility functions and also a matching function reflecting a preference of workers for private jobs. The latter introduces an asymmetry in matching. Consider the process of recruiting workers as an urn-ball process. There will be a distribution across workers of the number of jobs about which they have heard. Assume that a worker takes a public job only if there is not a private job he or she can get.[10] Thus, public jobs do not interfere directly with the filling of private jobs, although they interfere indirectly by decreasing the number of unemployed. (We will ignore quits directly from one job to another.) With this approach, the matching functions are:

(8.5) $$M = b(L - E - E^*)\{1 - \exp[-a(K - E)/b(L - E - E^*)]\}$$
$$M^* = b(L - E - E^*)\exp[-a(K - E)/b(L - E - E^*)]$$
$$\{1 - \exp[-a(K^* - E^*)/b(L - E - E^*)]\}.$$

Thus, the number of hirings for private jobs equals the fraction of workers ready to respond to a job offer who receive at least one private offer. This number is independent of the number of public jobs for a given level of unemployment. The number of hirings for public jobs equals the number of workers ready to respond who receive an offer of a public job and no offer of a private job.

Figure 8.1 shows the optimal number of public jobs as a function of the number of private jobs, as in equation (8.3), for two economies differing only in matching function.[11] The points marked * are the full optima assuming both jobs have the same costs, obtained by solving the first-order conditions for private and public jobs simultaneously. The location of the full optimum and the slope of the tradeoff both depend on the matching function, which affects the levels of private and public goods outputs as well as the extent to which more public good output comes at the expense of private good output. The upward

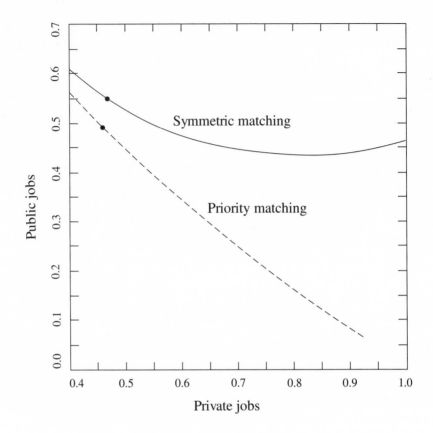

Figure 8.1. Optimal job creation.

slope of part of the locus shows some of the additional complexity that comes from reconciling both allocation and stabilization objectives; we are concerned with both the aggregate number of jobs and their division between sectors. Of course, an infinite horizon steady-state model is only a crude approximation to the richer model ultimately desired, but it gives the flavor of an optimal response to periods of prolonged low private demand for labor.

B. Labor Demand Shifts

In the model sketched above, there were too few or too many private jobs in total. No distinction was made among private jobs and no mechanism was described for influencing the number of jobs. Turning to reallocation, let us consider a circumstance in which a large increase or decrease in the value of output of some sector occurs. Think of peace breaking out. A large movement of labor between sectors begins. Such movements can come when job creation either leads or lags behind job destruction. Assume that job destruction comes first. The process of moving labor between sectors is rife with externalities. Search externalities are different in the two sectors. There is the desire to offset the bad income distribution impact of the shock (see, for example, Diamond, 1982b). Stickiness in wages will affect the rates of both job destruction and job creation. There is the degree of foresight in job creation in the expanding sector. These externalities leave lots of room for policies aimed at specific industries and workers, and for general policies which are not based on necessarily knowing the source of labor for a major expanding sector or the destination of labor from a major shrinking sector. In other words, there is likely to be a role for aggregate policies in improving (presumably speeding) the adjustment to a recognized shock. For full modeling, private adaptation to the existence of a policy of responding to recognized shocks would be included.

C. Built-In Stabilizers

If perfect stabilization is impossible, one is led to ask about the natural response of the economy to shocks. In this context, the theory of built-in stabilizers plays a central role. In his *Theory,* Musgrave models built-in stabilizers. Greater marginal tax rates lower the multiplier, making the economy less sensitive to some shocks. But greater marginal tax rates have greater distortions, lowering potential welfare. Thus, there is a tradeoff that could be modeled consistently. Built-in stabilizers have two properties. First, their effects occur quickly. Second, they interfere with the circular flow which relates demand to production. The model I use to present such a tradeoff has a somewhat odd structure, being made of parts readily available in the literature; but my purpose is to raise researchable questions, not answer them. In particular, the circular flow is missing. The model in Section A on prolonged low output focused on lags in realizing allocation possibilities as the central aspect of the response to shocks. In this section, the focus is on commitments to particular prices which prevent some reallocations after certain shocks. The question we shall examine is whether the failure of markets to clear results in a higher optimal tax rate than does market clearance.

In order to consider built-in stabilization as a response to short-run shocks, uncertainty must be explicitly considered in the model. A literature already exists on distorting taxation to provide insurance, paralleling the literature on optimal coinsurance. The new element raised is the presence of macro failures: to what extent does the failure of markets to clear change the theory of optimal coinsurance?[12] In order to have nonclearing markets, I will use a model of fixed (real) prices, although I believe this is only part of the story of macro difficulties.[13] In large part, I am building on modeling ideas presented by Lucas (1989), who assumes fixed nominal prices, and also on Salop and Stiglitz (1977), who use a two-price distribution.

When built-in stabilizers are used, the government deficit is a random variable. Thus, the optimal use of built-in stabilizers must reflect a shadow value on the deficit carried forward in time. Built-in stabilization will make sense only if current revenues have a greater variation in shadow value than the deficit carried forward; otherwise it would not be optimal to have the deficit fluctuate in the way I will model it. I will duck the problem of intertemporal modeling by assuming that the government can transfer resources between two states of nature.[14] This should yield similar results. I will ignore possible restrictions on the complexity of built-in stabilization rules. Built-in stabilization is assumed to occur more quickly than the rate at which prices are changed, with the need for incentives limiting the scope for stabilization. Serious development of this approach would need to model the available tax and transfer rules. Implicit in this model is the idea that changed command over resources is important, something not fully achievable by open-market operations, which are exchanges of equal values.

There is a continuum of identical potential suppliers of good x. Each can provide one unit at a utility cost c. The good will be traded for p units of good y. The utility of suppliers is $v(p) - c$. But the production decision must be taken before the state of nature is known. We assume an infinitely elastic supply of good x. Therefore, the expected value of the utility of suppliers will be a constant, which we normalize to zero. We can then ignore these suppliers in welfare calculations. It may be helpful to interpret these agents as workers and to interpret p as a real wage.

There is a continuum of suppliers of good y of measure one. There are two states of nature. If a supplier exerts no effort, output of that supplier is y in both states of nature. If a supplier exerts effort that costs e, output of that supplier equals y with probability π and equals y' with probability π', with $y < y'$. The occurrence of high output is perfectly correlated among suppliers exerting effort. It is assumed that it is socially worthwhile to induce effort by all suppliers; no mixed behavior outcomes are considered. This will be the incentive constraint for the government. Built-in stabilizers are assumed to work so quickly that the government can provide these suppliers with payments z and z' of good y in the two states. This is done subject to the government resource constraint

(8.6) $\pi z + \pi' z' = k,$

for some constant k, possibly negative. These payments are made conditional only on individual supply, although these are perfectly correlated. No use is made of this perfect correlation to improve incentives. This restriction is made to avoid modeling idiosyncratic uncertainty that would prevent unrealistic use of this correlation. If a single supplier deviates from supplying effort, it is assumed that the transfer z occurs in the good state rather than z'. Thus, the level of z must be low enough relative to z' for suppliers to make the effort e. Having $z > z'$ corresponds to a positive marginal tax rate, while $y + z < y' + z'$ corresponds to a marginal tax rate less than one.

Suppliers of good y care only about the consumption of x, $u(x)$, and the effort to permit the good state to occur. Since the decision to supply x is taken before the state is realized, consumption of good x would not vary across states if the market allowing trade between x and y cleared. Thus, the optimal choice of z and z' would solve the problem:

(8.7)   Max $u(x)$
$$\text{s.t. } \pi v[(y + z)/x] + \pi' v[(y' + z')/x] = c$$
$$\pi z + \pi' z' = k$$
$$\pi' u(x) - \pi' u[x(y + z)/(y' + z')] \geq e.$$

The first constraint is that suppliers are willing to provide good x, which trades, in aggregate, for $y + z$ units of good y in the bad state and $y' + z'$ units of good y in the good state. The second constraint is the government budget constraint across states. The third constraint is that suppliers of good y provide effort. This makes it clear that total income must be sufficiently lower in the bad state to induce effort. It is useful to define the prices that clear the markets:

(8.8) $p^* x = y + z$
$$p^{*'} x = y' + z'.$$

The cost of providing good x comes from both the labor cost c and the risk aversion of suppliers. If there were no incentive problem for the suppliers of good y, public supply could be chosen to eliminate uncertainty for the suppliers of good x. That is, if we ignore the incentive constraint, the optimal solution has $y + z$ equal to $y' + z'$.

We now examine the same problem under the assumption that the suppliers of good x must place a price on the good before realization of the state of nature. That is, we can think of workers committing themselves to particular real wages. It is assumed that demand is directed to the lowest-priced goods until all demand is used up. (It would be appropriate to explore the more realistic case where some purchases are made at high prices even though low-priced goods are available.) Thus, suppliers of the quantity x will price their goods at p and sell in both states. Suppliers of the quantity x' will price at p' and sell only in the good state. In the labor market interpretation, the unemployment rate in the bad state is $x'/(x + x')$. Equality of purchases and sales now becomes

$$(8.9) \qquad px = y + z$$
$$px + p'x' = y' + z'.$$

Thus, all of income is spent in both states. In order to induce these supplies of good x, the incentive must be adequate for suppliers setting both prices. We then have the supply constraints

$$(8.10) \qquad v[(y + z)/x] = c$$
$$\pi'v[(y' + z' - y - z)/x'] = c.$$

That is, the low-priced goods are sold in both states at price p. The high-priced goods are sold only in the good state at price p'. The high price is enough above the low price to cover the loss from making no sale in the bad state. This structure would seem more natural if there were idiosyncratic shocks that supported the use of two different pricing strategies, as well as the aggregate shocks being modeled.

It remains to describe the expected utility of and incentives for the y suppliers. In order to do this, we need to determine which consumers get the low-priced good in the good state. For simplicity, let us assume that everyone pays the average price. Expected utility is now

$$(8.11) \qquad \pi u(x) + \pi'u(x + x').$$

The incentive constraint is

$$(8.12) \qquad \pi'u(x + x') - \pi'u[(x + x')(y + z)/(y' + z')] = e.$$

Optimal stabilization is now the maximization of (8.11) subject to (8.6), (8.10), and (8.12). For comparison with (8.7), we can state the problem:

(8.13)   Max $\pi u(x) + \pi' u(x + x')$

$$\text{s.t. } v[(y + z)/x] = c$$
$$\pi' v[(y' + z' - y - z)/x'] = c$$
$$\pi z + \pi' z' = k$$
$$\pi' u(x + x') - \pi' u[(x + x')(y + z)/(y' + z')] \geq e.$$

To see the difference between these two problems, consider the case where both u and v are logarithms. The optimal z is simply the intersection of the government resource constraint and the incentive constraint for suppliers of good y. Thus, in both cases we have

(8.14) $e/\pi' = \ln[(y' + z')/(y + z)] = \ln[(y' + (k - \pi z)/\pi')/(y + z)].$

If it weren't for the incentive constraint, the government would increase z along the resource constraint. Even though government choice is the same in the two problems, the value of loosening the constraint is different in the two cases. With flexible prices, utility is $\ln(x)$ and the derivative of utility with respect to z along the resource constraint is

(8.15) $\Delta = \pi[1/(y + z) - 1/(y' + z')].$

With fixed prices, the derivative of expected utility is

(8.16) $\Delta' = \{\pi + \pi'[x/(x + x')]\}/(y + z)$
$$- (\pi + \pi')[x'/(x + x')]/(y' + z' - y - z)\}$$
$$= \Delta + \pi/(y' + z') + \pi'[x/(x + x')]/(y + z)$$
$$- (\pi + \pi')[x'/(x + x')]/(y' + z' - y - z)$$
$$= \Delta + \pi/(px + p'x') + \pi'/[p(x + x')]$$
$$- (\pi + \pi')/[p'(x + x')]$$
$$> \Delta.$$

Thus, while the discrete setup of this model resulted in the same government behavior with and without market clearance, the difference in the welfare costs of the incentive constraints in the two problems suggests that in a smoother model, one will have more insurance without market clearance. That is, the need for built-in stabilization will raise the optimal tax rate.

III. INFLATION

The models above were formulated in real terms. There was no allowance for the fact that transactions and contracts are in monetary units. Yet the Stabilization Branch needs to address significant average price level changes, as well as unemployment. To the extent that one is willing to address this problem in a market-clearing model, the analysis is less difficult. To incorporate the complexity of lack of market clearance along with the problems of average price changes is more difficult. It is common in monetary theory to think about the price level which clears markets rather than think about individual price setting. It is also common to ignore the complexity that comes from shifting relative prices. Were I to survey the existing literature involving interaction between the Stabilization and Allocation branches, I would probably start with the use of the inflation tax along with other distorting taxes as part of the optimal revenue-raising structure (Phelps, 1972, 1973; Woodford, 1990), although one might not think of the choice of a steady inflation rate as a stabilization issue. But I want to focus on situations where prices are set by individuals, not fictitious auctioneers. Let us look at two crucial points. One arises from recognizing that inflation comes from aggregating many price changes. The second comes from interactions between inflation rates and market power.

A. Price Adjustment Costs

I find it unlikely that the resource costs of changing prices play a significant role in the slow, erratic way in which prices respond to economic conditions. Nevertheless, as an example of the sort of second-best analysis I have in mind, consider a two-good model where the cost of changing prices is the only reason for not achieving the Walrasian optimum. The model is in continuous time. There is a constant labor supply of one which can be continuously and costlessly reallocated between production of two nondurable goods. There is an additive disutility, z_i, whenever consumer price i is changed. Prices are set by a central planner. There is a representative consumer. We denote the vector of consumer prices in money terms by $\mathbf{q}$ and the vector of producer prices in labor units by $\mathbf{p}$. Wages are paid in money, which is then spent to purchase consumer goods. Thus instantaneous utility from consumption can be written as $v[\mathbf{q}(t),I(t)]$. The demand vector, $\mathbf{x}[\mathbf{q}(t),I(t)]$, must satisfy the production constraint

$$(8.17) \qquad \mathbf{p}(t)\mathbf{x}[\mathbf{q}(t),I(t)] = 1.$$

Assume that the exogenous values $\mathbf{p}_i(t)$ are exponential with different rates. The government wants to set prices and income to maximize the discounted integral of v less the discounted sum of costs of price changes.

Since only relative prices of consumer goods matter, the government need not change both prices; it can change just the one with the lower cost of adjustment. Thus, in a two-good model the optimal (average) inflation rate might be positive or negative, but, except at the knife edge of equal adjustment costs, it cannot be zero.[15] This extreme finding goes away with more goods, but zero has no special claim for presumed optimality. Obviously, optimization of both prices and incomes still leaves a second-best problem.

B. Market Power

The discussion above focused on the cost of adapting to change, assuming a socially optimal adaptation. In addition to socially optimal adaptation, we need to examine nonoptimal adjustments to different inflation rates. In part, these adjustments come from the extent to which people do not perceive or understand the differential impact of different inflation rates.[16] I will say nothing about this, since I know no evidence about the extent to which people fail to understand the pricing process in the economy, and I know little theory to substitute for direct evidence. A second element is the way in which different inflation rates interact with market power—that is, the extent to which the deviation of the market outcome from some optimum varies with the average rate of inflation. For example, I have been told by Israeli friends that at sufficient inflation rates it becomes impossible to comparison shop, and this cuts competition. It is natural to capture this idea in a search model. Search models with inflation have been constructed by Benabou (1988, 1992), Casella and Feinstein (1990), and Diamond (1993).

In the third model, when firms price on a take-it-or-leave-it basis and it is costly to seek alternatives, some degree of market power can be exercised by firms. The presence of inflation and sticky prices will affect the degree of market power in equilibrium. Thus, as with taxes, the interaction between inflation and market power is important for evaluating different inflation rates. In the absence of inflation, market power extracts all consumer surplus from shoppers, whereas free entry implies a lack of profit for firms. Thus, inflation, which cuts into market power by having in place previously priced (but not yet sold) goods, improves welfare. A similar finding holds for deflation (Diamond and Felli, 1990). With all consumers identical, zero inflation is the worst possible outcome. As modeled by Benabou (1988), it is also true that the interaction of inflation and market power implies that inflation can have beneficial effects at sufficiently low rates.

Neither my discussion of individual price setting nor my remarks on general inflation have a strong fiscal flavor. It would be nice to integrate inflation into fiscal analysis by recognizing the differential inflation effects (in timing and perhaps level) of different taxes.[17] This is a familiar concern in countries contemplating removal of large subsidies because of revenue needs. Moreover, it was present in discussions in the United States in the 1970s. But I have never seen a balanced budget incidence analysis. What would be the consequence of a systematic increase in consumer goods subsidies financed by rising income taxes? Presumably the distortions that come from imperfect taxes and subsidies would overwhelm the gains from decreased inflation at some point. But would such a policy make sense on a one-time basis? Although I am not enamored of the idea, it could lead to a useful analysis. It might serve as a framework for evaluating the ''Tax-Based Incomes Policies'' that were so popular and that will probably return to the public discussion.

Researchers' growing understanding of a range of non-Walrasian models holds considerable long-run promise for improving resource allocation, when these models are used seriously in policy analysis.

9

Optimal Taxation and Public Policy

What are the lessons that one can learn from the optimal taxation literature—in particular, the literature on optimal income taxation—for the making of public policy?

I shall begin this chapter with a brief description of the nature and contribution of optimal taxation theory, including the current contribution of Mirrlees (Chapter 7) to that literature. Then, I will turn from the optimal commodity tax variant of the model and address its sibling, the optimal income tax model. I will examine a number of the underpinnings of the theory that constrain the relevance of some of its apparent conclusions for public policy, and will conclude by suggesting some extensions that the next generation of research would do well to pursue.

In discussing the optimal income tax literature, I will first argue that a common policy inference taken from that literature—that the less income tax progressivity the better—should be treated with skepticism. I suggest that those who put forth this policy recommendation erroneously interpret the insights from the theoretical literature on optimal income taxation. They inappropriately transform theoretical implications regarding the optimal shape of the *marginal tax rate schedule* into assertions regarding the structure of *average income tax rates*.[1]

Second, I will suggest that, because of the limitations of optimal income tax theory, policymakers should treat all policy inferences derived from it with circumspection. For example, one must have a broader view than that taken in the optimal income tax literature, in order to make an informed judgment on even the optimal structure of *marginal* income tax rates.

I. OPTIMAL COMMODITY TAXATION: THE PROBLEM AND THE THEORY

Optimal taxation theory—in both its commodity and income taxation variants—begins with a second-best world. The objective is to identify those public fiscal interventions that enable the government to secure revenue for socially worthwhile expenditures with the least sacrifice of economic well-being. The public sector optimizes within the constraints imposed by preexisting failures in the private sector.

Although that objective seems straightforward, it is not straightforward in a distorted general equilibrium world. Any intervention—say, the imposition of a sales tax on some commodity x to finance a public good—not only alters the price of x but also changes the prices of commodities related to x. With distortions in these markets, changes in efficiency (deadweight) losses occur throughout the economy, due to the change in tax policy. Hence, the issue: What change in fiscal measures will raise the requisite revenue with the least loss in economic well-being?

In attempting to answer this question, the optimal taxation literature has sought rules to guide fiscal policymakers. Because of the complexity of the problem, substantial simplifications have had to be made. Hence, parts of the economy had to be segregated from the rest in order to maintain analytical tractability, and the economy's aggregate resource constraint had to be specified as if known. The extent of responsiveness incorporated into supply and demand curves had to be taken into account, as well as the interrelationships among the level of demand (supply) in one market and the levels of demand (supply) in other markets. And in more advanced models, the way various commodities (or income) contribute to the utility of individuals in society—and the way individual utilities are aggregated to obtain social welfare—had to be specified.

Depending on the assumptions made, then, a number of optimal commodity taxation rules have been derived. A few examples will give the flavor:

The inverse elasticity rule. Given the need to collect some amount of revenue via taxes on commodities, set the tax rates so that the percentage reduction in the quantity demanded of each commodity is the same. This means that tax rates should be inversely proportional to (compensated) elasticities of demand—higher tax rates on goods with inelastic demands, and low tax rates on goods with high elasticities.[2]

The leisure-complementarity rule. When there are two commodities that are to be taxed, impose the higher tax on the commodity that is the more closely associated with the consumption of leisure time.[3]

The "if equity counts" rule. If, in addition to minimizing efficiency losses, society wishes to equalize the distribution of well-being, the taxes placed on commodities in whose consumption the well-to-do specialize should be higher than the taxes levied on the commodities on which the poor concentrate their spending.[4]

Since the early contributions that yielded these rules, the optimal commodity taxation literature has been extended in a large number of ways. Researchers have relaxed assumptions, introduced additional constraints and intertemporal considerations, and derived the implications for worlds in which some commodities are both consumed and used as inputs, or where duties on imported goods exist, or where there are preexisting "market failures" that cannot be undone, or where there are administrative costs associated with taxing commodities.[5]

Mirrlees' contribution in this volume (Chapter 7) uses the standard optimal commodity taxation model to address two important, though neglected, questions. First, when there is uncertainty about supply and demand conditions, and when tax rate and public expenditure levels are set ex ante, will an equilibrium exist? If not, what adjustments are necessary and what are their economic impacts? Second, in an economy with both distortionary taxes and lump-sum taxes (subsidies), will the optimal level of public expenditures be less than that in the same economy under first-best conditions? Is the social cost of a marginal dollar of public funds in a second-best economy greater than one?

Although his models extend the reach of optimal taxation theory in both domains, his findings are neither straightforward nor unambiguous; they yield no new optimal taxation rules. In the uncertainty case, a quite different—though unspecified—form of analysis is called for, and little light is shed on either the sign or the magnitude of the shadow price of the marginal dollar of public funds.[6] Mirrlees' efforts highlight the difficulties inherent in answering the questions which he himself has posed.

II. OPTIMAL INCOME TAXATION THEORY

The problem that is addressed by the literature on optimal income taxation is straightforward, and similar to that confronted in the literature searching out optimality conditions in commodity taxation: What should be the structure of an income tax that minimizes the loss in economic well-being—that leaves well-being as great as possible, given that some revenue needs to be collected by an income tax?[7] Or, more completely, knowing consumer preferences, technology, and market structure, and given a public revenue requirement to be raised by a distorting income tax (that is, lump-sum or ability taxes are ruled out), what is the efficient structure of the income tax?

When there is but a single representative consumer, the answer is as straightforward as the question: choose that combination of linear income tax cum refundable tax credit that simultaneously raises the required revenue and maximizes utility. That tax will have a single marginal tax rate and will yield a lower level of utility than a lump-sum tax which raises the same revenue. The reduction in utility associated with the income tax is—in monetary units—the deadweight loss of taxation.

This problem becomes interesting (and the progressivity issue arises) only when there are numerous heterogeneous consumers. Now a social welfare function is necessary, distributional issues become relevant, and allocative efficiency may cease to be the sole norm. When the optimal income tax literature assumes consumers who are heterogeneous in abilities and homogeneous in tastes over income and leisure, ignores distributional objectives through a utilitarian social welfare function with equal weights across consumers,[8] and allows only leisure demand choices to be distorted by the tax, the literature and the optimal rules are not very interesting: the single marginal tax rate across income levels should range from 0 to 100 percent, and some workers will find the net wage rate below their reservation wage.

Progressivity—defined as *marginal* tax rates which vary positively with income—is zero in this economy (though average tax rates may vary across income levels). As Sadka (1976) and Seade (1977) have demonstrated, however, the optimal marginal tax rate on the highest- and lowest-income individuals is zero. Indeed, even if this simple social welfare function is modified to permit higher weights on lower-income people, the optimal tax will have lower marginal rates on those with higher incomes than on those with lower incomes.

To reach more specific conclusions, assumptions regarding the separate components of the model (the parameters of the social welfare and utility functions, and the distribution of ability) must be made, and the structure of the optimal income tax falls out from calculations based on these assumptions.

Prominent papers in the literature employing such calculations[9] have yielded other propositions that have become closely associated with the optimal income tax approach to tax policy design: *marginal tax rates should be low (20–30 percent), and generally constant over the income distribution, but zero at the highest level.* (Indeed, if heterogeneity among individuals in terms of ability is admitted, the optimal marginal tax rate on the highest-ability individual is negative when different groups' abilities are not completely substitutable in production.) Even with strong egalitarian social welfare functions, this general structure has resulted, in large part because of the assumed high elasticity of substitution between leisure and consumption.

III. A COMMON POLICY INTERPRETATION OF OPTIMAL INCOME TAX RULES

A message that some have taken from the optimal income tax literature draws from the linearity (flat rate structure) of the tax structure and the proportional marginal tax rates across the distribution implied by this structure. Indeed, a good deal of that literature lends itself to that interpretation, defining tax progressivity in terms of marginal rates; given that definition, proportional—not progressive—marginal rates are implied.

That literature, however, also permits the optimal income tax rate schedule to have a negative intercept, in effect allowing a refundable tax credit for individuals at the bottom of the distribution. With such a negative intercept and proportional marginal tax rates, average tax rates will increase over the income distribution. If tax progressivity is defined in terms of average tax rates, an optimal linear income tax can also be a progressive tax.

Although the classic articles in this literature have been clear on these distinctions, numerous policy interpreters of that literature have not. They have taken the conclusions of early analyses (low progressivity) and the mathematical form of later analyses (linear tax schedules) and have persuaded themselves and others that flat taxes without income guarantees for the poor are optimal. Indeed, as Rosen has stated in his public finance text (1988b): "In popular discussions, a *linear income tax schedule* [constant marginal tax rates across the distribution] is often referred to as a *flat tax.*" And the flat-tax argument has come to be associated with the absence of tax progressivity—with reducing the role of the public sector in redistributing income. Colander (1979) put it even more strongly: "The most significant result of the optimal income tax discussion . . . [is] that . . . an optimal income tax should be close to proportional, and the income tax is less effective than thought for reducing inequalities."

Those advocating this view caricature the optimal income tax literature.

In effect, the common interpretation has not made the subtle distinction between a flat-rate tax and a *progressive* flat-rate tax. In short, the key policy message that some have taken from the optimal income tax literature is to keep marginal income tax rates low, avoid progressivity, and refrain from using the income tax for redistributive purposes. In much of the policy debate, the case for a progressive income tax based on "ability to pay" judgments and egalitarian tastes went out of vogue with the advent of optimal income tax theory.

IV. FURTHER CONSIDERATIONS

Read carefully, the optimal income tax literature has given us some guidance into thinking about the optimal level of tax progressivity, but has by no means resolved the issue. As Slemrod (1983b) has noted, optimal income tax models "suggest that a system which combines a constant marginal rate with a[n] . . . exemption level of income below which tax liability is negative may be close to optimal. This conclusion, though, is highly tentative" (p. 367).

Whatever lessons one does take from optimal taxation models derive directly from the assumptions on which any particular analysis rests. In the absence of empirical testability, if one is to accept the conclusions, one must be comfortable with the underlying assumptions. And the assumptions underlying the models are stringent ones. Moreover, in addition to the fundamental components of the determinants of optimal progressivity that the optimal income tax literature has identified—the variance in the distribution of endowments, the elasticity of labor supply, and the social aversion to inequality—there are a wide range of other issues that must be considered in determining the optimal degree of tax progressivity.

Some of these additional considerations clearly suggest that optimal progressivity is greater than is implied in the existing literature; others may suggest that it is less. In any case, a full-bodied and comprehensive treatment of the progressivity issue must entertain all of them.

1. The optimal income tax framework rests on cardinal individual utility functions that are homogeneous across individuals, and that are aggregated into social welfare functions. But individual utility functions seem inherently heterogeneous, and social welfare functions built only on cardinal individual utility functions seem to lack realism. Building normative statements on these propositions seems a far stretch.

2. The social welfare functions employed in the optimal tax literature enable only a narrow range of value judgments to be incorporated into the analysis.

Although various degrees of aversion to inequality are clearly relevant, concerns over deviations from equal opportunity and personal liberty should also be allowed to affect the design of tax structures.

3. The optimal income tax literature generally restricts the domain of revenue instruments to the income tax, and analyzes only the effect on social welfare of changes in the taxation of wage income. Is but a single tax base optimal, and do the conclusions regarding the optimal progressivity of income tax schedules hold if a variety of taxes are in place? In such a multiple-tax world, how is the degree of progressivity to be defined and measured?[10]

4. The ownership of wealth and its transmission are not addressed well by the standard static version of the theory, and in the face of ineffective estate taxes and constraints on other forms of income equalization, income tax progressivity may be a relatively attractive means of reducing inequities in the transmission of wealth.

5. The required assumption of zero administrative costs, no evasion, and no return from market power casts at least some of the lessons of optimal income tax theory into doubt when examples of these phenomena abound. Moreover, the difficulties of taxing capital gains at accrual, taxing real versus nominal gains, and assessing the value flow of the services from owner-occupied housing, household farm labor income, and the consumption of do-it-yourself activities are pervasive, administratively intractable, and neglected by the theory. Surely these considerations should enter any social calculus regarding the optimal level of income tax progressivity.

6. The generally held perception that income-leisure substitutions vary systematically with endowments suggests that marginal tax rates should vary systematically across individuals—that the uniform marginal tax rate prescription seems nonoptimal. What if work satisfaction, promotional possibilities, and lower health risks are positively correlated with endowments, implying lower labor supply sensitivity to tax rates for those with higher earnings capacities? Again, marginal tax progressivity may be in order within the optimal income tax framework; nonoptimal leisure may not be the only "bad" to be avoided.

7. It is hard to accept the implicit assumption that the "tax sensitivity" of different sources of income is constant. If, say, the wage rate is less sensitive to tax rates than are hours worked, and if high earners are more hours constrained than low earners, a higher marginal tax rate on high-income workers seems called for; it becomes a wage rate tax.[11]

8. Although the optimal income tax framework is static and builds on nondistorted markets, many decisions are made in an intertemporal context, and in

distorted markets. As Hubbard and Judd (1986) have shown, if the poorest consumers are liquidity constrained, an increase in marginal tax rates with an associated increase in the exemption level will increase consumption dollar-for-dollar with the increased exemption. Increasing the pro-poor impact of the income tax increases efficiency by reducing a preexisting distortion in the market.

9. Still other important considerations can be identified which may also alter the policy prescription. What if those in the population affected by the negative segment of the linear tax function—that is, recipients of the implicit refundable tax credit—are constrained by capital market imperfections from borrowing for human capital investments in education and training? And what if those investments yield social benefits in *excess* of the perceived private benefits, as much of the literature suggests?[12] In this case, an increase in the redistributional role of the tax will (by relaxing the capital market failure resulting in constrained purchases) lead to human capital investments for which the social gains exceed private gains. The tradeoff function reflecting this efficiency effect will be different from that reflecting only the labor supply effects of redistributive income taxation.[13]

10. Or again, what if the "safety net" created by the negative segment of the linear tax function (or by graduated marginal tax rates) conveys the public good called "security" from adverse changes in individual earnings?[14] In a market system, the subjective probability distribution of future earnings has a large variance. For risk-averse individuals, reducing this variance has value; for others, it does not. Private insurance markets accomplish some of this function, but few would argue that insurance markets enable heterogeneous individuals to secure the optimal amount of such variance reduction privately. An increase in income tax progressivity, measured by either marginal or average tax rates, would decrease the variance of this subjective probability distribution. The resulting increase in the public good "security" implies the optimality of a higher degree of progressivity in the income tax than would otherwise exist.[15] (Offsetting this, of course, is the potential for reduced precautionary private saving in response to the increased security.)

11. On a related point, what if the proposition argued so well by Abramovitz (1981)—that the safety net afforded by a welfare state enhances the possibility of technical change—is correct? This dynamic efficiency gain from an increase in the redistributive contribution of the income tax should also be reflected in designing the income tax structure.

12. Finally, consider the efficiency effects of progressivity in a world in which both a formal and a shadow economy are possible. Does increased progressivity lead to more shadow economy activity, or to less? There are arguments on both sides of this question, although results from a simple model indicate that a progressive linear income tax structure may induce an increase in unreported economic activities.[16] Irrespective of the direction of the impact, this efficiency consequence must also be taken into account in structuring income taxation.

V. CONCLUSION

I am in agreement with many other fiscal economists when I conclude that the policy advance on tax progressivity offered by the optimal income tax literature is genuinely ambiguous.[17] Hence, the suggestion that a simple flat-rate income tax (implying no progressivity) rests on the lessons from the optimal income tax literature, and that it is therefore superior to a progressive income tax, is both unwarranted and misleading.

In fact, the structure of the optimal income tax depends on several things: the parameters of the relevant utility and social welfare functions, the degree of inequality in abilities and capacities among the population, the domain of behavioral responses to progressivity that are admitted into the model, and the nature of preexisting constraints affecting decision makers imparted directly or indirectly by the tax. When sources of progressivity-induced efficiency effects beyond labor supply are introduced into the analysis—those associated with human capital effects, security as a public good, technological change, and the shadow economy, among others—the case for progressivity and a redistributive income tax may well not be a weak one. Only an appraisal of the full range of effects of tax progressivity—including both those effects captured in the formal models and those that are not—can lead to an informed and (in that sense at least) "optimal" income tax policy choice. Although such an appraisal awaits the development of optimal taxation models that are more comprehensive in their scope, it also cries out for more reliable empirical estimates of the components of the costs and benefits associated with a variety of tax structures, and of the behavioral responses to the incentives in these structures.

Joseph Pechman (1990), in his presidential address to the American Economic Association, stated his own position on the matter of income tax progressivity as follows: "Most people support tax progressivity on the ground that taxes should be levied in accordance with ability to pay, which is assumed to rise more than proportionately with income. Economists have . . . had trouble with the 'ability to pay' concept . . . I believe that the person on the street is right and that we should continue to rely on the income tax to raise revenue in an equitable manner.'' In the absence of more reliable guidance from both theory and empirical evidence, perhaps this is the best that the economics discipline can currently offer.

10

Reflections on Optimal Tax Theory

This chapter complements Chapters 7 and 9: "Optimal Taxation and Government Finance" by James Mirrlees, and "Optimal Taxation and Public Policy" by Robert Haveman. It addresses three questions raised by Mirrlees and Haveman: Is there a presumption that the second-best (when differential lump-sum taxation is impossible) level of a public good is lower than the first-best level? Can optimal tax theory be extended to address issues related to macroeconomic stabilization? And how has optimal tax theory contributed to public economics?

The chapter has two related themes. The first is that the primary contribution of optimal tax theory has been to provide a coherent theory of optimal economic policy. Following the method of optimal tax theory, optimal policy is solved for by maximizing a welfare function in which all desiderata are quantified subject to a complete description of the economy, which includes all relevant constraints—production possibilities, endowments, information, and politics. Contrary to the optimistic expectations early in its development, optimal tax theory has supplied little in the way of *concrete* guidance concerning the design of actual tax systems. Nevertheless, by providing a consistent and rigorous framework for normative analysis, it has contributed greatly not only to public economics but to applied economics generally.

The second theme concerns the methodological relationship between applied economic theory and public policy analysis. An applied theoretical model offers a way of conceptualizing and of focusing thought on *some* facets of a public policy issue. It does not, or should not, claim to capture all or even most of the important considerations relevant to a particular policy issue. The role of the policy economist is to draw together the insights derived from a variety of applied economic theoretical models and of econometric studies, as well as to consider practical issues that the academic literature has neglected, and then to recommend policy on the basis of this synthesis. It may be that some policy analysts have drawn too heavily on some simple optimal tax models in their policy prescriptions. Still, to criticize optimal tax *theory* for this reason is inappropriate.

Part I examines the first- and second-best levels of a public good, focusing on the contributions of the Mirrlees chapter. Part II considers stabilization policy and optimal tax theory, taking Mirrlees' discussion as the point of departure. And Part III responds to Haveman's chapter by providing a defense of optimal tax theory.

I. FIRST- AND SECOND-BEST LEVELS OF A PUBLIC GOOD

The first to address this issue were Stiglitz and Dasgupta (1971) and Atkinson and Stern (1974), who considered economies with a single representative consumer. First-best finance was lump-sum taxation. Second-best finance was optimal differential commodity taxation with an untaxed good. With optimal differential commodity taxation, the tax rates are chosen to equalize across taxed goods the social cost of raising an extra dollar of revenue—one dollar plus the marginal excess burden. As was recognized at the time, the comparison of the first- and second-best levels of a public good with a single consumer is practically uninteresting, since there is no good reason to rule out lump-sum taxation. The analysis was, however, considered interesting as progressing halfway toward examination of the issue with heterogeneous consumers.

These papers demonstrated that the second-best level of the public good can exceed the first-best; for example, if goods whose optimal tax rates are low are complementary with the public good, the switch from lump-sum to differential commodity taxation may stimulate demand for the public good sufficiently that the optimal level increases, even though the marginal cost is higher. Nevertheless, the general insight derived from these papers was that the higher cost of the public good in the second-best economy "typically" causes its optimal level to be lower.

The optimal commodity tax literature started by examining a representative consumer economy with an untaxed commodity (Ramsey, 1927; Corlett and Hague, 1953; Diamond and Mirrlees, 1971a, 1971b). By the mid-seventies, the models were extended to treat heterogeneous individuals—the many-person Ramsey tax problem (Feldstein, 1972; Diamond, 1975; and Mirrlees, 1975)—thus permitting the integration of efficiency and equity. It was assumed that the government cannot identify individuals or keep track of a specific individual's purchases; as a result, commodity taxation is anonymous and linear. It was also recognized that, *under these assumptions, although the government cannot impose differential lump-sum taxation, it can impose a uniform poll tax.* This is very important, since it implies that *the government then has a nondistortionary method of finance at the margin.*

The many-person Ramsey tax problem was subsequently extended to incorporate public goods (see, for example, Atkinson and Stiglitz, 1980). Remarkably, however, *the chapter by Mirrlees is the first*[1] *to examine the implications of having a nondistortionary method of finance at the margin in the second-best economy on the first-best (full lump-sum taxation) versus second-best level of public goods with heterogeneous consumers.*

There are generally two different approaches to the comparison of the first-versus the second-best provision of public goods: the first-order approach and the levels approach. The first-order approach entails only a comparison of the first-order conditions in the first- and second-best problems. The levels approach attempts to compare the actual levels of the public goods. Since this entails a comparison of two general equilibria, the analysis is more difficult, but the results are also more informative.

A. The First-Order Condition Approach

Mirrlees analyzes the problem using the first-order condition approach, and then using the levels approach. The basic procedure for the first-order condition approach is as follows. The Samuelson condition for the first-best level of the public good is $\Sigma MB = MC$. Since there is optimal lump-sum taxation, everyone has the same marginal utility of income and hence the same welfare weight. The first-order condition for the second-best level of the public good can be written as $\Sigma \widetilde{MB} - \phi = MC$, where MC is the resource cost of the public good, $\Sigma \widetilde{MB}$ is the *welfare-weighted*[2] sum of marginal benefits (since optimal lump-sum taxation is unavailable, individuals' marginal utilities of income differ at the second-best optimum), and ϕ is an additional term which shall be explained shortly. Then the two first-order conditions are compared. To simplify, assume that production possibilities are linear. Then the second-best level of the public good is greater than the first-best level if $(-\phi + \Sigma \widetilde{MB})_2 > \Sigma MB_1$, where subscript 2 denotes evaluation with the second-best set of taxes and subscript 1 denotes evaluation with the first-best set of taxes. This inequality can be decomposed:

$$(-\phi + \Sigma \widetilde{MB})_2 > \Sigma MB_1 \Leftrightarrow -\phi + (\Sigma \widetilde{MB} - \Sigma MB)_2$$
$$+ (\Sigma MB_2 - \Sigma MB_1) > 0.$$

The last term on the left-hand side of the second inequality is the difference in the welfare-unweighted sum of marginal benefits due to differences in the tax systems. The middle term is the difference between welfare-weighted and welfare-unweighted sum of marginal benefits under the second-best tax regime; it is positive if the covariance between welfare weights and marginal benefits is positive. Mirrlees focuses on the first term, $-\phi$.

In Mirrlees' chapter $\phi = Ht(\bar{x}_b m^* - \bar{x}_z)$, where H is the number of individuals or households, t is the vector of optimal commodity (excise) tax rates, $\bar{x}$ is the vector of mean commodity demands, b is lump-sum income, z is the level of the public good, m^* is the mean welfare-weighted marginal benefit from the public good, and subscripts denote partial derivatives. The variable $-\phi$ captures the *magnitude of the indirect revenue effect.* Suppose that the government raises the poll tax by one dollar, spending the extra revenue raised on the public good. This extra revenue comes directly from the poll tax and indirectly from commodity taxes. The *direct* revenue increase is H. The perturbation changes households' lump-sum income, as well as the level of the public good. In response, households adjust their consumption bundles, which alters the revenue raised from commodity taxes. The important point to note is that, by the envelope theorem, the indirect increase in revenue comes at no welfare cost. Thus, a positive indirect revenue effect can be viewed as either decreasing the marginal cost of the public good or as increasing the marginal benefit.

Atkinson and Stiglitz (1980, p. 497) clearly identify the indirect revenue effect in this context. Thus, Mirrlees' result is not new. He does, however, provide a more helpful discussion of the indirect revenue effect than do Atkinson and Stiglitz. He makes three interesting observations:

1. Suppose that commodity demands are independent of $z;$ that, for whatever reason, goods' tax rates exceed factor tax rates in absolute value (since $q \equiv p + t$, a factor tax which causes the consumer factor price to be lower than the producer factor price corresponds to a negative t); and that commodities are normal. Then the indirect revenue effect is negative. This indicates that the second-best level of the public good depends, inter alia, on the relative magni-

tude of factor and goods taxes (and, therefore, on whatever determines these relative magnitudes).

2. Continue, for the purposes of illustration, to assume that the indirect revenue effect is negative. Return to Mirrlees' first-order condition for the second-best level of the public good, with $MC = 1$:

(10.1a) $\Sigma \widetilde{MB} - \phi = 1.$

Atkinson and Stiglitz rewrite (10.1a) as

(10.1b) $\Sigma \widetilde{MB} = 1 + \phi$
$$= \varphi, \text{ with } \varphi \equiv 1 + \phi,$$

interpreting a negative indirect revenue effect as increasing the social cost of the public good. Mirrlees, in contrast, rewrites (10.1a) as

(10.1c)
$$\Sigma \widehat{MB} = 1, \text{ with } \widehat{MB} \equiv \frac{\Sigma \widetilde{MB} - \phi}{\Sigma \widetilde{MB}} \, \widetilde{MB},$$

interpreting a negative indirect revenue effect as effectively causing the social valuation of the public good, $\widehat{MB}$, to be lower than the "private valuation," $\widetilde{MB}$. Since tax rates (and hence the consumer prices of commodities) are high, individuals overvalue the public good.

3. Mirrlees points out that, since poll taxation is possible, no distortion terms enter the formula for the second-best level of the public good. The distortions are inframarginal rather than marginal.

Although these observations are insightful, they do not go very far toward identifying primitive conditions under which the second-best level of the public good is higher or lower than the first-best level. The first-order conditions are just too implicit.

B. The Levels Approach

Mirrlees' analysis here is characteristically elegant, clear, and insightful. He notes that with a poll tax, if everyone is identical the first- and second-best levels of the public good are the same. He then introduces a perturbation—a small amount of inequality—and compares the resulting change in the first- and second-best levels of the public good, under the simplifying assumption that utility is separable between public and private goods.

Individuals in the model are indexed by n (which can be interpreted as ability) and (with the assumed separability) have the utility functions $v(q,b,n) + g(z)$. Mirrlees demonstrates that the second-best level of the public good is higher than the first-best if $v_{bbn}/v_{bn} > \frac{1}{2}(v_{bbb}/v_{bb})$, and lower if the inequality is reversed.

Mirrlees supplies a rigorous proof. Here I shall provide a heuristic, approximate derivation in order to elucidate the result. I shall simplify by assuming that there are only two individuals and that production possibilities are linear. In the initial situation, $q = p$ (no commodity taxes), b and n are the same for both individuals, and z is the optimal level of the public good. Then, *with z at its initial level*, a small mean-preserving spread in n is introduced, which is captured by assuming that one individual's n is $n + \Delta$ and the other's is $n - \Delta$. After the perturbation, the second-best level of the public good is higher than the first-best level if the sum of the marginal benefits is greater at the second-best optimum than at the first-best optimum—that is, if $\Sigma MB_2 > \Sigma MB_1$.

Consider the *second best* initially. It turns out that for this perturbation, the effects from imposing differential commodity taxes are of higher order than the effects that are central; thus, we may assume that the public good is financed solely through a poll tax. Since, by assumption, the level of the public good and hence tax revenue are unaffected by the perturbation, the level of the poll tax is unaffected by the perturbation—label it $\bar{b}$. Thus,

(10.2a) $\Sigma MB_2 = MB(p,\bar{b},n + \Delta) + MB(p,\bar{b},n - \Delta)$

(10.2b) $\left. \dfrac{\partial \Sigma MB_2}{\partial \Delta} \right|_{\Delta=0} = (MB_n^+ - MB_n^-)_{\Delta=0} = 0$

(10.2c) $\left. \dfrac{\partial^2 \Sigma MB_2}{\partial \Delta^2} \right|_{\Delta=0} = (MB_{nn}^+ + MB_{nn}^-)_{\Delta=0} = (2MB_{nn})_{\Delta=0}.$

The effect of the perturbation on ΣMB_2 is second-order and its magnitude is given by (10.2c).

Consider next the *first-best* tax regime. The sum of the differential lump-sum taxes must raise the revenue to finance z—that is, $b^+ + b^- = 2\bar{b}$. Hence,

(10.3a) $\Sigma MB_1 = MB(p,b^+,n+\Delta) + MB(p,b^-,n - \Delta)$

(10.3b) $\left. \dfrac{\partial \Sigma MB_1}{\partial \Delta} \right|_{\Delta=0} = \left[MB_b^+\left(\dfrac{\partial b^+}{\partial \Delta}\right) + MB_n^+ + MB_b^-\left(\dfrac{\partial b^-}{\partial \Delta}\right) - MB_n^- \right]_{\Delta=0}$

$= 0,$

since $\partial b^+/\partial \Delta + \partial b^-/\partial \Delta = 0$. Now, the lump-sum taxes are chosen so that both individuals have the same marginal utility of income. Since marginal benefit equals $g'(z)$ divided by the marginal utility of income, both individuals must have the same marginal benefit:

(10.3c)
$$MB_b^+\left(\frac{\partial b^+}{\partial \Delta}\right) + MB_n^+ = MB_b^-\left(\frac{\partial b^-}{\partial \Delta}\right) - MB_n^-.$$

Combining (10.3c) and (10.3b) gives

(10.3d)
$$\frac{\partial b^+}{\partial \Delta} = -\frac{MB_n^+}{MB_b^+} \text{ and } \frac{\partial b^-}{\partial \Delta} = \frac{MB_n^-}{MB_b^-}.$$

Then

(10.3e)
$$\left.\frac{\partial^2 \Sigma MB_1}{\partial \Delta^2}\right|_{\Delta=0} = \left[MB_{bb}^+\left(\frac{\partial b^+}{\partial \Delta}\right)^2 + MB_b^+\frac{\partial^2 b^+}{\partial \Delta^2} + 2MB_{bn}^+\frac{\partial b^+}{\partial \Delta} + MB_{nn}^+ \right.$$

$$+ MB_{bb}^-\left(\frac{\partial b^-}{\partial \Delta}\right)^2 + MB_b^-\frac{\partial^2 b^-}{\partial \Delta^2} - 2MB_{bn}^-\frac{\partial b^-}{\partial \Delta}$$

$$\left. + MB_{nn}^- \right]_{\Delta=0}$$

$$= \left[2MB_{bb}\left(-\frac{MB_n}{MB_b}\right)^2 + 4MB_{bn}\left(\frac{-MB_n}{MB_b}\right) + 2MB_{nn} \right]_{\Delta=0},$$

using (10.3d) and $\partial^2 b^+/\partial \Delta^2 + \partial^2 b^-/\partial \Delta^2 = 0$ from the revenue constraint.

Combining results gives

(10.4)
$$(z_2 - z_1)_{\Delta=0} > 0 \Leftrightarrow \left.\frac{\partial^2 \Sigma MB_2}{\partial \Delta^2}\right|_{\Delta=0} > \left.\frac{\partial^2 \Sigma MB_1}{\partial \Delta^2}\right|_{\Delta=0}$$

$$\Leftrightarrow \left[2MB_{bb}\left(\frac{-MB_n}{MB_b}\right)^2 + 4MB_{bn}\left(\frac{-MB_n}{MB_b}\right) \right]_{\Delta=0} < 0.$$

Substituting $MB = g'/v_b$ gives a result very similar to Mirrlees'.

I have been unable to come up with a neat geometric characterization of the result. But the following geometric characterization provides some insight. Consider first the poll tax. The effect of the perturbation on the average marginal benefit is illustrated in Figure 10.1. From Figure 10.1, it is evident that the effect of the perturbation on the mean marginal benefit from the public good with the poll tax depends on the curvature of the $MB-$surface along $b = \bar{b}$. Next consider the first-best system of taxes. Figure 10.2 shows that in this case the effect of the perturbation on the mean marginal benefit from the public good depends on the curvature of marginal benefit contours.

In any event, the essential point made by Mirrlees is that even in an extremely simple situation which contains no obvious bias, the relative magnitude of the first- and second-best levels of the public good depends on higher-order (rather than concavity/convexity) curvature properties of the utility function, concerning which economic theory has little to say. With a finite amount of inequality, the comparison is further complicated by commodity taxes, the form of inequality aversion, and the form of the income distribution. Furthermore, the compari-

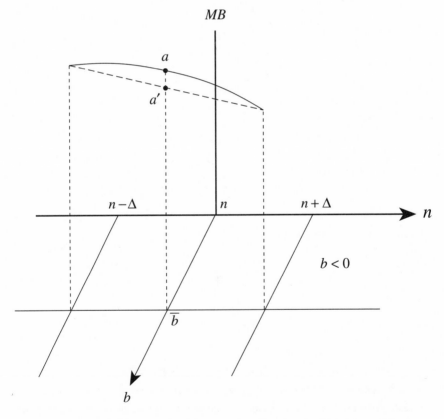

Figure 10.1. Effect of perturbation on average marginal benefit: poll tax.

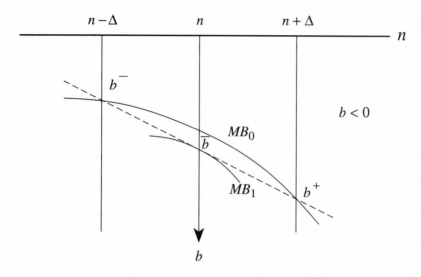

Figure 10.2. Effect of perturbation on average marginal benefit: first-best taxes.

son then depends on global rather than local higher-order curvature properties of the utility functions. Thus, it is safe to say that *there is no a priori presumption that the second-best (with the optimal poll tax) level of a public good is higher or lower than the first-best level.*

It is commonly argued that the second-best level of a public good is typically lower than the first-best level, on the grounds that in the former case the use of differential commodity taxation raises the private cost of public funds. Mirrlees demonstrates that this argument is fallacious. Differential commodity taxation *is* distortionary. But when the set of policy instruments includes a poll tax, it is always possible to finance the marginal unit of the public good via a rise in the poll tax. Thus, when both differential commodity taxes and a poll tax can be employed, taxation is nondistortionary *at the margin,* and it is distortion *at the margin* that affects the private cost of public funds.

II. STABILIZATION POLICY

For twenty years students received their first exposure to graduate public finance through Richard Musgrave's *Theory of Public Finance.* To these many generations of students, it must be striking that the Stabilization Branch of Musgrave's Fiscal Department has all but disappeared from public economics. Its disappearance is, I think, a quirk of intellectual history. The "new public economics" (now not so new) insisted on rigorous microfoundations—a requirement that was hard, if not impossible, to reconcile with the Keynesian macroeconomics of that era (the early 1970s), which Musgrave espoused. Since then, of course, the microfoundations of macroeconomics have been made much stronger. But stabilization policy has not yet been brought back into public economics. This is regrettable, since most fiscal policy analysis in macroeconomics provides a crude treatment of taxes and welfare economics.

In the first part of Chapter 7, Mirrlees takes a step toward bringing stabilization policy back into the fold, through optimal tax theory. He initially assumes that *nominal* excise tax rates, *nominal* lump-sum transfers, and *real* levels of government purchases are decided ex ante, in a static, uncertain environment. This leads to two related problems, on which Mirrlees focuses. First, at the time tax rates are set, the price level is unknown, since it is state-contingent. Second, it may be impossible to finance the predetermined level of real government purchases; in some states, there may exist no set of prices such that the ex ante government purchases can be financed, given the nominal ex ante tax rates and lump-sum transfers.

Mirrlees provides the following example: Production possibilities are given by $y = c + z$, where y is aggregate output of a generic good which may be either privately consumed, c, or used by the government, z. Output is produced using labor, l. The representative consumer's budget constraint is $(p + t)c = py(l) + b$, where b is the nominal lump-sum transfer and p is the endogenous price of y. The consumer decides on c and l *after* the realization of the state. The consumer's maximization problem is therefore

$$\max_{c,l} u(c,l) \text{ s.t. } (p + t)c = py(l) + b.$$

The nominal revenue raised is $tc - b$, and the quantity of public goods purchased is $(tc - b)/p$. For purpose of illustration, suppose that the utility function is Cobb-Douglas, $u = c^{1/2}(1 - l)^{1/2}$ (the individual has one unit of time), and that $y(l) = wl$, where w is the realization of the random marginal (= average) product of labor. Then, from the consumer's maximization problem,

$$1 - l = \frac{pw + b}{2pw} \text{ and } c = \frac{pw + b}{2(p + t)},$$

which imply that real tax revenue is

$$\frac{tc - b}{p} = \frac{ptw - tb - 2bp}{2(p + t)p}.$$

The price level adjusts such that (if feasible) this equals z. Thus, p solves

(10.5) $p^2(2z) + p(2tz - tw + 2b) + tb = 0.$

It is straightforward that if $tb > 0$ *and either* $(2tz - tw + 2b)^2 < 8tbz$ or $2tz - tw + 2b > 0$, then there is no real, positive solution to (10.5). This is the situation shown in Mirrlees' Figure 7.1.

Mirrlees demonstrates that a potential nonexistence problem may also arise if taxes and lump-sum transfers are indexed to prices. He then argues: ''An alternative view of [these potential nonexistence problems] is that we have found here lurking in the microeconomic optimal tax model some aspects of the macroeconomic problems of adjustment and stabilization, and that welfare maximization is not a satisfactory way of analyzing the policy issues in this context.''

In the remainder of this section, I shall dispute these two statements and discuss an alternative approach to stabilization policy from an optimal tax perspective.

The potential nonexistence problems that Mirrlees identifies are new and of some theoretical interest. But at the same time, they appear similar to a nonexistence problem that may arise in the standard optimal commodity tax problem. There, the government may commit itself to a technically feasible level of government expenditures whose cost exceeds the maximum amount that can be raised via taxation. In Mirrlees' model, nominal excise tax rates are fixed and there may be no price level for which enough revenue can be raised to finance a technically feasible level of government expenditures.

Mirrlees' model might be relevant to hyperinflated economies, but surely not to today's developed countries, where the magnitude of fluctuations is ''modest,'' the limits of fiscal capacity are far from being exceeded, and the political process works at least moderately well. If there were a significant downturn, the political process would be sufficiently responsive that fiscal capacity would not be exceeded; government expenditures, tax rates, transfers, and monetary policy would be adjusted appropriately. I think Mirrlees is barking up the wrong tree.

From one perspective, there is no problem at a conceptual level in developing a theory of optimal stabilization policy based on welfare maximization. Consider the economy as a mechanism that transforms a set of stochastic dynamic input signals into a set of stochastic dynamic output signals (various economic time series). The object is to tinker with the mechanism so as to maximize the expected discounted welfare associated with the output signals. This is an exercise in optimal dynamic feedback control. It may be difficult to make this conceptualization operational for policy purposes. But we should be very hesitant to reject the welfare maximization approach, since, like the assumption of rationality, it forces conceptual coherence.

The principal difficulty in developing a theory of optimal stabilization policy is to provide persuasive microfoundations not only for macroeconomics but also for the economic failures, market and nonmarket, which justify government intervention to stabilize the economy.

Macroeconomic fluctuations are not per se undesirable. They would occur in an Arrow-Debreu economy with uncertainty, which is well known to be Pareto-efficient, and with optimal lump-sum redistribution, to be optimal as well. There is a general perception, however, that macroeconomic fluctuations in developed economies are excessive—too large to be explained as the response of a well-behaved economy to the kinds of exogenous shocks that developed economies experience. As a result of some failure, either the economy magnifies these exogenous shocks or else it creates the fluctuations internally. Support for this view is provided by the persistence, importance, and cyclicality of involuntary unemployment, which has no place in an Arrow-Debreu economy.

What is the source of economic failure? There is no shortage of candidate culprits: sticky or fixed prices and wages (Benassy, 1985), job search externalities (Diamond, 1982a), coordination failure (Cooper and John, 1988), credit market imperfections (Greenwald and Stiglitz, 1990), staggered contracts (Taylor, 1980), implicit contracts (Arnott, Hosios, and Stiglitz, 1988), efficiency wages (Shapiro and Stiglitz, 1984), sunspots (Azariadis and Guesnerie, 1986), and so on. None has gained majority acceptance within the profession. Given this lack of consensus concerning appropriate microfoundations for macroeconomics, it would be misguided to search for the definitive theory of optimal stabilization policy. But the more limited goal of developing a theory of optimal stabilization policy based on any of the above microfoundations seems realistic.

Indeed, much work has been done along these lines; yet none of it provides a rich treatment of fiscal policy, or develops a theory of optimal stabilization policy which draws on optimal tax theory. In the model which follows, my aim is to show that this can be done. The model's microfoundations of the macroeconomy are much too simple, but they are at least consistent. I hope that the model will encourage others to incorporate optimal tax theory into models with richer microfoundations.

The reasoning underlying the model specification is as follows. The model needs to incorporate uncertainty and a source of market failure, and to provide a description of the economy compatible with optimal tax theory. The theory of moral hazard satisfies these requirements. The model describes a farm economy. A farmer's output depends on his effort and the weather which is imperfectly correlated over farms. Crop insurance is provided. This causes farmers to exert less effort, which in turn reduces average aggregate output and increases the variability of output. The efficiency loss associated with moral hazard can be mitigated through optimal taxation—for instance, by subsidizing agricultural inputs that reduce the probability of crop failure.

To set the stage, let's look at a preliminary model. The economy comprises identical individuals, each of whom farms a unit area of land. There is a single generic crop. Output per farm depends on both effort and the weather; specifically, there are two possible output levels: h (high) and l (low). Effort is decided before the weather is known. In good years, the probability of low output on a particular farm is $p_g(e)$ and in bad years is $p_b(e)$, with $p_i' < 0$, $p_i'' > 0$, $p_i(0) = \bar{p}_i < .5$, $i = g,b$, and $p_g(e) > p_b(e)$ for all e. Good and bad years occur with equal probability. Crop insurance is available. The insurer can observe whether a crop year was good or bad and the total quantity of insurance purchased by a farmer, but neither the weather nor the effort expended on a particular farm. Consequently, an insurance contract in aggregate state i specifies a premium β_i and a net payout α_i. The insurance must break even in a particular crop year.

Let y be post-insurance income and $U(y,e)$ be the utility function. Then an individual's expected utility is

$$(10.6) \qquad EU = \frac{1}{2}\left\{\sum_i [1 - p_i(e)]U_i^0 + p_i(e)U_i^1\right\},$$

where $U_i^0 \equiv U(h - \beta_i, e)$ and $U_i^1 \equiv U(l + \alpha_i, e)$. The first-order condition for e (an interior solution is assumed) is

$$(10.7) \qquad \left[\frac{1}{2}\sum_i p_i'(-U_i^0 + U_i^1)\right] + \left\{\frac{1}{2}\sum_i \left[(1 - p_i)\frac{\partial U_i^0}{\partial e} + p_i\frac{\partial U_i^1}{\partial e}\right]\right\} = 0,$$

which states that the expected marginal benefit from effort (the term in the first set of square brackets) equals the expected marginal cost (the term in the curved brackets). The solution to (10.7) may be written compactly as $e = e(\alpha_g, \alpha_b, \beta_g, \beta_b)$. Normally,[3] $\partial e/\partial \beta_i < 0$ and $\partial e/\partial \alpha_i < 0$; as more insurance is provided, the individual reduces effort. Substitution of the effort equation into (10.6) gives expected utility as a function of the terms of the insurance contract—that is, $V(\alpha_g, \alpha_b, \beta_g, \beta_b) \equiv \max_e EU(\alpha_g, \alpha_b, \beta_g, \beta_b)$.

The insurance is provided either by the government or by competitive insurance firms. In both cases, the insurance maximizes expected utility subject to the insurers at least breaking even *in each aggregate outcome*—that is,

$$(10.8) \qquad \max_{\alpha,\beta} V(\boldsymbol{\alpha},\boldsymbol{\beta}) \text{ s.t. } [1 - p_i(e)]\beta_i - p_i(e)\alpha_i \geq 0, \quad i = g,b.$$

(To simplify notation, we employ vectors where there is no ambiguity.) The details of the solution need not concern us here; they are provided in Arnott and Stiglitz (1986). Three qualitative features of the solution are important, however. First, moral hazard causes individuals to exert too little effort relative to the first best, where the insurance contract specifies effort.[4] Second, the equilibrium is *constrained* efficient; even though it entails too little effort relative to the first best, it is efficient conditional on the unobservability of effort: there is no market failure. And third, effort is positively related to mean aggregate output and negatively related to the variability of aggregate output. Consequently, relative to both the no-insurance and first-best situations, the provision of insurance under moral hazard is destabilizing.

We now enrich the model in a natural way to include multiple goods. The resulting equilibrium is constrained *inefficient,* and the inefficiency is remedied by optimal commodity taxation. The intuition is straightforward. The equilibrium with insurance provided under moral hazard entails individuals' expending too little effort relative to the first best. The efficiency loss associated with this distortion (relative to the first best) can be reduced by taxing substitutes to effort and subsidizing complements. The optimum balances these efficiency gains against the efficiency losses from not pricing goods at marginal cost. Since the taxation stimulates effort, and since effort is negatively related to the variability of output, then in our economy *optimal commodity taxation is stabilizing.* A complete analysis of optimal commodity taxation with moral hazard is provided in Arnott and Stiglitz (1986). Here we simply illustrate the result.

We augment the model by assuming that a unit of the generic output can be costlessly transformed into either a unit of agricultural input or a unit of one of two consumer goods. Let f be the quantity of the agricultural input employed, and c_{ij}^1 and c_{ij}^2 be the quantity of goods 1 and 2 consumed with aggregate outcome $i = g,b$ and output $j = h,l$. The agricultural input increases the probability of high output (that is, $p_i = p_i(e,f)$ with $\partial p_i/\partial f < 0$, $\partial^2 p_i/\partial f^2 > 0$, $i = g,b$). Consumption occurs after the outcome has been realized and insurance payments made. The government employs linear commodity taxes. Since the agricultural input is purchased before the realization of the outcome, its consumer price, q^f, is outcome-independent, and since the consumer goods are purchased after the realization of uncertainty, it is reasonable to assume that their consumer prices are outcome-contingent, q_i^1 and q_i^2. Since the demands for f and c are homogeneous of degree zero in post-insurance income and consumer prices, we need an additional normalization. There is no natural one; let it be $q_g^1 = 1$.

We shall skip the algebraic details. But it will be useful to explain the solution procedure. The consumer's maximization problem now has two stages. In the later stage, consumption decisions are made, taking e and f, consumer prices and the parameters of the insurance contract, as given. In the earlier stages the individual chooses e and f, taking into account the dependence of c on e and f, and taking consumer prices and the parameters of the insurance contract as given. It will simplify notation in what follows if we let x_{ij} be the transfer from the insurance company to the individual with aggregate output i and output j, and π_{ij} be the corresponding probability. Solving, one obtains $e = e(y,q)$ and so on. Hence,

$$(10.9) \qquad EU(y,q) = \sum_{ij} \pi_{ij}(y,q) V_{ij}(y,q).$$

where V_{ij} is expected utility with i,j. The social planner's problem is then to choose the parameters of the insurance contract, as well as consumer prices, so as to maximize expected utility subject to budget balance in each aggregate outcome

$$(10.10) \qquad B_i = \frac{-\displaystyle\sum_j \pi_{ij} x_{ij} + \sum_{k=1}^{2} \sum_j \pi_{ij}(q_i^k - 1)\, c_{ij}^k + \sum_j \pi_{ij}(q^f - 1)\, f}{\displaystyle\sum_j \pi_{ij}} = 0.$$

The solution (available upon request) is

(10.11)
$$-\sum_i \lambda_i \sum_j \pi_{ij} \left[(q^f - 1)\left(\frac{\partial f}{\partial q^f}\right)_\theta + \sum_{k=1}^{2} (q_i^k - 1)\left(\frac{\partial c_{ij}^k}{\partial q^f}\right)_\theta \right]$$

$$+ \sum_i \lambda_i \sum_j s_{ij} \left(\frac{\partial \pi_{ij}}{\partial q^f}\right)_\theta = 0$$

(10.12)
$$-\sum_i \lambda_i \sum_j \pi_{ij} \left[(q^f - 1)\left(\frac{\partial f}{\partial q_{i'}^k}\right)_\theta + \sum_{k=1}^{2} (q_i^k - 1)\left(\frac{\partial c_{ij}^k}{\partial q_{i'}^k}\right)_\theta \right]$$

$$+ \sum_i \lambda_i \sum_j s_{ij} \left(\frac{\partial \pi_{ij}}{\partial q_{i'}^k}\right)_\theta = 0,$$

where λ_i is the shadow price on the budget constraint with aggregate outcome i,

$$s_{ij} \equiv x_{ij} - (q^f - 1)f - \sum_{k=1}^{2} (q_i^k - 1)c_{ij}^k$$

is the net transfer from the government to the individual for ij, and $(\partial m/\partial q_n)_\theta$ denotes the change in m from a compensated change in q_n (the compensation occurs for all relevant i,j) and therefore captures the relevant substitution effects. Though they appear rather intimidating, eqs. (10.11) and (10.12) have an intuitive interpretation that has been alluded to earlier. The first term is the change in deadweight loss due to distorted consumer prices resulting from raising the consumer price of the good in question by one unit. The second term is the corresponding change in deadweight loss due to moral hazard. Thus, at the constrained optimum, the overall deadweight loss, relative to the first best, is minimized. Arnott and Stiglitz solve for the optimal tax rates in simple variants of their model with only one or two relative prices. They find (subject to minor qualifications) that accident-prevention goods and goods complementary to effort should be subsidized. In terms of the model presented, these results suggest that the agricultural input should be subsidized,[5] as well as the consumer good that is more complementary to effort.[6] This accords with the intuition given earlier that commodity taxation/subsidization is desirable to stimulate effort which is inefficiently low due to moral hazard.

   The above analysis has, I think, succeeded in its modest goal of demonstrating that optimal tax theory can be fruitfully employed in developing a theory of optimal stabilization policy.

   The model is much too simple, however. It is nondynamic.[7] It also ignores business cycles. Greenwald and Stiglitz (1990) cite four stylized facts that any satisfactory theory of business cycles, and hence of stabilization policy, should explain: (1) cyclical movements in real product wages; (2) cyclical patterns of output and investment, including inventories; (3) sensitivity of the economy to small perturbations; (4) persistence. To this list, I would add cyclical movements in unemployment. The model presented explains *none* of these stylized facts. To develop a satisfactory theory of optimal stabilization policy, it will be necessary to develop a satisfactory theory of business cycles. The book by Stokey and Lucas (1989) and the research by Greenwald and Stiglitz would appear to be good starting points.

Any theory of optimal policy has three essential ingredients: a rigorous model of general equilibrium, a fully specified welfare function, and market failure. These three ingredients essentially define optimal tax theory, which is, broadly interpreted, a theory of optimal economic policy. Thus, I contend that optimal tax theory is an *essential* component of any satisfactory theory of optimal stabilization policy.

I think the time is ripe for bringing stabilization policy back into public finance. Building on progress made in other branches of economics over the last two decades, we should be able to extend the basic static, certain optimal tax model to stochastic dynamic settings in ways that permit insightful and conceptually sound analyses of optimal stabilization policy.

We should be grateful to Mirrlees for advocating that the Stabilization Branch of Richard Musgrave's Fiscal Department be reopened.

III. IN DEFENSE OF OPTIMAL TAX THEORY

Twenty years ago, optimal tax theory was "in." Students packed the classrooms in graduate public finance courses, eager to learn about the revolution in the field. There was a sense of heady optimism. With a powerful new set of conceptual tools, there was the hope that significant advances would be made in solving for the optimal tax system.

The early models (1971–1974) were by and large encouraging. They gave rise to interesting, intelligible, and nontrivial results: tax goods according to their complementarity with leisure; tax goods such that the proportional reduction in consumption of all goods is the same; impose a marginal income tax rate of zero at the highest income level; and so on. These first-phase results have become part of the conventional wisdom and have formed the basis for some policy (see Chapter 9).

The next generation of models (1975–1980) were less encouraging. Not only did they indicate that the qualitative results of the earlier models were nonrobust,[8] but they also derived optimal tax formulas so implicit that they provided little insight into which goods should be taxed heavily and which lightly, or into the optimal progressivity of the income tax system.

The result was a decline of interest in the new public economics, as well as some disenchantment and rejection, and a shift within the field toward positive and more down-to-earth issues. Moreover, many of the contributors to optimal tax theory during its early incandescent phase moved on to other problems.

Optimal tax theory is now "out"—or perhaps down but not out. Atkinson and Stiglitz's textbook *Lectures on Public Economics,* the high-water mark of optimal tax theory, is now out of print in North America.

The time has now come to take a sober, second look at optimal tax theory. I believe that optimal tax theory made several very important and lasting general conceptual contributions to economic theory, especially to the economic theory of policy, but that its specific contributions to public economics, over and above its contributions to economics generally, have been slim.

A. The Contributions of Optimal Tax Theory

Optimal tax theory has had a profound and lasting effect on applied economic theory and practice. It has made five distinct contributions. First, by employing a cardinal welfare function, it permitted the integration of equity and efficiency in applied economics. Second, by formulating the optimal tax problem in a general equilibrium framework à la Arrow-Debreu, it catalyzed the use of general equilibrium analysis in applied economics. Third, by providing the first rigorous treatment of asymmetric information in applied economics, it stimulated application of the economics of information. Fourth, it gave rise to a richer and more reasonable view of the appropriate role of government in a market-oriented economy. And fifth, it provided rigorous foundations for the theory of the second best.

1. THE "NEW, NEW WELFARE ECONOMICS"

The new welfare economics, pioneered by Lionel Robbins (1932), declared that interpersonal utility comparisons were invalid. Economists were to restrict their attention to efficiency, since efficiency analysis is scientific, and were to eschew equity concerns, since they are metaphysical. This put normative economics in an intellectual straitjacket for more than thirty years; the discipline still suffers from this misguided attempt to expel value judgments from economics and to focus on efficiency. Policymakers could not, however, ignore equity. In policy analysis, equity was incorporated by tacking on an imprecise equity-efficiency tradeoff to the rigorous efficiency analysis.

The ''new, new welfare economics'' was developed primarily in the context of optimal tax theory, starting with Mirrlees' seminal paper on the optimal income tax. The basic idea of the new, new welfare economics is that value judgments should be admitted completely and explicitly, via a cardinal social welfare function. That way, efficiency and equity considerations can be integrated in policy analysis in a conceptually coherent manner. The equity-efficiency tradeoff can be formalized. Policy advisers may then offer policymakers a range of policy options from which they may choose on the basis of their values. By introducing a rigorous formulation of equity and a precise language for discussing equity and efficiency together, the new, new welfare economics has led to a considerable improvement in the clarity and quality of policy debate.

These points can be illustrated with reference to cost-benefit analysis. Some assumptions concerning distributional weighting have to be made. In the new welfare economics, since interpersonal utility comparisons are deemed invalid, Occam's Razor, or the principle of insufficient reason, is used to justify the assumption that ''a dollar is a dollar is a dollar.'' Furthermore, where equity considerations are evidently of importance, some discussion of equity effects is appended to the cost-benefit calculus. This procedure seems arbitrary and needlessly indirect at best.

Drèze and Stern (1987) provide an excellent description of the cost-benefit procedure employed in the new, new welfare economics. A project is accepted simply if it increases welfare. The general equilibrium of the economy is described as the solution to a welfare maximization problem subject to a complete listing of resource, informational, and political constraints. The Lagrange multipliers on the resource constraints (with an arbitrary normalization) are the appropriate shadow prices, and a small project should be accepted if it generates a profit evaluated using these shadow prices. The superiority of this approach compared to that of the new welfare economics is evident by contrasting the clarity of Drèze and Stern's treatment of the social rate of discount with the fuzziness of the earlier literature.

2. APPLIED GENERAL EQUILIBRIUM ANALYSIS

International trade theory deserves the credit for being the first applied field in economics to employ general equilibrium analysis. But prior to optimal tax theory, almost all general equilibrium analysis in trade theory was in the context of the $2 \times 2 \times 2$ Hecksher-Ohlin model. The first use of general equilibrium theory à la Arrow-Debreu in the applied economics literature was by Diamond and Mirrlees (1971a, 1971b) in their seminal papers on optimal commodity taxation. Since then, use of the Arrow-Debreu general equilibrium framework has become a quality standard in all branches of applied economics.

Prior to optimal tax theory, normative economic analysis not only separated equity and efficiency but also (with the exception of international trade theory) relied almost exclusively on partial equilibrium analysis. The conditions under which single-market partial equilibrium welfare analysis is valid—equality of the marginal utility of income across consumers, and either no distortions elsewhere in the economy or zero income and cross-price (between the commodity under consideration and other commodities) effects—are extremely restrictive. And the extension of partial equilibrium analysis to multiple markets is fraught with pitfalls. A well-known example is from optimal commodity tax theory. Partial equilibrium analysis gives rise to the inverse elasticity rule. But if all goods are taxable, a uniform tax is optimal, since it is equivalent to a lump-sum tax. General equilibrium is much easier to do correctly. Nowadays, almost all normative analysis of quality is done employing general equilibrium models. Optimal tax theory led the way in this changeover.

A major contribution to applied economics over the last twenty years has been the development of increasingly sophisticated and detailed general equilibrium simulation models. This development was spurred not only by improvements in computer technology but also by the switch to general equilibrium thinking by applied economists.

It is hard to overstate the importance of the general equilibrium revolution. The use of general equilibrium analysis not only enforces conceptual consistency—everything has to be accounted for—but also alters the focus of analysis from the single market to the whole economy. This change in perception has resulted in better economic analysis. And optimal tax theory was a major contributor to this revolution.

3. ASYMMETRIC INFORMATION IN APPLIED ECONOMICS

It is now generally acknowledged that asymmetries of information are pervasive and are a major determinant of the structure of economic organization. Recognition of the importance of asymmetric information occurred only very recently, however. Insurers must have had at least an inchoate understanding of moral hazard and adverse selection for thousands of years. And the preference revelation problem for public goods has long been recognized. But Arrow's paper on the welfare economics of medical care (1963) is arguably the first to discern the broad importance of asymmetric information.

In the subsequent decade, there were a number of important contributions to the literature on asymmetric information. One was Mirrlees' paper on the optimal income tax (1971). The problem facing the government is to raise a given amount of revenue, at the least cost in terms of social welfare, from a population of heterogeneous individuals who differ in ability. If there were symmetric information, the government would tax on the basis of ability, equalizing everyone's marginal utility of income. But it is assumed that the government cannot observe ability and instead bases its taxation on observable income. Then individuals have an incentive to cut back labor supplied so as to reduce their tax liability. Thus, redistribution has efficiency effects.

Mirrlees' paper was of historical importance in a number of respects. It was arguably the first paper on mechanism design (Vickrey's 1961 paper on auctions was not discovered until later), and can therefore be considered one of the cornerstones of the burgeoning literature on the subject. Intensive study of the optimal income tax problem has also led to a greatly improved understanding of equilibrium with adverse selection with multiple types or a continuum of types.

The paper had a major impact on policy analysis as well. It was the first to impose informational constraints on the government's policy design problem. It was also the first to analyze formally the equity-efficiency tradeoff. And consequently, it was the first to model explicitly the role of informational constraints in limiting the scope for redistribution.

The optimal commodity tax literature has contributed less to the theoretical and applied literatures on asymmetric information, but not insubstantially. That asymmetric information generally causes shadow prices to deviate from market prices was first recognized in the context of optimal commodity taxation. Issues related to linear versus nonlinear pricing were also scrutinized in the optimal commodity literature. With distortions, nonlinear commodity taxation is generally desirable but requires that an individual's total consumption be observable; where only anonymous transactions can be taxed, linear pricing is implied.

4. THE ROLE OF GOVERNMENT

A generation ago, the judgment of most North American economists was that, apart from the enforcement of law and of property rights, governments should intervene only to correct demonstrable market failures; governments should provide public goods, regulate natural monopolies, and internalize production and consumption externalities. This belief was based primarily on the First and Second Theorems of Welfare Economics, derived from the Arrow-Debreu model of general equilibrium. Most economists also considered that some *lump-sum* redistribution should be undertaken on ethical grounds.

The insights derived from optimal tax theory have led to a fundamental re-evaluation of the role of government. From the optimal income tax problem came the insight that *lump-sum redistribution is infeasible,* and consequently that *efficiency cannot be separated from equity.* Lump-sum redistribution must be based on *exogenous* characteristics of the individual, on the basis of which it is deemed fair to redistribute (ability in Mirrlees' model). Most such characteristics, however, are only imperfectly measurable. Redistribution is therefore based on measurable, *endogenous* characteristics of the individual (income in Mirrlees' model). But then individuals have an incentive to modify these characteristics so as to reduce their tax liability, which has efficiency effects.

The theory of optimal commodity taxation reinforced the insight that with an unalterable distortion, it is generally desirable to introduce offsetting distortions. For example, since redistribution via the optimal income tax distorts the labor-leisure tradeoff, it is generally desirable to impose a set of differential commodity taxes. Pursuit of this train of thought gave rise to the insight that the presence of asymmetric information upsets both the First and Second Theorems and causes shadow prices to deviate from market prices.

An implication of these results is that the *potential* scope for welfare-improving government intervention is considerable. But whereas previously it was judged that when the market fails, the government should intervene, it is now recognized that those factors (transaction costs, asymmetric information, and so on) which cause the market to fail have implications for the effectiveness of government intervention. Thus, the modern view is that economists should search for the efficient structure of economic organization, which will generally include some mix of market, government, and private, nonmarket institutions.

The role of government is a central issue in economics. The issue will never be resolved, but optimal tax theory has raised the level of the debate.

5. THEORY OF THE SECOND BEST

The theory of the second best is concerned with optimal policy response in the presence of unalterable distortions. Drawing together disparate second-best problems that had been treated, including Ramsey (1927) and Corlett and Hague

(1953) from the literature on taxation, Lipsey and Lancaster (1956) provided a general statement of the problem. But the formal development of the theory of the second best occurred almost entirely in the context of optimal taxation.

The theory of the second best is now widely employed in all branches of applied microeconomics. One common application is to public utility pricing and investment; there the distortion is a breakeven or similar constraint in the presence of decreasing costs. Another common application is to urban transportation, where the distortion is that cars do not pay for the congestion they cause (see, for example, Wilson, 1983). The results of second-best pricing—Ramsey pricing—are especially well known.

Insights derived from second-best theory—especially that policy rules derived from partial equilibrium analysis do not generally hold where there are distortions in other markets—are now found in almost all policy discussions. For example, twenty years ago most housing policy economists advocated minimal government intervention, whereas now they recognize that housing policy should be designed taking into account such distortions as the property tax, imperfect capital markets, and the infeasibility of lump-sum taxation.

Thus, optimal tax theory has profoundly altered the theory, philosophy, and practice of economic policy and has led to significant improvement in both academic and popular discussion of economic policy.

B. Optimal Income Tax Theory and Income Tax Policy

In Chapter 9, Haveman argues that optimal income tax theory has seriously misled policymakers into believing that income tax progressivity is undesirable. This has come about, he states, because the theory has neglected many important considerations, and because policymakers have incorrectly interpreted the optimal tax theory results concerning *marginal* progressivity to apply to *average* progressivity. Haveman appears to hold optimal income tax theory, and perhaps optimal income tax theorists as well, responsible for this unfortunate state of affairs.

I would like to take issue with two general points in Haveman's chapter. The first is that theory is to blame for policies that are misguided because they are designed on the basis of unrealistically simple models. The second is that elaboration of the optimal income tax model to incorporate realistic complications will (for any social welfare function) most likely increase optimal progressivity.

1. APPLIED THEORY AND POLICY ANALYSIS

I did not know that policymakers had interpreted the results of optimal income tax theory as implying that income tax progressivity is undesirable. A thorough reading of the optimal income tax literature suggests, instead, that quantitative and even qualitative results are nonrobust. This is argued particularly forcefully in Stiglitz (1982b): if income uncertainty is introduced, if there are two or more labor types (say, different kinds of ability) that are imperfect substitutes in production, or if income is measured with noise, then the qualitative properties of the optimal income tax model are altered. But for the sake of argument, let us suppose that policymakers have indeed based policy on misinterpretations of simple optimal tax models, which seems quite plausible.

Good theorists are typically not good policy advisers. The mark of the good theorist is an ability to develop a useful conceptualization clearly. This requires a combination of sound intuition concerning the mechanism of the economy and an ability to simplify and abstract. Simplification and abstraction entail focusing on some important facets of a problem, while ignoring others or paying them less attention than their empirical importance merits. Sound policy advising, meanwhile, requires good judgment concerning the relative importance of different aspects of a policy problem, sensitivity to political currents, and concern for practical detail. Thus, except for sound intuition, the qualities that make a good theorist are the antithesis of those that make a good policy adviser. A division of labor is therefore appropriate. Applied theorists should produce models and policy economists should use the insights derived from them (along with the results of econometric studies, and issues raised in public debate that have been ignored in the academic literature) as ingredients in their policy analysis.

According to this view, applied theorists have done their job well if they have produced a model that sheds new light on some policy issues. They should not be held responsible for any policies that derive from overstressing or misinterpreting their model's results. The responsibility lies rather with policy analysts, whose job it is to weigh the policy significance of a new model's results.

The issue is not that clear-cut, however, since many applied theorists make exaggerated claims for the policy relevance of their work. Many articles in applied theory present numerical examples and include some policy discussion. The intention of the numerical examples should be to show the sensitivity of results to certain parameters and to indicate the order of magnitude of various effects. But often applied theorists overstate the practical relevance of their numerical results, whether because they really believe that their models capture reality, or because they feel the need to oversell their product. Similarly, policy discussion in articles in applied theory should be presented as demonstrating how the model provides insights into a few features of a policy problem. Too often, however, the policy discussion is presented as being more comprehensive than it actually is, and caveats are often mumbled.

Policy analysts should have the common sense to discount inflated claims of policy relevance in articles in applied theory and to realize that famous theorists, while very smart, can be seriously deficient in policy sense. But at the same time, theorists need to be more circumspect and modest in their claims of policy relevance.

2. REALISTIC COMPLICATIONS AND PROGRESSIVITY

There are indeed many considerations relevant to the design of the income tax that optimal income tax theory has overlooked. Haveman lists a number of these neglected considerations which he feels should be incorporated into optimal income tax theory before it will provide reliable guidance concerning the optimal degree of progressivity. He argues that incorporation of these considerations would most likely support a more progressive income tax. Although his discussion is insightful, sensitive, and well informed, its balance is open to question.

A strong case can be made that the most important oversight of the basic income tax model is its neglect of administrative, "financial,"[9] and compliance costs. According to this view, the income tax system should be radically simplified. Much of the complexity of the tax system stems from its marginal progressivity.[10] The more steeply the marginal tax rate rises with income, the greater taxpayers' incentive to self-average their income, which they can do by altering the timing of their expenses and receipts. If, indeed, the administrative, financial, and compliance costs associated with marginal progressivity are high, then a demogrant system is called for, which combines a poll subsidy with a flat-rate tax and hence exhibits average progressivity.

A strong case can also be made that the search for the optimal degree of income tax progressivity is a will-o'-the-wisp. Since the simple optimal income tax model is nonrobust, a fortiori more complex models will be nonrobust. Even the *qualitative* results will depend on the details of the model's specification and on parameter values. Then determining the optimal degree of progressivity will require precise parameter estimates and testing of competing models. But given the lack of agreement among empirical studies concerning the magnitude of such basic parameters as labor supply elasticities, it is open to question whether the simultaneous dynamic processes of improvements in data, theory, and econometric method will converge to a consensus concerning the optimal degree of progressivity.

Notes

2. The Distribution of the Tax Burden

I am grateful to Jim Poterba, Frank Levy, John Hills, Julian Le Grand, and Nick Stern for their helpful comments during the writing of this chapter.

1. For a discussion of these studies, see, among others, Peacock and Shannon (1968), Prest (1968), Boreham and Semple (1976), O'Higgins (1980), Le Grand (1982, Appendix), and Le Grand (1987).
2. For an early attempt at the international comparison of results from such studies, see Clark and Peters (1964).
3. For reviews of the contribution of the Harberger model, see, among others, Mieszkowski (1969), McLure (1975a), and Kotlikoff and Summers (1987).
4. Specifically, $a_x \equiv \theta_{kx}\lambda_{lx} + \theta_{lx}\lambda_{kx}$ and $a_y \equiv \theta_{ky}\lambda_{ly} + \theta_{ly}\lambda_{ky}$.
5. For an equilibrium, we either have equality of the factor demands with supplies, or inequality with the relevant factor price zero. So if labor is in excess supply, then the wage would have to be zero.
6. A sufficient condition for the tax to be fully borne by labor, in this sense, is that the production functions and demand functions be Cobb-Douglas (of which Brittain's case is a subcase).
7. See Smolensky et al. (1987) for a discussion of the role of computable general equilibrium models in budget incidence studies.
8. This is one of the special cases considered by Harberger (1962, Part III).
9. This may happen in the case of a constant elasticity of substitution demand system, if D is sufficiently large so that the demand curve tends to a vertical line whose location depends on the weights of the goods in the utility function.

10. See MacLeod and Malcomson (1989), for further discussion of the contractual basis.

11. For an empirical analysis of the regional effects, see Golladay and Haveman (1977).

12. Efficiency wages were introduced into the Harberger model by Agell and Lundborg (1990). The model here differs in emphasizing the primary/secondary distinction, as in Van de Klundert (1988) and Atkinson (1988).

13. The equations $p_x = c_{lx}w_x + c_{kx}r$ and $p_y = c_{ly}(w_x + e(1 - q)/q) + c_{ky}r$ give (where $r = 1$) a curve which starts at $c_{kx}/[c_{ky} + c_{ly}e(1 - q)/q]$ and tends as $w_x \to \infty$ to c_{lx}/c_{ly}. The assumption about capital intensity means that it slopes down to the right.

14. The factor market equations are $c_{lx}x + c_{ly}y(1 + gU/V) = L$ and $c_{kx}x + c_{ky}y = K$. It is assumed that

$$\frac{c_{kx}}{c_{lx}} < \frac{K}{L} < \frac{c_{ky}}{c_{ly}(1 + gU/V)}.$$

15. The existence of unemployment introduces the question of transfer payments. If there is some form of unemployment insurance or assistance, then the specification of differential incidence needs reconsideration. Is it supposed that the value of these benefits is reduced to the extent of the forward shifting of the payroll tax (in which case real government spending is reduced), or is it the case, as Browning (1978) has argued, that these transfers are effectively indexed against such price changes? What interpretation is to be given to the alternative position with which the tax is being compared? Is it one in which transfer incomes would be reduced proportionately with other incomes?

16. For discussion of the conditions under which this may happen, see Grandmont (1986), and, for a more heuristic account, Day (1982).

17. This means that $s_1 < s_2$, and that the expression added to (2.28) is a positive multiple of $(dp_x/p_x - dp_y/p_y)$.

18. Convergence is guaranteed where s is constant (and the production function satisfies certain conditions). Where the savings rate is not constant, it is possible that the aggregate capital-labor ratio does not converge. We saw in Section E above that in an intergenerational accumulation model, there may be erratic growth; it would be interesting to explore its distributional implications.

19. V may be rewritten as G plus $w(1 - t)L$ divided by $(1 + h)$, the latter factor being the "discount" applied to earnings to allow for the cost of effort.

20. For a discussion of the interpretation of observed alcohol expenditure in the United Kingdom, see Atkinson et al. (1990).

21. More recent work suggests that the underrecording may be caused to a significant

degree by differential nonresponse to the survey, rather than underreporting by the respondents themselves. See Kemsley et al. (1980).

Comments on Chapter 2 by Frank Levy

My thanks go to Henry Aaron and Sheldon Danziger for helpful discussions.

1. The exact situation is slightly more complex than this sketch shows. Elderly families in 1949 did, in fact, have a moderately high rate of labor force participation. This rate has declined over time and thus has made some contribution to the proportion of families without earners.

2. For example, Moore, Zil, and Steif (1990) have examined young women's Armed Forces Qualification Test (AFQT) scores from the National Longitudinal Survey of Labor Market Experiences of Youth. For all young women (ages 22–30) in the sample, the mean AFQT score is defined as 100 with a standard deviation of 15. The mean for poor mothers, both on and off AFDC (Aid to Families with Dependent Children), is 86 (with a standard deviation of 15). In terms of occupational "fit," 55 percent of AFDC mothers have AFQT scores more than one s.d. below the mean score of women who are clerical/secretarial workers (mean 101), while 40 percent have scores more than one s.d. below the mean of women in service occupations (mean 96). (Note that these are all point-in-time estimates and therefore are weighted toward welfare recipients in the midst of long AFDC spells.)

3. The role of the trade deficit in increasing the return to education is emphasized in Levy (1988) and in Murphy and Welch (1988). Bound and Johnson (1989) believe that the increasing return is due to technological change—a shift away from unskilled workers in all sectors—and argue that the trade deficit per se is not a strong explanation.

4. In Roy's model, a person can either fish or hunt. Individuals vary in their fishing ability and hunting ability (though the two abilities are not necessarily positively correlated across individuals). Hunting is more "skilled," in the sense that hunting output varies with hunting ability more than fishing output varies with fishing ability.

5. At first glance, the relative gains of the elderly seem to contradict the way in which the elderly made up a quarter of the bottom quintile in both 1949 and 1987 (see the table in text). But in 1949, these bottom-quintile elderly families represented almost one-half of all elderly families. In 1987, the bottom-quintile elderly families represented only one-fourth of all elderly families.

6. My comments were written later in the week in which the article appeared.

7. See, for example, a January 1990 *Wall Street Journal* poll in which 73 percent of all respondents said that Japan was currently in a stronger economic position than the United States.

8. I wish to thank Patricia Graham for discussion of this point.

9. The National Opinion Research Center's General Social Survey for 1990 shows a widespread belief that current spending on education is too low among respondents with children (73 percent) as well as respondents under 35 without children (71 percent) and respondents 35 and over without children (63 percent).

3. Public Sector Dynamics

I am grateful to John Quigley, Gene Smolensky, Don Fullerton, and David Romer for their comments on early versions of this chapter.

1. See Bernheim (1987) for a recent survey of this literature.

2. See, for example, Stiglitz and Weiss (1981).

3. From the normative perspective, there have also been interesting contributions on the role of deficits and social security in spreading risks across generations. See, for example, Green (1977); Merton (1983); Brandts and de Bartolome (1992).

4. See, for example, Eaton and Gersovitz (1981) and Bulow and Rogoff (1989).

5. This assumes that the economy is dynamically efficient and on a sustainable path. Without efficiency, it could create additional wealth by creating additional debt. The recent literature has featured tests for the sustainability of government policy (for example, Hamilton and Flavin, 1986; Wilcox, 1989).

6. Indeed, evidence presented in Feldstein and Morck (1983) suggests that these liabilities are fairly accurately valued by the market.

7. Such a case arises when there are deferred capital income taxes, associated with such items and accelerated depreciation and, perhaps, with dividends taxes. In this situation (discussed more fully below), changes in market values may reflect changes in future government taxes.

8. See Auerbach, Gokhale, and Kotlikoff (1991) for an initial attempt at calculating such "generational accounts."

9. This characteristic holds even in an infinite horizon model (Judd 1987), since the consumption tax is imposed after "the" generation has accumulated some assets.

10. See, for example, Venti and Wise (1986), Feenberg and Skinner (1989), and Gale and Scholz (1990).

11. See Bhatia (1972); Feldstein (1983); Poterba (1987); Auerbach and Hassett (1991).

12. For a more recent econometric approach that incorporates the assumption of forward-looking behavior in estimating the impact of taxation, see Auerbach and Hassett (1992).

13. The result holds even if the *expected* return on the marginal investment exceeds the deductible interest rate because of risk, since the tax on the risk premium itself imposes no cost on the firm and, in an efficient capital market, has no real effects either (Gordon 1985).

14. A useful discussion of long-run incidence can be found in Kotlikoff and Summers (1987).

15. See Auerbach (1987) for further description of the act's corporate provisions.

16. See Auerbach (1989). Empirical tests of this hypothesis (Cutler 1988) yield some support but are inconclusive.

17. The same approach has been applied to the case of capital income taxation in an overlapping generations model by Kotlikoff et al. (1988), in which the social contract forbidding capital levies is sold by each generation to the next, and once broken cannot be replaced.

18. Feenberg and Rosen (1987), however, find little empirical support for this proposition.

19. For some preliminary analysis in this direction, see Auerbach and Kotlikoff (1987, ch. 11), and Auerbach et al. (1989).

4. Public Goods and the Invisible Hand

I thank Marcus Berliant for many discussions and also Robert M. Anderson, Jacques Drèze, Greg Engl, Theodore Groves, Mordecai Kurz, Todd Sandler, Dan Rubinfeld, and Jacques-François Thisse for useful comments.

1. Public goods may also be provided in a Nash equilibrium by self-interested parties who make voluntary contributions, rather than by a benevolent government or by profit-maximizing entrepreneurs. In general, the provision of public goods will be suboptimal. See Bliss and Nalebuff (1984) and Bergstrom, Blume, and Varian (1986).

2. In a variant of the club model, the member pays for "visits" to the club and can reduce the total payment by reducing the number of visits. "Visits" in the club model are similar to "lot size" in the local public good model, since varying visits varies the total price in the club model just as varying the lot size varies the total price in the local public goods model. But reducing the lot size in the local public goods model reduces the price without necessarily reducing the enjoyment of the public goods. In contrast, reducing the number of visits to a club reduces the member's enjoyment of the shared facilities that the club provides.

3. The original model of Buchanan, as well as many subsequent models, assumes that crowding is anonymous. See Cornes and Sandler (1986, Part IV), Boadway (1982), Berglas and Pines (1981), Bewley (1981), Pauly (1970), Scotchmer (1985a, 1985b), Wooders (1978, 1980), Scotchmer and Wooders (1987a).

4. See Ichiishi (1977, 1981, 1982, 1991), who models the firm as a cooperative venture and permits complementarities among workers of different types.

5. See Scotchmer and Wooders (1986) for examples and elaboration.

6. We notice that there cannot be private information about types in this model. If types were not observable, crowding externalities could not be nonanonymous.

7. This is done by Scotchmer and Wooders (1987b).

8. For example, see Berglas (1976) and Wooders (1989, "Tiebout equilibrium").

9. For example, see Wooders (1978, 1989, "competitive equilibrium"), where consumers are permitted to act cooperatively in forming new jurisdictions.

10. A literature is developing to show that in large games, utilities in the core will "almost" have equal treatment. See Engl and Scotchmer (1992), who show this in a model with transferable utility where agents are not characterized by type but can have any vector of characteristics. "Types" is a special case.

11. A similar proposition is proved by Scotchmer and Wooders (1987b) with a different condition 1 and a scale assumption. Wooders (1978, 1989) discusses equivalence of the core and a type of price equilibrium where consumers are permitted to cooperate in forming jurisdictions. It would be surprising if such a notion of equilibrium did not bear a close relationship to the core. See my comments on equilibrium concepts in Section A of Part I, above.

12. The notion of exhaustion appears in many papers, especially those on club theory, originating with the discussions of club economies given by Buchanan (1965), but also in discussions of private goods economies with U-shaped average cost. Most notions of exhaustion are defined with respect to the utility functions (or, in games, for the characteristic function), and imply that after some maximal size, the average utility payoff to increasing the size of the group increases very slowly or becomes negative. In contrast, the above definition of "exhaustion of blocking opportunities" applies to the game itself.

13. If utility is transferable, for each $\mathbf{n}$ there is a number $V(\mathbf{n})\in \mathbf{R}_+$ such that $\mathbf{u}\in W(\mathbf{n})$ iff $\mathbf{u} \cdot \mathbf{n} \leq V(\mathbf{n})$. The condition $\mathbf{u}\in W(r\mathbf{s})$ implies that $\mathbf{u} \cdot r\mathbf{s} \leq V(r\mathbf{s})$, and $\mathbf{u}\in w(\mathbf{s})$ implies that $\mathbf{u} \cdot \mathbf{s} \leq \sup_{r>0} V(r\mathbf{s})/r$.

14. The first conclusion, $(\mathbf{u} - \mathbf{u}') \cdot (\mathbf{N} - \mathbf{N}') \leq 0$, is proved by Scotchmer and Wooders (1989). The monotonicity inequalities $(\mathbf{u} - \mathbf{u}') \cdot (\mathbf{N} - \mathbf{N}') \leq 0$ and $(\mathbf{u} - \mathbf{u}') \cdot (\mathbf{s} - \mathbf{s}') \leq 0$ do not imply the comparative static result stated in the remaining part of the theorem; however, the inequalities (i) and (ii) in the proof underlie all these results.

15. Utility in the club economy can be represented as $U^i[g,\mathbf{n},x_i] = x_i + \varphi^i(g,\mathbf{n})$ for a suitable function φ^i.

16. For example, to prove their monotonicity result (and also to prove nonemptiness of the epsilon core) Scotchmer and Wooders (1988) use the condition that only coalitions smaller than a bound, say r^{**}, "matter." Versions of this condition are used in subsequent papers of Wooders as well. Such conditions are enough to ensure that blocking opportunities are exhausted, but are not required for the notion of "approximate" exhaustion of blocking opportunities defined by Engl and Scotchmer (1992), which underlies an even more general monotonicity relationship.

17. They define "approximate" exhaustion of the set Ω and show that $(\mathbf{u} - \mathbf{u}') \cdot (\mathbf{s} - \mathbf{s}') \leq \psi$ for ψ arbitrarily small. They also generalize the proportional

comparative statics described in Proposition 4.2. Using the conditions on N and N' described there, they show that $\gamma + u_1 > u'_1$, where γ can be arbitrarily small.

18. The club theory literature typically describes emptiness of the core as an "integer problem." See Pauly (1970b) for an early exposition of this problem.

19. Shapley and Shubik also define the related notion "strong epsilon core." For a proof that the strong epsilon core is nonempty in club economies with transferable utility, see Scotchmer and Wooders (1988).

20. Another tempting approach is to divide the remainder group of players among the groups of size n^*, so that the sizes of groups would be arbitrarily close to n^*. This would work if players were continuously divisible. However, if n must be an integer and if $n^* = 5$, groups with size "close" to n^* must have either 4 or 6 members— not arbitrarily close.

21. See Stiglitz (1977), Wildasin (1986), Starrett (1988), and Fujita (1989) for summaries and references. See also Brueckner (1983) and Pines (1991).

22. This literature implicitly assumes that relative prices for private goods (including the nonland portion of housing) are fixed, and that private goods can be summarized as a real value rather than a vector.

23. I have suppressed the endowments of land in this description, but Y_t exceeds y_t if consumers are endowed with land, as well as with private goods, and if they earn income in their capacities as landlords. Of course, there is no restriction that consumers must own the land they occupy.

24. Allocations are defined so that consumers of the same type in the same jurisdiction are treated equally. Of course, there might be only one consumer of each type, in which case N_t^j simply indicates whether that consumer occupies jurisdiction j.

25. The function m^t is well defined if U^t is strictly increasing in private goods and is unbounded as x_t becomes large. We will have $p(g) < \infty$ if m^t is decreasing in s and $m^t(g,s,u_t)$ becomes unbounded for s near zero. If $[Y_t - m^t(g,s,u_t)] / s < 0$ for all s and t, as when the public goods g are very unattractive, then $p(g) = 0$ and no consumers would occupy such a jurisdiction if offered.

26. See Fujita (1990) for an excellent discussion of bid rent functions as used in the tradition of urban economics.

27. The proof applies to allocations for which $s_t^j > 0$. If we assume, as in note 25, that $m^t(g,s,u_t)$ becomes unbounded as s comes close to zero, it follows immediately that an unbounded amount of private goods is required to achieve utilities $\{u_t\}$ if $s_t^j = 0$ and $N_t^j > 0$. Such allocations are therefore more costly than the LPGE, which will not have $s_t^j = 0$ when $N_t^j > 0$.

28. The numerators of the first and fourth expressions of (4.3) must include $-\tau^j$, since each consumer pays that amount. But the cost paid by landowners must now be diminished by the amount of revenue collected through the head tax, so that it becomes $-[c(g^j,N^j) - \tau^j N^j]$ instead of $-c(g^j,N^j)$. Thus, we have subtracted and added the same amount to the first and last expressions in (4.3).

29. I am grateful to Jacques Drèze for this example.

Comments on Chapter 4 by Daniel L. Rubinfeld

1. Groucho Marx once said he would not want to join any club that would accept him as a member. Nonexistence of equilibrium is discussed in greater detail in Rubinfeld (1987).
2. See Buchanan and Goetz (1972) and Flatters, Henderson, and Mieszkowski (1974) for further development of this point.
3. This point is made by Starrett (1988, p. 14).
4. See Mieszkowski and Toder (1983) for details. In this example, the western states have a large share of the coal market, but the general point would apply so long as there is some market power.
5. See, for example, Hamilton (1975).
6. See *Shapiro v. Thompson,* 394 U.S. 618 (1969).
7. See Courant and Rubinfeld (1979). See also Wilson (1984) for a related property tax analysis.
8. See Courant and Rubinfeld (1981) for details.

5. Federalism and Government Finance

1. In fact, mobility can, under certain circumstances, be a source of distortions. In a regional context, for example, if individuals must work in the same jurisdiction in which they reside, mobility can produce inefficient outcomes. See Flatters, et al. (1974) and Stiglitz (1977).
2. See Bradford and Oates (1975) for an attempt to quantify these gains.
3. A case in point is a state or local corporation income tax. Such a tax on mobile capital introduces troublesome and costly administrative complexities and is the likely source of locational inefficiencies. See McLure (1986b, 1986c).
4. See also Break's later treatment (1980, ch. 3) and Oates (1972, ch. 3).
5. For a useful (if now somewhat dated) survey and assessment of work on the flypaper effect, see Fisher (1982). See Quigley and Smolensky (1993) for a more recent treatment.
6. Whether or not this is, in fact, true is not wholly clear from the aggregate data. There appears to have been some slowing in the growth of state and local spending during the early 1980s, when federal grants were cut. A careful study of all this is needed.
7. For an excellent survey of the economics of the local public sector, see Rubinfeld (1987).
8. Mrs. Thatcher's introduction of a local poll tax in the United Kingdom—the source

of riots in the realm—can be justified on efficiency grounds from a Tiebout perspective!

9. Although much of this literature finds a high degree of capitalization of fiscal differentials, a recent and careful study by Yinger et al. (1988) has yielded estimates suggesting a much smaller extent of capitalization of property tax differentials among a sample of Massachusetts localities.

10. Pack and Pack (1978), in a study of Pennsylvania communities, find heterogeneity in excess of that which they view as consistent with a Tiebout world. However, it is unclear what "excessive" means in this context. Moreover, the extent of heterogeneity may be exaggerated somewhat by the measures used in the study.

11. Put more formally, it is the level of final services that enters as an argument in the individual utility functions.

12. See Oates (1989) for a summary and assessment of this later work.

6. The Study and Practice of Income Tax Policy

The authors acknowledge useful suggestions and comments from Henry Aaron, Walter Blum, George Break, John Due, Richard Goode, Daniel Halperin, Paul McDaniel, Peter Mieszkowski, Richard Musgrave, Ronald Pearlman, Harvey Rosen, Carl Shoup, John Witte, and Bernard Wolfman. The views expressed here should, however, be attributed only to the authors.

1. See Chapter 4 (Scotchmer) and Chapter 5 (Oates) for discussions of these issues. The federal income taxes accounted for 51.4 percent of federal receipts (national income and product accounts basis) in 1960, but only 43.8 percent in 1986. From providing almost a third of income tax revenues, the corporate income tax slipped to providing less than 20 percent.

2. See Chapter 8 (Diamond) for a discussion of stabilization issues.

3. The introduction, Parts I and III, and Section B of Part IV were written primarily by McLure; Part II and Section A of Part IV were written primarily by Zodrow.

4. Much of this was brought together in undergraduate textbooks on government finance by Rolph and Break (1961) and Due (1959). For a retrospective view on the conventional wisdom that guided much academic thinking during this period, as well as the historical development of the U.S. income tax system, see Witte (1985).

5. This discussion draws on the retrospective view in Aaron (1989, p. 10). We do not discuss the benefit principle, which is generally agreed to be of little relevance for federal income taxation. Musgrave (1959a) emphasized the need to distinguish clearly between the allocative and redistributive roles of fiscal policies.

6. See Ramsey (1927) and Lipsey and Lancaster (1956).

7. See Corlett and Hague (1953–54).

8. Musgrave (1959a, chs. 7, 11, and 12) did make this distinction.

9. Income taxation allows no deductions for saving; by comparison, amounts saved are explicitly excluded from the base of a direct consumption-based tax. See, for example, U.S. Treasury (1977), Institute for Fiscal Studies (1978), and Bradford (1986).

10. Musgrave (1959a, pp. 161–164) was more sympathetic to a consumption-based tax than most of his peers; he reviewed the literature on the choice between income and consumption, including Kaldor's "spirited and imaginative book" *An Expenditure Tax* (1955) and the philosophical musings of Hobbes about whether taxation should be based on what is taken from the pot (consumption) instead of what is put in (income). Simons (1938) argued that a comprehensive income tax is desirable because it promotes personal liberty and equality.

11. For some, resolution of the equity issue depended crucially on whether gifts and estates would be exempt from tax or included in taxable consumption; this issue also arises in the income tax context.

12. See Slitor (1973), which includes a brief discussion of the 1942 study of a possible expenditure tax conducted by the U.S. Department of the Treasury.

13. These issues are discussed in Musgrave (1959a, ch. 8). We follow American practice in using the term "Haig-Simons," even though Schanz (1896) had stated the same principles earlier.

14. See, for example, Smith (1961, ch. 7) and Musgrave (1959a, p. 174). For contrary views on this important issue, see Mieszkowski (1972) and McLure (1975b).

15. Seven papers were included in the *Tax Revision Compendium;* see, for example, Groves (1959), Surrey (1959a, 1959b), and Smith (1959).

16. See Surrey (1959a), Lyon and Eustice (1962), and Eustice (1964) on the difficulty of distinguishing between capital gains and ordinary income under certain circumstances.

17. See, for example, Groves (1959), Musgrave (1959b, p. 2, 231), and Simons (1950, p. 44).

18. Musgrave (1959a), however, devoted an entire chapter to the theoretical microeconomic effects of taxation on saving. The last third of his treatise is devoted to macroeconomic aspects of fiscal policies.

19. Richard Goode noted this last point in correspondence with the authors.

20. See, for example, the essentially standard lists in Paul (1956), Pechman (1959a), Surrey (1959a), and U.S. Congress, Joint Economic Committee (1961). Paul lists nine items: municipal bonds; interest on life insurance; percentage depletion and intangible drilling costs; deductions for personal taxes, mortgage interest, and consumer interest; income splitting; deferred compensation, pensions, and fringe benefits; use of closely held corporations; preferential treatment of long-term capital gains; and evasion via personal consumption expenditures deducted as business expense and failure to report interest and dividends. Surrey's list is similar, but includes the exclusion of up to $50 of dividends and the 4 percent credit for divi-

dends received, special provisions for the elderly, deductions for charitable contributions, casualty losses, and medical expenses. The *Tax Revision Compendium* contained seven papers on the exemption of interest on state and local bonds.

21. See Kahn (1959), Brazer (1959), and Heller (1959). For a more recent discussion, see Andrews (1972).

22. See Kahn (1959).

23. See, for example, Pechman (1959a).

24. Pechman (1959b) considers the loss of imputed income and the added expenses that result when the spouse works, but not the disincentive effects.

25. The early work on "ability-to-pay" taxation cited in Musgrave (1959a, pp. 95–108) suggested that the progressivity of the income tax structure should be determined by requiring equal "sacrifice" of utility by individuals with identical utility functions characterized by diminishing marginal utility of income. If the criterion were equal marginal sacrifice and if incentive effects were ignored, marginal tax rates of 100 percent should be applied to all high-income individuals until all required revenues were raised (Edgeworth, 1897). Under the less extreme requirements of equal proportionate or equal absolute sacrifice, declining marginal utility of income does not suffice to justify progressive taxation; the rapidity of decline must exceed a certain threshold to justify progressivity. Such analysis suffered from being based on the assumption that the utility of income is measurable and comparable across individuals. By 1960 (or even before) attempts to base progressivity on the sacrifice doctrine had been discarded by most tax economists. Most economists would probably have shared Musgrave's views (1959a, p. 109) on the foundations of progressive taxation: "the principle of ability to pay . . . becomes a question of social value." For further discussion, see Witte (1985, pp. 32–36).

26. The *Economic Report of the President* for 1962 noted that the consumer price index (CPI) had risen, on average, less than 1.5 percent per year from 1951 to 1960. By comparison, the *Economic Report of the President* for 1992 indicates that from 1968 to 1985 the CPI rose by about 6.75 percent per year; from 1973 to 1981 it rose by about 9.25 percent per year. Whereas the prime interest rate was barely 3 percent during the former period, during the latter it was almost 10 percent.

27. See Killingsworth (1983), Hausman (1985), and Pencavel (1986) for surveys of the literature on the effects of taxation on labor supply.

28. Hausman's methods and results have been controversial; for a highly critical evaluation, see Heckman (1983).

29. By comparison, Harberger (1964) estimated that the total excess burden of taxes on labor supply was roughly 2.5 percent of tax revenues.

30. For example, see Section E of Part II, below.

31. See King (1980), Kotlikoff (1984), and Sandmo (1985) for surveys.

32. See David and Scadding (1974) for a discussion of these results; the invariance of saving with respect to the rate of return was often referred to as Denison's Law.

33. See also Hall (1968).

34. See Auerbach and Kotlikoff (1983b), Auerbach, Kotlikoff, and Skinner (1983), and Auerbach and Kotlikoff (1987) for various extensions to the strict life-cycle model employed by Summers, including the addition of an endogenous labor-leisure choice and the assumption of perfect foresight (rather than myopic expectations). See Seidman (1983) for the inclusion of bequests in the individual utility function, and Kotlikoff and Summers (1981) on the importance of doing so.

35. See also the response by Boskin (1978b and 1980) to his critics.

36. For a survey of the effects of taxation on risk taking, see Sandmo (1985).

37. See also Boadway (1987) and Bradford and Fullerton (1981).

38. For a recent survey, see Zodrow (1991).

39. These uncertainties obviously complicate attempts at business-individual tax integration; for a recent discussion, see Gerardi, Graetz, and Rosen (1990).

40. Sinn (1991) argues, however, that it is possible to construct models in which the existence of share repurchases is consistent with the new view.

41. For recent surveys, see Shoven and Whalley (1984) and Whalley (1988), as well as Chapter 2, above.

42. See also Brown (1939) for an extremely perceptive early analysis of tax incidence that anticipates some of the key results of later research.

43. See Mieszkowski (1969) and McLure (1975a) for reviews of these developments.

44. The latter analysis focuses on the implications of considerations of risk for incidence analysis, building on the work of Gordon (1985).

45. Note also that such large excess burdens complicate the determination of the conditions for the optimal allocation of resources to the public sector; see Atkinson and Stern (1974).

46. See Musgrave, Carroll, Cook, and Frane (1951), Musgrave, Case, and Leonard (1974), Devarajan, Fullerton, and Musgrave (1980), Pechman and Okner (1974), and Pechman (1985). For criticism of this approach, see Prest (1955). Browning (1978) and Browning and Johnson (1979) make incidence assumptions that are radically different from those traditionally employed. These authors followed the path-breaking work by Colm and Tarasov (1940).

47. See also the discussion in Chapter 2 (Atkinson) above.

48. See Kotlikoff and Summers (1987) and Chapter 3 (Auerbach) for surveys of dynamic incidence models.

49. Lyon (1989), however, finds a positive relationship between firm values and the introduction of investment tax credits, suggesting that the negative asset price effect stressed by Auerbach and Kotlikoff may be offset by the positive effect on firm values of the prospect of excess returns to new investment subject to the tax credit.

50. For surveys, see Sandmo (1976), Mirrlees (1976), Atkinson and Stiglitz (1980), Auerbach (1985), and Stern (1987a, 1987b).

51. See Rosen (1988a) for a recent discussion.

52. For simulation results under alternative tax treatments, see Feenberg and Rosen (1983).

53. See Slemrod (1990) for a discussion of conditions under which production taxes might be desirable.

54. Note that under certain circumstances, tax reform may be Pareto-improving so that the issue of reform-induced redistributions does not arise; see Guesnerie (1977) and Dixit (1979).

55. For recent surveys, see Zodrow and McLure (1991); Zodrow (forthcoming, b).

56. For example, see Musgrave (1959a), Goode (1977), and Pechman (1987). As indicated earlier, consumption taxation has in the past generally been identified with indirect (sales) taxation, and thus with regressivity. This confusion has long since been dispelled; at least within the tax policy community, it is recognized that a direct consumption tax is probably feasible. In such a tax regime, progressive rates could be used to achieve any degree of progressivity thought desirable.

57. For example, see U.S. Department of the Treasury (1977), Institute for Fiscal Studies (1978), Mieszkowski (1980), Hall and Rabushka (1983, 1985), Aaron and Galper (1985), Bradford (1986), McLure (1988), and McLure, Mutti, Thuronyi, and Zodrow (1990).

58. The government is assumed to balance its budget in each period and thus is unable to affect aggregate saving.

59. An earlier, if less developed, statement of the concept of "special relief" or tax "preference," defined as "a departure from a standard," can be found in Wolfman (1965).

60. See Surrey (1973) and Surrey and McDaniel (1985) for the development of the tax expenditure concept.

61. As noted by Break (1982, 1985), defining what is "normal" and what is "special" is not a simple task. In its 1983 budget the Reagan administration did not include the ITC and ACRS as tax expenditures, arguing that they were part of the "reference" tax structure. The Joint Committee on Taxation and the Congressional Budget Committee continued to use the "normal structure" of previous years and thus to classify these provisions as tax expenditures. The 1986 and subsequent budgets of the Reagan administration reported estimates of tax expenditures based on both pre-1983 and post-1982 concepts. The Bush administration continued this practice.

62. Both Walter Blum and Paul McDaniel, in conversation and correspondence with the authors, noted the role of computers in facilitating the growth of the tax shelter business. Computers have made possible the design of new and sophisticated financial instruments and the rapid calculation of the benefits of various shelter schemes under a variety of assumptions.

63. See, for example, Halperin (1986).

64. Thus, if there is no inflation and the interest rate is 10 percent, a taxpayer subject to a 50 percent marginal tax rate pays an after-tax interest rate of 5 percent [10 ×

$(1 - 0.5)]$. If the inflation rate is 10 percent and the nominal interest rate is 20 percent, the after-tax real rate of interest is zero $[20 \times (1 - 0.5) - 10]$. A smaller increase in the nominal interest rate would produce a negative real after-tax interest rate. The nominal interest rate must increase to 30 percent for the real after-tax interest cost to be 5 percent $[30 \times (1 - 0.5) - 10]$. See also Steuerle (1985) and Steuerle (1992, esp. pp. 48–51).

65. See the evidence on inflation and interest rates reported in note 26 above.

66. McLure (1989, p. 62) describes this as the "vampire approach" to dealing with tax shelters: "to be safe when dealing with a vampire, one drives a stake through the heart, hangs a cross around the neck, places a mirror over the eyes, and fills the coffin with wolfsbane."

67. We are indebted to Walter Blum for this insight. Koppelman (1989, p. 103) notes that "abusive tax shelters . . . generally have no economic reality . . . The PAL [passive activity loss] rules . . . were created to defeat virtually all tax shelters, whether regular or abusive."

68. Several of the tax policy lawyers who reviewed an earlier draft of this paper expressed the view that they and their colleagues would be much less likely than economists to favor consumption-based direct taxation and that many do not support investment incentives. It may also be necessary to differentiate among economists by age. Younger economists tend to be much more favorably inclined than their older colleagues toward consumption-based taxation and incentives for saving and investment.

69. Needless to say, we are not using the term "liberal" in its traditional European sense, which is essentially synonymous with laissez-faire. For speculations on the cause of this shift in views, see McLure (1984).

70. This is taken largely from Pechman (1987, App. A). Witte (1985) provides further details on the evolution of tax policy, as well as commentary on the politics of tax reform.

71. House Ways and Means Committee and Senate Finance Committee (1969).

72. In actuality the rate could go to approximately 50 percent, because long-term gains caused a reduction in the amount of earned income subject to the maximum rate of 50 percent.

73. This problem was first recognized only eight years after enactment of the income tax in 1913, when deduction of the expense of carrying tax-exempt securities was disallowed in 1921.

74. Witte (1985, pp. 190–198) describes the political debate that produced the 1976 law. He notes (p. 198) that "the growing perception of a capital crisis set the stage for the next five years of tax politics," culminating in the 1981 act.

75. For further discussion, see Witte (1985, pp. 204–217).

76. See Rudder (1983) and Witte (1985).

77. Feldstein (1981) had advocated the use of accelerated depreciation as a surrogate for inflation adjustment on simplicity grounds.

78. Richard Musgrave, reflecting in private conversation on the tax proposals in President George Bush's 1993 budget, has suggested that the 1986 act may be the high-water mark of tax policy based on the Haig-Simons definition of income. Reflecting on the complexity of the 1986 act, McLure (1988) has asked whether the act was "Tax Reform's Finest Hour or the Death Throes of the Income Tax."

79. The highest marginal rate was, however, actually 33 percent; it was paid by upper-middle-income taxpayers.

80. Walter Blum has noted in conversations with the authors that this was only the logical conclusion of a historical development in which the definition of capital gains was tightened to make it increasingly difficult to recharacterize ordinary income as capital gains—a ruse that was all too easy in the early days of the income tax.

81. One commentator questioned this statement, "given the conservative bias of accountants. It is not illogical to believe that true economic income can't be less than book income." We continue to believe it strange and inappropriate to base tax liabilities on whatever accounting conventions happen to underlie the reported income of a particular firm, rather than on uniform legislated standards.

82. For a list of provisions for which no change was proposed, see U.S. Department of the Treasury (1984, vol. 1, p. 147).

83. For more on the economics and politics of the 1986 act, see McLure and Zodrow (1987).

84. This paragraph is based on the authors' personal experience in the Office of Tax Policy.

85. Indeed, one could argue that the "humpbacked" individual marginal rate structure of the 1986 act (rates of 15, 28, 33, and 28 percent) reflected prescriptions for qualitatively similar rate patterns in the optimal tax literature; we suspect one would be hard-pressed to find evidence of this particular link between theory and policy.

86. By comparison, the emphasis placed on providing uniform treatment of various forms of taxable investment income during the debate, in order to avoid tax-induced misallocations of capital (providing a level playing field), has been questioned. As noted above, so long as some forms of income from capital—notably housing—go untaxed, it is not generally desirable to subject all other forms of capital income to uniform taxation. For this reason, McLure (1986a) has called the politically sacrosanct tax treatment of owner-occupied housing the Achilles' heel of tax reform.

87. See Aaron (1989, p. 11). Aaron also considers and rejects the possibility that policy makers are ignorant of recent theoretical advances. He acknowledges, but does not discuss at length, the proposition that many provisions of the tax law are so gross as to offend both old and new principles.

88. This school is sometimes called the fiscal exchange school. The terminology is unfortunate, since it suggests inaccurately that the school follows in the tradition of Wicksell. 89.

89. For a discussion of this point, see Hettich and Winer (1985).

90. Steuerle (1992, p. 84) continues in a footnote, "Many academic researchers failed to get involved in detailed structural issues, partly because they were ignorant of the many details of tax and expenditure law and often couldn't incorporate such details into their simple models of the economy, even if they were aware of them. In a self-deceptive way, issues became defined as unimportant because they weren't in one's economic model." Writing in a different context (about articles in legal periodicals written by law professors), Eustice (1989, pp. 17–18) makes a similar point: "Tax policy discussions without technical expertise are, at best, impractical, and, at worst, highly dangerous."

91. Several of the tax lawyers commenting on an earlier draft of this chapter noted the complexity created by preferential taxation of capital gains, an issue they are in a better position than economists to judge. Eustice (1989) wrote in 1976, "the decision to tax capital gains at a lower preferential rate is an enormous engine for complexity in the current law."

92. It is, however, possible to overemphasize redistribution. Musgrave (1987) has suggested that the base broadening of the 1986 act should have been combined with less rate reduction, especially for high-income taxpayers. McLure (1990, p. 174) has responded with three words: "dead on arrival."

93. Thus, Slemrod (1990, p. 167) writes: "I suspect that the ascendancy of uniform taxation . . . is due to the lack of strong evidence pointing to a clear alternative and the sense that a uniform tax system is less susceptible to political pressures favoring tax changes that serve special interests and are unrelated to optimal tax considerations."

94. See the discussion in Birnbaum and Murray (1987, pp. 11–13) of the role played by Robert McIntyre of Citizens for Tax Justice in publicizing the fact that Fortune 500 companies were paying no taxes, often as a result of safe harbor leasing and the generous provisions for capital recovery (ACRS and the ITC) contained in the 1981 act. Information for publicly held corporations was taken from annual financial statements. Because of confidentiality requirements, similar information on individual high-income participants in tax shelter partnerships was not available. See, however, the next paragraph.

95. See McLure (1989) for a more detailed discussion of how changes in the legislative process have contributed to complexity and for further references to the literature on the legislative process and simplification.

96. This does not mean that the tax-writing committees have less power. The increased use of the tax system to achieve social objectives has increased the power of the committees. The tax-writing committees can combine tax-increasing and -decreasing measures in a revenue-neutral manner; this may help explain the growth of tax expenditures. Because they control much of spending (especially on social security), they can make deals involving revenue-neutral changes in both taxes and expenditures. On this, see Steuerle (1992, pp. 77–79).

97. Birnbaum and Murray (1987, p. 260) quote Bob Packwood, former chairman of the Senate Finance Committee, to this effect: "Common Cause simply has everything upside down when they advocate 'sunshine laws' . . . When we're in the sunshine, as soon as we vote, every trade association in the country gets out their mailgrams and their phone calls in twelve hours, and complains about the members' votes. But when we're in the back rooms, the senators can vote their conscience. They vote what they think is good for the country. Then they go out to the lobbyists and say, 'God, I fought for you. I did everything I could. But Packwood just wouldn't give in, you know. It's so damn horrible.' "

98. Weidenbaum (1988, pp. 95–96) and Birnbaum and Murray (1987, p. 241) describe how special provisions of the 1986 act were tailored to benefit only one taxpayer, without naming the beneficiary. For example, General Motors was described as an "automobile manufacturer that was incorporated in Delaware on October 13, 1916." Other breaks were provided for projects with particular Farmers Home Administration Code numbers and for companies taking specified actions on certain dates.

99. See also note 91 above on the lack of professional support for this proposal among tax lawyers, who best understand how complicated it makes compliance and administration. For a survey of economic research on taxation of capital gains, see Zodrow (forthcoming, b).

100. For a complete analysis of the 1986 act, see Birnbaum and Murray (1987), Conlan et al. (1990), and Steuerle (1992).

101. For further development of this theme, see Steuerle (1992).

7. Optimal Taxation and Government Finance

1. Atkinson and Stiglitz (1980) provide an account of the theory.

2. Using a multiplier λ for the constraint $\mathbf{F}(\mathbf{y},z) = 0$, we set the derivatives of $\Sigma_h v^h - \lambda \mathbf{F}$ equal to zero. The derivative of v^h with respect to q is $-v_b^h x^h$, by Roy's famous identity. The derivative with respect to z is, by definition of marginal rates of substitution m, $v_b^h m^h$. We therefore get the three equations

$$-\sum_h v_b^h x^h = \lambda F_y \sum_h x_q^h, \quad \sum_h v_b^h m^h = \lambda \left[F_y \sum_h x_z^h + F_z \right], \quad \sum_h v_b^h$$

$$= \lambda F_y \sum_h x_b^h,$$

which yield (7.2a) and (7.2b) on dividing the first and second by the third, and using $\mathbf{p} = \mu \mathbf{F}_y$, $\mathbf{r} = \mu \mathbf{F}_z$ for some scalar μ.

3. The consumer budget constraints $\mathbf{q} \cdot \mathbf{x}^h = b$ imply, on differentiating with respect to $\mathbf{q}$ and b, $\mathbf{q} \cdot \mathbf{x}_q^h = -x$ and $\mathbf{q} \cdot \mathbf{x}_b^h = 1$. Consequently $\mathbf{t} \cdot \mathbf{x}_q^h = (\mathbf{q} - \mathbf{p}) \cdot \mathbf{x}_q^h = -\mathbf{x}^h - \mathbf{p} \cdot \mathbf{x}_q^h$; and $\mathbf{t} \cdot \mathbf{x}_b^h = (\mathbf{q} - \mathbf{p}) \cdot \mathbf{x}_b^h = 1 - \mathbf{p} \cdot \mathbf{x}_b^h$. Averaging over the population, and defining $x^* = \Sigma_h v_b^h x^h / \Sigma_h v_b^h$, we get equation (7.2c) in the text.

4. Some policy variables are set later in the day than others. So far as I know, all tax and subsidy rates are set in advance, though I dare say there may have been one or two occasions where a tax rate was changed retrospectively. But it may be useful to identify some policy variables as being (relatively) ex post. Automatic stabilizers will be discussed briefly below.

5. A paper by J. D. Wilson (1991) has now appeared which, like this chapter, considers the question for an economy in which the government is allowed to use a uniform lump-sum subsidy. Wilson's analysis covers some of the same ground as this one, concluding that the cost of public expenditure may well be less in a second-best economy than in one with first-best taxation. On the question which kind of tax environment would justify the higher level of public expenditure, Wilson obtains definite results for two interesting examples. Below, I obtain general results valid only for economies with a small degree of inequality. Our results are therefore complementary.

6. An interesting example is Ballard, Shoven, and Whalley (1985), where the premium on the cost of public expenditure is estimated for the United States, with a computable general equilibrium model of Ramsey type.

7. Their proposition concerns a two-good economy with identical consumers, for whom the utility of a public good is additively separable from the utility of private goods. In this economy, there is a fixed level of lump-sum tax. Commodity taxes and the level of expenditure on the public good are chosen optimally. The optimal level of public-good expenditure is shown to be a decreasing function of the lump-sum tax, in the neighbourhood of the optimal lump-sum tax (that is, the amount required to finance the public good). The restriction to a two-good economy is in fact unnecessary: the same proposition is true whatever the number of goods in the economy. Since the interesting model is the many-person economy discussed in the text, I omit the proof for that more general case.

8. King (1986) has also examined the conditions for optimal provision of public goods in the many-person optimal tax model. He derives them in a different form from the one used here. I comment on his interpretation below.

8. Integrating Allocation and Stabilization Budgets

This chapter draws heavily on my ongoing research collaborations with Olivier Blanchard and Jim Mirrlees. I am grateful to Cary Brown, Nick Stern, and Jim Poterba for helpful comments, to Doug Galbi for research assistance, and to the National Science Foundation for financial support.

1. Although this conception was important for the development of my writings in this area, the key analytical step initially was the realization that the use of the indirect utility function permitted a one-consumer analysis to be interpreted as a many-consumer analysis (Diamond and Mirrlees, 1971a, 1971b).

2. With this formulation, it is easy to see that the envelope theorem implies that, generically, the optimum includes some distorting taxes unless income distribution cannot be improved, even by lump-sum taxes.

3. Conceivably, some economists believe that constant money growth will solve all stabilization problems, as in the models of Robert Lucas (1972, 1989). I find it almost as hard to believe that some economists might think this as to believe that this is true about the economy. It is possible that constant growth is the best that can be done, just as one might conclude that a constant-rate VAT is better than varying rates; but before one can address this possibility, one needs a model that has some realism in addressing the tradeoffs involving more complexity and more diversity.

4. If it were adequate to think about allocation in terms of inflation and unemployment, it would be impossible to explain the enormous dissatisfactions with centrally planned economies that have had zero inflation and zero unemployment.

5. Tracking down this paper required the serendipity of Haveman's presence when I presented an earlier version of my arguments. I had remembered its content, the approximate publication date, and the journal, but could not remember the author.

6. For an approach to benefit-cost analysis based on fixed-price equilibria, see Drèze (1984).

7. In a standard Keynesian macro model, employment is equal to labor demand. In a typical analysis of unemployment compensation, the response of employment to changes in policy parameters depends only on labor supply. Both of these can't be right. Probably, neither is. Search theory offers a framework that can be used for both questions.

8. For estimates of the aggregate matching function for the United States, see Blanchard and Diamond (1989, 1990).

9. This assumption is made for clarity of presentation, ignoring the important impact of public investment on jobs.

10. For a discussion of the urn-ball approach to multiple applications for jobs and the derivation of the obverse of this matching function, see Blanchard and Diamond (forthcoming).

11. For this calculation, logarithmic utility functions were used, with the same coefficients on employment in both types of jobs. The symmetric matching function was taken to be Cobb-Douglas in unemployment and vacancies.

12. In posing the question this way, I am naturally led to assume individual optimization in the face of risk, ignoring the complications that come from failures to understand the workings of the economy.

13. I expect that an analysis of built-in stabilizers could also be conducted on the basis of finance constraints—for example, as modeled by Greenwald and Stiglitz (1988).

14. For another analysis of optimal taxation with separate states of nature, see Diamond and Mirrlees (1992).

15. Contrast this approach with the view that higher inflation involves a cost of more frequent price changes (for example, Fischer and Modigliani, 1978).

16. Consider the greater apparent willingness of the American public to accept cancellation of Social Security cost-of-living adjustments rather than accept benefit cuts. Consider contracts in nominal terms that do not change as inflation rates vary, such as the maximum pay cut for baseball players without free agency under the major league basic agreement.

17. For evidence of the nonneutrality of tax changes, see Poterba, Rotemberg, and Summers (1986).

9. Optimal Taxation and Public Policy

I would like to acknowledge the helpful comments of Henry Aaron, Richard Arnott, Anthony Atkinson, Peter Diamond, Walter Hettich, Charles McLure, Richard Musgrave, James Poterba, and Barbara Wolfe.

1. In this sense, my comments are an attempt to answer the question recently posed by Rosen (1988a): "Does progressive taxation survive optimal tax theory?"

2. This rule is sometimes referred to as the "Ramsey rule," after the author of one of the earliest and most insightful papers in this area (Ramsey, 1927).

3. If available leisure time itself could be taxed, there would be no distortions in the composition of outputs in the economy; such a tax would be a lump-sum tax. Hence, if leisure time itself cannot be taxed, impose the tax on the good that is most closely associated with leisure time. This rule is also known as the Corlett-Hague rule, named after its authors in another prominent article (Corlett and Hague, 1953).

4. This rule is often known as the Diamond-Feldstein rule, again named after those whose models incorporated the assumptions from which the rule was derived (Diamond, 1975; Feldstein, 1972).

5. See Auerbach (1985) for an excellent review of recent developments in the optimal taxation literature.

6. Mirrlees' answer to the first question is that under conditions of uncertainty an equilibrium may not exist (for given tax rates, planned public expenditures may exceed tax revenues), and price level adjustments will be necessary. In his words, issues of "stickiness," "robustness," and speed of "convergence" arise. Although Mirrlees tells us that some "kind of analysis" is required to identify a "means of adjustment that will bring the economy rapidly to equilibrium, without serious side effects," he says only that the welfare function analysis so central to the optimal-taxation literature does not provide the answer. He provides few other clues.

The second question has a somewhat more satisfying but equally ambiguous answer. When both distortionary and lump-sum taxes (subsidies) coexist, the cost of public expenditure need not be higher in a second-best than in a first-best world, and may be lower. Because marginal public revenue costs are equal across all sources, the nondistortionary tax (subsidy) option defines marginal cost. Mirrlees gives us two additional ways of reaching this same general conclusion. The first involves the incorporation of price level effects related to distortionary taxation. The second takes the form of an analytical demonstration that when the utility of a public good is additively separable from the utility of private goods and when there is a (very) small degree of inequality (in consumer characteristics), the social cost of a marginal dollar of public revenue may be greater than, less than, or equal to one. In this case, the answer depends on a variety of both unobserved and unmeasured price levels, marginal expenditure weights, and indirect effects of public expenditures on tax revenues. Although the conclusion that there is no general answer to the marginal social cost of public funds is not new (see Wilson, 1991), Mirrlees' analytic approach is.

7. The basic literature in this field stems from Mirrlees' 1971 study, and includes Atkinson (1973), Sheshinski (1972), and Stern (1976).

8. Or incorporates inequality aversion tastes into a social welfare function of the utilitarian variety through an adjustment in the rate of diminishing marginal utility of income. Richard Arnott emphasized this point to me.

9. Mirrlees (1971), Atkinson (1973), and Stern (1976).

10. I owe this point to Walter Hettich.

11. See Krause-Junk (1987).

12. See Haveman and Wolfe (1984).

13. Those underlying phenomena which generate capital market imperfections may themselves have implications for the optimal income tax. In this case, simply assuming the existence of these imperfections may be too facile.

14. See Varian (1980).

15. An insightful empirical analysis of the welfare gains attributable to the reduction in uncertainty (security) attributable to the U.S. and German tax transfer systems is Bird (1991).

16. See Neck, Schneider, and Hofreither (1988).

17. Stiglitz (1982b) put it this way: "The main qualitative properties of . . . analyses of the optimal tax structure are clearly not robust to . . . attempts to make the theory more 'realistic'. . . There is much more to be done. Until a more general theory is developed, none of the qualitative results can be accepted as a basis of policy . . . The extreme sensitivity of the results to the changes in the assumptions suggests that results which are sufficiently clear and robust to form the basis of policy may well not be obtained; rather, the objective of future research should perhaps be the clarification of the important dimensions of choice (risk taking, effort, etc.) affected by the income tax structure and the trade-offs which emerge."

10. Reflections on Optimal Tax Theory

1. The paper by Wilson (1991) was written independently.
2. The welfare weight is

$$\frac{\partial \Psi}{\partial v^h} \alpha^h \div \frac{1}{H} \sum_h \frac{\partial \Psi}{\partial v^h} \alpha^h,$$

where Ψ is the social welfare function, v^h is the utility of household h, and α^h the marginal utility of income of household h.

3. And always with separable and event-independent utility:

$$EU = \frac{1}{2} \left\{ \sum_i [1 - p_i(e)]u(y_i^0) + p_i(e)u(y_i^1) \right\} - e.$$

4. The provision of insurance under moral hazard causes a substitution effect away from effort. With nonseparable utility, there are also income effects which can operate in either direction, depending on the risk aversion properties of the utility function.

5. Unless this causes the individual to reduce effort to such an extent that the probability of accident increases.

6. Which goods will be taxed and which subsidized depends on the normalization employed for consumer prices.

7. Stern (1992) provides an excellent discussion of the issues involved in extending optimal tax theory from a static to a dynamic environment.

8. Stiglitz (1982b) provides an excellent discussion of the fragility of the results derived in the early optimal income tax literature.

9. By "financial" costs, I mean the taxpayer's costs of altering his financial affairs without altering his real activities—relabeling income, changing the timing of receipts and expenditures, altering organizational form and financial structure, and so on.

10. This is argued forcefully in Blum and Kalven's book, *An Uneasy Case for Progressive Taxation.*

References

Aaron, Henry J. 1985. Some Further Thoughts on Recapture of Excess Depreciation. *Tax Notes* 28, no. 3 (July): 315–321.

—— 1989. Politics and the Professors Revisited. *American Economic Review* 79, no. 2 (May): 1–15.

—— 1990. Alternate Roads to Consumption Taxation: Administration Versus Tax Structure. In *Heidelberg Congress on Taxing Consumption*. Berlin: Springer-Verlag.

Aaron, Henry J., and Harvey Galper. 1985. *Assessing Tax Reform*. Washington, D.C.: Brookings Institution.

Abel, Andrew. 1982. Dynamic Effects of Permanent and Temporary Tax Policies in a Q Model of Investment. *Journal of Monetary Economics* 9 (May): 353–373.

Abramovitz, Moses. 1981. Welfare Quandaries and Productivity Concerns. *American Economic Review* 71: 1–17.

Agell, J., and P. Lundborg. 1990. Fair Wages, Involuntary Unemployment and Tax Policies in the Simple General Equilibrium Model. Unpublished paper.

Alesina, Alberto. 1987. Macroeconomic Policy in a Two-Party System as a Repeated Game. *Quarterly Journal of Economics* 102 (August): 651–678.

Altonji, Joseph, Fumio Hayashi, and Laurence J. Kotlikoff. 1988. Is the Extended Family Altruistically Linked? Mimeo.

Andrews, William D. 1972. Personal Deductions in an Ideal Income Tax. *Harvard Law Review* 86 (December): 309–385.

—— 1974. A Consumption-Type or Cash Flow Personal Income Tax. *Harvard Law Review* 87 (April): 1113–1188.

Arnott, R., and J. Stiglitz. 1986. Moral Hazard and Optimal Commodity Taxation. *Journal of Public Economics* 29: 1–24.

Arnott, R., A. Hosios, and J. Stiglitz. 1988. Implicit Contracts, Labor Mobility and Unemployment. *American Economic Review* 78: 1046–1066.

Arrow, K. 1963. Uncertainty and the Welfare Economics of Medical Care. *American Economic Review* 53: 941–973.

Atkinson, Anthony B. 1970. On the Measurement of Inequality. *Journal of Economic Theory* 2: 244–263.

———— 1973. How Progressive Should Income Tax Be? In *Essays in Modern Economics*, ed. Michael Parkin and A. R. Nobay. London: Longman.

———— 1977. Optimal Taxation and the Direct Versus Indirect Tax Controversy. *Canadian Journal of Economics* 10 (November): 590–606.

———— 1980. The Distribution of Income and the Taxation of Inheritance. In *Public Policy and the Tax System,* ed. G. A. Hughes and G. M. Heal. London: Allen and Unwin.

———— 1988. The Economics of Unemployment Insurance. Presidential address to the Econometric Society.

———— 1990. The Design of Direct Taxation and Family Benefits. *Journal of Public Economics* 41: 3–29.

Atkinson, Anthony B., and F. Bourguignon. 1987. Income Distribution and Differences in Needs. In *Arrow and the Foundation of the Theory of Economic Policy,* ed. G. R. Feiwel. London: Macmillan.

Atkinson, Anthony B., J. Gomulka, and N. H. Stern. 1990. Spending on Alcohol. *Economic Journal* 100, no. 402: 808–827.

Atkinson, Anthony B., J. Gomulka, and H. Sutherland. 1988. Grossing-Up FES Data for Tax-Benefit Models. In *Tax-Benefit Models,* ed. A. B. Atkinson and H. Sutherland. London: STICERD, London School of Economics.

Atkinson, Anthony B., M. A. King, and H. Sutherland. 1983. The Analysis of Personal Taxation and Social Security. *National Institute Economic Review* (November).

Atkinson, Anthony B., and Agnar Sandmo. 1980. Welfare Implications of the Taxation of Savings. *Economic Journal* 90 (September): 529–549.

Atkinson, Anthony B., and N. Stern. 1974. Pigou, Taxation and Public Goods. *Review of Economic Studies* 41: 119–128.

Atkinson, Anthony B., and Joseph E. Stiglitz. 1972. The Structure of Indirect Taxation and Economic Efficiency. *Journal of Public Economics* 1 (April): 97–119.

———— 1976. The Design of Tax Structure: Direct Versus Indirect Taxation. *Journal of Public Economics* 6 (July–August): 55–75.

———— 1980. *Lectures on Public Economics.* New York: McGraw-Hill.

Auerbach, Alan J. 1979a. The Optimal Taxation of Heterogeneous Capital. *Quarterly Journal of Economics* 93 (November): 489–612.

———— 1979b. Wealth Maximization and the Cost of Capital. *Quarterly Journal of Economics* 93 (August): 433–446.

———— 1979c. A Brief Note on a Non-Existent Theorem about the Optimality of Uniform Taxation. *Economics Letters* 3: 49–52.

———— 1983a. Corporate Taxation in the United States. *Brookings Papers on Economic Activity* 14, no. 2: 1451–1505.

———— 1983b. Taxation, Corporate Financial Policy and the Cost of Capital. *Journal of Economic Literature* 21 (September): 905–940.

———— 1984. Taxes, Firm Financial Policy, and the Cost of Capital: An Empirical Analysis. *Journal of Public Economics* 23 (February–March): 27–57.

———— 1985. The Theory of Excess Burden and Optimal Taxation. In *Handbook of Public Economics,* vol. 1, ed. Alan J. Auerbach and Martin Feldstein. Amsterdam: North-Holland.

———— 1986. The Dynamic Effects of Tax Law Asymmetries. *Review of Economic Studies* 53 (April): 205–225.

———— 1987. The Tax Reform Act of 1987 and the Cost of Capital. *Journal of Economic Perspectives* 1 (Summer): 73–86.

———— 1989. Tax Reform and Adjustment Costs: The Impact on Investment and Market Value. *International Economic Review* 30 (November): 939–962.

Auerbach, Alan J., Jagadeesh Gokhale, and Laurence J. Kotlikoff. 1991. Generational Accounts: A Meaningful Alternative to Deficit Accounting. In *Tax Policy and the Economy,* vol. 5, ed. D. Bradford. Cambridge, Mass.: MIT Press, for National Bureau of Economic Research.

Auerbach, Alan J., and Kevin Hassett. 1982. Tax Policy and Business Fixed Investment in the United States. *Journal of Public Economics* 47: 141–170.

———— 1991. Corporate Savings and Shareholder Consumption. In *National Saving and Economic Performance,* ed. D. Bernheim and J. Shoven. Chicago: University of Chicago Press.

Auerbach, Alan J., and Laurence J. Kotlikoff. 1983a. Investment versus Savings Incentives: The Size of the Bang for the Buck and the Potential for Self-Financing Tax Cuts. In *The Economic Consequences of Government Deficits,* ed. L. H. Meyer. Boston: Kluwer-Nijoff.

———— 1983b. National Savings, Economic Welfare, and the Structure of Taxation. In *Behavioral Simulation Methods in Tax Policy Analysis,* ed. Martin Feldstein. Chicago: University of Chicago Press.

———— 1987. *Dynamic Fiscal Policy.* Cambridge, Mass.: Harvard University Press.

Auerbach, Alan J., Laurence J. Kotlikoff, Robert Hagemann, and Giuseppe Nicoletti. 1989. The Dynamics of an Aging Population: The Case of Four OECD Countries. *OECD Economic Studies* 12 (Spring): 97–130.

Auerbach, Alan J., Laurence J. Kotlikoff, and Jonathan Skinner. 1983. The Efficiency

Gains from Dynamic Tax Reform. *International Economic Review* 24 (February): 81–100.

Azariadis, Costas, and Roger Guesnerie. 1986. Sunspots and Cycles. *Review of Economic Studies* 53: 725–737.

Bagwell, Kyle, and B. Douglas Bernheim. 1988. Is Everything Neutral? *Journal of Political Economy* 96 (April): 308–338.

Bagwell, Laurie S., and John Shoven. 1989. Cash Distributions to Shareholders. *Journal of Economic Perspectives* 3 (Summer): 129–140.

Ball, Laurence, and David Romer. 1989. Are Prices Too Sticky? *Quarterly Journal of Economics* 104 (August): 507–524.

Ballard, Charles L. 1988. The Marginal Efficiency Cost of Redistribution. *American Economic Review* 78 (December): 1019–1033.

Ballard, Charles L., Don Fullerton, John B. Shoven, and John Whalley. 1985. *A General Equilibrium Model for Tax Policy Evaluation.* Chicago: University of Chicago Press.

Ballard, Charles L., John B. Shoven, and John Whalley. 1985a. General Equilibrium Computations of the Marginal Welfare Costs of Taxes in the United States. *American Economic Review* (March): 128–138.

———— 1985b. The Total Welfare Cost of the United States Tax System: A General Equilibrium Approach. *National Tax Journal* 38 (June): 125–140.

Ballentine, J. Gregory, and Ibrahim Eris. 1975. On the General Equilibrium Analysis of Tax Incidence. *Journal of Political Economy* 83 (June): 633–644.

Barro, Robert J. 1974. Are Government Bonds Net Wealth? *Journal of Political Economy* 82 (November–December): 1095–1117.

———— 1979. On the Determination of the Public Debt. *Journal of Political Economy* 87 (October): 940–971.

———— 1991. Economic Growth in a Cross Section of Countries. *Quarterly Journal of Economics* 106 (May): 407–443.

Barro, Robert J., and David B. Gordon. 1983. Rules, Discretion and Reputation in a Model of Monetary Policy. *Journal of Monetary Economics* 12 (July): 101–121.

Barsky, Robert, N. Gregory Mankiw, and Steven Zeldes. 1986. Ricardian Consumers with Keynesian Properties. *American Economic Review* 76 (September): 676–691.

Bartik, Timothy. 1991. *Who Benefits from State and Local Economic Development Policies?* Kalamazoo, Mich.: W. J. Upjohn.

Benabou, Roland. 1988. Search, Price Setting and Inflation. *Review of Economic Studies* 55: 353–373.

———— 1992. Inflation and Efficiency in Search Markets. *Review of Economic Studies* 59: 299–329.

Benassy, J. P. 1982. *The Economics of Market Disequilibrium.* New York: Academic Press.

Berglas, E. 1976. Distribution of Tastes and Skills and the Provision of Local Public Goods. *Journal of Public Economics* 6: 409–423.

———— 1982. User Charges, Local Public Services, and Taxation of Land Rents. *Public Finance* 37: 178–188.

———— 1984a. Quantities, Qualities, and Multiple Public Services in the Tiebout Model. *Journal of Public Economics* 25: 299–322.

———— 1984b. Resource Constraint, Replicability and Mixed Clubs: A Reply. *Journal of Public Economics* 23: 391–397.

———— and D. Pines. 1981. Clubs, Local Public Goods, and Transportation Models: A Synthesis. *Journal of Public Economics* 15: 141–162.

Bergstrom, Theodore, Lawrence Blume, and Hal Varian. 1986. On the Private Provision of Public Goods. *Journal of Public Economics* 29: 25–49.

Berkovec, James, and Don Fullerton. 1992. A General Equilibrium Model of Housing, Taxes, and Portfolio Choice. *Journal of Political Economy* 100 (April): 390–429.

Berliant, Marcus, Y. Y. Papageorgiou, and Ping Wang. 1990. On Welfare Theory and Urban Economics. *Regional Science and Urban Economics* 20: 245–261.

Berliant, Marcus, and Thijs, ten Raa. 1991. On the Continuum Approach of Spatial and Some Local Public Goods or Product Differentiation Models: Some Problems. *Journal of Economic Theory* 55: 95–120.

Bernheim, B. Douglas. 1987. Ricardian Equivalence: An Evaluation of Theory and Evidence. In *NBER Macroeconomics Annual,* ed. S. Fischer. Cambridge, Mass.: MIT Press, for National Bureau of Economic Research.

Bewley, Truman T. 1981. A Critique of Tiebout's Theory of Local Public Expenditures. *Econometrica* 49: 713–740.

Bhatia, Kul B. 1972. Capital Gains and the Aggregate Consumption Function. *American Economic Review* 62 (December): 866–879.

Bird, Edward. 1993. *The Welfare Cost of Income Uncertainty: A Nonparametric Analysis of Households in the United States and Western Germany.* Boulder, Colo.: Westview Press.

Bird, Richard M. 1980. Income Redistribution through the Fiscal System: The Limits of Knowledge. *American Economic Review, Papers and Proceedings* 70: 77–81.

———— 1986. *Federal Finance in Comparative Perspective.* Toronto: Canadian Tax Foundation.

Birnbaum, Jeffrey, and Alan Murray. 1987. *Showdown at Gucci Gulch.* New York: Random House.

Bjerke, K. 1964. Redistribution of Income in Denmark before and after the War. In *Income Redistribution and the Statistical Foundations of Economic Policy,* ed. C. Clark and G. Stuvel. London: Bowes and Bowes.

Blanchard, O., and P. A. Diamond. 1989. The Beveridge Curve. *Brookings Papers on Economic Activity* 1: 1–74.

―――― 1990. The Aggregate Matching Function. In *Growth/Productivity/Unemployment: Essays to Celebrate Bob Solow's Sixty-Fifth Birthday,* ed. P. Diamond. Cambridge, Mass.: MIT Press.

―――― Forthcoming. Ranking, Unemployment Duration, and Wages. *Review of Economic Studies.*

Blanchard O., and S. Fischer. 1989. *Lectures on Macroeconomics.* Cambridge, Mass.: MIT Press.

Blinder, Alan S., and Angus Deaton. 1985. The Time-Series Consumption Function Revisited. *Brookings Papers on Economic Activity* 2: 465–511.

Blinder, Alan S., and Robert M. Solow. 1974. Analytical Foundations of Fiscal Policy. In *The Economics of Public Finance,* ed. A. Blinder et al. Washington, D.C.: Brookings Institution.

Bliss, Christopher, and Barry Nalebuff. 1984. Dragon Slaying and Ballroom Dancing: The Private Supply of a Public Good. *Journal of Public Economics* 25: 1–12.

Blum, Walter J. 1955. Simplification of the Federal Income Tax Law. *Tax Law Review* 10: 239–253.

Blum, Walter J., and H. Kalven. 1953. *The Uneasy Case for Progressive Taxation.* Chicago: University of Chicago Press.

Blume, Lawrence, Daniel L. Rubinfeld, and Perry Shapiro. 1984. The Taking of Land: When Should Compensation Be Paid? *Quarterly Journal of Economics* 94 (February): 71–92.

Boadway, Robin W. 1982. On the Method of Taxation and the Provision of Local Public Goods: Comment. *American Economic Review* 72: 846–851.

―――― 1987. The Theory and Measurement of Effective Tax Rates. In *The Impact of Taxation on Business Activity,* ed. Jack Mintz and Douglas D. Purvis. Kingston, Ontario: John Deutsch Institute.

Boadway, Robin W., and Frank R. Flatters. 1982. *Equalization in a Federal State: An Economic Analysis.* Ottowa: Economic Council of Canada.

Boreham, A. J., and M. Semple. 1976. Future Development of Work in the Government Statistical Service on the Distribution and Redistribution of Household Income. In *The Personal Distribution of Incomes,* ed. A. B. Atkinson. London: Allen and Unwin.

Boskin, Michael J. 1972. The Incidence of the Payroll Tax: An Alternative Approach. Stanford University Centre for Research in Economic Growth, Memorandum 136.

―――― 1975. Efficiency Aspects of the Differential Tax Treatment of Market and Household Economic Activity. *Journal of Public Economics* 4: 1–25.

―――― 1978a. Taxation, Saving and the Rate of Interest. *Journal of Political Economy* 86 (April): S3–S27.

―――― 1978b. Comments and Discussion. *Brookings Papers on Economic Activity* 3: 694–700.

———— 1980. Comments. In *What Should Be Taxed: Income or Expenditure?* ed. Joseph A. Pechman. Washington, D.C.: Brookings Institution.

Boskin, Michael J., and Eytan Sheshinski. 1983. Optimal Tax Treatment of the Family: Married Couples. *Journal of Public Economics* 20 (April): 281–297.

Bound, John, and George Johnson. 1989. Changes in the Structure of Wages during the 1980's: An Evaluation of Alternative Explanations. Cambridge, Mass.: National Bureau of Economic Research, Working Paper 2983.

Bradbury, Katharine L., Helen F. Ladd, Mark Perrault, Andrew Reschovsky, and John Yinger. 1984. State Aid to Offset Fiscal Disparities across Communities. *National Tax Journal* 37, no. 2 (June): 151–170.

Bradford, David F. 1978. Factor Prices May Be Constant but Factor Returns Are Not. *Economic Letters* 1: 199–203.

———— 1981. The Incidence and Allocation Effects of a Tax on Corporate Distributions. *Journal of Public Economics* 15, no. 1 (February): 1–22.

———— 1986. *Untangling the Income Tax.* Cambridge, Mass.: Harvard University Press.

Bradford, David F., and Don Fullerton. 1981. Pitfalls in the Construction and Use of Effective Tax Rates. In *Depreciation, Inflation, and the Taxation of Income from Capital,* ed. Charles R. Hulten. Washington, D.C.: Urban Institute Press.

Bradford, David F., R. A. Malt, and Wallace E. Oates. 1969. The Rising Cost of Local Public Services: Some Evidence and Reflections. *National Tax Journal* 22 (June): 185–202.

Bradford, David F., and Wallace E. Oates. 1971. The Analysis of Revenue Sharing in a New Approach to Collective Fiscal Decisions. *Quarterly Journal of Economics* 85 (August): 416–439.

———— 1975. Suburban Exploitation of Central Cities and Governmental Structure. In *Redistribution through Public Choice,* ed. H. Hochman and G. Peterson. New York: Columbia University Press.

Brandts, Jordi, and Charles A. M. de Bartolome. 1992. Population Uncertainty, Social Insurance, and Actual Bias. *Journal of Public Economics* 47 (April): 361–380.

Brazer, Harvey E. 1959. The Deductibility of State and Local Taxes under the Individual Income Tax. *Tax Revision Compendium.* Washington, D.C.: Government Printing Office.

Break, George F. 1957. Income Taxes and Incentives to Work: An Empirical Study. *American Economic Review* 48 (September): 529–549.

———— 1959. Income Tax Rates and Incentives to Work and to Invest. *Tax Revision Compendium.* Washington, D.C.: Government Printing Office.

———— 1967. *Intergovernmental Fiscal Relations in the United States.* Washington, D.C.: Brookings Institution.

———— 1974. The Incidence and Economic Effects of Taxation. In *The Economics of Public Finance,* ed. A. Blinder et al. Washington, D.C.: Brookings Institution.

—— 1980. *Financing Government in a Federal System.* Washington, D.C.: Brookings Institution.

—— 1982. Issues in Measuring the Level of Government Economic Activity. *American Economic Review* 72, no. 2 (May): 288–295.

—— 1985. The Tax Expenditure Budget: The Need for a Fuller Accounting. *National Tax Journal* 38 (September): 261–265.

Break, George F., and Joseph A. Pechman. 1975. *Federal Tax Reform: The Impossible Dream?* Washington, D.C.: Brookings Institution.

Brennan, Geoffrey, and James Buchanan. 1980. *The Power to Tax: Analytical Foundations of a Fiscal Constitution.* Cambridge: Cambridge University Press.

Brittain, J. A. 1972. *The Payroll Tax for Social Security.* Washington, D.C.: Brookings Institution.

Brown, Charles C., and Wallace E. Oates. 1987. Assistance to the Poor in a Federal System. *Journal of Public Economics* 32 (April): 307–330.

Brown, E. Cary. 1948. Business-Income Taxation and Investment Incentives. In *Income, Employment and Public Policy: Essays in Honor of Alvin H. Hansen.* New York: Norton.

Brown, H. G. 1939. The Incidence of a General Output or a General Sales Tax. *Journal of Political Economy* 47, no. 2: 254–262.

Browning, Edgar K. 1978. The Burden of Taxation. *Journal of Political Economy* 86 (August): 649–671.

Browning, Edgar K., and William J. Johnson. 1979. *The Distribution of the Tax Burden.* Washington, D.C.: American Enterprise Institute.

—— 1984. The Trade-Off between Equality and Efficiency. *Journal of Political Economy* 92 (April): 175–203.

Brueckner, Jan K. 1983. Property Value Maximization and Public Sector Efficiency. *Journal of Urban Economics* 14: 1–16.

Brueckner, Jan K., and Kangoh Lee. 1989. Club Theory with a Peer-Group Effect. *Regional Science and Urban Economics* 19 (August): 399–420.

Buchanan, James M. 1950. Federalism and Fiscal Equity. *American Economic Review* 40, no. 4 (September): 583–599.

—— 1952. Federal Grants and Resource Allocation. *Journal of Political Economy* 60 (June): 208–217.

—— 1965. An Economic Theory of Clubs. *Economica* 33: 1–14.

—— 1977. Why Does Government Grow? In *Budgets and Bureaucrats: The Source of Governmental Growth,* ed. T. Borcherding. Durham, N.C.: Duke University Press.

Buchanan, James M., and Charles Goetz. 1972. Efficiency Limits of Fiscal Mobility: An Assessment of the Tiebout Model. *Journal of Public Economics* 1: 25–43.

Buhmann, B., L. Rainwater, G. Schmaus, and T. Smeeding. 1988. Equivalence Scale, Well-Being, Inequality, and Poverty. *Review of Income and Wealth* 34: 115–142.

Buiter, Willem H. 1983. Measurement of the Public Sector Deficit and Its Implications for Policy Evaluation and Design. *IMF Staff Papers* 30 (June): 306–349.

Bulow, Jeremy, and Kenneth Rogoff. 1989. A Constant Recontracting Model of Sovereign Debt. *Journal of Political Economy* 97 (February): 155–178.

Bulow, Jeremy, Kenneth Rogoff, and L. H. Summers. 1986. A Theory of Dual Labor Markets with Application to Industrial Policy, Discrimination, and Keynesian Unemployment. *Journal of Labor Economics* 4: 376–414.

Carroll, Christopher, and Lawrence H. Summers. 1989. Consumption Growth Parallels Income Growth: Some New Evidence. Cambridge, Mass.: National Bureau of Economic Research, Working Paper 3090.

Carruth, A. A., and A. J. Oswald. 1987. On Union Preferences and Labour Market Models: Insiders and Outsiders. *Economic Journal* 97: 431–445.

Case, Anne. 1993. Interstate Tax Competition after TRA86. *Journal of Policy Analysis and Management* 12, no. 1: 136–148.

Casella, Alessandra, and Jonathan S. Feinstein. 1990. Economic Exchange during Hyperinflation. *Journal of Political Economy* 98: 1–27.

Cazenave, P., and C. Morrisson. 1978. Justice et Redistribution. *Economica.* Paris.

Central Statistical Office. (U.K.) 1988. The Effects of Taxes and Benefits on Household Income. *Economic Trends* 422: 89–118.

Chamley, Christophe, and Heraklis Polemarchakis. 1984. Assets, General Equilibrium and the Neutrality of Money. *Review of Economic Studies* 51 (January): 129–138.

Chari, V. V., Lawrence J. Christiano, and Patrick J. Kehoe. 1990. Optimal Taxation of Capital and Labor Income in a Stochastic Growth Model. Federal Reserve Bank of Minneapolis, Working Paper 465.

Chernick, Howard A. 1979. An Economic Model of the Distribution of Project Grants. In *Fiscal Federalism and Grants-in-Aid,* ed. P. Mieszkowski and W. Oakland. Washington, D.C.: Urban Institute.

Chirinko, Robert S. 1986. Business Investment and Tax Policy: A Perspective on Existing Models and Empirical Results. *National Tax Journal* 39 (June): 137–155.

———— 1987. The Ineffectiveness of Effective Tax Rates on Business Investment: A Critique of Feldstein's Fisher-Schultz Lecture. *Journal of Public Economics* 32, no. 3 (April): 369–387.

Chirinko, Robert S., and Robert Eisner. 1983. Tax Policy and Investment in Major U.S. Macroeconomic Econometric Models. *Journal of Public Economics* 20 (March): 139–166.

Clark, C., and G. H. Peters. 1964. Income Redistribution Through Taxation and Social Services: Some International Comparisons. In *Income Redistribution and the Statistical Foundations of Economic Policy,* ed. C. Clark and G. Stuvel. London: Bowes and Bowes.

Colander, David. 1979. A Note on Optimal Income Taxation. *American Economist* 23, no. 1: 59–64.

Colm, Gerhard, and Helen Tarasov. 1940. *Who Pays the Taxes?* Temporary Economic Committee, Monograph 3. Investigation of the Concentration of Economic Power, 76th Congress, 3rd Session, Washington, D.C.

Conlan, Timothy J., Margaret T. Wrightson, and David R. Beam. 1990. Taxing Choices: The Politics of Tax Reform. Washington, D.C.: CQ Press.

Cooper, R., and A. John. 1988. Coordinating Coordination Failures in Keynesian Models. *Quarterly Journal of Economics* 103: 441–463.

Corlett, W. J., and D. C. Hague. 1954. Complementarity and the Excess Burden of Taxation. *Review of Economic Studies* 21: 21–30.

Cornes, Richard, and Todd Sandler. 1986. *The Theory of Externalities, Public Goods and Club Goods.* Cambridge: Cambridge University Press.

Courant, Paul N., and Daniel L. Rubinfeld. 1978. On the Measurement of Benefits in an Urban Context: Some General Equilibrium Issues. *Journal of Urban Economics* 5: 346–356.

———— 1981. On the Welfare Effects of Tax Limitation. *Journal of Public Economics* 16: 289–316.

Courant, Paul N., and Edward M. Gramlich. 1990. The Impact of the TRA on State and Local Fiscal Behavior. In *Do Taxes Matter? The Impact of the Tax Reform Act of 1986,* ed. Joel Slemrod. Cambridge, Mass.: MIT Press.

Courant, Paul N., Edward M. Gramlich, and Daniel L. Rubinfeld. 1979. The Stimulative Effects of Intergovernmental Grants: Or Why Money Sticks Where It Hits. In *Fiscal Federalism and Grants-in-Aid,* P. Mieszkowski and W. Oakland. Washington, D.C.: Urban Institute.

Cover, James Peery. 1988. Asymmetric Effects of Positive and Negative Money-Supply Shocks. University of Alabama, mimeo.

Craig, Steven G., and Robert P. Inman. 1982. Federal Aid and Public Education: An Empirical Look at the New Fiscal Federalism. *Review of Economics and Statistics* 64, no. 4 (November): 541–552.

———— 1986. Federalism, Welfare, and the "New" Federalism: State Budgeting in a Federalist Public Economy. In *Studies in State and Local Public Finance,* ed. Harvey S. Rosen. Chicago: University of Chicago Press.

Cumberland, John. 1981. Efficiency and Equity in Interregional Environmental Management. *Review of Regional Studies* 2: 1–9.

Cutler, David. 1988. Tax Reform and the Stock Market: An Asset Price Approach. *American Economic Review* 78 (December): 1107–1117.

Dasgupta, P. S., and J. E. Stiglitz. 1971. On Optimal Taxation and Public Production. *Review of Economic Studies* 39: 87–103.

David, Paul, and John L. Scadding. 1974. Private Saving: Ultra-Rationality, Aggregation, and Denison's Law. *Journal of Political Economy* 82, no. 2 (March–April), Part 1: 225–249.

Davidson, Carl, and Lawrence Martin. 1985. General Equilibrium Tax Incidence under

Imperfect Competition: A Quantity-Setting Supergame Analysis. *Journal of Political Economy* 93 (December): 1212–1223.

Davidson, Carl, Lawrence Martin, and S. Matusz. 1988. The Structure of Simple General Equilibrium Models with Frictional Unemployment. *Journal of Political Economy* 96: 1267–1293.

Davies, James, France St-Hilaire, and John Whalley. 1984. Some Calculations of Lifetime Tax Incidence. *American Economic Review* 74 (September): 633–649.

Day, R. H. 1982. Irregular Growth Cycles. *American Economic Review* 72: 406–414.

Deaton, Angus S. 1979. Optimally Uniform Commodity Taxes. *Economics Letters* 2: 357–361.

——— 1981. Optimal Taxes and the Structure of Preferences. *Econometrica* 49 (September): 1245–1260.

——— 1987. Econometric Issues for Tax Design in Developing Countries. In *The Theory of Taxation for Developing Countries,* ed. David Newberry and Nicholas Stern. Oxford: Oxford University Press, for the World Bank.

Deaton, Angus S., and Nicholas H. Stern. 1985. Optimally Uniform Commodity Taxes, Taste Differences, and Lump-Sum Grants. *Economics Letters* 20: 263–266.

de Bartolome, Charles A. M. 1990. Equilibrium and Inefficiency in a Community Model with Peer Group Effects. *Journal of Political Economy* 98 (February): 110–133.

Debreu, Gerard. 1959. *Theory of Value.* New York: Wiley.

DeLong, J. Bradford, and Lawrence H. Summers. 1986a. Are Business Cycles Symmetrical? In *The American Business Cycle: Continuity and Change,* ed. Robert J. Gordon. Chicago: University of Chicago Press.

——— 1986b. The Changing Cyclical Variability of Economic Activity in the United States. In *The American Business Cycle: Continuity and Change,* ed. Robert J. Gordon. Chicago: University of Chicago Press.

——— 1991. Equipment Investment and Economic Growth. *Quarterly Journal of Economics* 106 (May): 445–502.

Devarajan, Shantayanan, Don Fullerton, and Richard A. Musgrave. 1980. Estimating the Distribution of Tax Burdens: A Comparison of Different Approaches. *Journal of Public Economics* 13 (April): 155–182.

Diamond, Peter A. 1965. National Debt in a Neoclassical Growth Model. *American Economic Review* 55: 1125–1150.

——— 1970. Incidence of an Interest Income Tax. *Journal of Economic Theory* 2 (September): 211–224.

——— 1975. A Many-Person Ramsey Rule. *Journal of Public Economics* 4 (November): 335–342.

——— 1980. An Alternative to Steady State Comparisons. *Economics Letters* 5: 7–9.

——— 1982. Wage Determination and Efficiency in Search Equilibrium. *Review of Economic Studies* 49: 217–227.

——— 1982a. Protection, Trade Adjustment Assistance, and Income Distribution. In

Import Competition and Response, ed. J. Bhagwati. Chicago: University of Chicago Press.

———— 1984. *A Search-Equilibrium Approach to the Microfoundations of Macroeconomics.* Cambridge, Mass.: MIT Press.

———— 1993. Search, Sticky Prices, and Inflation. *Review of Economic Studies* 60: 53–68.

Diamond, Peter A., and Leonardo Felli. 1990. Search, Sticky Prices, and Deflation. Unpublished.

Diamond, Peter A., and James A. Mirrlees. 1971a. Optimal Taxation and Public Production, I: Production Efficiency. *American Economic Review* 61 (March): 8–27.

———— 1971b. Optimal Taxation and Public Production, II: Tax Rules. *American Economic Review* 61, no. 2 (June): 261–278.

———— 1974. Private Constant Returns and Public Shadow Prices. *Review of Economic Studies* 42: 41–47.

———— 1992. Optimal Taxation of Identical Consumers When Markets are Incomplete. In *Economic Analysis of Markets and Games,* ed. P. Dasgupta, D. Gale, O. Hart, and E. Maskin. Cambridge, Mass.: MIT Press.

Dixit, Avinash K. 1976a. *The Theory of Equilibrium Growth.* Oxford: Oxford University Press.

———— 1976b. Public Finance in a Keynesian Temporary Equilibrium. *Journal of Economic Theory* 12: 242–258.

———— 1979. Price Changes and Optimum Taxation in a Many-Person Economy. *Journal of Public Economics* 11 (April): 143–157.

Dixit, Avinash K., and Joseph E. Stiglitz. 1977. Monopolistic Competition and Optimum Product Diversity. *American Economic Review* 67 (June): 297–308.

Doeringer, P. B., and M. J. Piore. 1971. *Internal Labor Markets and Manpower Analysis.* Lexington, Mass.: Heath.

Domar, Evsey D., and Richard A. Musgrave. 1944. Proportional Income Taxation and Risk-Taking. *Quarterly Journal of Economics* 58 (May): 388–422.

Drazen, A. 1986. Optimal Minimum Wage Legislation. *Economic Journal* 96: 774–784.

Drèze, J. H. 1984. Second-Best Analysis with Markets in Disequilibrium: Public Sector Pricing in the Keynesian Regime. In *The Performance of Public Enterprises: Concepts and Measurements,* ed. M. Marchand and P. Pestieau. Amsterdam: North-Holland.

Drèze, J. H., and E. Greenberg. 1980. Hedonic Coalitions: Optimality and Stability. *Econometrica* 48 (May): 987–1004.

Drèze, J. H., and N. Stern. 1987. The Theory of Cost-Benefit Analysis. In *Handbook of Public Economics,* vol. 2, ed. A. Auerbach and M. Feldstein. Amsterdam: North-Holland.

Driffill, E. John, and Harvey S. Rosen. 1983. Taxation and Excess Burden: A Life Cycle Perspective. *International Economic Review* 24, no. 3 (October): 671–683.

Due, John F. 1959. *Government Finance: An Economic Analysis,* revised edition. Homewood, Ill.: Irwin.

Eaton, Jonathan, and Mark Gersovitz. 1981. Debt with Potential Repudiation: Theoretical and Empirical Analysis. *Review of Economic Studies* 48 (April): 289–309.

Eberts, Randall W., and Timothy J. Gronberg. 1981. Jurisdictional Homogeneity and the Tiebout Hypothesis. *Journal of Urban Economics* 10 (September): 227–239.

——— 1988. Can Competition among Local Governments Constrain Government Spending? *Economic Review* 24, no. 1: 2–9. Federal Reserve Bank of Cleveland.

Economic Report of the President. 1962. Washington, D.C.: U.S. Government Printing Office.

Economic Report of the President. 1992. Washington, D.C.: U.S. Government Printing Office.

Edel, Matthew, and Elliott Sclar. 1974. Taxes, Spending, and Property Values: Supply Adjustment in a Tiebout-Oates Model. *Journal of Political Economy* 82 (September–October): 941–954.

Edgeworth, F. Y. 1897. The Pure Theory of Taxation. *Economic Journal* 7 (December): 550–571. Reprinted in F. Y. Edgeworth, *Papers Relating to Political Economy,* vol. 2. London: Macmillan, 1925.

Eisner, Robert, and Paul Pieper. 1984. A New View of Federal Debt and Budget Deficits. *American Economic Review* 74 (March): 11–29.

Ellickson, B. 1973. A Generalization of the Pure Theory of Public Goods. *American Economic Review* 63: 417–432.

——— 1977. The Politics and Economics of Decentralization. *Journal of Urban Economics* 4: 135–149.

Ellwood, David. 1988. *Poor Support.* New York: Basic Books.

Engl, G., and S. Scotchmer. 1992. The Core and the Hedonic Core: Equivalence and Comparative Statics. Institute for Business and Economic Research, Working Paper 92–197. University of California, Berkeley.

Epple, D., R. Filimon, and T. Romer. 1983. Housing, Voting, and Moving: Equilibrium in a Model of Local Public Goods with Multiple Jurisdictions. *Research in Urban Economics* 3: 59–90.

Eustice, James S. 1964. Contract Rights, Capital Gain, and Assignment of Income: The *Ferrer* Case. *Tax Law Review* 20: 1–76.

——— 1989. Tax Complexity and the Tax Practitioner. *Tax Law Review* 45, no. 1 (Fall): 7–24. Reprinted with minor additions from *California CPA Quarterly,* September 1976.

Evans, Owen J. 1983. Tax Policy, the Interest Elasticity of Saving, and Capital Accumulation: Numerical Analysis of Theoretical Models. *American Economic Review* 73 (June): 398–410.

Evans, Paul. 1987. Do Budget Deficits Raise Nominal Interest Rates? Evidence from Six Countries. *Journal of Monetary Economics* 20 (September): 281–300.

Fair, Ray C. 1978. The Effect of Economic Events on Votes for President. *Review of Economics and Statistics* 60 (May): 159–173.

Fazzari, Steven M., R. Glenn Hubbard, and Bruce C. Peterson. 1988. Financing Constraints and Corporate Investment. *Brookings Papers on Economic Activity* 19, no. 1: 141–195.

Feenberg, Daniel R., and Harvey S. Rosen. 1983. Alternative Tax Treatments of the Family: Simulation Methodology and Results. In *Behavioral Simulation Methods in Tax Policy Analysis,* ed. Martin Feldstein. Chicago: University of Chicago Press.

—— 1987. Tax Structure and Public Sector Growth. *Journal of Public Economics* 32 (March): 185–201.

Feenberg, Daniel R., and Jonathan Skinner. 1989. Sources of IRA Saving. In *Tax Policy and the Economy,* vol. 3, ed. Lawrence Summers. Cambridge, Mass.: MIT Press, for National Bureau of Economic Research.

Feldstein, Martin. 1972. Distributional Equity and the Optimal Structure of Public Prices. *American Economic Review* 62: 32–36.

—— 1973. Tax Incentives, Corporate Saving and Capital Accumulation in the United States. *Journal of Public Economics* 2 (April): 159–171.

—— 1974a. The Incidence of a Capital Income Tax in a Growing Economy with Variable Savings Rates. *Review of Economic Studies* (October): 505–513.

—— 1974b. Tax Incidence in a Growing Economy with Variable Factor Supply. *Quarterly Journal of Economics* 88 (November): 551–573.

—— 1976a. On the Theory of Tax Reform. *Journal of Public Economics* 6, no. 1 (July–August): 77–104.

—— 1976b. Compensation in Tax Reform. *National Tax Journal* 29 (June): 123–130.

—— 1976c. Personal Taxation and Portfolio Composition: An Econometric Analysis. *Econometrica* 44 (July): 631–650.

—— 1978. The Welfare Cost of Capital Income Taxation. *Journal of Political Economy* 86, no. 2 (April): S29-S51.

—— 1981. Adjusting Depreciation in an Inflationary Economy: Indexing versus Acceleration. *National Tax Journal* 34, no. 1 (March): 29–43.

—— 1982. Inflation, Tax Rules and Investment: Some Econometric Evidence. *Econometrica* 50 (July): 825–862.

—— 1985. The Second Best Theory of Capital Income Taxation. Cambridge, Mass.: National Bureau of Economic Research, Working Paper 1781.

—— 1987. Tax Rates and Business Investment: Reply. *Journal of Public Economics* 32, no. 3 (April): 89–96.

Feldstein, Martin, and Lawrence Summers. 1979. Inflation and the Taxation of Capital Gains in the Corporate Sector. *National Tax Journal* 32 (December): 445–470.

Feldstein, Martin, and Randall Morck. 1983. Pension Funding Decisions, Interest Rate

Assumptions, and Share Prices. In *Financial Aspects of the U.S. Pension System,* ed. Z. Bodie and J. Shoven. Chicago: University of Chicago Press.

Filimon, R., T. Romer, and H. Rosenthal. 1982. Asymmetric Information and Agenda Control: The Bases of Monopoly Power and Public Spending. *Journal of Public Economics* 17: 51–70.

Fischel, William A. 1975. Fiscal and Environment Considerations in the Location of Firms in Suburban Communities. In *Fiscal Zoning and Land Use Controls: the Economic Issues,* ed. Edwin S. Mills and Wallace E. Oates. Lexington, Mass: Lexington Books.

———— 1981. Is Local Government Structure in Large Urbanized Areas Monopolistic or Competitive? *National Tax Journal* 34 (March): 95–104.

———— 1990. Fiscal Zoning Is Alive in the Suburbs and Makes the Property Tax a Benefit Tax. Unpublished.

———— 1992. Property Taxation and the Tiebout Model: Evidence for the Benefit View from Zoning and Voting. *Journal of Economic Literature* 30, no. 1 (March): 171–177.

Fischer, Stanley. 1980. Dynamic Inconsistency, Cooperation, and the Benevolent Dissembling Government. *Journal of Economic Dynamics and Control* 2 (February): 93–107.

———— and Franco Modigliani. 1978. Towards an Understanding of the Real Effects and Costs of Inflation. *Weltwirtschaftliches Archiv* 114, no. 4: 810–833.

Fischer, Stanley, and Lawrence H. Summers. 1989. Should Governments Learn to Live with Inflation? *American Economic Review* 79 (May): 382–387.

Fisher, Irving. 1939. Double Taxation of Savings. *American Economic Review* 29 (March): 16–33.

Fisher, Ronald C. 1982. Income and Grant Effects on Local Expenditure: The Flypaper Effect and Other Difficulties. *Journal of Urban Economics* (November): 324–345.

Flatters, Frank, Vernon Henderson, and Peter Mieszkowski. 1974. Public Goods, Efficiency, and Regional Fiscal Equalization. *Journal of Public Economics* 3: 99–112.

Forbes, Kevin F., and Ernest M. Zampelli. 1989. Is Leviathan a Mythical Beast? *American Economic Review* 79 (June): 587–596.

Forte, Francesco, and Alan Peacock. 1985. *Public Expenditure and Government Growth.* Oxford: Basil Blackwell.

Franzén, T., K. Lövgren, and I. Rosenberg. 1975. Redistribution Effects of Taxes and Public Expenditures in Sweden. *Swedish Journal of Economics* 77: 31–55.

Friedman, Benjamin. 1978. Crowding Out or Crowding In? Economic Consequences of Financing Government Deficits. *Brookings Papers on Economic Activity* 9, no. 3: 593–641.

Friedman, Milton. 1962. *Capitalism and Freedom.* Chicago: University of Chicago Press.

Fujita, Masahisa. 1990. *Urban Economic Theory.* Cambridge: Cambridge University Press.

Fullerton, Don. 1982. On the Possibility of an Inverse Relationship between Tax Rates and Government Revenues. *Journal of Public Economics* 19 (October): 3–22.

——— 1987. The Indexation of Interest, Depreciation and Capital Gains and Tax Reform in the United States. *Journal of Public Economics* 32, no.1 (February): 25–51.

Fullerton, Don, and Roger H. Gordon. 1983. A Reexamination of Tax Distortions in General Equilibrium Models. In *Behavioral Simulation in Tax Policy Analysis,* ed. Martin Feldstein. Chicago: University of Chicago Press.

Fullerton, Don, and Yolanda K. Henderson. 1984. Incentive Effects of Taxes on Income from Capital: Alternative Policies in the 1980s. In *The Legacy of Reaganomics,* ed. Charles R. Hulten and Isabel V. Sawhill. Washington, D.C.: Urban Institute Press.

Fullerton, Don, Thomas A. King, John B. Shoven, and John Whalley. 1980. Corporate and Personal Tax Integration in the U.S.: Some Preliminary Findings. In *Microeconomic Simulation Models for Public Policy Analysis,* vol. 2, ed. Robert H. Haveman and Kevin Hollenbeck. New York: Academic Press.

Fullerton, Don, and Diane Lim Rogers. 1992. *Who Bears the Lifetime Tax Burden?* Washington, D.C.: Brookings Institution.

Fullerton, Don, John B. Shoven, and John Whalley. 1983. Replacing the U.S. Income Tax with a Progressive Consumption Tax: A Sequenced General Equilibrium Approach. *Journal of Public Economics* 20 (February): 3–23.

Gale, William G., and John Karl Scholz. 1990. IRAs and Household Saving. Mimeo.

Galper, Harvey, and Eric Toder. 1984. Transfer Elements in the Taxation of Income from Capital. In *Economic Transfers in the United States,* ed. Marilyn Moon. Chicago: University of Chicago Press, for National Bureau of Economic Research.

Gerardi, Gerry, Michael J. Graetz, and Harvey S. Rosen. 1990. Corporate Integration Puzzles. *National Tax Journal* 43 (September): 307–314.

Gillespie, W. I. 1965. Effect of Public Expenditure on the Distribution of Income. In *Fiscal Federalism,* ed. R. A. Musgrave. Washington, D.C.: Brookings Institution.

Golladay, F. L., and R. H. Haveman. 1977. *The Economic Impacts of Tax-Transfer Policy.* New York: Academic Press.

Goode, Richard. 1946. *The Postwar Corporation Tax Structure.* Washington, D.C.: Government Printing Office.

——— 1951. *The Corporation Income Tax.* New York: Wiley.

——— 1977. The Economic Definition of Income. In *Comprehensive Income Taxation,* ed. Joseph A. Pechman. Washington, D.C.: Brookings Institution.

——— 1980. The Superiority of the Income Tax. In *What Should Be Taxed: Income or Expenditure?* ed. Joseph A. Pechman. Washington, D.C.: Brookings Institution.

Goodspeed, Timothy. 1989. A Re-examination of the Use of Ability to Pay Taxes by Local Governments. *Journal of Public Economics* 38 (April): 319–342.

Gordon, Roger. 1983. An Optimal Taxation Approach to Fiscal Federalism. *Quarterly Journal of Economics* 97: 567–586.

———— 1985. Taxation of Corporate Capital Income: Tax Revenues versus Tax Distortions. *Quarterly Journal of Economics* 100 (February): 1–27.

Goulder, Lawrence H., John B. Shoven, and John Whalley. 1983. Domestic Tax Policy and the Foreign Sector: The Importance of Alternative Foreign Sector Formulations to Results from a General Equilibrium Tax Analysis Model. In *Behavioral Simulation Methods in Tax Policy Analysis,* ed. Martin Feldstein. Chicago: University of Chicago Press.

Graetz, Michael J. 1977. Legal Transitions: The Case of Retroactivity in Income Taxation. *University of Pennsylvania Law Review* 126 (November): 47–87.

Gramlich, Edward M. 1977. Intergovernmental Grants: A Review of the Empirical Literature. In *The Political Economy of Fiscal Federalism,* ed. W. Oates. Lexington, Mass.: Heath-Lexington.

———— 1985a. Reforming U.S. Federal Fiscal Arrangements. In *American Domestic Priorities: An Economic Appraisal,* ed. John M. Quigley and D. Rubinfeld. Berkeley: University of California Press.

———— 1985b. The Deductibility of State and Local Taxes. *National Tax Journal* 38, no. 4: 447–465.

———— 1987a. Subnational Fiscal Policy. In *Perspectives on Local Public Finance,* ed. John M. Quigley. London: JAI Press.

———— 1987b. Federalism and Federal Deficit Reduction. *National Tax Journal* 40 (September): 299–313.

Grandmont, J. M. 1986. Periodic and Aperiodic Behaviour in Discrete One-Dimensional Dynamical Systems. In *Contributions to Mathematical Economics,* ed. W. Hildenbrand and A. Mas-Collel. New York: North-Holland.

Gravelle, J. G., and L. J. Kotlikoff. 1989. The Incidence and Efficiency Costs of Corporate Taxation when Corporate and Noncorporate Firms Produce the Same Good. *Journal of Political Economy* 97: 749–780.

Green, Jerry. 1977. Mitigating Demographic Risk through Social Insurance. Cambridge, Mass.: National Bureau of Economic Research, Working Paper 215.

Greenwald, Bruce, and Joseph Stiglitz. 1988. Imperfect Information, Finance Constraints, and Business Fluctuations. In *Finance Constraints, Expectations, and Macroeconomics,* ed. M. Kohn and S. C. Tsiang. Oxford: Clarendon Press.

———— 1990. Macroeconomic Models with Equity and Credit Rationing. In *Asymmetric Information, Corporate Finance and Investment,* ed. R. G. Hubbard. Chicago: University of Chicago Press.

Groves, Harold M. 1959. Taxation of Capital Gains. In *Tax Revision Compendium.* Washington, D.C.: Government Printing Office.

Guesnerie, Roger. 1977. On the Direction of Tax Reform. *Journal of Public Economics* 6 (July–August): 77–104.

Hahn, F. H. 1965. On Two-Sector Growth Models. *Review of Economic Studies* 32: 339–346.

Hall, Robert E. 1968. Consumption Taxes versus Income Taxes: Implications for Economic Growth. In *Proceedings of the National Tax Association–Tax Institute of America Annual Conference on Taxation,* ed. S. J. Bowers. Columbus, Ohio: National Tax Association.

———— 1988. Intertemporal Substitution in Consumption. *Journal of Political Economy* 96 (April): 339–357.

Hall, Robert E., and Dale W. Jorgenson. 1967. Tax Policy and Investment Behavior. *American Economic Review* 57 (June): 391–414.

Hall, Robert E., and Alvin Rabushka. 1983. *Low Tax, Simple Tax, Flat Tax.* New York: McGraw-Hill.

———— 1985. *The Flat Tax.* Stanford, Calif.: Hoover Institution Press.

Halperin, Daniel. 1986. Interest in Disguise: Taxing the Time Value of Money. *Yale Law Journal* 95, no. 3: 506–552.

Hamilton, Bruce W. 1975. Zoning and Property Taxation in a System of Local Governments. *Urban Studies* 12: 205–211.

———— 1976. Capitalization of Intrajurisdictional Differences in Local Tax Prices. *American Economic Review* 66 (December): 743–753.

———— 1983. The Flypaper Effect and Other Anomalies. *Journal of Public Economics* 22 (December): 347–361.

Hamilton, Bruce W., Edwin S. Mills, and David Puryear. 1975. The Tiebout Hypothesis and Residential Income Segregation. In *Fiscal Zoning and Land Use Controls,* ed. E. Mills and W. Oates. Lexington, Mass.: Heath-Lexington.

Hamilton, Jonathan H. 1986. The Flypaper Effect and the Deadweight Loss from Taxation. *Journal of Urban Economics* 19, no. 2 (March): 148–155.

Hamilton, William, and Marjorie Flavin. 1986. On the Limitations of Government Borrowing: A Framework for Empirical Testing. *American Economic Review* 70 (September): 808–819.

Hansson, Ingemar, and Charles Stuart. 1989. Why Is Investment Subsidized? *International Economic Review* 30 (August): 549–559.

Harberger, Arnold C. 1962. The Incidence of the Corporation Income Tax. *Journal of Political Economy* 70 (June): 215–240.

———— 1964. Taxation, Resource Allocation and Welfare. In *The Role of Direct and Indirect Taxes in the Federal Revenue System,* ed. John F. Due. Princeton, N.J.: Princeton University Press.

———— 1980. Tax Neutrality in Investment Incentives. In *The Economics of Taxation,* ed. Henry J. Aaron and Michael J. Boskin. Washington, D.C.: Brookings Institution.

Harris, J. R., and M. Todaro. 1970. Migration, Unemployment, and Development. *American Economic Review* 60: 126–142.

Hart, O. D. 1982. A Model of Imperfect Competition with Keynesian Features. *Quarterly Journal of Economics* 97: 109–138.

Hart, O. D., and J. H. Moore. 1988. Property Rights and the Nature of the Firm. London: STICERD Theoretical Economics Workshop, Discussion Paper 174, London School of Economics.

Hartman, David G. 1985. Tax Policy and Foreign Direct Investment. *Journal of Public Economics* 26 (February): 107–121.

Hartzmark, Michael, and Eugene Steuerle. 1981. Individual Income Taxation, 1947–49. *National Tax Journal* 34, no. 2 (June): 145–166.

Hausman, Jerry A. 1981a. Exact Consumer's Surplus and Deadweight Loss. *American Economic Review* 71 (September): 662–676.

———— 1981b. Labor Supply. In *How Taxes Affect Economic Behavior,* ed. Henry J. Aaron and Joseph A. Pechman. Washington, D.C.: Brookings Institution.

———— 1985. Taxes and Labor Supply. In *Handbook of Public Economics,* vol. 1, ed. Alan J. Auerbach and Martin Feldstein. Amsterdam: North-Holland.

Haveman, Robert, and John Krutilla. 1967. Unemployment, Excess Capacity, and Benefit-Cost Investment Criteria. *Review of Economics and Statistics* 44: 382–392.

Haveman, Robert, and Barbara Wolfe. 1984. Schooling and Economic Well-Being: The Role of Nonmarket Effects. *Journal of Human Resources* 19: 377–408.

Hayashi, Fumio. 1987. Tests for Liquidity Constraints: A Critical Survey and Some New Observations. In *Advances in Econometrics,* vol. 2, ed. T. Bewley. Cambridge: Cambridge University Press.

Heckman, James J. 1983. Comment. In *Behavioral Simulation Methods in Tax Policy Analysis,* ed. Martin Feldstein. Chicago: University of Chicago Press.

Heil, James. 1991. Searching for Leviathan Revisited. *Public Finance Quarterly* 19 (July): 334–346.

Heller, Walter W. 1959. Deductions and Credits for State Income Taxes. In *Tax Revision Compendium.* Washington, D.C.: Government Printing Office.

Hellmuth, William F., Jr. 1959. The Corporate Income Tax Base. In *Tax Revision Compendium.* Washington, D.C.: Government Printing Office.

Helms, L. J. 1985. The Effect of State and Local Taxes on Economic Growth: A Time Series–Cross Section Approach. *Review of Economic Statistics* 67, no. 4 (November): 497–511.

Hendershott, Patric H., and Sheng Cheng Hu. 1983. The Allocation of Capital between Residential and Nonresidential Uses: Taxes, Inflation, and Capital Market Constraints. *Journal of Finance* 38: 795–812.

Henderson, J. Vernon. 1986. The Time of Regional Development. *Journal of Development Economics* 23, no. 2 (October): 275–292.

———— 1991. Will Homeowners Impose Property Taxes? Unpublished.

Hettich, Walter, and Stanley Winer. 1985. Blueprints and Pathways: The Shifting Foundations of Tax Reform. *National Tax Journal* 38 (December): 423–445.

Hill, J. K. 1984. Comparative Statics in General Equilibrium Models with a Unionized Sector. *Journal of International Economics* 16: 345–356.

Hirschman, Albert. 1973. The Changing Tolerance for Income Inequality in the Course of Economic Development. *Quarterly Journal of Economics* 87 (November): 544–566.

Holcombe, Randall C., and Asghar Zardkoohi. 1981. The Determinants of Federal Grants. *Southern Economic Journal* 48 (October): 393–399.

Holland, Daniel. 1969. The Effect of Taxation on Effort: The Results for Business Executives. In *Proceedings of the National Tax Association–Tax Institute of America Annual Conference on Taxation,* ed. S. J. Bowers. Columbus, Ohio: National Tax Association.

Holmlund, B., and P. Lundborg. 1989. Unemployment Insurance Schemes for Reducing the Natural Rate of Unemployment. *Journal of Public Economics* 38: 1–15.

Howrey, E. Philip, and Saul H. Hymans. 1978. The Measurement and Determination of Loanable-Funds Saving. *Brookings Papers on Economic Activity* 3: 655–685.

——— 1980. The Measurement and Determination of Loanable-Funds Saving. In *What Should Be Taxed: Income or Expenditure?* ed. Joseph A. Pechman. Washington, D.C.: Brookings Institution.

Hoyt, W., and E. Smolensky. 1989. The Distributed Effects of Revenue Structures. In *Changes in Revenue Structures.* Detroit: Wayne State University Press.

Hubbard, Glenn, and Kenneth Judd. 1986. Liquidity Constraints, Fiscal Policy, and Consumption. *Brookings Papers on Economic Activity* 1: 1–60.

Hulten, Charles R., and Robert A. Klayman. 1988. Investment Incentives in Theory and Practice. In *Uneasy Compromise: Problems of a Hybrid Income-Consumption Tax,* ed. Henry J. Aaron, Harvey Galper, and Joseph A. Pechman. Washington, D.C.: Brookings Institution.

Hulten, Charles R., and Frank C. Wykoff. 1981. Economic Depreciation and Accelerated Depreciation: An Evaluation of the Conable-Jones 10–5–3 Proposal. *National Tax Journal* 34 (March): 45–60.

Ichiishi, Tatsuro. 1977. Coalition Structure in a Labor-Managed Market Economy. *Econometrica* 45, no. 2: 341–361.

——— 1981. A Social Coalitional Equilibrium Existence Lemma. *Econometrica* 49, no. 2: 369–377.

——— 1982. Management versus Ownership, I. *International Economic Review* 23, no. 2: 323–337.

——— 1991. *The Cooperative Nature of the Firm.* Cambridge: Cambridge University Press.

Inman, Robert P. 1987. Markets, Government and the "New" Political Economy. In *Handbook of Public Economics,* vol. 2, ed. Alan J. Auerbach and Martin Feldstein. Amsterdam: North-Holland.

——— 1988. Federal Assistance and Local Services in the United States: The Evolution of a New Federalist Fiscal Order. In *Fiscal Federalism: Quantitative Studies*, ed. H. Rosen. Chicago: University of Chicago Press.

———— 1989. The Local Decision to Tax: Evidence from Large U.S. Cities. *Regional Science and Urban Economics* 119, no. 3 (August): 455–492.

Inman, Robert P., and Daniel L. Rubinfeld. 1991. Fiscal Federalism in Europe: Lessons from the United States Experience. Cambridge, Mass.: National Bureau of Economic Research, Working Paper 3941.

Institute for Fiscal Studies. 1978. *The Structure and Reform of Direct Taxation*. London: Allen and Unwin.

Johnson, H. G. 1971. *The Two-Sector Model of General Equilibrium*. London: Allen and Unwin.

Johnson, H. G., and P. M. Mieszkowski. 1970. The Effects of Unionization on the Distribution of Income: A General Equilibrium Approach. *Quarterly Journal of Economics* 84: 539–561.

Jones, R. W. 1965. The Structure of Simple General Equilibrium Models. *Journal of Political Economy* 73: 557–572.

———— 1971. Distortions in Factor Markets and the General Equilibrium Model of Production. *Journal of Political Economy* 79: 437–459.

Jorgenson, Dale W. 1963. Capital Theory and Investment Behavior. *American Economic Review* 53 (May): 247–259.

Judd, Kenneth. 1987. The Welfare Cost of Factor Taxation in a Perfect-Foresight Model. *Journal of Political Economy* 95 (August): 675–709.

———— 1989. Optimal Taxation in Dynamic Stochastic Economies: Theory and Evidence. Hoover Institution, mimeo.

Kadane, J. B. 1975. Statistical Problems of Merged Data Files. Office of Tax Analysis, Paper 6. Washington, D.C.: U.S. Treasury Department.

Kahn, Harry C. 1959. Personal Deductions in the Individual Income Tax. In *Tax Revision Compendium*. Washington, D.C.: Government Printing Office.

Kaldor, Nicholas. 1955. *An Expenditure Tax*. London: Allen and Unwin.

———— 1956. Alternative Theories of Distribution. *Review of Economic Studies* 23: 83–100.

Kaplow, Louis. 1989. Horizontal Equity: Measures in Search of a Principle. *National Tax Journal* 42 (June): 139–154.

Katz, Michael L., and Harvey S. Rosen. 1985. Tax Analysis in an Oligopoly Model. *Public Finance Quarterly* 13 (January): 3–19.

Kay, J. A. 1990. Tax Policy: A Survey. *Economic Journal* 100: 18–75.

Kehoe, T. J., and J. Serra-Puche. 1983. A Computational General Equilibrium Model with Endogenous Unemployment: An Analysis of the 1980 Fiscal Reform in Mexico. *Journal of Public Economics* 22: 1–26.

Kehoe, T. J., and S. Whalley. 1985. Uniqueness of Equilibrium in Large-Scale Numerical General Equilibrium Models. *Journal of Public Economics* 28: 247–254.

Kemsley, W. F. F., R. U. Redpath, and M. Holmes. 1980. *Family Expenditure Survey Handbook.* London: Her Majesty's Stationery Office.

Keynes, John Maynard. 1936. *The General Theory of Employment, Interest, and Money.* New York: Harcourt, Brace and World.

Killingsworth, Mark R. 1983. *Labor Supply.* Cambridge: Cambridge University Press.

King, David. 1984. *Fiscal Tiers: The Economics of Multi-Level Government.* London: Allen and Unwin.

King, Mervyn A. 1974. Taxation and the Cost of Capital. *Review of Economic Studies* 41 (January): 21–35.

—— 1977. *Public Policy and the Corporation.* London: Chapman and Hall.

—— 1980. Savings and Taxation. In *Public Policy and the Tax System,* ed. G. A. Hughes and G. M. Heal. London: Allen and Unwin.

—— 1983. Welfare Analysis of Tax Reforms Using Household Data. *Journal of Public Economics* 21: 183–214.

—— 1986. A Pigovian Rule for the Optimum Provision of Public Goods. *Journal of Public Economics* 30: 273–291.

—— 1988. Tax Arbitrage and the Life-Cycle of Firms. Walras-Bowley Lecture.

—— 1989. Economic Growth and the Life-Cycle of Firms. Unpublished.

King, Mervyn A., and Don Fullerton, eds. 1984. *The Taxation of Income from Capital: A Comparative Study of the U.S., U.K., Sweden and West Germany.* Chicago: University of Chicago Press.

King, Mervyn A., and Mark Robson. 1989. Endogenous Growth and the Role of History. Cambridge, Mass.: National Bureau of Economic Research, Working Paper 3151.

Klundert, T., van de. 1988. Wage Differentials and Employment in a Two-Sector Model with a Dual Labour Market. Unpublished.

Koppelman, Stanley A. 1989. At-Risk and Passive Activity Limitations: Can Complexity Be Reduced? *Tax Law Review* 45 (Fall): 97–120.

Kotlikoff, Laurence J. 1984. Taxation and Savings: A Neoclassical Perspective. *Journal of Economic Literature* 22 (December): 1576–1629.

—— 1986. Deficit Delusion. *The Public Interest* 84 (Summer): 53–65.

Kotlikoff, Laurence J., Torsten Persson, and Lars Svensson. 1988. Social Contracts as Assets: A Possible Solution to the Time-Consistency Problem. *American Economic Review* 78 (September): 662–677.

Kotlikoff, Laurence J., and Lawrence H. Summers. 1981. The Role of International Transfers in Aggregate Capital Accumulation. *Journal of Political Economy* 89 (August): 706–732.

—— 1987. Tax Incidence. In *Handbook of Public Economics,* vol. 2, ed. Alan J. Auerbach and Martin Feldstein. Amsterdam: North-Holland.

Krause-Junk, Gerold. 1987. Optimal Taxation: A Beautiful Cul-de-Sac? In *The Rele-*

vance of Public Finance for Policy-Making, ed. H. van der Kar and B. Wolfe. Detroit: Wayne State University Press.

Krzyzaniak, Marian. 1967. The Long-Run Burden of a General Tax on Profits in a Neo-Classical World. *Public Finance* 22: 472–491.

Krzyzaniak, Marian, and Richard A. Musgrave. 1963. *The Shifting of the Corporation Income Tax: An Empirical Study of Its Short-Run Effect upon the Rate of Return.* Baltimore: Johns Hopkins University Press.

Kydland, Finn E., and Edward C. Prescott. 1977. Rules Rather than Discretion: The Inconsistency of Optimal Plans. *Journal of Political Economy* 85 (June): 473–491.

Ladd, Helen F. 1993. State Responses to the TRA86 Revenue Windfalls: A New Test of the Flypaper Effect. *Journal of Policy Analysis and Management* 12, no. 1: 82–103.

Ladd, Helen F., and Fred C. Doolittle. 1982. Which Level of Government Should Assist the Poor? *National Tax Journal* 35 (September): 323–336.

Ladd, Helen F., and John Yinger. 1989. *America's Ailing Cities: Fiscal Health and the Design of Urban Policy.* Baltimore: Johns Hopkins University Press.

Lampman, Robert J. 1959. Taxation and the Size Distribution of Income. In *Tax Revision Compendium.* Washington, D.C.: Government Printing Office.

Le Grand, J. 1982. *The Strategy of Equality.* London: Allen and Unwin.

——— 1987. Measuring the Distributional Impact of the Welfare State: Methodological Issues. In *Not Only the Poor,* ed. R. E. Goodin and J. Le Grand. London: Allen and Unwin.

Levy, Frank. 1985. Affluence, Altruism and Happiness in the Postwar Period. In *Horizontal Equity and Economic Welfare,* ed. Martin David and Timothy Smeeding. Chicago: University of Chicago Press.

——— 1988a. *Dollars and Dreams.* New York: Norton.

——— 1988b. Incomes, Families and Living Standards. In *American Living Standards: Threats and Challenges,* ed. Robert E. Litan, Robert Z. Lawrence, and Charles L. Schultze. Washington, D.C.: Brookings Institution.

Lindbeck, Assar. 1985. Redistribution Policy and the Expansion of the Public Sector. *Journal of Public Economics* 28: 309–328.

Lindbeck, Assar, and D. J. Snower. 1988. *The Insider-Outsider Theory.* Cambridge, Mass.: MIT Press.

Lipsey, R., and K. Lancaster. 1957. The General Theory of the Second Best. *Review of Economic Studies* 24: 11–32.

Lucas, Robert E., Jr. 1972. Expectations and the Neutrality of Money. *Journal of Economic Theory* 4: 103–124.

——— 1976. Econometric Policy Evaluation: A Critique. In *The Phillips Curve and Labor Markets,* ed. K. Brunner and A. Meltzer. Amsterdam: North-Holland.

———— 1989. The Effects of Monetary Shocks when Prices Are Set in Advance. University of Chicago, unpublished.

Lucas, Robert E., Jr., and Nancy L. Stokey. 1983. Optimal Fiscal and Monetary Policy in an Economy without Capital. *Journal of Monetary Economics* 8: 55–94.

———— 1989. *Recursive Methods in Economic Dynamics.* Cambridge, Mass.: Harvard University Press.

Lyon, Andrew B. 1989. The Effect of the Investment Tax Credit on the Value of the Firm. *Journal of Public Economics* 38 (March): 227–247.

Lyon, Charles S., and James S. Eustice. 1962. Assignment of Income: Fruit and Tree as Irrigated by the P. G. Lake Case. *Tax Law Review* 17: 293–430.

MacLeod, W. B., and J. Malcomson. 1989. Wage Premiums and Profit Maximisation in Efficiency Wage Models. CLE Discussion Paper 337, London School of Economics.

MaCurdy, Thomas, David Green, and Harry Paarsch. 1990. Assessing Empirical Approaches for Analyzing Taxes and Labor Supply. *Journal of Human Resources* 25: 415–490.

Magee, S. P. 1976. *International Trade and Distortions in Factor Markets.* New York: Marcel Dekker.

Mankiw, N. Gregory. 1987. The Optimal Collection of Seignorage: Theory and Evidence. *Journal of Monetary Economics* 20 (September): 327–341.

McDonald, I. M., and R. M. Solow, 1985. Wages and Employment in a Segmented Labor Market. *Quarterly Journal of Economics* 100: 1115–1141.

McLure, Charles E., Jr. 1967. The Interstate Exporting of State and Local Taxes: Estimates for 1962. *National Tax Journal* 20 (March): 49–77.

———— 1969. The Inter-Regional Incidence of General Regional Taxes. *Public Finance* 24: 457–484.

———— 1970. Taxation, Substitution, and Industrial Location. *Journal of Political Economy* 78 (January–February): 112–132.

———— 1971. The Theory of Tax Incidence with Imperfect Factor Mobility. *Finanzarchiv* 30, no. 1: 27–48.

———— 1974. A Diagrammatic Exposition of the Harberger Model with One Immobile Factor. *Journal of Political Economy* 82, no. 1 (January–February): 56–82.

———— 1975a. General Equilibrium Incidence Analysis: The Harberger Model after Ten Years. *Journal of Public Economics* 4, no. 2 (February): 125–161.

———— 1975b. Integration of the Personal and Corporate Income Taxes: The Missing Element in Tax Reform Proposals. *Harvard Law Review* 88 (January): 532–582.

———— 1979. *Must Corporate Income Be Taxed Twice?* Washington, D.C.: Brookings Institution.

———— 1984. The Evolution of Tax Advice and the Taxation of Capital in the USA. *Government and Policy* 2: 251–269.

——— 1985. Rationale Underlying the Treasury Proposals. In *Economic Consequences of Tax Simplification*. Boston: Federal Reserve Bank of Boston.

——— 1986a. The Tax Treatment of Owner-Occupied Housing: The Achilles' Heel of Tax Reform. In *Tax Reform and Real Estate*, ed. James R. Follain. Washington, D.C.: Urban Institute Press.

——— 1986b. *Economic Perspectives on State Taxation of Multijurisdictional Corporations*. Arlington, Va.: Tax Analysts.

——— 1986c. Tax Competition: Is What's Good for the Private Goose also Good for the Public Gander? *National Tax Journal* 39 (September): 341–348.

——— 1988. The 1986 Act: Tax Reform's Finest Hour, or Death Throes of the Income Tax? *National Tax Journal* 41, no. 3 (September): 303–315.

——— 1989. The Budget Process and Tax Simplification/Complication. *Tax Law Review* 45, no. 1 (Fall): 25–95.

——— 1990. International Aspects of Tax Policy for the Twenty-First Century. *American Journal of Tax Policy* 8, no. 2 (Fall): 167–185.

McLure, Charles E., Jr., Jack Mutti, Victor Thuronyi, and George R. Zodrow. 1988. *The Taxation of Income from Business and Capital in Colombia*. Bogotá: Ministerio de Hacienda y Credito Publico; and Durham, N.C.: Duke University Press, 1990.

McLure, Charles E., Jr., and George R. Zodrow. 1987. Treasury-I and the Tax Reform Act of 1986: The Economics and Politics of Tax Reform. *Journal of Economic Perspectives* 1, no. 1 (Summer): 37–58.

——— 1990. Administrative Advantages of the Individual Tax Prepayment Approach to the Direct Taxation of Consumption. In *Heidelberg Congress on Taxing Consumption*. New York: Springer-Verlag.

McWhinney, Edward. 1965. *Comparative Federalism*, second edition. Toronto: University of Toronto Press.

Meade, James E. 1955a. *Mathematical Supplement to Trade and Welfare*, vol. 2. Oxford: Oxford University Press.

——— 1955b. *The Theory of International Economic Policy*, vol. 2: *Trade and Welfare*. London: Oxford University Press.

Meltzer, Allan. 1988. *Keynes's Monetary Theory: A Different Interpretation*. Cambridge: Cambridge University Press.

Merton, Robert C. 1983. On the Role of Social Security as a Means for Efficient Risk Sharing in an Economy where Human Capital is Not Tradeable. In *Financial Aspects of the U.S. Pension System*, ed. Z. Bodie and J. Shoven. Chicago: University of Chicago Press.

Metcalf, Gilbert C. 1993. Tax Exporting, Federal Deductibility, and State Tax Structure. *Journal of Policy Analysis and Management*, 12, no. 1: 109–126.

Mieszkowski, Peter. 1967. On the Theory of Tax Incidence. *Journal of Political Economy* 75 (June): 250–262.

——— 1969. Tax Incidence Theory: The Effects of Taxes on the Distribution of Income. *Journal of Economic Literature* 7 (December): 1103–1124.

——— 1972. Integration of the Corporate and Personal Income Taxes: The Bogus Issue of Shifting. *Finanzarchiv* 31: 256–297.

——— 1980. The Advisability and Feasibility of an Expenditure Tax System. In *The Economics of Taxation,* ed. Henry J. Aaron and Michael J. Boskin. Washington, D.C.: Brookings Institution.

——— 1983. Energy Policy, Taxation of Natural Resources, and Fiscal Federalism. In *Assignment in Federal Countries,* ed. Charles E. McLure, Jr. Canberra: Australian National University Press.

Mieszkowski, Peter, and Eric Toder. 1983. Taxation of Energy Resources. In *Fiscal Federalism and the Taxation of Natural Resources,* ed. Charles E. McLure, Jr., and Peter Mieszkowski. Lexington, Mass.: Heath.

Mieszkowski, Peter, and George R. Zodrow. 1989. Taxation and the Tiebout Model: The Differential Effects of Head Taxes, Taxes on Land Rents, and Property Taxes. *Journal of Economic Literature* 27 (September): 1098–1146.

Mintz, Jack, and Henry Tulkens. 1986. Commodity Tax Competition between Member States of a Federation. *Journal of Public Economics* 29: 133–172.

Mirrlees, James A. 1971. An Exploration in the Theory of Optimum Income Taxation. *Review of Economic Studies* 38 (April): 175–208.

——— 1975. Optimal Commodity Taxation in a Two-Class Economy. *Journal of Public Economics* 4: 27–33.

——— 1976. Optimal Tax Theory: A Synthesis. *Journal of Public Economics* 6 (November): 327–358.

Moffitt, Robert. 1984. The Effects of Grants-in-Aid on State and Local Expenditures: The Case of AFDC. *Journal of Public Economics* 23 (April): 279–305.

Moore, Kristin A., Nicholas Zill, and Thomas Stief. 1990. The Effects of the Family Support Act on Child Development. Paper prepared for the annual meetings of the Population Association of America, Toronto.

Mossin, J. 1968. Taxation and Risk-Taking: An Expected Utility Approach. *Economica* 35 (February): 74–82.

Munnell, Alicia H. 1980. The Couple versus the Individual under the Federal Personal Income Tax. In *The Economics of Taxation,* ed. Henry J. Aaron and Michael J. Boskin. Washington, D.C.: Brookings Institution.

Murphy, Kevin, and Finis Welch. 1988. Wage Differentials in the 1980's: The Role of International Trade. Mimeo.

Musgrave, Richard A. 1959a. *The Theory of Public Finance: A Study in Public Economy.* New York: McGraw-Hill.

——— 1959b. How Progressive Is the Income Tax? In *Tax Revision Compendium.* Washington, D.C.: Government Printing Office.

——— 1961. Approaches to a Fiscal Theory of Political Federalism. In *National Bu-*

reau of Economic Research, *Public Finance: Needs, Sources, and Utilization.* Princeton, N.J.: Princeton University Press.

———— 1964. Estimating the Distribution of the Tax Burden. In *Income Redistribution and the Statistical Foundations of Economic Policy,* ed. C. Clark and G. Stuvel. London: Bowes and Bowes.

Musgrave, Richard A., ed. 1965. *Essays in Fiscal Federalism.* Washington, D.C.: Brookings Institution.

———— 1981. Leviathan Cometh—Or Does He? In *Tax and Expenditure Limitations,* ed. H. Ladd and T. N. Tideman. Washington, D.C.: Urban Institute.

———— 1982. Tax Reform or Tax Deform. In *Tax Policy Options for the 1980s,* ed. Wayne R. Thirsk and John Whalley. Toronto: Canadian Tax Foundation.

———— 1983. Who Should Tax, Where, and What? In *Tax Assignment in Federal Countries,* ed. Charles E. McLure, Jr. Canberra: Australian National University Press.

———— 1987. Short of Euphoria. *Journal of Economic Perspectives* 1, no. 1 (Summer): 59–71.

Musgrave, Richard A., J. J. Carroll, L. D. Cook, and L. Frane. 1951. Distribution of Tax Payments by Income Groups: A Case Study for 1948. *National Tax Journal* 4 (March): 1–53.

Musgrave, Richard A., Karl E. Case, and Herman Leonard. 1974. The Distribution of Fiscal Burdens and Benefits. *Public Finance Quarterly* 2 (July): 259–311.

Musgrave, Richard A., and P. B. Musgrave. 1989. *Public Finance in Theory and Practice,* fifth edition. New York: McGraw-Hill.

Musgrave, Richard A., and Mitchell Polinsky. 1970. Revenue Sharing—A Critical View. In *Financing State and Local Governments.* Boston: Federal Reserve Bank of Boston.

Neary, J. P. 1978. Dynamic Stability and the Theory of Factor Market Distortions. *American Economic Review* 68: 671–682.

Neck, R., F. Schneider, and M. Hofreither. 1988. The Consequences of Progressive Income Taxation for the Shadow Economy: Some Theoretical Considerations. Johannes Kepler University of Linz, Austria, Working Paper 8810.

Newbery, David, and Nicholas Stern. 1987. *The Theory of Taxation for Developing Countries.* Oxford: Oxford University Press, for the World Bank.

Newman, R. J., and D. H. Sullivan. 1988. Econometric Analysis of Business Tax Impacts on Industrial Location: What Do We Know and How Do We Know It? *Journal of Urban Economics* 23, no. 2 (March): 215–234.

Nicholson, J. L. 1964. *Redistribution of Income in the United Kingdom in 1959, 1957 and 1953.* Cambridge: Bowes and Bowes.

Niskanen, William. 1975. Bureaucrats and Politicians. *Journal of Law and Economics* 18 (December): 617–643.

Noiset, Luc, and William Oakland. 1992. The Local Taxation of Capital: Are Local Communities Shooting Themselves in the Foot? Unpublished.

Nordhaus, William D. 1975. The Political Business Cycle. *Review of Economic Studies* 42 (April): 169–190.

Oakland, William. 1987. Theory of Public Goods. In *Handbook of Public Economics,* vol. 2, ed. Alan J. Auerbach and Martin Feldstein. Amsterdam: North-Holland.

Oates, Wallace E. 1968. The Theory of Public Finance in a Federal System. *Canadian Journal of Economics* 1 (February): 37–54.

———— 1969. The Effects of Property Taxes and Local Public Spending on Property Values: An Empirical Study of Tax Capitalization and the Tiebout Hypothesis. *Journal of Political Economy* 77 (November–December): 957–971.

———— 1972. *Fiscal Federalism.* New York: Harcourt, Brace, Jovanovich.

———— 1977. The Use of Local Zoning Ordinances to Regulate Population Flows and the Quality of Local Services. In *Essays in Labor Market Analysis,* ed. O. Ashenfelter and W. Oates. New York: Wiley.

———— 1979. Lump Sum Intergovernmental Grants Have Price Effects. In *Fiscal Federalism and Grants-in-Aid,* ed. P. Mieszkowski and W. Oakland. Washington D.C.: Urban Institute.

———— 1980. The Role of Intergovernmental Grants in the U.S. Economy with Special Attention to Countercyclical Policy. In U.S. Congress, Joint Economic Committee, *Special Study on Economic Change,* vol. 6, *Federal Finance: The Pursuit of American Goals.* Washington, D.C.: Government Printing Office.

———— 1981. On Local Finance and the Tiebout Model. *American Economic Review* 71 (May): 93–98.

———— 1985. Searching for Leviathan: An Empirical Study. *American Economic Review* 75 (September): 748–757.

———— 1989a. Searching for Leviathan: A Reply and Some Further Reflections. *American Economic Review* 79 (June): 578–583.

———— 1989b. The Theory of Regulatory Federalism: The Case of Environmental Management. Unpublished.

———— and Robert M. Schwab. 1988. Economic Competition among Jurisdictions: Efficiency-Enhancing or Distortion-Inducing? *Journal of Public Economics* 35 (April): 333–354.

O'Higgins, M. 1980. The Distributive Effects of Public Expenditure and Taxation: An Agnostic View of the CSO Analyses. In *Taxation and Social Policy,* ed. C. Sandford, C. Pond, and R. Walker. London: Heinemann.

Okner, B. A. 1972. Constructing a New Data Base from Existing Microdata Sets: The 1966 Merge File. *Annals of Economic and Social Measurement* 1: 325–342.

Okun, A. M. 1975. *Equality and Efficiency.* Washington, D.C.: Brookings Institution.

Pack, Howard, and Pack, Janet R. 1978. Metropolitan Fragmentation and Local Public Expenditures. *National Tax Journal* 31 (December): 349–362.

Paul, Randolph. 1956. Erosion of the Tax Base and Rate Structure. *Tax Law Review* 11: 203–222.

Pauly, M. V. 1967. Clubs, Commonality and the Core: An Integration of Game Theory and the Theory of Public Goods. *Economica* 34: 314–324.

———— 1970a. Optimality, "Public" Goods, and Local Governments: A General Theoretical Analysis. *Journal of Political Economy* 78: 572–585.

———— 1970b. Cores and Clubs. *Public Choice* 9: 53–65.

———— 1973. Income Redistribution as a Local Public Good. *Journal of Public Economics* 2 (February): 35–58.

Peacock, A. T., and R. Shannon. 1968. The Welfare State and the Redistribution of Income. *Westminster Bank Review:* 30–46.

Pechman, Joseph A. 1959a. What Would a Comprehensive Income Tax Yield? In *Tax Revision Compendium.* Washington, D.C.: Government Printing Office.

———— 1959b. Income Splitting. In *Tax Revision Compendium.* Washington, D.C.: Government Printing Office.

———— 1966. *Federal Tax Policy.* Washington, D.C.: Brookings Institution.

———— 1970. Revenue Sharing Revisited. In *Financing State and Local Governments.* Boston: Federal Reserve Bank of Boston.

Pechman, Joseph A., ed. 1980. *What Should Be Taxed: Income or Expenditure?* Washington, D.C.: Brookings Institution.

———— 1985. *Who Paid the Taxes, 1966–85?* Washington, D.C.: Brookings Institution.

———— 1987. *Federal Tax Policy,* Fifth edition. Washington, D.C.: Brookings Institution.

———— 1990. The Future of the Income Tax. *American Economic Review* 80, no. 1 (March): 1–20.

Pechman, Joseph A., and Benjamin A. Okner. 1974. *Who Bears the Tax Burden?* Washington, D.C.: Brookings Institution.

Peltzman, Sam, and T. Nicolaus Tideman. 1972. Local versus National Pollution Control: Note. *American Economic Review* 62 (December): 959–963.

Pencavel, John. 1986. Labor Supply of Men: A Survey. In *Handbook of Labor Economics,* ed. Orley Ashenfelter and R. Layard. Amsterdam: North-Holland.

Persson, Mats, Torsten Persson, and Lars Svensson. 1987. Time Consistency of Fiscal and Monetary Policy. *Econometrica* 55 (November): 1419–1431.

Persson, Torsten, and Lars Svensson. 1989. Checks and Balances on the Government Budget. *Quarterly Journal of Economics* 104 (May): 325–346.

Phelps, Edmund S. 1972. *Inflation Policy and Unemployment Theory.* New York: Norton.

———— 1973. Inflation in the Theory of Public Finance. *Swedish Journal of Economics* 75: 67–82.

Phelps, Edmund S., and Robert A. Pollak. 1968. On Second-Best National Saving and Game-Equilibrium Growth. *Review of Economic Studies* 35 (April): 185–199.

Piggott, J. R., and J. Whalley. 1985. *Applied General Equilibrium Analysis: An Application to UK Tax Policy.* New York: Cambridge University Press.

Pines, David. 1991. Tiebout without Politics. *Regional Science and Urban Economics* 21, no. 3 (November): 469–489.

Pissarides, C. 1979. Job Matchings with State Employment Agencies and Random Search. *Economic Journal* 89: 818–833.

Plumb, William T. 1971. The Federal Income Tax Significance of Corporate Debt: A Critical Analysis and a Proposal. *Tax Law Review* 26: 369–640.

Poterba, James M. 1987. Tax Policy and Corporate Saving. *Brookings Papers on Economic Activity* 18, no. 2: 455–503.

——— 1989. Lifetime Incidence and the Distributional Burden of Excise Taxes. *American Economic Review* 79 (May): 325–330.

Poterba, James A., Julio Rotemberg, and Lawrence H. Summers. 1986. A Tax-Based Test for Nominal Rigidities. *American Economic Review* 76 (September): 659–675.

Poterba, James M., and Lawrence H. Summers. 1985. The Economic Effects of Dividend Taxation. In *Recent Advances in Corporate Finance,* ed. E. Altman and M. Subrahmanyam. Homewood, Ill,: Irwin.

——— 1987. Finite Lifetimes and the Effects of Budget Deficits on National Saving. *Journal of Monetary Economics* 20: 369–391.

Prest, A. R. 1955. Statistical Calculations of Tax Burdens. *Economica* (new series) 22, no. 87 (August): 234–245.

——— 1968. The Budget and Interpersonal Distribution. *Public Finance* 23: 80–98.

Quigley, John M., and Eugene Smolensky. 1993. Conflicts among Levels of Government in a Federal System. *Public Finance/Finances Publiques* 47 (Suppl.): 202–215.

Ramsey, Frank P. 1927. A Contribution to the Theory of Taxation. *Economic Journal* 37 (March): 47–61.

Reynolds, M., and Eugene Smolensky. 1976. *Public Expenditures, Taxes and the Distribution of Income.* New York: Academic Press.

Robbins, L. 1932. *An Essay on the Nature and Significance of Economic Science.* London: Macmillan.

Rogers, Carol Ann. 1987. Expenditure Taxes, Income Taxes and Time-Inconsistency. *Journal of Public Economics* 32 (March): 215–230.

Rogoff, Kenneth. 1989. Reputation, Coordination and Monetary Policy. In *Handbook of Modern Business Cycle Theory,* ed. R. Barro. Cambridge, Mass.: Harvard University Press.

——— 1990. Equilibrium Political Budget Cycles. *American Economic Review* 80 (March): 21–36.

Rolph, Earl R., and George F. Break. 1961. *Public Finance.* New York: Roland Press.

Romer, David. 1988. What Are the Costs of Excessive Deficits? *NBER Macroeconomics Annual* 3: 63–98.

Romer, Paul. 1986. Increasing Returns and Long-Run Growth. *Journal of Political Economy* 94 (October): 1002–1037.

Romer, Thomas, and Howard Rosenthal. 1979. Bureaucrats versus Voters: On the Political Economy of Resource Allocation by Direct Democracy. *Quarterly Journal of Economics* 93 (November): 563–587.

Rosen, Harvey S. 1978. The Measurement of Excess Burden with Explicit Utility Functions. *Journal of Political Economy* 86 (April): S121–S136.

——— 1988a. Does Progressive Taxation Survive Optimal Tax Theory? Manuscript.

——— 1988b. *Public Finance.* Homewood, Ill.: Irwin.

Roseveare, H. 1973. *The Treasury.* London: Allen and Unwin.

Roy, A. D. 1951. Some Thoughts on the Distribution of Earnings. *Oxford Economic Papers* 3: 135–146.

Rubinfeld, D. L. 1987. The Economics of the Local Public Sector. In *Handbook of Public Economics,* vol. 2, ed. A. Auerbach and M. Feldstein. Amsterdam: North-Holland.

Rudder, Catherine E. 1983. Tax Policy: Structure and Choice. In *Making Economic Policy in Congress,* ed. Allen Schick. Washington, D.C.: American Enterprise Institute for Public Policy Research.

Ruggles, N., and R. Ruggles. 1974. A Strategy for Merging and Matching Micro-Data Sets. *Annals of Economic and Social Measurement* 3: 353–371.

Sadka, Efraim. 1976. On Income Distribution, Incentive Effects, and Optimal Taxation. *Review of Economic Studies* 9: 261–268.

Salop, S., and J. Stiglitz. 1977. Bargains and Ripoffs: A Model of Monopolistically Competitive Price Dispersion. *Review of Economic Studies* 44: 493–510.

Samuel, H. 1919. The Taxation of the Various Classes of the People. *Journal of the Royal Statistical Society* 82, no. 2: 143–182.

Samuelson, Paul A. 1951. Theory of Optimal Taxation: Memorandum to the U.S. Treasury, 1951. *Journal of Public Economics* 30 (July 1986): 137–144.

——— 1958. An Exact Consumption-Loan Model of Interest with or without the Social Contrivance of Money. *Journal of Political Economy* 66: 467–482.

——— 1964. Tax Deductibility of Economic Depreciation to Insure Invariant Valuations. *Journal of Political Economy* 72 (December): 604–606.

Sandmo, Agnar. 1974. A Note on the Structure of Optimal Taxation. *American Economic Review* 64 (September): 701–706.

——— 1976. Optimal Taxation: An Introduction to the Literature. *Journal of Public Economics* 6 (July–August): 37–54.

——— 1985. The Effects of Taxation on Savings and Risk Taking. In *Handbook of Public Economics,* vol. 1, ed. Alan J. Auerbach and Martin Feldstein. Amsterdam: North-Holland.

Schanz, Georg. 1896. Der Einkommenbegriff und die Einkommensteuergesetze. *Finanz Archiv* 13: 1–87.

Schwab, Robert M., and Wallace Oates. 1991. Community Composition and the Provision of Local Public Goods: A Normative Analysis. *Journal of Public Economics* 44: 217–237.

Scotchmer, Suzanne. 1985a. Profit Maximizing Clubs. *Journal of Public Economics* 27: 25–45.

———— 1985b. Two-Tier Pricing of Shared Facilities in a Free-Entry Equilibrium. *Rand Journal* 16, no. 4: 456–472.

———— 1986. Local Public Goods in an Equilibrium: How Pecuniary Externalities Matter. *Regional Science and Urban Economics* 16: 463–481.

———— 1990. Cost-Benefit Analysis at the Local Level. Teaching notes. University of California, Berkeley.

Scotchmer, Suzanne, and M. H. Wooders. 1986. Optimal and Equilibrium Groups. Discussion Paper, Institute of Economic Research, Harvard University.

———— 1987a. Competitive Equilibrium and the Core in Club Economies with Anonymous Crowding. *Journal of Public Economics* 34, no. 2 (November): 159–173.

———— 1987b. Competitive Equilibrium and the Core in Club Economies with Nonanonymous Crowding. Mimeo.

———— 1988. Monotonicity in Games that Exhaust Gains to Scale. IMSSS Working Paper 525, Stanford University.

Seade, J. 1977. On the Shape of Optimum Tax Schedules. *Journal of Public Economics* 7: 203–236.

Seidman, Laurence S. 1983. Taxes in a Life Cycle Growth Model with Bequests and Inheritances. *American Economic Review* 73 (June): 437–441.

Shapiro, Carl, and Joseph E. Stiglitz. 1984. Equilibrium Unemployment as a Worker Discipline Device. *American Economic Review* 74: 433–444.

Shapiro, Matthew. 1984. The Dynamic Demand for Capital and Labor. *Quarterly Journal of Economics* 101 (August): 513–541.

Shapley, L. S., and M. Shubik. 1966. Quasi-Cores in a Monetary Economy with Non-Convex Preferences. *Econometrica* 34: 305–327.

Shephard, R. W. 1944. A Mathematical Theory of the Incidence of Taxation. *Econometrica* 12: 1–18.

Sheshinski, Eytan. 1972. The Optimum Linear Income Tax. *Review of Economic Studies* 39 (July): 297–302.

Shorrocks, A. F. 1983. Ranking Income Distributions. *Economica* 50: 3–17.

Shoup, Carl S. 1969. *Public Finance.* Chicago: Aldine.

———— 1972. Quantitative Research in Taxation and Government Expenditure. In *Public Expenditures and Taxation.* New York: Columbia University Press.

Shoven, John B. 1976. The Incidence and Efficiency Effects of Taxes on Income from Capital. *Journal of Political Economy* 84 (December): 1261–1284.

———— 1984. Applied General-Equilibrium Models of Taxation and International

Trade: An Introduction and Survey. *Journal of Economic Literature* 22 (September): 1007–1051.

Shoven, John B., and John Whalley. 1972. A General Equilibrium Calculation of the Effects of Differential Taxation of Income from Capital in the U.S. *Journal of Public Economics* 1 (November): 281–321.

Sichel, Daniel E. 1989. Business Cycle Asymmetry: A Deeper Look. Economic Activity Working Paper 93, Board of Governors of the Federal Reserve System.

Simons, Henry C. 1938. *Personal Income Taxation.* Chicago: University of Chicago Press.

――― 1950. *Federal Tax Reform.* Chicago: University of Chicago Press.

Sims, C. 1972. Comments. *Annals of Economic and Social Measurement* 1: 343–345.

Sinn, Hans-Werner. 1991. Taxation and the Cost of Capital: The "Old View," the "New View" and Another View. In *Tax Policy and the Economy,* vol. 5, ed. David F. Bradford. Cambridge, Mass.: MIT Press.

Sjoblom, Kriss. 1985. Voting for Social Security. *Public Choice* 45: 225–240.

Skinner, Jonathan. 1988. The Welfare Cost of Uncertain Tax Policy. *Journal of Public Economics* 37 (November): 129–145.

Skinner, Jonathan, and Daniel Feenberg. 1990. The Impact of the 1986 Tax Reform on Personal Saving. In *Do Taxes Matter: The Impact of the Tax Reform Act of 1986,* ed. Joel Slemrod. Cambridge, Mass.: MIT Press.

Slemrod, Joel. 1983a. A General Equilibrium Model of Taxation with Endogenous Financial Behavior. In *Behavioral Simulation Methods in Tax Policy Analysis,* ed. Martin Feldstein. Chicago: University of Chicago Press.

――― 1983b. Do We Know How Progressive the Income Tax System Should Be? *National Tax Journal* 36: 361–369.

――― 1990. Optimal Taxation and Optimal Tax Systems. *Journal of Economic Perspectives* 4, no. 1 (Winter): 157–178.

Slitor, Richard E. 1973. Administrative Aspects of Expenditures Taxation. In *Broad-Based Taxes: New Options and Sources,* ed. Richard A. Musgrave. Baltimore: Johns Hopkins University Press.

Smith, Dan Throop. 1959. Tax Treatment of Capital Gains. In *Tax Revision Compendium.* Washington, D.C.: Government Printing Office.

――― 1961. *Federal Tax Reform.* New York: McGraw-Hill.

――― 1980. Statement. In *Committee on Ways and Means, Hearings on the Tax Restructuring Act of 1979.* Washington, D.C.: Government Printing Office.

Smolensky, E., W. Hoyt, and S. Danziger. 1987. A Critical Survey of Efforts to Measure Budget Incidence. In *The Relevance of Public Finance for Policy-Making.* Detroit: Wayne State University Press.

Solow, Robert M. 1956. A Contribution to the Theory of Economic Growth. *Quarterly Journal of Economics* 70 (February): 65–94.

Sonstelie, J. C., and P. R. Portney. 1978. Profit Maximizing Communities and the Theory of Local Public Expenditure. *Journal of Urban Economics* 5: 263–277.

Starrett, David A. 1980. On the Method of Taxation and the Provision of Local Public Goods. *American Economic Review* 70: 380–392.

——— 1981. Land Value Capitalization in Local Public Finance. *Journal of Political Economy* 89: 306–327.

——— 1982. Long Run Savings Elasticities in the Life Cycle Model. Stanford University Research Paper 24.

——— 1988. *Foundations of Public Economics.* Cambridge: Cambridge University Press.

Stern, Nicholas H. 1976. On the Specification of Models of Optimum Income Taxation. *Journal of Public Economics* 6 (July–August): 123–162.

——— 1987a. The Theory of Optimal Commodity and Income Taxation: An Introduction. In *The Theory of Taxation for Developing Countries,* ed. David Newbery and Nicholas Stern. Oxford: Oxford University Press, for the World Bank.

——— 1987b. Aspects of the General Theory of Tax Reform. In *The Theory of Taxation for Developing Countries,* ed. David Newbery and Nicholas Stern. Oxford: Oxford University Press, for the World Bank.

——— 1990. From the Static to the Dynamic: Some Problems in the Theory of Taxation. Paper presented to the International Seminar in Public Economics, Delhi, India.

——— 1992. From Static to Dynamic Taxation. *Journal of Public Economics* 47: 273–297.

Steuerle, Eugene C. 1985. *Taxes Loans and Inflation: How the Nation's Wealth Becomes Misallocated.* Washington, D.C.: Brookings Institution.

——— 1992. *The Tax Decade: How Taxes Came to Dominate the Public Agenda.* Washington, D.C.: Urban Institute Press.

Steuerle, Eugene C., and Michael Hartzmark. 1981. Individual Income Taxation. *National Tax Journal* 34, no. 2 (June): 145–166.

Stiglitz, Joseph E. 1969a. Distribution of Income and Wealth among Individuals. *Econometrica* 37: 382–397.

——— 1969b. The Effects of Income, Wealth and Capital Gains Taxation on Risk-Taking. *Quarterly Journal of Economics* 83 (May): 262–283.

——— 1973. Taxation, Corporate Financial Policy and the Cost of Capital. *Journal of Public Economics* 2 (February): 1–34.

——— 1976. The Corporation Tax. *Journal of Public Economics* 5 (April–May): 303–311.

——— 1977. The Theory of Local Public Goods. In *The Economics of Public Services,* ed. M. Feldstein and R. Inman. New York: Wiley.

——— 1982a. Alternative Theories of Wage Determination and Unemployment. In *The Theory and Experience of Economic Development,* ed. M. Gersovitz et al. London: Allen and Unwin.

—— 1982b. Self-Selection and Pareto Efficient Taxation. *Journal of Public Economics* 17: 213–240.

—— 1983. Some Aspects of the Taxation of Capital Gains. *Journal of Public Economics* 21 (July): 257–294.

—— 1987. Pareto Efficient and Optimal Taxation and the New New Welfare Economics. In *Handbook of Public Economics,* vol. 2, ed. A. Auerbach and M. Feldstein. Amsterdam: North-Holland.

Stiglitz, Joseph E., and P. Dasgupta. 1971. Differential Taxation, Public Goods, and Economic Efficiency. *Review of Economic Studies* 38: 151–174.

Stiglitz, Joseph E., and Andrew Weiss. 1981. Credit Rationing in Markets with Imperfect Information. *American Economic Review* 71 (June): 393–410.

Summers, Lawrence H. 1981a. Capital Taxation and Accumulation in a Life Cycle Growth Model. *American Economic Review* 71: 533–544.

—— 1981b. Taxation and Corporate Investment: A Q-Theory Approach. *Brookings Papers on Economic Activity* 12, no. 1: 67–127.

Surrey, Stanley S. 1959a. Definitional Problems in Capital Gains. In *Tax Revision Compendium.* Washington, D.C.: Government Printing Office.

—— 1959b. The Federal Tax Base for Individuals. In *Tax Revision Compendium.* Washington, D.C.: Government Printing Office.

—— 1973. *Pathways to Tax Reform.* Cambridge, Mass.: Harvard University Press.

—— 1981. Our Troubled Tax Policy: False Routes and Proper Paths to Change. *Tax Notes* 12, no. 5 (February): 179–197.

Surrey, Stanley S., and Paul R. McDaniel. 1985. *Tax Expenditures.* Cambridge, Mass.: Harvard University Press.

Tabellini, Guido, and Alberto Alesina. 1990. Voting on the Budget Deficit. *American Economic Review* 80 (March): 37–49.

Taylor, J. 1980. Aggregate Dynamics and Staggered Contracts. *Journal of Political Economy* 88: 1–24.

Terborgh, George. 1959. Tax Depreciation. In *Tax Revision Compendium.* Washington, D.C.: Government Printing Office.

Tiebout, Charles, M. 1956. A Pure Theory of Local Expenditures. *Journal of Political Economy* 64: 416–424.

Tirole, J. 1988. *The Theory of Industrial Organization.* Cambridge, Mass.: MIT Press.

Tobin, James. 1958. Liquidity Preference as Behavior Towards Risk. *Review of Economic Studies* 25 (February): 65–87.

—— 1961. Money, Capital and Other Stores of Value. *American Economic Review* 51 (May): 26–37.

Triest, Robert K. 1990. The Effect of Income Taxation on Labor Supply in the United States. *Journal of Human Resources* 25: 491–516.

U.S. Congress, House Committee on Ways and Means. 1959. *Tax Revision Compendium*. Washington, D.C.: Government Printing Office.

———— 1969. *Tax Reform Act of 1969* (H.R. 13270), H.R. Report 413, 91st Congress, 1st Session. Washington, D.C.: Government Printing Office.

———— and Senate Finance Committee. 1969. *U.S. Treasury Department Tax Reform Studies and Proposals*. Washington, D.C.: Government Printing Office.

U.S. Congress, Joint Committee on Taxation. 1975. *Overview of Tax Shelters*. Washington, D.C.: Government Printing Office.

———— 1983. *Background on Tax Shelters*. Washington, D.C.: Government Printing Office.

———— 1984. *Proposals Relating to Tax Shelters and Other Tax-Motivated Transactions*. Washington, D.C.: Government Printing Office.

U.S. Congress, Joint Economic Committee. 1961. *The Federal Revenue System: Facts and Problems*. Washington, D.C.: Government Printing Office.

U.S. Department of Commerce, Bureau of the Census. 1952. *U.S. Census of Population: 1950*. Washington, D.C.: Government Printing Office.

———— 1975. *Historical Statistics of the United States: Colonial Times to 1970*. Washington, D.C.: Government Printing Office.

———— 1989. *Money Income of Households, Families and Persons: 1987*. Current Population Reports, series P-60, no. 162. Washington, D.C.: Government Printing Office.

———— 1977. *Blueprints for Basic Tax Reform*. Washington, D.C.: Government Printing Office. Also available as David F. Bradford and the U.S. Treasury Tax Policy Staff, *Blueprints for Basic Tax Reform*. Arlington, Va.: Tax Analysts, 1984.

———— 1984. *Tax Reform for Fairness, Simplicity and Economic Growth*. Washington, D.C.: Government Printing Office.

U.S. Department of the Treasury. 1985a. *Taxes Paid by High-Income Taxpayers and the Growth of Partnerships*. Reprinted in *Tax Notes* 28 (August): 717–720.

———— 1985b. *The President's Tax Proposals to the Congress for Fairness, Growth and Simplicity*, vols. 1–3. Washington, D.C.: Government Printing Office.

Vandendorpe, Adolph L., and Ann F. Friedlaender. 1976. Differential Incidence in the Presence of Initial Distorting Taxes. *Journal of Public Economics* 6 (October): 205–229.

Varian, Hal. 1980. Redistributive Taxation as Social Insurance. *Journal of Public Economics* 14: 49–68.

Venti, Steven, and David Wise. 1986. Tax-Deferred Accounts, Constrained Choice, and the Estimation of Individual Saving. *Review of Economic Studies* 53 (August): 579–601.

Vickrey, William. 1939. Averaging of Income for Income Tax Purposes. *Journal of Political Economy* 47 (June): 379–397.

———— 1947. *Agenda for Progressive Taxation*. New York: Ronald Press.

———— 1961. Counterspeculation, Auctions, and Competitive Sealed Tenders. *Journal of Finance* 16: 8–37.

Warr, Peter, and Brian Wright. 1981. The Isolation Paradox and the Discount Rate for Public Investment. *Quarterly Journal of Economics* 96 (February): 129–145.

Warren, Alvin C., Jr. 1979. Integration of the Individual and Corporate Income Taxes. In *Federal Tax Simplification,* ed. Charles H. Gustafson. Philadelphia, Pa.: American Law Institute.

———— 1981. The Relation and Integration of Individual and Corporate Income Taxes. *Harvard Law Review* 94, no. 4 (February): 717–800.

Weidenbaum, Murray. 1988. *Rendezvous with Reality: The American Economy after Reagan.* New York: Basic Books.

Whalley, John. 1988. Lessons from General Equilibrium Models. In *Uneasy Compromise: Problems of a Hybrid Income-Consumption Tax,* ed. Henry J. Aaron, Harvey Galper, and Joseph A. Pechman. Washington, D.C.: Brookings Institution.

White, Michelle, J. 1975a. Firm Location in a Zoned Metropolitan Area. In *The Political Economy of Fiscal Federalism,* ed. Edwin S. Mills and Wallace E. Oates. Lexington, Mass.: Heath.

———— 1975b. Fiscal Zoning in Fragmented Metropolitan Areas. In *The Political Economy of Fiscal Federalism,* ed. Edwin S. Mills and Wallace E. Oates. Lexington, Mass.: Heath.

Wilcox, David W. 1989. The Sustainability of Government Deficits: Implication of the Government Borrowing Constraint. *Journal of Money, Credit and Banking* 21 (August): 291–306.

Wildasin, David. 1979. Local Public Goods, Property Values, and Local Public Choice. *Journal of Urban Economics* 6: 521–534.

———— 1986. *Urban Public Finance.* New York: Academic Press.

———— 1987. Theoretical Analysis of Local Public Economics. In *Handbook of Urban Economics,* ed. Edwin Mills. Amsterdam: North-Holland.

———— 1989. Interjurisdictional Capital Mobility: Fiscal Externality and a Corrective Subsidy. *Journal of Urban Economics* 25, no. 2 (March): 193–212.

Willis, Arthur. 1959. Treatment of Partners and Partnerships. In *Tax Revision Compendium.* Washington, D.C.: Government Printing Office.

Wilson, J. 1983. Optimal Road Capacity in the Presence of Unpriced Congestion. *Journal of Urban Economics* 13: 337–357.

———— 1991. Optimal Public Good Provision with Limited Lump-Sum Taxation. *American Economic Review* 81: 153–165.

Witte, John F. 1985. *The Politics and Development of the Federal Income Tax.* Madison: University of Wisconsin Press.

Wolfman, Bernard. 1965. Federal Tax Policy and the Support of Science. *University of Pennsylvania Law Review* 114, no. 2 (December): 171–186.

Wooders, M. H. 1978. Equilibria, the Core, and Jurisdiction Structures in Economies with a Local Public Good. *Journal of Economic Theory:* 18, no. 2 (August): 328–348.

——— 1980. The Tiebout Hypothesis: Near Optimality in Local Public Goods Economies. *Econometrica* 48, no. 6: 1467–1485.

——— 1983. The Epsilon Core of a Large Replica Game. *Journal of Mathematical Economics* 2: 277–300.

——— 1989. A Tiebout Theorem. *Mathematical Social Sciences* 18: 33–55.

Woodford, Michael. 1990. The Optimum Quantity of Money. In *Handbook of Monetary Economics,* ed. B. Friedman and F. H. Hahn. Amsterdam: North-Holland.

Wright, Colin. 1969. Saving and the Rate of Interest. In *The Taxation of Income from Capital,* ed. Arnold C. Harberger and Martin J. Bailey. Washington, D.C.: Brookings Institution.

Yinger, John, Howard S. Bloom, Axel Borsch-Supan, and Helen F. Ladd. 1988. *Property Taxes and House Values.* San Diego: Academic Press.

Yinger, John, and Helen F. Ladd. 1989. The Determinants of State Assistance to Central Cities. *National Tax Journal* 42 (December): 413–428.

Zax, Jeffrey S. 1989. Is There a Leviathan in Your Neighborhood? *American Economic Review* 79 (June): 560–567.

Zodrow, George R. 1981. Implementing Tax Reform. *National Tax Journal* 4: 401–418.

——— 1985. Optimal Tax Reform in the Presence of Adjustment Costs. *Journal of Public Economics* 27: 211–220.

——— 1986. Implementing Tax Reform: The Intergenerational Carryover Problem. *National Tax Journal* 9: 419–504.

——— 1988. The Windfall Recapture Tax: Issues of Theory and Design. *Public Finance Quarterly* 16 (October): 387–424.

——— 1990. The Choice between Income and Consumption: Efficiency and Horizontal Equity Aspects. In *The Personal Income Tax: Phoenix from the Ashes?* ed. Sijbren Cnossen and Richard Bird. Amsterdam: North-Holland.

——— 1991. On the "Traditional" and "New" Views of Dividend Taxation. *National Tax Journal* 44, no. 4, pt. 2: 497–509.

——— 1992. Grandfather Rules and the Theory of Optimal Tax Reform. *Journal of Public Economics* 49, no. 2: 163–190.

——— Forthcoming, a. Economic Analysis of Capital Gains Taxation: Realizations, Revenues, Efficiency and Equity. *Tax Law Review.*

——— Forthcoming, b. Reflections on the Consumption Tax Option. In *Taxation Issues of the 1990s,* ed. John G. Head. Sydney: Australian Tax Foundation.

Zodrow, George R., and Charles E. McLure, Jr. 1991. Implementing Direct Consumption Taxes in Developing Countries. *Tax Law Review* 46, no. 4: 405–487.

Zodrow, George R., and Peter Mieszkowski. 1986. Pigou, Tiebout, Property Taxation, and the Underprovision of Local Public Goods. *Journal of Urban Economics* 19: 296–315.

Acknowledgments

The year 1990 was important to the field of public finance for at least three reasons: it marked the thirtieth anniversary of the publication of Richard Musgrave's *Theory of Public Finance,* the retirement of George Break from the faculty of the University of California, Berkeley, and the appointment of Joseph Pechman as Distinguished Regents' Professor at Berkeley. A conference was planned to take stock of the major developments in the field since publication of Musgrave's *Theory,* the definitive statement of knowledge at the beginning of the 1960s.

We invited a number of eminent scholars in the field to a three-day meeting on the Berkeley campus. Shortly after the program was established (and the week before he was to have assumed his duties at Berkeley), Joe Pechman died in Washington, D.C. The original planning of the conference owed much to Pechman's influence and enthusiasm, as well as to the suggestions of Break and Musgrave. This volume grew out of their efforts and was inspired by their work. We can only hope that it lives up to their high standards.

The conference was held in April 1990 and included several roundtable presentations on the relationship between theory and tax policy and between theory and public expenditure policy. Early drafts of most of the chapters in this book were presented at the conference. We commissioned three additional chapters afterward.

This volume could not have been undertaken without the intellectual leadership provided by George Break, Richard Musgrave, and Joseph Pechman over their long and distinguished careers. They did much to define the field of public finance and to give it form and substance in the 1960s. We hope this book attests to their enormous influence and also indicates the subsequent progress that has been made.

* * *

As this work took shape, we were assisted by many individuals and organizations. The principal financial support for the research was provided by the Jefferson Lectureship on American Democracy at the University of California, Berkeley. We thank both the lectureship and its chairman, Thomas Leonard. Additional financial aid was provided by the Institute for Governmental Studies (IGS), the Institute for Business and Economic Research (IBER), and the Center for Real Estate and Urban Economics (CREUE) at Berkeley. We are grateful to Nelson Polsby, Richard Sutch, and Kenneth Rosen, the directors of IGS, IBER, and CREUE, respectively, for their generous and sustained assistance.

Special thanks go to Berkeley's Graduate School of Public Policy and to the Department of Economics for additional financial and logistic support. The efforts of Maria Pann, who provided logistic and editorial help during the long period of preparation of this volume, were especially valuable. Chris Redfern proofed the final copy with customary precision.

Index